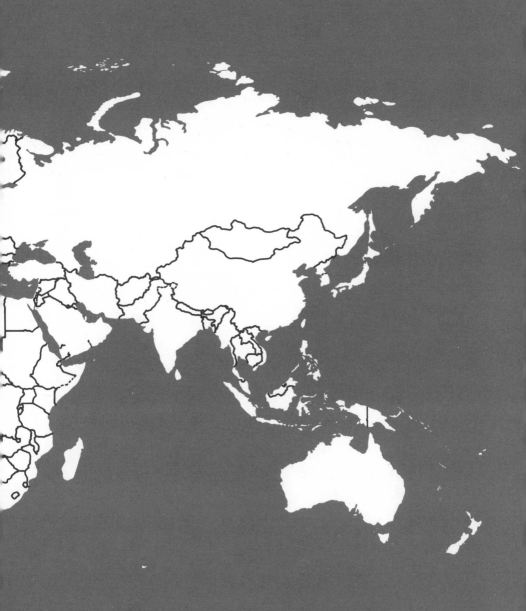

Syria
a country study

Federal Research Division
Library of Congress
Edited by
Thomas Collelo
Research Completed
April 1987

On the cover: Ivory head of a prince from Ugarit,
ca. 14th century B.C.

Third Edition, 1988; First Printing, 1988.

Library of Congress Cataloging in Publication Data

Syria, a country study.

(Area handbook series) (DA pam ; 550-47)
Bibliography: p. 295.
Includes index.
1. Syria. I. Collelo, Thomas, 1948-   . II. Library of Congress.
Federal Research Division. III. Series: DA pam ; 550-47.

DS93.S953   1988   956.91'04   87-600488

Headquarters, Department of the Army
DA Pam 550-47

For sale by the Superintendent of Documents, U.S. Government Printing Office
Washington, D.C. 20402

Foreword

This volume is one in a continuing series of books now being prepared by the Federal Research Division of the Library of Congress under the Country Studies—Area Handbook Program. The last page of this book lists the other published studies.

Most books in the series deal with a particular foreign country, describing and analyzing its political, economic, social, and national security systems and institutions, and examining the interrelationships of those systems and the ways they are shaped by cultural factors. Each study is written by a multidisciplinary team of social scientists. The authors seek to provide a basic understanding of the observed society, striving for a dynamic rather than a static portrayal. Particular attention is devoted to the people who make up the society, their origins, dominant beliefs and values, their common interests and the issues on which they are divided, the nature and extent of their involvement with national institutions, and their attitudes toward each other and toward their social system and political order.

The books represent the analysis of the authors and should not be construed as an expression of an official United States government position, policy, or decision. The authors have sought to adhere to accepted standards of scholarly objectivity. Corrections, additions, and suggestions for changes from readers will be welcomed for use in future editions.

Carol Migdalovitz
Acting Chief
Federal Research Division
Library of Congress
Washington, D.C. 20540

Acknowledgments

The authors wish to acknowledge the contributions of the following individuals who wrote the 1978 edition of *Syria: A Country Study:* Larraine Newhouse Carter, "Historical Setting;" Richard F. Nyrop, "The Society and Its Environment;" Darrel R. Eglin, "The Economy;" R.S. Shinn, "Government and Politics;" and James D. Rudolph, "National Security." Their work provided the organization and structure of the present volume, as well as substantial portions of the text.

The authors are grateful to individuals in various government agencies and private institutions who gave of their time, research materials, and expertise to the production of this book. The authors also wish to thank members of the Federal Research Division staff who contributed directly to the preparation of the manuscript. These people include Helen C. Metz, the substantive reviewer of all the textual material; Richard F. Nyrop, who reviewed all drafts and served as liaison with the sponsoring agency; and Martha E. Hopkins, who edited the manuscript and managed production. Also involved in preparing the text were editorial assistants Barbara Edgerton, Monica Shimmin, and Izella Watson, Andrea Merrill, who performed the final prepublication editorial review, and Editorial Experts, which compiled the index. Diann Johnson, of the Library of Congress Composing Unit, prepared the camera-ready copy, under the supervision of Peggy Pixley.

Invaluable graphics support was provided by David P. Cabitto, assisted by Sandra K. Cotugno and Kimberly A. Lord. Susan M. Lender reviewed the map drafts, and Harriet R. Blood prepared the final maps. Special thanks are owed to Paulette A. Marshall, who designed the cover artwork and the illustrations on the title page of each chapter.

The authors would like to thank several individuals who provided research and operational support. Sisto M. Flores supplied information on ranks and insignia; Patricia A. Rigsbee assisted in obtaining economic data; Jonathan Tetzlaff was instrumental in the planning and selecting the word-processing system; and Stephen Cranton installed the equipment and trained the authors to use it.

Finally, the authors acknowledge the generosity of the many individuals and public and private agencies who allowed their photographs to be used in this study. We are indebted especially to those persons who contributed original work not previously published.

Contents

Preface

Like its predecessor, this study is an attempt to treat in a concise and objective manner the dominant social, political, economic, and military aspects of contemporary Syrian society. Sources of information included scholarly journals and monographs, official reports of governments and international organizations, foreign and domestic newspapers, and numerous periodicals. Relatively up-to-date economic data were available from official Syrian sources, but, in general, this information conflicted with that in other sources. Chapter bibliographies appear at the end of the book; brief comments on some of the more valuable sources suggested as possible further reading appear at the end of each chapter. Measurements are given in the metric system; a conversion table is provided to assist those readers who are unfamiliar with metric measurements (see table 1, Appendix). A glossary is also included.

The transliteration of Arabic words and phrases follows a modified version of the system adopted by the United States Board on Geographic Names and the Permanent Committee on Geographic Names for British Official Use, known as the BGN/PCGN system. The modification is a significant one, however, in that diacritical markings and hyphens have been omitted. Moreover, some geographical locations, such as the cities of Aleppo, Damascus, Homs, and Latakia, are so well known by those conventional names that their formal names—Halab, Dimashq, Hims, and Al Ladhiqiyah, respectively, are not used, although the latter names are used for the provinces (see fig. 1).

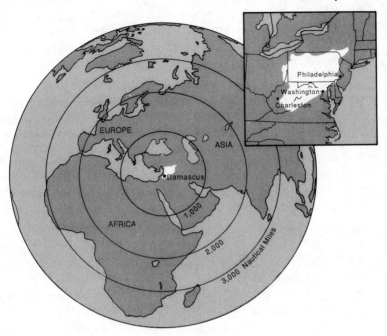

Country Profile

Country

Formal Name: Syrian Arab Republic.

Short Form: Syria.

Term for Citizens: Syrians.

Capital: Damascus.

Geography

Size: About 185,180 square kilometers.

Topography: Country consists of coastal zone divided by narrow double mountain range from large eastern region that includes various mountain ranges, large desert regions, and Euphrates River basin.

Society

Population: Approximately 10.6 million in 1986, including about 250,000 Palestinian refugees. Growth rate estimated at about 3.7 percent per year, one of the world's highest.

Education: Nearly full enrollment in compulsory tuition-free public schools at primary level. School system consists of six years of primary, three years of lower secondary, and three years of upper secondary education. Four major universities and various teacher-training and vocational institutes, all government owned and operated. Adult literacy rate estimated at over 60 percent.

Health: Gastrointestinal ailments, trachoma, and infectious diseases prevalent; considerable progress has been made in control of malaria. Severe shortage of medical and paramedical personnel.

Languages: Official language, Arabic, mother tongue of about 90 percent of population, understood by most others. Kurdish (Kirmanji), Armenian, Turkic, and Syriac spoken by minorities; French and English spoken by educated elites in major urban areas.

Religion: Estimated 85 percent of population adheres to some form of Islam. About 13 to 15 percent of Muslims are Alawis (see Glossary); less than 1 percent, Shias (see Glossary); and remainder, Sunnis (see Glossary). About 10 percent of population observes some form of Christianity, and about 3 percent are Druzes (see Glossary). Small numbers of Jews, Yazidis, and others.

Economy

Gross Domestic Product (GDP): LS75.1 billion (for value of the Syrian pound—see Glossary) in 1984 (LS7,600 per capita). Real growth rate of GDP 6.3 percent a year from 1953 to 1976, but averaged 9.7 percent a year throughout 1970s. Real growth peaked at 10.2 percent in 1981 but declined sharply to 3.2 percent in 1982 and –2.1 percent in 1984 as falling world oil prices, drought, and physical and financial constraints slowed economic growth.

Agriculture: Historically most important source of employment. Agriculture's share of labor force declined from 53 percent in 1965 to 30 percent in 1984 as service and commercial sectors dominated economy. Agriculture's contribution to GDP fell from 30 percent in 1963 to 17.7 percent in 1985. Irrigated area less than 10 percent of that cultivated. Sharp swings in production because of differences in rainfall. Main products: cotton, wheat, and barley. Farming primarily by private sector.

Industry: Growth rate of industrial sector 8.3 percent between 1953 and mid-1970s. Manufacturing (including extractive industries) contributed 22.4 percent of GDP in 1976 but fell to 13.4 in 1984. Crude oil production small by world standards but important to industrial growth and development. Discovery of high-quality oil at Dayr az Zawr in mid-1980s gives hope for economic recovery in 1990s. New emphasis on phosphate production in mid-1980s. Industry based on chemicals, cement, food processing, and textiles. Most large-scale industry owned by state.

Imports: LS16.2 billion in 1984. Public sector accounted for 79 percent of imports in 1984. Major imports: oil, machinery, metal products, materials for processing, and foods.

Exports: LS7.4 billion in 1984. Major exports: crude oil, cotton, and phosphates.

Major Trade Areas: Eastern Europe, Soviet Union, Western Europe, Arab states, and Iran.

Balance of Payments: Heavily dependent on foreign economic credits and grant aid from Arab states and Iran.

Exchange Rates: Official (used generally for government imports) LS3.92 to US$1 in early 1987. Parallel (used for commercial deals, but gradually being replaced by tourist rate) LS5.40 to US$1. Tourist (previously available only to visitors, in 1987 applied to many commercial and diplomatic transactions) LS9.75 to US$1. "Neighboring country" (exchange rate of Syrian pound in Jordanian and Lebanese markets and inside Syria; also applied to private sector imports under barter trade agreements) LS21.50 to US$1 (August 1986).

Transportation and Communications

Roads: In 1985 over 25,000 kilometers of roads, 18,000 of which were paved. Main areas linked, but network required continuous and intensive development.

Railroads: 2,013 kilometers in 1984. Standard gauge (1,686 kilometers) crossed northern part of country from coast to Iraq border in northeast (via Aleppo). Narrow gauge in southwest served Damascus with tracks into Lebanon and Jordan.

Ports: Tartus most important—8.8 million tons of cargo in 1984. Also served as country's crude oil export terminal. Latakia handled 1.7 million tons of cargo in 1984. Baniyas was oil port and site of large refinery.

Pipelines: Two international crude-oil pipelines, one from Iraq and one from Saudi Arabia, both terminating in Lebanon. Domestic crude-oil pipeline from oil fields in northeast to port of Tartus via Homs (refinery). Three lines for petroleum products from Homs refinery to Damascus, Aleppo, and Latakia.

Communications: Good domestic and international telecommunications service.

Government and Politics

Government: Governmental system based on Permanent Constitution of March 13, 1973. Theoretically, power divided into executive, legislative, and judicial spheres, but all institutions overshadowed by preeminence of president (reelected February 10, 1985, in national referendum for seven-year term), who was head of state, chief executive, and secretary of ruling Baath (Arab Socialist Resurrection) Party. People's Council, 195-member parliament, popularly elected in 1986 for term of four years. Judiciary based on amalgam of Ottoman, French, and Islamic laws and practices. Some legal rights abrogated under state of martial law, in effect since 1963.

Politics: Baath Party—popular name for ruling party—provided ideological rationale for Syrian socialism and pan-Arabism. Directed by twenty-one-member Regional Command (top national decision-making body of party) led by regional secretary. Party allied in coalition with minor parties (including communist) through framework of National Progressive Front. Dominant aspect of political system pivotal role of military as real source and guarantor of power. Disproportionately significant role played by country's largest minority, Alawis, who held many key positions in armed forces, Baath Party, and government.

Administrative Divisions: Divided into thirteen provinces, each consisting of capital, districts, and subdistricts.

Foreign Affairs: Arab-Israeli conflict remained paramount foreign policy concern, Syrian objective being to secure withdrawal of Israeli forces from the occupied territories, to restore sovereignty over Israeli-annexed Golan Heights, and to ensure full political self-determination for Palestinians. In attempting to resolve Arab-Israeli issue, Syria seeks unilateral strategic and military parity with Israel to negotiate from position of strength. Syria attempts to exert regional dominance over its Arab neighbors, focusing on Lebanon, which it has partially occupied since 1976.

National Security

Armed Forces: In 1985 army, 396,000 regulars (300,000 reserves); navy, 4,000 regulars (2,500 reserves); and air force, 100,000 regulars (37,500 reserves). Compulsory thirty-month conscription for males.

Combat Units and Major Equipment: In 1985, army consisted of five armored divisions (with one independent armored brigade), three mechanized divisions, one infantry-special forces division, and ten airborne-special forces independent brigades; weapons included over 4,100 Soviet-built tanks and 95 surface-to-air missile (SAM) batteries. Navy weapons included forty-one vessels, including two or three Soviet submarines and twenty-two missile attack craft. Air force weapons included 650 combat aircraft in 9 fighter and 15 interceptor squadrons.

Military Budget: In 1985 equivalent of US$4.2 billion. Approximately 21.1 percent of GNP; 42 percent of government expenditures. In 1986 $3.7 billion for national security, including armed forces and internal security agencies.

Police and Internal Security Agencies: Single national police force for routine duties. Numerous internal security forces under umbrella of National Security Directorate. Sizes unknown.

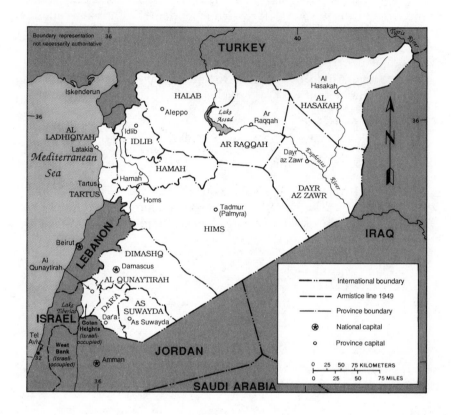

Figure 1. Administrative Divisions

Introduction

FROM INDEPENDENCE in 1946 through the late 1960s, Syria stood out as a particularly unstable country in a geographic region noted for political instability. Illegal seizures of power seemed to be the rule as Syrians were governed under a series of constitutions and the nation's political direction made several abrupt ideological lurches. Therefore, when Minister of Defense Hafiz al Assad assumed authority in yet another coup in November 1970, many believed his regime was merely one more in a long string of extralegal changes of government. Indeed, because of the coup's similarity to previous ones, at the time there was little evidence to suggest otherwise. Nonetheless, from 1970 until mid-1987, Assad has provided Syria with a period of uncommon stability, all the more remarkable when viewed against the backdrop of the nation's postindependence history of political turbulence.

Although uncertainty and internal tension are threads that run through Syrian history, not all conflict has been negative. From the earliest days of civilization to more recent times, struggle among various indigenous groups as well as with invading foreigners has resulted in cultural enrichment. Phoenicians, Canaanites, Assyrians, and Persians are but a few of the peoples who have figured prominently in this legacy. As significant were the contributions of Alexander the Great and his successors and the Roman and Byzantine rulers (see Ancient Syria, ch. 1).

But as great as these considerable foreign influences were, few would disagree that the most important additions to Syria's rich culture were made following the death of the Prophet Muhammad, when Arab conquerors brought Islam to Greater Syria (see Glossary). By A.D. 661, Muawiyah, the governor of Syria, had proclaimed himself caliph, or temporal leader, and established Damascus as the seat of the Umayyad Empire. Thus began a dynasty whose realm stretched as far west as southern France and as far east as Afghanistan, an expanse of territory that surpassed even that which Rome had held a few centuries earlier. Thirteen hundred years after his death, the memory of Muawiyah and his accomplishments still stirs pride and respect in Syria. Likewise, the image of the great Muslim general Saladin (Salah ad Din al Ayubbi), who defeated the Christian Crusaders in 1187, is deeply imprinted on the Syrian psyche.

These native heroes notwithstanding, it was foreign domination that determined the political boundaries of present-day Syria. First the Ottoman Turks, then after World War I the French, and, more recently, the Israelis shaped the contours of the nation, breaking off chunks of what was Greater Syria and repositioning borders to leave the configuration of the contemporary state. In spite of these territorial changes, support for a return to the glory that was Greater Syria and a development of a powerful nation-state has remained strong. Syrians share a vision of a pan-Arab entity—the unification of all Arab brethren throughout the region (see Political Orientations, ch. 4).

Despite the rhetoric and idealism, in Syria, as in many developing nations, strife between and among communities has hindered development of a genuine national spirit. Also, the importance of regional, sectarian, and religious identities as the primary sources of loyalty have frustrated nation-building. Although about 85 percent of Syrians were Muslims, in 1987 most scholars agreed that the domination of Assad's small Alawi (see Glossary) sect over the larger Sunni (see Glossary) community was at the root of much of the internal friction, even though ethnic issues also accounted for a certain amount of tension. Other significant minorities that contributed to social tensions were Druzes (see Glossary), Kurds, Armenians, and Circassians (see The Peoples, ch. 2).

Although internal discord is a fact of life in every country in the Middle East, it is difficult to imagine that dissent in any of them could have been met more brutally than it was in Syria in the 1980s. One dissident group was the Muslim Brotherhood, a Sunni fundamentalist, antigovernment movement whose popularity grew markedly in the late 1970s. Unlike Islamic fundamentalist movements in certain other Middle Eastern countries, the Muslim Brotherhood opposed the Assad regime not so much for its secularism as for its sectarian favoritism. To protest Alawi domination, the Muslim Brotherhood and other like-minded groups undertook a series of violent attacks against the Baath (Arab Socialist Resurrection) Party government. After Assad's attempts at negotiation failed, Muslim Brotherhood attacks increased in frequency, and the government responded in kind. Using his armed forces, in late 1981 Assad finally isolated Muslim Brotherhood adherents in their strongholds of Aleppo and Hamah (see fig. 1). In February 1982, with no regard for civilian safety, the full force of the Syrian army was brought to bear on the rebels in Hamah. Entire sections of the city, including the architecturally magnificent ancient quarter, were reduced to rubble by tank and artillery fire, as upward of 25,000 citizens were killed. This lesson in abject obedience was not lost on the populace, for as of mid-1987, the Muslim Brotherhood and its antigovernment allies were almost moribund (see The

Assad Era, ch. 1; Ethnic and Religious Opposition Movements, ch. 5).

Other violent stresses on internal stability occurred later in 1982. In June, Israel invaded Lebanon with the stated aim of driving away Palestine Liberation Organization (PLO) guerrillas from Israel's northern border. After a few days of fighting and constant Israeli advances, it became obvious that Israel's goal was not merely the creation of a security zone, but rather the complete destruction of the PLO or at least its forced expulsion from Lebanon. In achieving this objective, armed confrontation with Syrian forces was inevitable. Although some of the Syrian units gave a good accounting against the Israel Defense Forces (IDF), in general the IDF overwhelmed the Syrians. This domination was nowhere more evident than in air battles over the Biqa Valley in which the Israeli Air Force destroyed nineteen air defense sites and downed more than eighty Syrian aircraft, while losing only two aircraft (see Syrian-Israeli Hostility, ch. 5). Despite these setbacks, as the only Arab leader to stand up to the Israeli assault, Assad gained the respect of other Middle Eastern states. The defeats were not enough to induce Syria to withdraw its forces from Lebanon, and eventually it worked out a modus vivendi with the IDF.

But for Syria there was no relief from internal pressures. Having weathered a "miniwar" in Lebanon, in 1983 another crisis arose when in November Assad suffered a severe heart attack that hospitalized him for several months. In February 1984, in a premature effort to succeed his brother, Rifaat al Assad moved his Defense Companies (now called Unit 569) into positions around the capital. Fighting broke out but soon subsided; however, in May it erupted once more in Latakia. As Hafiz al Assad recovered and reasserted his authority, he neutralized political opportunists (including his brother) while making changes in the Baath Party and army hierarchies. To restore faith in his regime, Assad began promoting a personality cult, the net effect of which was to identify government with Hafiz al Assad rather than to encourage government through political and social institutions (see Post-1982 Political Developments, ch. 4). Thus, in 1987 many concerns remained about succession and about whether or not Syria could peacefully survive the loss of Assad as the adhesive that held together the diverse elements of society.

An added concern was the perilous state of the economy (see Period of Economic Retrenchment, 1986–90, ch. 3). Years of drought in the early 1980s had effectively stymied agricultural growth. By the time production began to rebound in the mid-1980s, commodity prices for Syria's agricultural goods were dropping.

Furthermore, the fledgling oil industry was retarded by the world-wide slump in petroleum prices and by Syria's own decision to cease pipeline transportation of Iraqi oil, thus surrendering lucrative transit fees. Moreover, Syria's stance in the Iran-Iraq War and its intransigence on other regional matters so angered wealthier Arab nations that they reduced financial support to the Assad regime.

And perhaps most salient, the need to provision tens of thousands of troops stationed in Lebanon and to maintain strong defenses against Israel caused a crushing defense burden. Although figures on defense outlays varied widely, in the late 1980s they apparently accounted for anywhere from one-third to just over one-half of all government spending. Regardless of which figure is accepted, clearly military spending was inhibiting development by diverting funds from desperately needed social programs.

The armed forces have played a central role in Syria's recent social and political history. As in many Third World countries, the army has provided minorities with a channel for upward mobility. Alawis in particular used this route of social advancement, and by the early 1960s they held influential positions in the military government. When in 1966 General Salah al Jadid overthrew General Amin al Hafiz, a Sunni, for the first time in the modern era an Alawi ruled Syria. Jadid, in turn, was overthrown in 1970 by Assad, another Alawi. Since then Assad has seen to it that only trusted relatives or friends, most of them Alawis, occupied or controlled politically sensitive or powerful positions. Similarly, because the armed forces are both the mainstay of his regime and the most likely threat to it, Assad has been deferential to the needs of the military forces and has raised the standard of living for those in uniform (see Conditions of Service, Morale, and Military Justice, ch. 5).

In addition to domestic discord, Syria has been subjected to many external strains. Not the least of these has been Syria's long-standing engagement in Lebanon. Although some analysts saw this involvement as part of a desire to recreate Greater Syria, others viewed it as a pragmatic manifestation of Assad's ambitions toward regional hegemony. Regardless of motive, Syria's presence in Lebanon presented dangers and opportunities. The principal problem was that the worsening Lebanese situation jeopardized the safety of Syrian troops and drained Syria's fragile economy. Nevertheless, at various times since 1976, Syrian intervention has had the positive effect of quelling some of the violence that has swept Lebanon and raised faint hopes of peace. Such positive intervention occurred most recently in February 1987, when Assad sent his forces into West Beirut to restore order to the Muslim half of the city (see Syria and the Lebanese Crisis, 1975–87, ch. 5).

Some scholars call Syria a nation of contradictions with good reason. Certainly these are inconsistencies in Syria's regional and international politics (see Foreign Policy, ch. 4). In spite of the pan-Arab ideology that is at the heart of the ruling Baath Party principles, Syria was one of only two Arab states (Libya being the other) supporting non-Arab Iran against Iraq in the Iran-Iraq War. In addition, Syria's steadfast refusal to negotiate with Israel ever since the June 1967 War and its support for radical Palestinian factions have set it apart from most of the Arab world.

In foreign relations, Syria proved it could be a supportive friend or obstinate foe—in fact, sometimes both within a short period of time. For example, every few years Syria seemed to begin a rapprochement with Jordan and Iraq, its neighbors to the south and east, but these thaws in otherwise cool relations have been short. Likewise, relations with various Lebanese and Palestinian factions have blown hot and cold.

Certainly the Soviet Union has found Assad a less than pliable client. Throughout the Soviet-Syrian relationship, Assad has taken much more in military assistance than the Soviets have received in terms of influence in Syria or the rest of the region. For the most part, Soviet efforts to dominate Syrian political and even military activities have had limited success (see Syria–Soviet Relations, ch. 4).

In 1987 Assad was thought by many to be an enigma, thus his nickname, "the sphinx." Having survived the tribulations of seventeen years of rule, he deserved his reputation as a wily and able politician. Diplomatic and practical when circumstances called for these qualities, Assad could also be manipulative and merciless, especially with regime opponents. Syrian dissidents in exile or regional political enemies have not been immune from Assad's intelligence and security networks. Insofar as Assad has assented to terrorist training in Syrian-controlled Lebanon and even on Syrian soil, he most likely has at his disposal a pool of individuals willing to carry out certain violent missions. Clearly, media attention given to Syria's complicity in terrorist incidents in Western Europe in the mid-1980s has underscored such activity (see Sponsorship of Terrorism, ch. 5).

In summary, in mid-1987 Syria was enjoying a period of unprecedented internal stability. In many ways, Assad had very nearly realized his ambitions for leadership in regional affairs. Syria was a key to the Palestinian problem and to any resolution of the Arab-Israeli dispute; it was also at the vortex of the Lebanese situation. Furthermore, it was making its presence felt in the Iran-Iraq War. Its economy, although by no means burgeoning, was at least resilient in the face of difficult circumstances. And even though its international image was tarnished because of its association with terrorism, that, too, was improving as a result of Syria's crackdown on Shia (see Glossary) extremists in Lebanon. Most troublesome, perhaps, was the unresolved question of who would succeed the somewhat frail president. It was uncertain if any successor could overcome the conflicts that were sure to surface after Assad or could maintain the nation's pace of development.

August 31, 1987   Thomas Collelo

Chapter 1. Historical Setting

Fragment of relief plaque, ca. 2500 B.C., Tall Hariri

PRESENT-DAY SYRIA constitutes only a small portion of the ancient geographical Syria. Until the twentieth century, when Western powers began to carve out the rough contours of the contemporary states of Syria, Lebanon, Jordan, and Israel, the whole of the settled region at the eastern end of the Mediterranean Sea was called Syria, the name given by the ancient Greeks to the land bridge that links three continents. For this reason, historians and political scientists usually use the term *Greater Syria* (see Glossary) to denote the area in the prestate period.

Historically, Greater Syria rarely ruled itself, primarily because of its vulnerable position between the Mediterranean Sea and the desert. As a marchland between frequently powerful empires on the north, east, and south, Syria was often a battlefield for the political destinies of dynasties and empires. Unlike other parts of the Middle East, Greater Syria was prized as a fertile cereal-growing oasis. It was even more critical as a source of the lumber needed for building imperial fleets in the preindustrial period.

Even though it was exploited politically, Greater Syria benefited immeasurably from the cultural diversity of the peoples who came to claim parts or all of it and who remained to contribute and participate in the remarkable spiritual and intellectual flowering that characterized Greater Syria's cultures in the ancient and medieval periods. Incorporating some of the oldest continuously inhabited cities in the world, Greater Syria was in a unique position to foster intellectual activities. By 1400 B.C., Damascus, Aleppo, Hamah, Byblos, Jaffa, Homs, Gaza, Tyre, and Sidon already had been established; some of these cities had flourished for many centuries. Because Greater Syria was usually ruled by foreigners, the inhabitants traditionally identified themselves with their cities, and in contemporary Syria each city continues to have a unique sociopolitical character.

A recurrent theme of Greater Syria's history has been the encounters between Eastern and Western powers on its soil. Even in the ancient period, it was the focus of a continual dialectic, both intellectual and bellicose, between the Middle East and the West. During the medieval period, this dialectic was intensified as it became colored by diametrically opposed religious points of view regarding rights to the land. The Christian Byzantines contended with Arabs and later the Christian Crusaders competed with Muslim Arabs for land they all held sacred.

The advent of Arab Muslim rule in A.D. 635 provided the two major themes of Syrian history: the Islamic religion and the world community of Arabs. According to traditionalist Muslims, the greatest period of Islamic history was the time of the brief rule of Muhammad—the prototype for the perfect temporal ruler—and the time of the first four caliphs (known as *rashidun*, meaning rightly guided), when man presumably behaved as God commanded and established a society on earth unequaled before or after. During this period religion and state were one, and Muslims ruled Muslims according to Muslim law. The succeeding Umayyad (661–750) and Abbasid (750–1258) caliphates were extensions of the first period and proved the military and intellectual might of Muslims. The history of Greater Syria in the early medieval period is essentially the history of political Islam at one of its most glorious moments—the period of the Umayyad caliphate when the Islamic empire, with its capital at Damascus, stretched from the Oxus River (present-day Amu Darya) in Central and West Asia to southern France.

A different view of Syrian history denies that the greatness of the Arab past was a purely Islamic manifestation. The history of the Arabs began before the coming of Muhammad, and that which the Arabs achieved during the Umayyad and Abbasid empires was evidence not only of the rich inheritance from Greek and Roman days but also of the vitality of Arab culture.

Since independence in 1946, Syria's history has been dominated by four overriding factors. First is the deeply felt desire among Syrian Arabs—Christian and Muslim alike—to achieve some kind of unity with the other Arabs of the Middle East in fulfillment of their aspirations for regional leadership. Second is a desire for economic and social prosperity. Third is a universal dislike of Israel, the creation of which Syrians feel was forcibly imposed by the West and which they view as a threat to Arab unity (see Foreign Policy, ch. 4). The fourth issue is the dominant political role of the military.

Ancient Syria

The first recorded mention of Greater Syria is in Egyptian annals detailing expeditions to the Syrian coastland to log the cedar, pine, and cypress of the Ammanus and Lebanon mountain ranges in the fourth millennium B.C. Sumer, a kingdom of non-Semitic peoples at the southern boundary of ancient Babylonia, also sent expeditions in the third millennium B.C., chiefly in search of cedar from the Ammanus and gold and silver from Cilicia. The Sumerians most probably traded with the Syrian port city of Byblos,

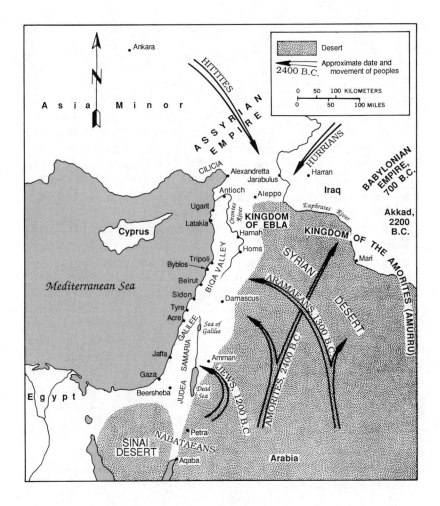

Figure 2. Ancient Syria

which was also negotiating with Egypt for exportation of timber
and the resin necessary for mummification.

An enormous commercial network linking Anatolia, Mesopotamia, Egypt, the Aegean, and the Syrian coast was developed. The
network was perhaps under the aegis of the kingdom of Ebla ("city
of the white stones"), the chief site of which was discovered in 1975
at Tall Mardikh, sixty-four kilometers south of Aleppo (see fig. 2).
Numerous tablets give evidence of a sophisticated and powerful
indigenous Syrian empire, which dominated northern Syria and
portions of lower Mesopotamia, Anatolia, and Iran. Its chief rival

5

was Akkad in southern Mesopotamia, which flourished about 2300 B.C. In addition to identifying another great cultural and political power for the period—and an independent Syrian kingdom at that—the discovery of Ebla has had other important ramifications. The oldest Semitic language was thought to have been Amorite, but the newly found language of Ebla, a variant of Paleo-Canaanite, is considerably older. Ebla twice conquered the city of Mari, the capital of Amurru, the kingdom of the Semitic-speaking Amorites. After protracted tension between Akkad and Ebla, the great king of Akkad, Naram Sin, destroyed Ebla by fire in about 2300. Naram Sin also destroyed Arman, which may have been an ancient name for Aleppo.

Amorite power was effectively eclipsed in 1600, when Egypt mounted a full attack on Greater Syria and brought the entire region under its suzerainty. During the fifteenth and fourteenth centuries, the area was in tremendous political upheaval because of the growing Assyrian power pressing from the east and invasions from the north of Hittites who eventually settled in north and central Syria.

Another Semitic-speaking people, the Canaanites, may have been part of the same migration that brought the Amorites into Syria from northern Arabia in approximately 2400. The Amorites came under the influence of Mesopotamia, whereas the Canaanites, who had intermarried with indigenous Syrians of the coast, were probably under the initial influence of Egypt.

The descendants of the intermarriages between Canaanites and coastal Syrians were the Phoenicians, the greatest seafaring merchants of the ancient world. The Phoenicians improved and developed iron tools and significantly advanced the art of shipbuilding. Their mastery of the seas allowed them to establish a network of independent city-states; however, these entities were never united politically, partially because of the continual harassment from Hittites to the north and Egyptians to the southwest. The name given to their land—Canaan in Hurrian, Phoenicia in Greek—refers to the fabulously valued purple dye extracted from mollusks found at that time only on the Syrian coast. From this period, purple became the color of the robes of kings because only they and other small groups of the ancient Middle Eastern elite could afford to purchase the rare dye. The wealth that was derived in part from the dye trade sparked the economic flame that made it possible for Greater Syrian city-states to enjoy a wide measure of prosperity.

Many of Greater Syria's major contributions to civilization were developed during the ancient period. Syria's greatest legacy, the alphabet, was developed by Phoenicians during the second millennium. The Phoenicians introduced their thirty-letter alphabet to the Aramaeans, among other Semitic-speaking people, and to the Greeks, who added letters for vowels not used in the Semitic languages.

The Phoenicians, somewhat pressed for space for their growing population, founded major colonies on the North African littoral, the most notable of which was Carthage. In the process of founding new city-states, they discovered the Atlantic Ocean.

The Aramaeans had settled in Greater Syria at approximately the end of the thirteenth century B.C., approximately the same time at which the Jews, or Israelites, migrated to the area. The Aramaeans settled in the Mesopotamian-Syrian corridor to the north and established the kingdom of Aram, biblical Syria. As overland merchants, they opened trade to southwestern Asia, and their capital at Damascus became a city of immense wealth and influence. At Aleppo they built a huge fortress, still standing. The Aramaeans simplified the Phoenician alphabet and carried their language, Aramaic, to their chief areas of commerce. Aramaic displaced Hebrew in Greater Syria as the vernacular (Jesus spoke Aramaic), and it became the language of commerce throughout the Middle East and the official language of the Persian Empire. Aramaic continued to be spoken in the Syrian countryside for almost 1,000 years, and in the 1980s it remained in daily use in a handful of villages near the Syrian-Lebanese border. A dialect of Aramaic continues to be the language of worship in the Syrian Orthodox Church.

The plethora of city-states in Greater Syria could not withstand the repeated attacks from the north by the powerful Assyrian Empire, which under the leadership of Nebuchadnezzar finally overwhelmed them in the eighth century. Assyrian aggressors were replaced by the conquering Babylonians in the seventh century and by the then-mighty Persian Empire in the sixth century. Under the aegis of the Persian Empire, Syria had a measure of self-rule, as it was to have under a succession of foreign rulers from that time until independence in the twentieth century. When Alexander the Great conquered the Persian Empire in 333, local political powers—which probably would have continued to contest for control of Greater Syria—were effectively shattered, and the area came into the strong cultural orbit of Western ideas and institutions.

At Alexander's death, the empire was divided among five of his generals. General Seleucus became heir to the lands formerly under Persian control, which included Greater Syria. The Seleucids ruled for three centuries and founded a kingdom with its capital at Damascus, which later became referred to as the Kingdom of Syria.

Seleucus named many cities after his mother, Laodicea; the greatest became Latakia, a major Syrian port.

Enormous numbers of Greek immigrants flocked to the Kingdom of Syria. Syrian trade was vastly expanded as a result of the newcomers' efforts, reaching into India, the Far East, and Europe. The Greeks built new cities in Syria and colonized existing ones. Syrian and Greek cultures synthesized to create Near Eastern Hellenism, noted for remarkable developments in jurisprudence, philosophy, and science.

Replacing the Greeks and the Seleucids, Roman emperors inherited already thriving cities—Damascus, Palmyra (present-day Tadmur), and Busra ash Sham in the fertile Hawran Plateau south of Damascus. Under the emperor Hadrian, Syria was prosperous, and its cities were major trading centers; Hawran was a well-watered breadbasket. After making a survey of the country, the Romans established a tax system based on the potential harvest of farmlands; it remained the key to the land tax structure until 1945. The Romans gave Syria some of the grandest buildings in the world, as well as aqueducts, wells, and roads that are still in use.

Neither the Seleucids nor the Romans ruled the area without conflict. The Seleucids had to deal with powerful Arab peoples, the Nabataeans, who had established an empire at Petra (in present-day Jordan) and at Busra ash Sham. The Romans had to face the Palmyrenes, who had built Palmyra, a city even more magnificent than Damascus and the principal stop on the caravan route from Homs to the Euphrates.

By the time the Romans arrived, Greater Syrians had developed irrigation techniques, the alphabet, and astronomy. In A.D. 324, the emperor Constantine moved his capital from Rome to Byzantium, renaming it Constantinople (present-day Istanbul). From there the Byzantines ruled Greater Syria, dividing it into two provinces: Syria Prima, with Antioch as the capital and Aleppo the major city; and Syria Secunda, ruled frequently from Hamah. Syria Secunda was divided into two districts: Phoenicia Prima, with Tyre as the capital; and Phoenicia Secunda, ruled from Damascus. The ruling families of Syria during this period were the Ghassanids, Christian Arabs loyal to Byzantium, from whom many Syrians now trace descent.

Byzantine rule in Syria was marked by constant warfare with the Persian Sassanian Empire to the east. In these struggles, Syria often became a battleground. In 611 the Persians succeeded in invading Syria and Palestine, capturing Jerusalem in 614. Shortly thereafter, the Byzantines counterattacked and retook their former possessions. During the campaign, the Byzantines tried to force

Greek Orthodoxy on the Syrian inhabitants, but were unsuccessful. Beset by financial problems, largely as a result of their costly campaigns against the Persians, the Byzantines stopped subsidizing the Christian Arab tribes guarding the Syrian steppe. Some scholars believe this was a fatal mistake, for these tribes were then susceptible to a new force emanating from the south—Islam.

The Byzantine heritage remains in Syria's Christian sects and great monastic ruins. In the fourth century A.D., Roman emperor Theodosius destroyed the temple to Jupiter in Damascus and built a cathedral in honor of John the Baptist. The huge monastery at Dayr Simaan near Aleppo, begun by Simeon Stylites in the fifth century, is perhaps the greatest Christian monument built before the tenth century.

Muslim Empires

During the first decades of the seventh century, Muhammad, a merchant from Mecca, converted many of his fellow Arabs to a new religion, Islam, which was conceived as the continuation and fulfillment of the Judeo-Christian tradition (see Muslims, ch. 2). By 629 the religious fervor and pressures of an expanding population impelled Muslim Arab tribes to invade lands to the north of the Arabian Peninsula. They called these lands *bilad ash sham,* the country or land of Sham—the name Arabs often used to designate

9

Damascus. The word *sham* derives from the Arabic word for dignity, indicating the high regard most Arabs have had for Damascus. Arabs, including Syrians, have referred to Syria by this name ever since and call Syrians Shamis.

In 635 Damascus surrendered to the great Muslim general, Khalid ibn al Walid. Undermined by Persian incursions, religious schisms, and rebellions in the provinces caused by harsh rule, Byzantium could offer little resistance to Islam.

In succeeding centuries, Muslims extended and consolidated their rule in many areas, and by 1200 they controlled lands from the Atlantic to the Bay of Bengal, from central Russia to the Gulf of Aden. Wherever they went, they built mosques, tombs, forts, and beautiful cities. The ruins of such structures are found widely in Greater Syria, a heartland of Islamic and Arab culture.

Muhammad made Medina his first capital, and it was here that he died. Leadership of the faithful fell to Abu Bakr (632–34), Muhammad's father-in-law and the first of the four orthodox caliphs, or temporal leaders of the Muslims. Umar followed him (634–44) and organized the government of captured provinces. The third caliph was Uthman (644–56), under whose administration the compilation of the Quran was accomplished. Among the aspirants to the caliphate was Ali, Muhammad's cousin and son-in-law, whose supporters felt he should be the Prophet's successor. Upon the murder of Uthman, Ali became caliph (656–61). After a civil war with other aspirants to the caliphate, Ali moved his capital to Mesopotamia and was later assassinated at Al Kufah. Ali's early followers established the first of Islam's dissident sects, the Shias (from Shiat Ali, party of Ali). Those who had accepted the successions before and after Ali remained the orthodox of Islam; they are called Sunnis—from the word *sunna,* meaning orthodox.

Umayyad Caliphate

After Ali's murder in 661, Muawiyah—the governor of Syria during the early Arab conquests, a kinsman of Uthman, and a member of the Quraysh tribe of the Prophet—proclaimed himself caliph and established the Umayyad caliphate with its capital at Damascus. From there he conquered Muslim enemies to the east, south, and west and fought the Byzantines to the north. Muawiyah is considered the architect of the Islamic empire and a political genius. Under his governorship, Syria became the most prosperous province of the caliphate. Muawiyah created a professional army and, although rigorous in training them, won the undying loyalty of his troops for his generous and regularly paid salaries. Heir to Syrian shipyards built by the Byzantines, he established the caliphate's first navy. He also conceived and established an efficient government, including a comptroller of finance and a postal system.

Muawiyah cultivated the goodwill of Christian Syrians by recruiting them for the army at double pay, by appointing Christians to many high offices, and by appointing his son by his Christian wife as his successor. His sensitivity to human behavior accounted in great part for his political success. The modern Syrian image of Muawiyah is that of a man with enormous amounts of *hilm*, a combination of magnanimity, tolerance, and self-discipline, and of *duha* (political expertise)—qualities Syrians continue to expect of their leaders. By 732 the dynasty he founded had conquered Spain and Tours in France and stretched east to Samarkand and Kabul, far exceeding the extent of the Roman Empire (see fig. 3). Thus, Damascus achieved a glory unrivaled among cities of the eighth century.

The Umayyad Muslims established a military government in Syria and used the country primarily as a base of operations. They lived aloof from the people and at first made little effort to convert Christians to Islam. The Umayyads administered the lands in the manner of the Byzantines, giving complete authority to provincial governors.

In the administration of law, the Umayyads followed the traditions set by the Hellenistic monarchies and the Roman Empire. The conqueror's law—in this case Muslim law (sharia)—applied only to those of the same faith or nationality as the conquerors. For non-Muslims civil law was the law of their particular *millet* (separate religious community, also called *milla*); religious leaders administered the law of the *millet*. This system prevailed throughout Islam and has survived in Syria's legal codes (see Muslims, ch. 2; Constitutional Framework, ch. 4).

During the eighty-nine years of Umayyad rule, most Syrians became Muslims, and the Arabic language replaced Aramaic. The Umayyads minted coins, built hospitals, and constructed underground canals to bring water to the towns. The country prospered both economically and intellectually. Foreign trade expanded, and educated Jews and Christians, many of them Greek, found employment in the caliphal courts, where they studied and practiced medicine, alchemy, and philosophy.

Succeeding Caliphates and Kingdoms

Under later dissolute caliphs, the Umayyad dynasty began to decline at a time when both Sunni and Shia Muslims in Iran began to press against Umayyad borders. By 750 the Abbasids, whose

11

forces originated in Khorasan (in northeast Iran), had conquered the Umayyads and established the caliphate in Baghdad. As a result, Syria became a province of an empire.

Abbasid rule over Syria, however, was precarious and often challenged by independent Muslim princes. The greatest of these was Abu Ali Hasan, who founded a kingdom known as the Hamdanid. A Shia, he established his capital at Aleppo, and the Abbasids recognized him as Sayf ad Dawlah (meaning sword of the state). The Hamdanid dynasty ruled throughout the tenth century and became famous for its achievements in science and letters. In Europe it was known for its persistent attacks against Constantinople. The Hamdanid kingdom fell in 1094 to Muslim Seljuk Turks invading from the northeast.

During the same period, the Shia Fatimids established themselves in Egypt and drove north against Syria. The Fatimids were less tolerant of subject peoples than their predecessors. Intolerance reached its height under the caliph Abu Ali Mansur al Hakim (966–1021), who destroyed churches and caused Christians to flee to the mountains. When he announced his divinity, his mother murdered him. In the secluded valleys of Mount Hermon in Syria, his followers found tribesmen to adopt his religion, the ancestors of Syria's present-day Druzes (see Glossary).

Muslim rule of Christian holy places, overpopulation, and constant warfare in Europe prompted the Crusades, the first major Western colonial venture in the Middle East. Between 1097 and 1144 Crusaders established the principalities of Edessa, Antioch, Tripoli, and the Latin Kingdom of Jerusalem. The politically fragmented area was an easy conquest for the Europeans. The first Muslim threat to European entrenchment came not from within Greater Syria but from Zangi, the amir (see Glossary) of Mosul (in modern Iraq). Zangi took Edessa in 1144, and his son, Nur ad Din (light of the faith), secured Damascus, extending the realm from Aleppo to Mosul. When the last Shia Fatimid caliph died, Nur ad Din secured Egypt as well. Eliminating Sunni-Shia sectarianism, the political rivalry that had so aided the European venture, he invoked jihad, holy war, as a unifying force for Arabs in Greater Syria and Egypt.

The jihad was to liberate Jerusalem, the third holiest city to Muslims, who call it Bayt al Quds (house of holiness) in memory of Muhammad's stopping there on his night journey to heaven. It fell to Nur ad Din's lieutenant, Saladin (Salah ad Din al Ayubbi, meaning rectitude of the faith), to recapture Jerusalem. Saladin, a Kurd, unified Syria and Egypt, a necessary preliminary and, after many setbacks, captured Mosul, Aleppo, and the string of

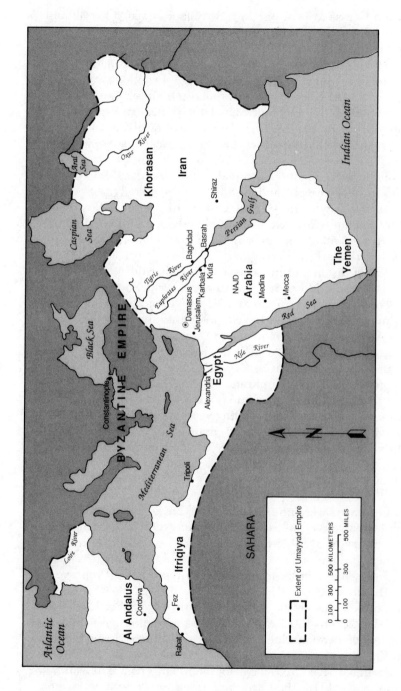

Figure 3. Umayyad Empire, A.D. 661–750

cities from Edessa to Nasihin. In 1187 Saladin took Al Karak (also known as Krak des Chevaliers), a Crusader fort on the route between Homs and Tripoli held by the infamous Reginald of Chatillon, who had broken treaties, molested Saladin's sister, and attacked Mecca for the purpose of obtaining the Prophet's body and exhibiting it at Al Karak for a fee. Saladin besieged Jerusalem on September 20, 1187, and nine days later Jerusalem surrendered. Saladin's behavior and his complete control of his troops earned him the respect of Jerusalemites and the epithet "flower of Islamic chivalry."

Saladin inflicted mighty blows against the Crusaders, raised Muslim pride and self-respect, and founded the Ayyubid dynasty, which was to govern Egypt until 1260. During his lifetime, he created harmony among Muslims in the Middle East and gained a position of affection and honor among them that remains strong to the present, particularly in Syria.

When Saladin died of malaria in 1192, his rule extended from the Tigris River to North Africa and south to the Sudan. Saladin's death brought this unity to an end. His Ayyubid successors quarreled among themselves, and Syria broke into small dynasties centered in Aleppo, Hamah, Homs, and Damascus. By the fourteenth century, after repelling repeated invasions by Mongols from the north, the Mamluk sultans of Egypt, successors to the Ayyubids, ruled from the Nile to the Euphrates. Their great citadels and monuments still stand, although Tamerlane's destruction of much of Damascus in 1402 seriously damaged such edifices as the Great Umayyad Mosque. In 1516 the Ottoman sultan in Turkey defeated the Mamluks at Aleppo and made Syria a province of a new Muslim empire.

Ottoman Empire

The Ottomans were nomadic Muslim Turks from Central Asia who had been converted to Islam by Umayyad conquerors in the eighth century. Led by Uthman (whence the Western term *Ottoman*), they founded a principality in 1300 amid the ruins of the Mongol-wrecked Seljuk Empire in northwest Turkey. Fifty years later, Uthman's successors invaded Europe. In 1453 they conquered Constantinople and in the sixteenth century conquered all of the Middle East. From 1300 to 1916, when the empire fell, thirty-six sultans, all descendants of Uthman, ruled much of the Muslim world. Europeans referred to the Ottoman throne as the Sublime Porte, a name derived from a gate of the sultan's palace in Istanbul.

Beginning in 1516, the Ottomans ruled Syria through pashas, who governed with unlimited authority over the land under their

Al Karak (Krak des Chevaliers)
Courtesy Embassy of Syria

control, although they were responsible ultimately to the Sublime
Porte. Pashas were both administrative and military leaders. So
long as they collected their taxes, maintained order, and ruled an
area not of immediate military importance, the Sublime Porte left
them alone. In turn, the pashas ruled smaller administrative districts through either a subordinate Turk or a loyal Arab. Occasionally, as in the area that was to become Lebanon, the Arab
subordinate maintained his position more through his own power
than through loyalty. Throughout Ottoman rule, there was little
contact with the authorities except among wealthier Syrians who
entered government service or studied in Turkish universities.

The system was not particularly onerous to Syrians because the
Turks respected Arabic as the language of the Quran and accepted
the mantle of defenders of the faith. Damascus was made the major
entrepôt for Mecca, and as such it acquired a holy character to
Muslims because of the *baraka* (spiritual force or blessing) of the
countless pilgrims who passed through on the hajj, the pilgrimage
to Mecca (see Muslims, ch. 2).

Ottoman administration often followed patterns set by previous
rulers. Each religious minority—Shia Muslim, Greek Orthodox,
Maronite, Armenian, and Jewish—constituted a *millet*. The religious heads of each community administered all personal status
law and performed certain civil functions as well.

15

The Syrian economy did not flourish under the Ottomans. At times, attempts were made to rebuild the country, but on the whole, Syria remained poor. The population decreased by nearly 30 percent, and hundreds of villages virtually disappeared into the desert. At the end of the eighteenth century, only one-eighth of the villages formerly on the register of the Aleppo *pashalik* (domain of a pasha) were still inhabited. Only the area now known as Lebanon achieved economic progress, largely resulting from the relatively independent rule of the Druze amirs.

Although impoverished by Ottoman rule, Syria continued to attract European traders, who for centuries had imported spices, fruits, and textiles from the Middle East to the West. By the fifteenth century, Aleppo was the Middle East's chief marketplace and had eclipsed Damascus in wealth, creating a rivalry between the two cities that continues.

With the traders from the West came missionaries, teachers, scientists, and tourists whose governments began to clamor for certain rights. France demanded the right to protect Christians, and in 1535 Sultan Sulayman I granted France several "capitulations"—extraterritorial rights that developed later into political semiautonomy, not only for the French but also for the Christians protected by them. The British acquired similar rights in 1580 and established the Levant Company in Aleppo. By the end of the eighteenth century, the Russians had claimed protective rights over the Greek Orthodox community.

The Ottoman Empire began to show signs of decline in the eighteenth century. By the nineteenth century, European powers had begun to take advantage of Ottoman weakness through both military and political penetration, including Napoleon's invasion of Egypt, subsequent British intervention, and French occupation of Lebanon. Economic development of Syria through the use of European capital—for example, railroads built largely with French money—brought further incursions.

Western penetration became decidedly political after the Druze uprising in the Syrian province of Lebanon in 1860. The revolt began in the north as a Maronite Christian peasant uprising against Christian landlords. As the revolt moved southward to the territories where the landlords were Druzes, the conflagration acquired an intersectarian character, and the Druzes massacred some 10,000 Maronites. France sent in troops and removed them a year later only after the European powers had forced the Sublime Porte to grant new laws for Lebanon. By the Statute of 1861, for the first time Mount Lebanon was officially detached from Syria, and its administration came increasingly under the control of France.

*Mosque of Sultan
Sulayman I in Damascus
Courtesy Embassy of Syria*

Because of European pressure as well as the discontent of the Syrian people, the Ottoman sultans enacted some reforms during the nineteenth century. The Egyptian occupation of Syria from 1831 to 1839 under the nominal authority of the sultan brought a centralized government, judicial reform, and regular taxation. But Ibrahim Pasha, son of the Egyptian ruler, became unpopular with the landowners because he limited their influence and with the peasants because he imposed conscription and taxation. He was eventually driven from Syria by the sultan's forces. Subsequent reforms of Turkish sultan Mahmud II and his son were more theoretical than real and were counteracted by reactionary forces inside the state as well as by the inertia of Ottoman officials. Reforms proved somewhat successful with the Kurds and Turkomans in the north and with the Alawis (see Glossary) around Latakia, but unsuccessful with the Druzes—who lived in the Jabal Druze (present-day Jabal al Arab), a rugged mountainous area in southwest Syria—who retained their administrative and judicial autonomy and exemption from military service.

Although further reform attempts generally failed, some of the more successful endure. Among them are the colonization of Syria's frontiers, the suppression of tribal raiding, the opening of new lands to cultivation, and the beginnings of the settlement of the beduin tribes. Attempts to register the land failed, however, because of the peasants' fear of taxation and conscription.

Sultan Abdul Hamid II (1876–1909), sometimes known as Abdul Hamid the Damned, acquired a reputation as the most oppressive Ottoman sultan. Opponents died quickly; taxes became heavy. Abdul Hamid tried to earn the loyalty of his Muslim subjects by preaching pan-Islamic ideas, and in 1908, by completing the Hejaz Railway between Istanbul and Medina. However, the sultan's cruelty— coupled with that of his deputy in Acre, known in Syria as The Butcher—and increasing Western cultural influences set the stage for the first act of Arab nationalism. World War I opened the next.

World War I, Arab Nationalism, and The French Mandate

The period from the outbreak of World War I in 1914 to the granting of France's mandate over Syria by the League of Nations in 1922 was marked by a complicated sequence of events and power politics during which Syrians achieved a brief moment of independence. Syrian intellectuals, many of them graduates of European and European- or American-run universities, were urging the study of Arab history, literature, and language. Also, groups of Syrians publicly demanded decentralization of Ottoman administration and administrative reform. As Ottoman governors such as Jamal Pasha suppressed them, Syrians went underground and demanded complete Arab independence. One of the first secret groups to form was Al Jamiyah al Arabiyah al Fatat (The Young Arab Society, known as Al Fatat, not to be confused with the present-day Al Fatah, or Fatah, of the Palestine Liberation Organization—PLO), of which Prince Faysal, son of Sharif Husayn of Mecca, was a member. Another group was Al Ahd (The Covenant), a secret association of Arab army officers.

Following the outbreak of World War I, Jamal Pasha determined to tighten his control over Syria. Attacking dissidents ruthlessly, he arrested Al Fatat members. Twenty-one Arabs were hanged in the city squares of Damascus and Beirut on the morning of May 6, 1916. The event is commemorated as Martyrs' Day, a national holiday in Syria and Lebanon.

Events leading to Syria's independence began in the Arabian Peninsula. The British—anxious for Arab support against the Ottomans in the war and desiring to strengthen their position vis-à-vis the French in the determination of the Middle East's future—asked Sharif Husayn, leader of the Hashimite lineage and an Ottoman appointee over the Hejaz, to lead the Arabs in revolt. In return the British gave certain assurances, which Husayn interpreted as an endorsement of his eventual kingship of the Arab world. From the Arab nationalists in Damascus came pleas for the

Hashimites to assume leadership. Husayn accepted, and on June 5, 1916, the Hejazi tribesmen, led by Husayn's sons and later advised by such British officers as T.E. Lawrence, rose against the Turks. In October 1918, Faysal entered Damascus as a popular hero.

Faysal, as military governor, assumed immediate control of all Syria except for the areas along the Mediterranean coast where French troops were garrisoned. In July 1919, he convened the General Syrian Congress, which declared Syria sovereign and free. In March 1920, the congress proclaimed Faysal king of Syria.

Faysal and his Syrian supporters began reconstructing Syria. They declared Arabic the official language and proceeded to have school texts translated from Turkish. They reopened schools and started new ones, including the Faculty of Law at the Syrian University and the Arab Academy in Damascus. Also, Faysal appointed a committee to begin drawing up a constitution.

In the areas still held by the French, Syrians continued to revolt. In the Jabal an Nusayriyah around Latakia in the northwest, there had been an uprising against French troops in May 1919. Along the Turkish border, the nationalist leader Ibrahim Hannanu incited another rebellion in July 1919. The French defeated these attempts, but not before Hannanu and Faysal had acquired permanent places in Syrian history as heroes.

Three forces worked against Arab nationalism and Faysal's budding Arab monarchy. One was Britain's earlier interest in keeping eastern Mesopotamia under its control, both to counter Russian influence in the north and to protect oil interests in the area. The second was Zionism and the Jewish interest in Palestine. Although Britain had promised to recognize "an independent Arab State or a Confederation of Arab States" in the Sykes-Picot Agreement of May 16, 1916 (not published until later—see below), in the Balfour Declaration of 1917 it had also promised Zionists a "national home" in Palestine. The two promises were in direct conflict. The third force was France's determination to remain a power in the Middle East. Earlier in the war, the French, British, Italians, and Russians had met secretly to decide the fate of Arab lands. After the Russian Revolution, the Bolsheviks published secret diplomatic documents, among them the Sykes-Picot Agreement. In this agreement, signed only six months after the British had vaguely promised Husayn an Arab kingdom, Britain and France agreed to give the French paramount influence in what became Syria and Lebanon; the British were to have predominance in what became Transjordan and Iraq.

At the Versailles Peace Conference in 1919, Woodrow Wilson asked that the Arab claims to independence be given consideration, and Faysal was invited to present the Arab cause. Faysal's pleas were unavailing, however, as was a report recommending Syrian independence under Faysal or a United States mandate over the country. Disappointed by his failure at Versailles, Faysal returned to Damascus and declared again that Syria was nevertheless free and independent.

France and Britain refused to recognize Syria's independence, and the Supreme Allied Council, meeting in San Remo, Italy, in April 1920, partitioned the Arab world into mandates as prearranged by the earlier Sykes-Picot Agreement. Syria became a French mandate, and French soldiers began marching from Beirut to Damascus. Arab resistance was crushed, and on July 25, 1920, the French took Damascus. Faysal fled to Europe and did not return to the Middle East until the British made him king of Iraq in 1921. Faysal's brother Abdullah was recognized by the British as the amir of the region that became known as Transjordan. The boundaries of these states were thus drawn unilaterally by the European Allies after World War I. Syria had experienced its brief moment of independence (1919–20), the loss of which Syrians blamed on France and Britain. These events left a lasting bitterness against the West and a deep-seated determination to reunite Arabs into one state. This was the primary basis for modern Arab nationalism and the central ideological concept of future pan-Arab parties, such as the Baath (Arab Socialist Resurrection) Party and the Arab National Movement. Aspects of the ideology also were evolved in the 1950s and 1960s by Gamal Abdul Nasser of Egypt.

French-British rivalry in the Middle East continued after the two countries had divided the area into spheres of influence at San Remo. In their mandate, the French sought to increase their strength by supporting and separating religious minorities and thereby weakening the Arab nationalist movement. France originally planned to establish three sectarian states: an Alawi state in the north, a Sunni Muslim state in the center, and a Druze state in the south. The three were eventually to be incorporated into a federal Syria. France did create a Christian state in the area of Mount Lebanon. The Sunni Muslim state never materialized. Instead, in 1926 the French, working with Maronite leaders, expanded the original boundaries of the Christian state to create Lebanon. To the east, the Biqa Valley, predominantly populated by Muslims, was added; to the west, the Christian state was expanded to the coast and incorporated the cities of Tripoli, Beirut, Sidon, and Tyre.

The rest of Syria was divided into five semiautonomous areas— the Jabal Druze, Aleppo, Latakia, Damascus, and the city of

Alexandretta (present-day Iskenderun)—which accentuated religious differences and cultivated regional, as opposed to national pan-Arab, sentiment (see Religious Life, ch. 2). The Druzes were given administration of the Jabal Druze, the area of their greatest concentration. The northern coastal region and the Jabal an Nusayriyah (where there was a concentration of Alawis, Syria's largest religious minority) were united in the state of Latakia (present-day Al Ladhiqiyah Province). North of Latakia, the district of Alexandretta (the present-day Turkish province of Hatay), home of some Turks, had a separate government. In the area to the south, in Palestine, European Jews were promised a Jewish homeland. Opposition by nationalistic Arabs to the many divisions proved fruitless, and Arab nationalists became isolated in Damascus.

French rule was oppressive. The franc became the base of the economy, and currency management was in the hands of French bankers concerned with French, rather than Syrian, shareholders and interests. The French language became compulsory in schools, and pupils were required to sing the "Marseillaise." Colonial administrators attempted to apply techniques of administration learned in North Africa to the more sophisticated Arabs of Syria. Nearly every feature of Syrian life came under French control.

The Syrians were an embittered, disillusioned people whose leaders kept them in ferment. Shaykh Salih ibn Ali led the Alawis in intermittent revolt; Shaykh Ismail Harir rebelled in the Hawran; Sultan Pasha al Atrash, kinsman of the paramount chief of the Druzes, led continual resistance in the Jabal Druze, most notably in 1925; and Mulhim Qasim led resistance in the mountains around Baalbek. The revolts, however, were not necessarily expressions of desire for unified Syrian independence. They were uprisings by individual groups—Alawis, Druzes, and beduins—against foreign interference, comparable to those earlier fomented against the Ottomans.

In Damascus, Arab nationalism was led by educated, wealthy Muslims who had earlier supported Faysal. Their grievances against the French were many, but chief among them were French suppression of newspapers, political activity, and civil rights and the division of Greater Syria into several political units. They also objected to French reluctance to frame a constitution for Syria that would provide for the eventual sovereignty that the League of Nations mandate had ordered. When the Iraqis gained an elected assembly from the British in March 1924, Syrian Arabs became even more distressed. On February 9, 1925, as a placating move, the French permitted the nationalists to form the People's Party. Led by Faris al Khuri, they demanded French recognition of eventual Syrian independence, unity of the country, greater stress on education, and the granting of civil liberties.

The most immediate issue was Syrian unity, since France had divided the country into six parts. In 1925 Aleppo and Damascus provinces were joined, and in 1926 Lebanon became an independent republic under French control. The League of Nations in its session in Rome in February–March 1926 stated: "The Commission thinks it beyond doubt that these oscillations in matters so calculated to encourage the controversies inspired by the rivalries of races, clans and religions, which are so keen in this country, to arouse all kinds of ambitions and to jeopardize serious moral and material interests, have maintained a condition of instability and unrest in the mandated territory.'

Devastating proof of the miscalculations of the French burst into the open with the 1925 Druze revolt. The Druzes had many complaints, but chief among them was the foreign intervention in Druze affairs. The Ottomans had never successfully subdued these mountain people; although split among themselves, they were united in their opposition to foreign rule. Led by Sultan Pasha al Atrash, Druzes attacked and captured Salkhad on July 20, 1925, and on August 2 they took the Druze capital, As Suwayda.

News of the Druze rebellion spread throughout Syria and ignited revolts in Aleppo and Damascus among Syrian nationalists, who pleaded with Atrash to attack the Syrian capital. In October the Druzes invaded the Damascus region; nationalist leaders led their own demonstrations; and the French began systematic bombardment of the city, resulting in the death of 5,000 Syrians. The rebellion collapsed by the end of the year, and reluctant order replaced open revolt.

The return of order gave the French military government an opportunity to assist Syrians in self-government, an obligation demanded of France by the League of Nations. In 1928 the French allowed the formation of the National Bloc (Al Kutlah al Wataniyah), composed of various nationalist groups centered in Damascus. The nationalist alliance was headed by Ibrahim Hannanu and Hashim Atassi and included leading members of large landowning families. One of the most extreme groups in the National Bloc was the Istiqlal (Independence) Party, a descendant of the old Al Fatat secret society of which Shukri al Quwatly was a leading member. Elections of that year for a constituent assembly put the National Bloc in power, and Hannanu set out to write a constitution. It provided for the reunification of Syria and ignored the authority of the French. In 1930 the French imposed the constitution minus articles that would have given Syria unified self-government.

22

The rolling countryside of Al Ladhiqiyah Province,
home to many of Syria's Alawis
Courtesy Embassy of Syria

Syrian nationalists continued to assert that they at least should have a treaty with France setting forth French aims, since Britain and Iraq had signed such a treaty in 1922. Unrest after the death of the nationalist leader Hannanu at the end of 1935, followed by a general strike in 1936, brought new negotiations for such a treaty. Under Leon Blum's liberal-socialist government in France, the two countries worked out the Syrian-French Treaty of Alliance in 1936. The French parliament never ratified the treaty, yet a feeling of optimism prevailed in Syria as the first nationalist government came to power with Atassi as president.

During 1937 Syria's drive for independence seemed to be advancing under National Bloc leadership. France allowed the return of the Jabal Druze and Latakia to the Syrian state and turned over many local government functions to the Syrian government. French administration during the previous years had given some advantages to the Syrians. It had built modern cities in Damascus and Aleppo and roads and schools throughout much of the country; and it had partially trained some Syrians as minor bureaucrats. French cultural influence spread in the schools, in the press, and even in the style of dress; social and economic conditions slowly improved.

Under the French, Syria became a refuge for persecuted groups from neighboring countries. Most of the Kurdish population arrived between 1924 and 1938, fleeing Kemalist rule in Turkey. The major immigration of Armenians occurred between 1925 and 1945 as a result of similar persecution. Assyrians, under attack in Iraq in 1933, settled in eastern Syria (see Kurds; Armenians; Others, ch. 2).

Although the country appeared to be on the verge of peace, true calm evaded Syria. Claims by Turkey to Alexandretta, Arab revolts in Palestine, an economic crisis caused by depreciation of the French franc, and lack of unity among Syrians served to undermine the stability of the Syrian government. The National Bloc was split by rivalries. Abdul Rahman Shahabandar, a leading nationalist, formed a rival organization in 1939 to compete for Syrian political leadership, but he was assassinated a year later. Separatist movements in the Jabal Druze found French support and antagonized the nationalists.

During the course of the Syrian-French treaty discussions in 1936, Turkey had asked for reconsideration of the situation in Hatay—at that time the Syrian province of Alexandretta—which had a large Turkish minority and already had been given a special administrative system under the Franco-Turkish Agreement of Ankara (sometimes called the Franklin-Bouillon Agreement) in 1921. The case was submitted to the League of Nations, which in 1937 decided that Alexandretta should be a separate, self-governing political state. Direct negotiations between Turkey and France ended on July 13, 1939, with France agreeing to absorption of Alexandretta by Turkey. Disturbances broke out in Syria against France and the Syrian government, which Syrian nationalist leaders felt had not adequately defended their interests. Syrian president Atassi resigned, parliamentary institutions were abolished, and France governed an unruly Syria through the Council of Directors. Latakia and the Jabal Druze were again set up as separate units. The French government officially declared it would not submit the Syrian-French treaty to the French Chamber of Deputies for ratification.

World War II and Independence

The capitulation of France in June 1940 brought Vichy-appointed General Henri Dentz as high commissioner and a new cabinet headed by Khalid al Azm, a wealthy landlord from an old Damascus family who was to play a leading role in Syrian politics twenty-two years later. Despite continued German military successes elsewhere, British and Free French forces supported by troops of the Transjordan Arab Legion defeated the Vichy forces in both Syria and Lebanon. Control then passed to Free French authorities.

A view of Damascus

The entry of Allied troops brought a promise from the Free French leader, General Charles de Gaulle, of eventual independence, although de Gaulle declared that so far as he was concerned, the mandate would remain in existence until a new French government legally brought it to an end. When the Syrians elected a new parliament in 1943 with the National Bloc in control, the parliament elected Quwatly as president of Syria.

During 1944 the Syrian government took over the functions of fourteen administrative departments that had been under direct French control since 1920. These included those dealing with customs, social affairs, excise taxes, control of concessionary companies, and supervision of tribes. France retained control of social, cultural, and educational services as well as the Troupes Spéciales du Levant (Levantine Special Forces), which were used for security purposes. Despite French opposition, the Soviet Union in July and the United States in September 1944 granted Syria and Lebanon unconditional recognition as sovereign states; British recognition followed a year later. These Allied nations pressured France to evacuate Syria.

The new Syrian government demanded either the immediate and unconditional transfer of the Troupes Spéciales du Levant to Syrian control or their disbandment and threatened to form a national army unless such action were taken. But France made withdrawal of the troops dependent on Syria's signing a treaty giving France a privileged position in the country.

In January 1945, the Syrian government announced the formation of a national army and in February declared war on the Axis powers. In March the nation became a charter member of the United Nations (UN), an indication of its sovereign status, and, in April, affirmed its allegiance to the idea of Arab unity by signing the pact of the League of Arab States (Arab League).

The way in which the French left Syria, however, increased the already bitter feelings the Syrians had toward France. France was adamant in its demand that its cultural, economic, and strategic interests be protected by treaty before agreeing to withdraw the Troupes Spéciales du Levant. In May 1945, demonstrations occurred in Damascus and Aleppo and, for the third time in twenty years, the French bombed and machine-gunned the ancient capital. Serious fighting broke out in Homs and Hamah as well. Only after Britain's prime minister Winston Churchill threatened to send troops to Damascus did General de Gaulle order a cease-fire. A UN resolution in February 1946 called on France to evacuate. The French acceded and, by April 15, 1946, all French troops were off Syrian soil. On April 17, Syria celebrated Evacuation Day; the date is a national holiday.

After Independence

The legacy of ancient Syria, the Arab empire, Ottoman rule, and the French Mandate left the people of Syria with loyalties to both their own nation and their neighbors. During the period of the French Mandate, Syria's leaders—though often competing with each other for power—were generally united in their single goal of freedom from French rule. Conflicts between diverse groups were postponed, as Syrian unity was essential for the independence fight.

When the French departed, however, unity among the leaders disappeared. Aleppines contested with Damascenes for dominance in commercial and political life; the Druzes pledged allegiance to Druzes, the Kurds to Kurds, and tribal peoples to tribal institutions. Alawis, the poorest yet largest of the minorities, tried to rebel from Sunni Muslim control. Rural leaders contended with urban leaders; the progressive, increasingly secularized, younger generation vied with the older, religious-minded leaders. Politicians differed over the kind of government Syria should have—monarchy or republic, parliamentary or presidential democracy.

Although most leaders agreed that the Syria they inherited was merely a part of a larger Arab nation, they disagreed on the form such a nation should take. Trade-minded Aleppines preferred Iraq and the Hashimites, as did some of the older leaders who had joined Faysal in 1918. Young, educated Damascenes rejected the Hashimites, who they felt were backed by the British. The cultural heritage of France and the American ideals of democracy induced many Syrians to look westward for friendship. Others looked northward to the Soviet Union, which from the Syrian point of view had no record of intrigue in the Arab world.

Syria began its independent life under the presidency of Quwatly, backed by a splintered parliament without real leadership. The nation's first crisis was the independence of Israel, fruit of the Balfour Declaration and the Sykes-Picot Agreement. In May 1948, Syrian troops invaded Israel in conjunction with other Arab armies.

Toward the end of 1948, Syrian politicians became profoundly disappointed with their government's failure not only to defeat Israel but also to regain the former province of Alexandretta, to free blocked assets in France, and to maintain an independent currency. Prime Minister Azm tried to cut army expenditures, find backing for the Syrian pound, and construct a new pipeline from Iraq to the Syrian coast. He failed in all of these efforts.

The year 1949 was one of dramatic instability for Syria. On March 30, Brigadier General Husni az Zaim, army chief of staff, staged the first of Syria's numerous coups. He was cheered by the political opposition and the urban masses who were tired of high prices and an inept bureaucracy. Zaim, first backed by the British and then by the French, was recognized by Arab and Western governments and was elected president of Syria after abolishing political parties and proposing himself as the only candidate. He ratified an agreement with the Trans–Arabian Pipeline Company (Tapline) and declared himself ready to support a Middle Eastern-North Atlantic Treaty Organization if the United States would give economic support to the area.

Although Zaim was deposed less than five months later in a countercoup, his brief whirlwind rule was crowded with constructive action as well as oppressive measures. His achievements included the start of construction on the Euphrates River project to bring water to Aleppo; initiation of the Latakia harbor project; building of new roads and hospitals; framing of new civil laws, commercial laws, and penal codes; granting of suffrage to women and abolition of private *waqfs* (charitable religious endowments). But Zaim's personal ambition depleted the treasury and lost him political support.

Syria's second coup was led by Brigadier General Sami al Hinnawi, who arrested Zaim and Prime Minister Muhsin al Barazi on August 14, 1949. After a trial before the Council of War, both were executed. Under the provisional government of Atassi, a new electoral law was adopted, and women voted for the first time in the election of November 15–16, 1949. Although Hinnawi's coup returned Syrian government to civilian politicians, the army remained watchful in the background.

Shishakli Dictatorship

On December 19, 1949, army leadership changed hands when Colonel Adib Shishakli arrested Hinnawi and accused him of conspiring with a foreign power—Iraq—against Syrian interests. While the army waited, civilian politicians tried to stabilize the government, and on September 4, 1950, the Constituent Assembly approved a new constitution and reconstructed itself as the Chamber of Deputies. But the leaderless civilians were unable to maintain authority. Inflation produced dissatisfaction in the cities, and hoarding, unemployment, and rioting followed. An economic dispute with the Lebanese, who were opposed to Syria's protective tariffs policy, led to the breaking of the seven-year-old economic agreement between the countries. Increasing opposition to army influence—Shishakli demanded that the minister of defense be his specially selected follower, Major General Fawzi Silu—forced Shishakli's hand. On November 28, 1951, he arrested the cabinet ministers and appointed Silu prime minister. From that point on, Shishakli exercised blatant dictatorial control, tightening his hold over the civil service and the courts and legislating by decree. On April 6, 1952, he abolished all political parties and tried to fill the vacuum by creating his own party—the Arab Liberation Movement (ALM).

In a July 1953 referendum, Syrians approved a new constitution, making Syria a presidential republic with Shishakli as president. The subsequent Chamber of Deputies was packed with ALM deputies, the other parties having boycotted the election.

Signs that Shishakli's regime would collapse appeared at the end of 1953 with student strikes and the circulation of unusually virulent pamphlets urging sedition. The major political parties, meeting at Homs in September, agreed to resist and overthrow Shishakli. Trouble developed among the Druzes, and Shishakli declared martial law. The army, infiltrated by Shishakli's opponents, staged Syria's fourth coup, on February 25, 1954, and restored the 1949 government.

Radical Political Influence

The ouster of Shishakli brought out once more the conflicts among the diverse political elements of the country. Cabinet succeeded cabinet as shifting coalitions of conservatives on the one hand and left-wing socialists on the other hand vied for supremacy. By 1955 the balance began to swing in favor of left-wing elements, notably the Baath Party and the Syrian Communist Party, the only parties in Syria with effective organizations and definite platforms and the only ones not based on sectarian interests. Their platforms coincided on some issues, and they sometimes cooperated in achieving their goals: economic and political reform aimed at dislodging the ineffective entrenched leadership that was at once quasi-feudal, mercantile, and Western connected; Arab unity; and close cooperation with the Soviets to counter alleged Western designs on the Arab homeland.

Anti-Western sentiment had been ever-present in independent Syria, resulting from deep disappointment over perceived British betrayal at Versailles and resentment of French policies under the mandate. It had reached a high pitch after the creation of Israel, considered another example of Western connivance against the Arabs, but was subdued by the pro-Western Shishakli. In 1955 it was vocal again under the stimulation of local politicians and Soviet propaganda. The British-French-Israeli invasion of the Sinai in late 1956 gave it additional impetus.

The gradual ascendance to power of left-wing radicals brought close relations with the Soviet Union and other communist countries. Several barter agreements were signed between 1954 and 1956; cultural agreements were concluded, missions were exchanged, and an arms deal was signed in 1956. At the same time, Syria became increasingly isolated from its Arab neighbors.

During 1957 the conservatives were virtually eliminated as a political factor. In May they suffered a crushing defeat in by-elections after four traditionally conservative representatives were convicted of conspiracy. Later that year, conservatives failed in an effort to form an effective coalition in parliament to counter the radicals, and conservative and moderate army officers failed to dislodge known Communists from strategic posts in the army. By the end of 1957, Baathists, with their Communist and other left-wing allies, were in control of the government.

The success of the radicals in gaining control resulted largely from close cooperation between the Baathists and the Communists. The Communists had been growing rapidly in number and strength as popularity of the East and dislike of the West grew, and, by the end of 1957, they threatened Baathist domination of the radical alliance. Moderates in Syria and abroad feared an imminent Communist takeover. The Baathists became alarmed when a new radical party was formed to counter their influence and to cooperate with the Communists. The last months of 1957 saw a fierce behind-the-scenes struggle for supremacy within the radical camp.

United Arab Republic

Seeing no way to preserve its position through domestic maneuvering, the government turned to Egypt's president Nasser for help. Discussions about a union between Syria and Egypt had been held in 1956 but had been interrupted by the Suez crisis. The subject was brought up again in December 1957, when the Baath Party announced that it was drafting a bill for union with Egypt. Although the Baath Party knew that Nasser's declared hostility to political parties would mean the end of its legal existence, it calculated that the group most affected would be the Communists, whose counterparts in Egypt were being ruthlessly persecuted. The Baathists expected Nasser to dissolve all parties but envisaged a special role for themselves in the new state because of their continued support of Nasser and their identification with his views. For his part, Nasser was reluctant to burden himself with a troubled Syria and agreed to the union only after a Syrian delegation convinced him of the seriousness of the communist threat. The union of Syria and Egypt in the United Arab Republic (UAR) was announced on February 1, 1958, and later ratified by a plebiscite in each country.

The form in which the UAR emerged was not what the Baathists had envisioned. One of Nasser's conditions for union was that the two countries be completely integrated, not just federated as the Syrians proposed, and Syria soon found itself dominated by the stronger, more efficient Egypt. The Provisional Constitution of 1958 called for a unitary cabinet and a 600-member assembly, composed of 400 Egyptians and 200 Syrians, half of the members being drawn from the then-existing national assemblies. Syria and Egypt were designated regions of the UAR, each headed by an appointed executive council. Nasser was unanimously chosen president of the republic, and two of the four vice presidents were Syrians, one of them Akram Hawrani, leader of the Baath Party. The first cabinet included fourteen Syrians out of thirty-four members, all of them leading politicians and military figures whom Nasser wanted removed from their bases of power. As expected, all political parties were dissolved; but the Baathists did not find themselves in the favored position they expected. The UAR was completely run by Nasser.

Although a number of nationalization and land reform measures had been implemented in Syria, Nasser felt that socialist reform and integration with Egypt were moving too slowly and, in October 1959, appointed Egyptian vice president Abdul Hakim Amir to supervise policy in Syria. The Syrians, however, were increasingly

*The Euphrates Dam, partially financed by the Soviet Union
and built with Soviet technical assistance
Courtesy Embassy of Syria*

dissatisfied with Egypt's domination. Egyptians took over a large number of the important administrative posts in Syria, and Syrian army officers were transferred to Egypt while Egyptians took posts in Syria. Growing political unrest in Syria was exacerbated by an economic crisis brought about by prolonged drought. Nasser made little apparent effort to placate Syrian dissatisfaction and continued with his planned integration of the UAR. On September 28, 1961, a military coup was staged in Damascus, and Syria seceded from the UAR.

Coups and Countercoups, 1961–70

The military coup again brought out all the competing factions and interest groups. In December 1961, all political groups except the Communists and pro-Nasser factions participated in a general election for a constituent assembly. Although party labels were not used, only a few known Baathists were elected to an assembly dominated by moderates and conservatives.

The new assembly elected Nazim al Qudsi president of the republic, and he in turn named a conservative, Maruf Dawalibi, prime minister. In January 1962, the assembly repealed major sections of a July 1961 decree that had nationalized various industrial and commercial firms, and, in February, it amended in favor of the landlords the land-reform measures that had been implemented during the period of union.

The new government succeeded in pleasing few and alienating many, and, on March 28, 1962, there was another military coup. President Qudsi resigned, as did the prime minister and the cabinet, and the executive and legislative functions of the government were taken over by an organization called the General Command of the Army and Armed Forces. Demonstrations against this new coup broke out in several of the major cities, and, on April 5, the seven military officers who had organized and implemented the coup were sent into exile by other military leaders. On April 10, Qudsi resumed the presidency.

The events between April and September were confusing. According to some factions, the assembly had been dissolved; other groups contended that the assembly had voluntarily resigned; and still others asserted that the assembly continued to exist although it was not allowed to meet. A new prime minister formed a government that restored several of the socialist measures of the UAR period but banned all political parties.

By early September 1962 clashes between pro-Nasser and anti-Nasser elements had become more violent and more frequent, as had the student demonstrations and terrorist bombings. On September 13, President Qudsi appointed Azm as the new prime minister and allowed the National Assembly, supposedly defunct, to convene at his residence. In its single session, the assembly confirmed Azm's appointment and approved three seemingly contradictory measures: first, the reinstated Constituent Assembly was to be called the Constitutional Assembly; second, the government could legislate in the absence of the assembly; and, third, the government was granted the authority to dissolve the assembly with the understanding that new elections would be held within one year. On September 20 the assembly was again dissolved.

Although Azm included representatives of all political factions except the extreme pro-Nasser group in this cabinet, he was unable to govern effectively, and, by early 1963, four of the seven military officers who had been exiled after their successful coup in March 1962 made another coup attempt. This time they were unsuccessful, and they again went into exile. Their abortive coup was poorly planned and elicited no discernible support from the military, but in February, the government attempted to purge the army of an estimated 120 officers who were believed to pose a threat. On March 8, there was yet another coup by the military, and on March 9, Salah ad Din al Bitar, who with Michel Aflaq had founded the Baath Party in the 1940s, became prime minister for the first of several times.

Bitar included five pro-Nasserites in his cabinet, but in early May these five ministers were forced to resign, and 47 officers and 1,000 noncommissioned officers who were believed to be pro-Nasser were forced out of the army. On May 11, Bitar resigned, but a week later, he returned to form a new government. During May and June 1963, the situation continued to be confused, and July 17–18, an estimated 2,000 Nasserites attempted a coup. The fighting was intense for a few hours in Damascus, but the coup was crushed. Major General Amin al Hafiz—a Sunni Baathist army officer who had risen with the neo-Baathists—emerged as the strongman, serving as commander in chief of the armed forces, president of the National Council of the Revolutionary Command (subsequently known as the National Council of the Revolution—NCR), deputy prime minister, minister of defense, minister of the interior, and deputy military governor. On August 4, Bitar formed another government, his third in six months.

The attempted coup marked a turning point in the country's domestic affairs. It was the first time that a coup or coup attempt had resulted in widespread violence and loss of life. On July 19, eight army officers and twelve civilians were convicted in summary trials before revolutionary security courts and were executed by firing squads the same day. This pattern of violence was to be repeated by the Baathists in seizing and retaining power.

On November 11, 1963, Bitar again resigned, and Hafiz became prime minister, retaining as well the other posts he previously held. By April 1964, urban unrest had again become serious. In Hamah, for example, the military measures taken to suppress the uprisings resulted in what Hafiz described as "frightful carnage." On May 14, Hafiz resigned as prime minister but retained his other posts, and Bitar formed another government.

Between May 1964 and February 1966, there were frequent changes of government, reflecting the contest for power between the centrist and leftist wings of the Baath Party. The occasional urban and town riots, student disorders, and pro-Nasser demonstrations were sternly repressed. During this period, Hafiz continued to dominate the public scene, but two other Baathist generals, both Alawis, began to exercise decisive power. On February 23, 1966, these two generals, Salah al Jadid and Hafiz al Assad, joined Nureddin Atassi in a coup that placed the more extremist wing of the Baath Party in power.

Neo-Baath Dominance, 1963–66

During the period of union with Egypt, the first stimulus for revival of the Syrian Baath Party came from a group of Syrian officers stationed in Egypt who styled themselves the Military Committee. This committee at one time or another included a Sunni, Amin al Hafiz; a Druze, Hamad Ubayd; and two Alawis, Muhammad Umran and Jadid. After the secession from the UAR in 1961, the Syrian Baath Party was formally reestablished at a party congress in May 1962. At this time, Hawrani was dismissed from the party on doctrinal grounds for opposing Arab unity. After the coup, these Baathist associates progressively moved to displace the coup leaders from the senior positions in the army and the newly formed, self-appointed, and largely anonymous National Council of the Revolutionary Command. It was with this body that effective power rested and not with Bitar's cabinet, as was clearly demonstrated in the provisional constitution decreed on March 24, 1963, and in its replacement promulgated on April 25, 1964.

The coming to power of the Baath Party in 1963 is sometimes referred to as the Baath Revolution, though the March 8 coup was not executed by the Baathists and did not actually initiate the great social revolution postulated in Baathist ideology. In any case, the party was supreme, but factionalism continued within the Baathist regime.

Five major centers of power existed in Syria. The National Council of the Revolutionary Command, preeminent in 1963, was changed by the Constitution of 1964 into the NCR, was enlarged in membership, and became an appointed legislative body. Highest authority was vested in the five-man Presidency Council elected from its membership. Other power centers included the Ministry of Defense and the top army command echelon, the government structure of prime minister and cabinet, and the Baath Party's Regional Command and National Command. The dominant clique at any time had representation in all of them; many officials held multiple offices with positions in two or more power centers; and top-level coordination of the centers was accomplished, in effect, by an interlocking directorate.

Broad factional differences developed between pan-Arab nationalist adherents to the old-guard Baath leadership of Aflaq and Bitar on the one hand and those who became known as regionalists, emphasizing Syria first, on the other hand. A principal area of contention was their attitudes toward Arab unity, specifically toward some kind of reunion with Egypt or union with Iraq or both.

Aflaq's nationalists varied from strong to moderate in their support of union, although they wanted it on their own terms and at a rapid rate, as a high priority. In contrast, the regionalists, while giving lip service to unity, varied from weak moderates favoring a go-slow approach to opponents of union. In the regionalist camp were the rising Alawi Baath officers Jadid, Assad, and Umran.

The neo-Baathists as a whole believed that the nationalization and land reform measures started under Nasser but reversed during the conservative interregnum of September 1961 to March 1963 should be restored. The question centered on the rate of movement toward socialism. Aflaq's adherents favored a moderate, slow approach, whereas the regionalists tended to favor extensive measures quickly carried out. The regionalists became known as radicals, the radical wing, or "the extremists." They also inclined to the establishment of closer, more exclusive ties with the Soviet Union than the old guard, which viewed an exclusive Soviet position of influence as nothing but a new form of imperialism.

Discussions with President Nasser in Cairo resulted on April 17, 1963, in a statement of intent to form a union of Syria, Egypt, and Iraq. This venture, however, collapsed by July 22. In Syria a major pro-Nasserite military coup attempt in early July was put down with severity by Hafiz, the minister of the interior and military governor. This coup attempt served thereafter to justify Baathist monopolization of power; it confirmed the change in style from the pre-1963 pattern of relatively bloodless coups and marked the advent to the top power position of Hafiz, who was to become a virtual dictator for the next two and one-half years.

On July 27, 1963, Hafiz acquired the additional titles of president of the National Council of the Revolutionary Command, president of the republic, commander in chief, and minister of defense. He was also a member of both the Regional Command and the National Command of the Baath Party. In November he became prime minister, although from time to time he called on civilians, such as Bitar and Yusuf Zuayyin, to hold this post.

From the outset, Hafiz aligned himself with Aflaq's old-guard civilian wing of the party, which was dominant in the National Command. This was to their mutual benefit, and the civilian leadership allowed the military Baathists a free hand in purging and structuring the forces into an "ideological army" (see Syrian-Israeli Hostility, ch. 5). Coordination between military and civilian party functions was restricted to the top level. This free-hand policy proved to be a mistake for the civilian leadership. Ties of party discipline with the military wing were dissolved, and an intensifying military-civilian split developed. In a reversal of positions, the military Baathists became sponsors of the civilian old guard, which then found itself in the role of junior partner.

During party congresses from 1962 to 1964, strong bids for power were made by a new Marxist faction of the party, which, although finally overcome in party maneuvering, exerted influence and precipitated events having lasting effects. At the congress of October 1963, propositions evincing a new ideological tone were adopted. Identity with "oppressed peoples everywhere" was declared, in contrast to the old Baathist limitation to the Arab nation, and terms such as *class struggle, scientific socialism,* and *popular struggle* were injected. These generic Marxist phrases were not, in fact, employed in the sense commonly understood in Marxist dialectic but were considerably altered by an Arab nationalist context. Their use, nevertheless, indicated a left-wing drift in the Baath Party. In particular, the notion of popular struggle was used to support the Maoist doctrine of the "people's war of liberation," which became a tenet of neo-Baathist ideology in its endorsement of the Palestinian guerrilla movements against Israel.

The regionalist side of the political spectrum welcomed the aspects of the leftward drift in ideology that both mitigated the intense Arab unity theme of the old guard and called for a more intense commitment to nationalization and socialism. The military Baathists welcomed the leftist doctrinal rationale for subordinating individual liberties to the society as a whole. The military, however, took strong exception to the left wing's demand for exclusion of the military from politics and to personal assaults on the "rightist character" of many Baathist officers.

Hafiz and the inner core of the Military Committee, along with Aflaq and Bitar's old guard, successfully engineered the expulsion of the Marxist wing from the party's Regional Command at a conference early in February 1964 and from the National Command later the same month. A new fifteen-member Regional Command was then formed and included seven officers of the Military Committee.

Hafiz sought to balance his position by developing support among different factions, even including the politically excommunicated Hawrani, and he made considerable use of both Alawi and Druze officers. In November 1963, he installed the Alawi Baathist Jadid in the key post of army chief of staff. Jadid emerged as a staunch regionalist.

Hafiz's right-hand man in the Baath military-political structure was Umran, another Alawi but of a different tribe from that of Jadid, and Umran's quietly rising associate, Hafiz al Assad. By the end of 1964, Umran had reversed his stance on several issues, including the matter of Hawrani and union, and was then at odds with Hafiz. He was removed from party position but allowed to take the post of ambassador to Spain.

At the party convention of April 1965, the military and civilian branches of the regional party were constitutionally merged, and the top post of secretary general of the Regional Command passed to Jadid. The contention between the older Aflaq-Bitar Baathists and the regionalists had long been organizationally reflected in contention between the National Command and the Regional Command over the location of principal party power. Assumption of control of the Regional Command by Jadid brought to that post an Alawi who was a senior military officer, the strong man of the shadowy Military Committee, and the staunchest proponent of regionalist Baathism.

The Baath Redirections of 1966 and 1970

By the summer of 1965, Hafiz began seeking to limit the influence of the Alawis and Druzes. His own political orientation had begun to shift toward compromise, moderation, union, and the slowing down of socialism. In September 1965, he removed Jadid from the post of army chief of staff, but the latter entrenched himself in his party position as secretary general of the Regional Command. On December 21, 1965, the National Command dissolved the Regional Command and removed Jadid's three supporters from the five-man Presidency Council.

At the same time, Hafiz dismissed the cabinet of Prime Minister Zuayyin, who had become a regionalist. He then called on the perennial Bitar to form a new cabinet (his fifth) and recalled General Umran as minister of defense. On Hafiz's authority, extensive transfers of Jadid's supporters in the army were planned. On February 18, 1966, Aflaq condemned the Jadid faction for "degenerating into regional separatism" and (although he himself had assisted the process) for the military usurpation of party and government power from the civilian leadership. Thus, the stage was set for a confrontation between the two parts of the Baath Party.

On February 23, 1966, Jadid, the Regional Command, and their army units seized the government in the bloodiest of the many coups d'état since 1949. The general public, however, displayed no inclination to fight for one Baathist military faction against the other.

Hafiz, wounded in the fighting, was arrested and imprisoned; the old National Command was denounced and expelled; and Aflaq and Bitar were read out of the party. Later released, both took refuge in Lebanon. One of the first acts of the Regional Command after seizing the radio station was the announcement of the appointment of Major General Hafiz al Assad as minister of defense.

On March 1, 1966, a new government was formed. Jadid remained outside the formal structure of government, directing affairs through his position as party leader. So as not to appear as an outright military dictatorship, the regime designated prominent regionalist Baath civilians to office: Nureddin Atassi as president of the republic; Yusuf Zuayyin again as prime minister; and Ibrahim Makhus as foreign minister. All were physicians and representatives of the urban intellectuals. The first two were Sunnis; Makhus, an Alawi. In the Regional Command, the top five positions were held by Jadid, Atassi, Zuayyin, Makhus, and Assad, in that order.

On September 8, 1966, a military countercoup attempt was led by a Druze, Salim Hatum, a leading partner of Jadid in the February 23 coup. Although Hatum's men actually arrested President Atassi, the army chief of staff Major General Ahmad Suwaydani, and Jadid himself, the attempt failed when Assad threatened to send the air force against Hatum's forces. The Workers' Battalions, a proletarian national guard organized by Khalid al Jundi and influenced by the Chinese Red Guard concept, also declared for Jadid. Agreement was reached between the factions for an exchange of prisoners, and on the following morning, Hatum and his associates fled to Jordan. He returned to Syria in early June 1967 to fight, he said, against Israel; he was arrested and shot.

The traumatic defeat of the Syrians and Egyptians in the June 1967 War with Israel discredited the radical socialist regimes of Nasser's Egypt and Baathist Syria. The Jadid faction, which included Atassi, Zuayyin, and Makhus, was particularly hurt. The defeat strengthened the hands of the moderates and the rightists and was the catalyst for Assad's ascent in Syria.

In the fall of 1968, open controversy developed between Assad, reportedly representing a moderate faction centered in the military, and extremists of Jadid's civilian regime. Although Jadid's power in the party remained strong, in March 1969 an ostensible compromise was reached between Assad and Jadid. The new government formed in May made minor concessions to broadening the political base but represented no real change in domestic or foreign policy. The rank order in the party's hierarchy remained unchanged. Assad continued as minister of defense. A number of Syrian Communists were arrested, and their leader, Khalid Bakdash, again left the country.

The conflict between the Jadid civilian wing and the Assad military wing of the party continued through 1970, and the government, although reported to be widely unpopular, remained in firm control of the country. From time to time, different measures bore the influence of the two factions. Party purges had decimated the air force, which suffered from a critical pilot shortage, and Assad succeeded in restoring to duty a number of air force pilots who had been retired for political reasons. The Regional Command headed by Jadid, rather than the Ministry of Defense, retained complete control of its institutionalized Palestine guerrilla force, As Saiqa (The Thunderbolt) (see Special and Irregular Armed Forces, ch. 5).

In its radical revolutionary role, the regime proclaimed support for the guerrilla movements but, while polemically assailing Jordan and Lebanon for their efforts to control Palestinian guerrillas in their territories, did not hesitate to control the guerrillas in Syria. As Saiqa was not allowed to launch operations from Syrian soil against Israel because of the danger of reprisal, but it was frequently used within Syria for party security purposes.

In inter-Arab affairs, the Jadid and Assad factions largely negated one another. Syria remained at odds with most Arab states, especially Jordan, Lebanon, and Iraq.

In September 1970, the Jordanian Army launched attacks on PLO camps and on Palestinian refugee camps that were under the control of PLO units; most were in the vicinity of Amman. King Hussein of Jordan ordered the assaults in response to efforts by the PLO to implement its avowed policy of deposing Hussein and other Arab monarchs. The hostilities in Jordan—which became known by the PLO and its supporters as Black September—had a profound impact on the Arab world and particularly on the government in Syria.

During the civil war, which lasted 10 days, Syria sent some 200 tanks (nominally of the Palestine Liberation Army—PLA) to aid the PLO forces. Iraq, Syria's Baathist rival, had a force of about 12,000 men stationed near Az Zarqa northeast of Amman; these troops did not participate in the fighting and withdrew to Iraq a few days later. The United States dispatched the Sixth Fleet to the eastern Mediterranean, and the Israeli Air Force openly assumed a posture of military preparedness. Most important, the Syrian air force refused to provide air cover to the Syrian tank brigade, which came under severe attacks first by the Jordanian Air Force and then by the Jordanian Army. On September 23 and 24, the Syrian expeditionary force withdrew from the battle zone and returned to Syria.

Syria's military fiasco in Jordan reflected political disagreement within the ruling Baath leadership. The Jadid faction argued for full support of and participation with the PLO in Jordan; Assad and his associates opposed such action. For a variety of reasons, not the least of which was fear of a devastating Israeli reprisal, Assad refused to commit his air force to support the tank units. Jadid and his supporters were militarily and politically humiliated.

The Baath Party's tenth congress, held in Damascus, lasted two weeks and ended November 12, 1970. This conference, labeled an extraordinary session of the National Command, underscored Jadid's continuing control of the party apparatus. It adopted resolutions reaffirming the government's position in internal and foreign affairs and censuring Assad and his chief of staff, Major General Mustafa Tlas, on the grounds of improper military influence in the government.

On November 13, 1970, army units arrested Jadid, Atassi, and Zuayyin along with several others and seized the centers of communication without effective opposition. Although a few minor demonstrations occurred, the overthrow was virtually bloodless. Jadid was detained under guard; Atassi, in house arrest. The others were soon released.

On November 16, the Regional Command of the Baath Party issued a statement saying that the change that had occurred was a transfer of power within the party showing that the party's progressive rank and file were stronger than the misdirected forces of dictators. A new party congress was to be convened to reorganize the party; a national front government was to be organized under revised Baathist leadership; and a people's council, or legislature, was to be formed within three months. Continued support for the Palestinian cause was affirmed.

On November 19, 1970, the Regional Command announced the designation of Ahmad al Khatib, a respected but hitherto little-known politician, as acting chief of state and of Lieutenant General Assad as prime minister and minister of defense. Assad then formed a twenty-six-member cabinet, consisting of about one-half Assad Baathists and the balance scattered among Socialists, Nasserites, independents, and Communists. This cabinet met for the first time on November 23, 1970. In a press interview, Assad claimed that the change in government had been neither a coup nor the result of political conflict along the lines of military-civilian division but a natural development in the party's revolutionary movement, often referred to as the "Corrective Movement."

The Assad Era

Soon after taking power, Assad moved quickly to create an organizational infrastructure for the government. In February 1971, the 173-member People's Council was organized, the Baath Party taking 87 seats; the remaining seats were divided among the "popular organizations" and other minor parties. In March 1971, the Baath Party held its regional congress and elected the twenty-one-member Regional Command headed by Assad. That same month, by a national referendum, Assad was elected president for a seven-year term, and in April, Major Abdul Rahman Khulayfawi was designated prime minister with Mahmud al Ayyubi as vice president. The transfer of power from Jadid to Assad was widely regarded as a conservative and moderating movement away from communist radicalism.

In foreign affairs, Syria's relations with the Soviet Union, strained toward the end of 1970, improved dramatically in 1971 and 1972. Syria's relations with other Arab states, particularly Egypt and Libya, became more cordial, as demonstrated by the April 1971 formation of the short-lived Federation of Arab Republics, made up of Syria, Egypt, and Libya.

In March 1972, the Progressive National Front was formed. It consisted of the Baath Party and four non-Baathist groups: the Syrian Arab Socialist Union, a Nasserite group under Jamal Atassi; the Socialist Union Movement under Jamal Sufi; the Arab Socialist Party, composed of the followers of the Baathist Akram Hawrani; and the Syrian Communist Party under Khalid Bakdash.

In March 1973, the Permanent Constitution went into effect, further strengthening Assad's already formidable presidential authority. However, the Assad regime was not without underlying tension. This tension stemmed from sectarian differences between the majority Sunni Muslims and the minority Alawis; but it had much wider implications, not the least of which were political. The immediate focus of the opposition to the regime was the demand by Sunni Muslims that Islam be declared the state religion in the constitution. The draft constitution that was adopted by the People's Council at the end of January 1973 had no provision to that effect. Viewing the constitution as the product of an Alawi-dominated, secular, Baathist ruling elite, Sunni militants staged a series of riots in February 1973 in conservative and predominantly Sunni cities such as Hamah and Homs. A number of demonstrators were killed or wounded in clashes between the troops and demonstrators.

As a result of these demonstrations, the Assad regime had the draft charter amended to include a provision that the president of Syria must be a Muslim. Implicit in this amendment was a declaration that Alawis are Muslims—a formula not accepted by many Sunni Muslims. The draft was approved in a popular referendum held in mid-March for formal promulgation. Assad's compromise, coupled with the government's effective security measures, calmed the situation, but sporadic demonstrations continued through April 1973.

Other major developments in 1973 included the holding in March of parliamentary elections for the People's Council, the first since 1962, and the Syrian-Egyptian war against Israel in October. Syrian forces acquitted themselves better against the Israeli forces in the October 1973 War than in the 1967 one; in fact, the war was widely regarded in Syria as a "victory" and helped to boost Syrian morale substantially. Moreover, in 1974, as a result of the disengagement agreement, Syria recovered parts of the Golan Heights it initially had lost to Israel.

In foreign affairs, the Assad regime charted a pragmatic and increasingly independent course. It maintained close ties with the Soviet Union and East European states, ensuring a sustained flow of Soviet military aid, especially after the October 1973 War. At the same time, Assad moved to improve Syrian relations with Jordan and with the United States and other Western nations.

In May 1973, diplomatic relations with Britain, severed in 1967, were fully restored. Relations with the United States, also severed in 1967, were normalized in June 1974. Two months later, diplomatic ties with the Federal Republic of Germany (West Germany) were resumed after having been severed in 1965, when the West German government exchanged ambassadors with Israel. Meanwhile, relations with Jordan grew progressively more cordial, so that in August 1975 Syria and Jordan announced the establishment of a joint supreme command to direct political and military action against Israel.

Perhaps the severest test of the Assad regime came in the latter half of the 1970s as a result of Syrian intervention in the Lebanese Civil War. During 1976 Assad was firmly resolved to stabilize the volatile Lebanese situation by providing troops, first unilaterally and later as part of the Lebanese-based peacekeeping Arab Deterrent Force (ADF). The Syrian intervention, in effect on the side of the Lebanese Christian right against the Palestinians and the Muslim left, tended to aggravate relations with other Arab countries, Egypt and Iraq in particular. In addition, the intervention in Lebanon was economically costly for Syria and not popular domestically, and a cease-fire was arranged in October 1976. Even so, in early 1987, Syrian troops still controlled large portions of eastern Lebanon.

Domestically, Assad's supremacy remained unassailable. He brooked no opposition, and his control of the Baath Party and the military and security organizations was complete. All political activities continued to be closely monitored by the party and a multiplicity of intelligence and security forces (see Civil Police and Internal Security Apparatus, ch. 5). The regime did not rely primarily on coercion, however; the Baath Party sought, with mixed results, to evolve into a truly mass-based organization. The peasants, workers, and revolutionary intellectuals continued to receive

A devastated street in Beirut during the Lebanese Civil War
Courtesy As'ad AbuKhalil

much rhetorical attention, and the party's high command continued to explore the relative merits of socialism for the Syrian economy.

The regime's responsiveness to public opinion after 1976 apparently was prompted by three factors: first, renewed concern about the persistence of sectarian tensions; second, an economic slowdown stemming from the burden of military intervention in Lebanon as well as the considerable decline and uncertainty of foreign aid from other Arab oil states; and, finally, signs of corruption in the higher echelons of the government and state-run economic enterprises. In August 1976, official concern was manifested when Prime Minister Mahmud al Ayyubi was replaced by Abdul Rahman Khulayfawi, a Sunni who formerly headed the cabinet (1971–72) and who was also highly popular among army officers for his honesty and thoroughness.

A major test of the regime's popularity came in August 1977, when Syrians went to the polls to elect the People's Council for a four-year term (1977–81). Election results gave cause for concern; the voter turnout was dismally low even by Syrian standards. It was estimated to range from 4 to 6 percent of the 4 million eligible voters, even though the polls were kept open an extra day because of the low turnout.

The election indicated the public's unhappiness with the government, an unhappiness that prompted Assad to institute what came to be known as his "anticorruption campaign." To this end, the Committee for the Investigation of Illegal Profits was formed. Opposition to the regime did not abate, however, and, on November 1, 1977, Ali ibn Abid al Ali, an Alawi professor of agriculture at the University of Aleppo and a close friend of Assad, was assassinated.

In February 1978, Assad was reelected for a second seven-year term (1978–85). However, his reelection coincided with the beginning of a period of domestic unrest. Even Assad's inner circle showed signs of dissolution; one of the first was the dismissal of Naji Jamil, who was air force commander, chief of the National Security Council, and deputy defense minister. His replacement was Brigadier General Muhammad Khawli, chief of air force intelligence and an Alawi. On March 30, 1978, the cabinet of Khulayfawi was dismissed, and Muhammad Ali al Halabi was asked to form a new cabinet. No significant changes were made in cabinet membership.

The most important opposition groups during this period were Sunni Muslim organizations, whose membership was drawn from urban Sunni youth. The largest and most militant of these groups was the Muslim Brotherhood. Other organizations included the Aleppo-based Islamic Liberation Movement, established in 1963; the Islamic Liberation Party, originally established in Jordan in the 1950s; Muhammad's Youth; Jundallah (Soldiers of God); and Marwan Hadid's group, established in Hamah in 1965, often referred to as At Tali'a al Muqatila (Fighting Vanguard). All, it is rumored, received financial assistance from private sources in Saudi Arabia, the Persian Gulf countries, and the revolutionary committees in Iran. It is also speculated that they received weapons smuggled from Iraq and Lebanon and training and assistance from Al Fatah of the Palestine Liberation Organization (PLO).

In addition to the militant Muslim opposition, there was opposition from intellectuals and professional associations, whose purpose was not to overthrow the regime but to reform it. The first time such groups challenged the government was on March 31, 1980, in Aleppo and Hamah. Additional opposition came from expatriate Syrian politicians, mostly Sunni Baath politicians of the pre-1966 era who opposed the military and sectarian nature of the government and its drift away from Arab nationalist policies. The leader of this group was Bitar, the cofounder of the Baath Party.

In the spring of 1980, these nonmilitant professional groups formed a loose alliance called the National Democratic Gathering and demanded freedom of the press, freedom of political action, promulgation of civil law with the ending of the state of emergency, and free parliamentary elections. The alliance had no contact with the Muslim Brotherhood and was considered a peaceful alternative to it.

In the late 1970s and early 1980s, there were a number of religiously motivated violent attacks, many instigated by the Muslim Brotherhood and directed at Assad's regime, members of the ruling Baath Party, and members of the Alawi religious sect. At the outset, rather than blaming the Muslim Brotherhood, the government blamed Iraq and disaffected Palestinians for these acts, and it retaliated by holding public hangings in September 1976 and June 1977.

In the spring of 1979, the Muslim Brotherhood claimed credit for a series of attacks on persons, usually Alawis, and government and military installations. The most serious attacks occurred in June 1979 when Muslim Brotherhood gunmen killed fifty Alawi cadets at the military academy in Aleppo. This clearly showed the Muslim Brotherhood's capability and determination. After this incident, the government resolved to crush the opposition and did so ruthlessly. Nevertheless, support for the Muslim Brotherhood grew over the next two years, and operations against Syrian government officials and installations increased in number and severity and included, for the first time, attacks on Soviet military and civilian advisers in Syria.

Terrorist acts by the militant Sunni Muslims during this period centered on urban centers such as Damascus, Hamah, Homs, and the coastal cities of Latakia and Tartus. In March 1980, the attacks were directed at widespread targets, most effectively in Aleppo. The violence reached its height on March 5. Although Aleppo was the primary target, violence spread to Hamah, Homs, and Dayr az Zawr, where Baath Party and military installations were attacked. In June 1980 an attempt was made on Assad's life.

Government security forces tried to uproot the Muslim Brotherhood from Hamah and Aleppo in late March and early April 1981. A large-scale search operation resulted in the deaths of 200 to 300 people and the destruction of sections of both cities. Tight security measures were implemented; membership in the Muslim Brotherhood was made a capital offense, the use of motorcycles was banned in some cities (they were used by the Muslim Brotherhood in hit-and-run attacks), and under the guise of holding a general census, the Ministry of the Interior ordered all citizens fourteen years of age and older to obtain new identity cards. In addition, a series of political, economic, and social measures were aimed at improving the regime's image and gaining more popular support.

In February 1982, the Muslim Brotherhood ambushed government forces who were searching for dissidents in Hamah. Several thousand Syrian troops, supported by armor and artillery, moved into the city and crushed the insurgents during two weeks of bloodshed. When the fighting was over, perhaps as many as 10,000 to 25,000 people lay dead, including an estimated 1,000 soldiers. In addition, large sections of Hamah's old city were destroyed. This battle led to the establishment of the National Alliance for the Liberation of Syria, which included the Muslim Brotherhood, the Islamic Front, the pro-Iraqi wing of the Baath Party, and other independent political figures. The destruction of Hamah and the ruthlessness of Assad's measures apparently has had a chastening effect on Syria's estimated 30,000 Muslim Brotherhood sympathizers.

In the 1980s, Syria continued to rely heavily on the Soviet Union, which resupplied the Syrian armed forces with sophisticated weapons, and with which it concluded the Treaty of Friendship and Cooperation on October 8, 1980. This relationship did not evolve, however, to either country's complete satisfaction. As of early 1987, Syria had not granted the Soviets permanent port facilities, and, although the Soviets had pledged to defend Syria if it were attacked by Israel, it refused to support a Syrian blitz on the Golan Heights (see Foreign Policy, ch. 4).

Since the outbreak of the Iran-Iraq War in 1980, Syria has aligned itself with Iran, to the chagrin of the moderate Arab countries. Despite this alienation, Syria has been receiving generous amounts of financial aid from Saudi Arabia, which hopes that the funding will moderate Syria's radical policies. In addition, since 1982 Syria has been receiving a substantial amount of oil from Iran as repayment for its support and as compensation for the closure of the Iraqi oil pipeline, which runs through Syria (see Foreign Trade, ch. 3).

Syrian-Israeli relations were tense during the early 1980s. In December 1981, Israel formally annexed the Golan Heights; in June 1982, Israel invaded Lebanon and destroyed Syrian surface-to-air missiles deployed in the Biqa Valley as well as about seventy-nine Syrian MiG–21 and MiG–23 aircraft (see Syrian-Israeli Hostility, ch. 5).

In late 1986, Syria faced a multitude of domestic and foreign challenges, some more threatening than others. The economy, for example, was in steady decline as a result of, among other factors, a chronic balance of payments deficit, foreign exchange shortages, a three-year-long drought, low commodity prices, and reduced subsidies from other Arab states (see Growth and Structure of the Economy, ch. 3). Because President Assad was in uncertain health, aspirants appeared to be maneuvering to succeed him (see Political Dynamics, ch. 4). In foreign relations, Syria remained fairly

A section of Hamah, before and after the devastating government assault

isolated from other Arab states, while considerable numbers of Syrian troops were stationed in Lebanon, entangled in that country's conflict (see Syria and the Lebanese Crisis, 1975–87, ch. 5). Furthermore, because Egypt was at peace with Israel and because Iran and Iraq were preoccupied with their war, Syria assumed a major role in the Arab-Israeli dispute; in fact, some Western observers openly speculated about renewed Syrian-Israeli hostilities over the Golan Heights. Meanwhile, on the basis of investigations of incidents that had occurred in Europe, the United States and some West European governments were accusing the Syrian regime of actively supporting international terrorism (see Sponsorship of Terrorism, ch. 5). Thus, in the late 1980s, serious uncertainty remained concerning Syria's future.

*   *   *

Scholarly works on modern Syria are relatively few, considering the importance of the country. Much of the best material available is in periodical literature. The single most authoritative study is Tabitha Petran's *Syria*, which offers comprehensive analyses of

47

the effect on Syria of its temporary union with Egypt, the development of the Baath revolution, and the response of Syria to its traumatic 1967 defeat by the Israelis. John F. Devlin has written a work critical to a complete understanding of the Baath, *The Ba'th Party: A History from Its Origins to 1966*. In the same genre is Patrick Seale's *The Struggle for Syria*. A.L. Tibawi's *A Modern History of Syria, Including Lebanon and Palestine* has excellent coverage of the period from the Ottomans up to, but not including, the June 1967 War. John Bagot Glubb's *Syria Lebanon Jordan* is a sensitive study reflecting the author's knowledge of the area, gained from decades of experience as commander of Jordan's Arab Legion. Philip K. Hitti's *Syria: A Short History* remains the best single source for the ancient and medieval periods. Robin Fedden's *Syria and Lebanon* is a reflective account of his travels there, interwoven with major cultural themes of Syria's ancient and medieval periods. Well-written accounts of events that have taken place in Syria in the 1970s and 1980s can be found in Devlin's *Syria: Modern State in an Ancient Land* and in the *Middle East Contemporary Survey*, edited by Colin Legum et al. (For further information and complete citations, see Bibliography.)

Chapter 2. The Society and Its Environment

A pilgrim flask found in the Antioch region, ca. A.D. 1250

SYRIAN SOCIETY IS a mosaic of social groups of various sizes that lacks both a consistent stratification system linking all together and a set of shared values and loyalties binding the population into one nation. Distinctions of language, region, religion, ethnicity, and way of life cut across the society, producing a large number of separate communities, each marked by strong internal loyalty and solidarity. Although about two-thirds of the people are Arabic-speaking Sunni Muslims, they do not constitute a unitary social force because of the strongly felt differences among beduin, villager, and urban dweller. A perceptive observer has spoken of the "empty center" of Syrian society, a society lacking an influential group embodying a national consensus.

The ethnic and religious minorities, none of which amounts to more than 15 percent of the population, nevertheless form geographically compact and psychologically significant blocs that function as distinct social spheres and dominate specific regions of the country. Because the religious groups in each locality function as largely independent social universes, a "minority mentality," characterized by suspicion toward those of different groups, is widespread among both minority group members and those of the majority group living in minority-dominated areas where they are therefore outnumbered. Psychologically and politically, religious distinctions are by far the most significant ones. In all groups, loyalty to one's fellow members, rather than to a larger Syrian nation, is a paramount value.

The religious communities are more than groups of coworshipers; they are largely self-contained social systems that regulate much of the daily life of their members and receive their primary loyalty. The independence of the religious communities is a distinctly divisive force in society. Although Islam provides the central symbolic and cultural orientation for about 85 percent of Syrians, minority communities, most with a long history in the region, maintain cultural and religious patterns outside the Muslim consensus.

The religions, sects, and denominations differ widely in formal doctrine and belief. Nevertheless, there exists in Syria a stratum of folk belief and practice common to rural and uneducated persons of many religions. Members of various groups hold certain common beliefs in saints and spirits and observe related practices, such as exorcism and visitation of shrines, regardless of the disapproval of the orthodox religious authorities.

51

In addition to linguistic and religious dissimilarities, three forms of traditional social and ecological organization further divide the society. Most Syrians, including many members of religious and ethnic minorities, inhabit rural villages and earn their living as subsistence farmers. A dwindling number live the admired nomadic life of the beduin, or tribesman. The remainder, including a substantial number of recent migrants from the countryside, live in cities and towns, many of which date from ancient times. Each of these three represents a distinct, usually hereditary, way of life, followed by particular social groups and separated from the others by such social barriers as marriage restrictions, education, and occupation.

The ascent to power of minority groups and their implementation of Baathist policies of secularism and socialism have left most non-Muslims financially better off than the average Syrian, putting them in an anomalous position. On the one hand, many have reasserted their solidarity with Syria's opposition to Israel, the West, alleged imperialism, and capitalism. On the other hand, some observers have noted an exodus of numerous urban businessmen, professionals, and managers, particularly Christians and non-Arabs. In response, during the mid- and late 1970s, the government encouraged the return of these émigrés and attempted to develop a climate more favorable to them.

Successive Syrian regimes have attempted to consolidate a Syrian national identity by eliminating the centrifugal effects of sectarianism. Despite these efforts, Syria's postindependence history is replete with conflict between minority groups and the central government.

In part this conflict can be attributed to the French Mandate administration, from which Syria inherited a system of parliamentary representation similar to that of Lebanon, in which specific seats were allocated to Christians, Kurds, Druzes, Alawis, Circassians, Turkomans, and Jews. These ethnic and religious groups were guaranteed 35 of the parliament's 142 seats. Minority groups also protested what they believed to be infringement on their political rights and in 1950 successfully blocked efforts by the Sunni Muslim president to declare Islam the official state religion. A 1953 bill finally abolished the communal system of parliamentary representation; subsequent legislation eliminated separate jurisdictional rights in matters of personal and legal status that the French had granted certain minority groups.

The struggle to balance minority rights and Sunni Islamic majority representation remained a paramount theme in Syrian domestic affairs. In 1987 the Syrian government was dominated by

President Hafiz al Assad's Alawi minority. The secular social-ism of the ruling Baath (Arab Socialist Resurrection) Party de-emphasized Islam as a component of Syrian and Arab nation-alism. However, Baath ideology prescribed that non-Muslims respect Islam as their "national culture."

In 1986 educational and cultural institutions remained under close governmental supervision. Such institutions were designed to further government objectives by raising the general level of edu-cation and literacy, strengthening awareness of Arab cultural achievements, building public support for official policies resting on the principles of the ruling Baath Party, and seeking to foster a sense of Syrian national unity. Public bodies serving these objectives multiplied during the late 1960s and by the mid-1980s included the ministries of education, higher education, informa-tion, and culture and national guidance. Their activities were com-plemented by several directorates, authorities, and planning boards. In the consolidated budget for fiscal year 1985, about LS 3.4 bil-lion (for value of the Syrian pound—see Glossary), or 14.5 per-cent of the government's expenditure, was earmarked for educa-tion. Despite the educational system's failure to achieve the govern-ment's goals, education remained an important channel of upward mobility for minorities.

Geography and Population

Throughout its history, Syria's political and economic impor-tance has been largely attributable to its position at the crossroads of three continents and several cultures. Because of its strategic geographic location, Syria continued to be a focus of transit trade among many countries of the Middle East and to be a vital factor in Arab politics and in Arab-Israeli hostilities.

The area includes about 185,180 square kilometers of deserts, plains, and mountains. It is divided into a coastal zone—with a narrow, double mountain belt enclosing a depression in the west—and a much larger eastern plateau. The climate is predominantly dry; about three-fifths of the country has less than twenty-five cen-timeters of rain a year. Fertile land is the nation's most important natural resource, and efforts have been made, and in the 1980s were continuing, to increase the amount of arable land through irrigation projects (see Agriculture, ch. 3).

In mid-1986, the population was estimated at 10.6 million, including beduin and Palestinian refugees, and was increasing at an annual rate of approximately 3.7 percent a year. The Syrian government encourages population increase, even though such increase tends to offset improvements in the national standard of living. In the mid-1980s, double-digit inflation cut real income and eroded some of the gains in the standard of living achieved in the late 1970s. Despite austerity budgets, the government boosted annual price subsidies for essential commodities to a total of LS1.4 billion and continued to maintain a safety net of health, welfare, and public housing services.

Social welfare and development projects have been concentrated in rural areas. Although in 1970 only 10 percent of rural dwellers had access to electricity, by the mid-1980s, electricity had been brought to virtually every village. However, progress lagged in providing sewage disposal, potable water, and health facilities to rural areas. City dwellers benefited from the proximity of medical, transportation, and educational facilities but suffered from a severe housing shortage. In addition, municipal services such as sanitation were inadequate for the rapidly growing urban population.

Increasing government responsibility in the field of social welfare has been consistent with the program of the Baath Party to create a socialist society. Official initiative in economic and social improvements has been reflected in substantial allocations set aside for these purposes in development plans. However, government-financed projects designed to bring about these improvements tended to be delayed because of frequent cabinet changes and shifting emphases within development budgets.

The principle of linking long-term economic development to social welfare has been voiced in official statements—calling for a better geographic distribution of industrial production and social services—accompanying development plans. Persistent welfare problems, however, arising from rural poverty and urban crowding and compounded by rapid population growth and the influx of refugees, often necessitated the diversion of funds earmarked for long-term planning to ad hoc relief measures.

Land, Water, and Climate

Along the Mediterranean, a narrow coastal plain stretches south from the Turkish border to Lebanon. The flatness of this littoral, covered with sand dunes, is broken only by lateral promontories running down from the mountains to the sea (see fig. 4). Syria claims a territorial limit of thirty-five nautical miles off its Mediterranean coastline.

The Jabal an Nusayriyah, a mountain range paralleling the coastal plain, average just over 1,212 meters; the highest peak in the range, Nabi Yunis, is about 1,575 meters. The western slopes catch moisture-laden western sea winds and are thus more fertile

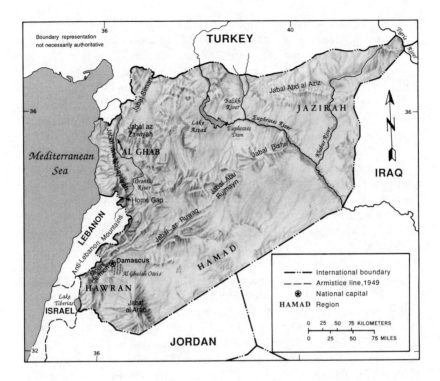

Figure 4. Physical Features

and more heavily populated than the eastern slopes, which receive only hot, dry winds blowing across the desert. Before reaching the Lebanese border and the Anti-Lebanon Mountains, the Jabal an Nusayriyah range terminates, leaving a corridor—the Homs Gap—through which run the highway and railroad from Homs to the Lebanese port of Tripoli. For centuries the Homs Gap has been a favorite trade and invasion route from the coast to the country's interior and to other parts of Asia. Eastward, the line of the Jabal an Nusayriyah is separated from the Jabal az Zawiyah range and the plateau region by the Al Ghab depression, a fertile, irrigated trench crossed by the meandering Orontes River.

Inland and farther south, the Anti-Lebanon Mountains rise to peaks of over 2,700 meters on the Syrian-Lebanese frontier and spread in spurs eastward toward the plateau region. The eastern slopes have little rainfall and vegetation and merge eventually with the desert.

In the southwest, the lofty Mount Hermon (Jabal ash Shaykh), also on the border between Syria and Lebanon, descends to the

55

Hawran Plateau—frequently referred to as the Hawran—that receives rain-bearing winds from the Mediterranean. All but the lowest slopes of Mount Hermon are uninhabited, however. Volcanic cones, some of which reach over 900 meters, intersperse the open, rolling, once-fertile Hawran Plateau south of Damascus and east of the Anti-Lebanon Mountains. Southwest of the Hawran lies the high volcanic region of the Jabal al Arab (formerly known as the Jabal Druze) range, home of the country's Druze population (see Druzes, this ch.).

The entire eastern plateau region is intersected by a low chain of mountains—the Jabal ar Ruwaq, the Jabal Abu Rujmayn, and the Jabal Bishri—extending northeastward from the Jabal al Arab to the Euphrates River. South of these mountains lies a barren desert region known as the Hamad. North of the Jabal ar Ruwaq and east of the city of Homs is another barren area known as the Homs Desert, which has a hard-packed dirt surface.

Northeast of the Euphrates River, which originates in the mountains of Turkey and flows diagonally across Syria into Iraq, is the fertile Jazirah region that is watered by the tributaries of the Euphrates. The area underwent irrigation improvements during the 1960s and 1970s, and it provides substantial cereal and cotton crops. Oil and natural gas discoveries in the extreme northeastern portion of the Jazirah have significantly enhanced the region's economic potential.

The country's waterways are of vital importance to its agricultural development. The longest and most important river is the Euphrates, which represents more than 80 percent of Syria's water resources. Its main left-bank tributaries, the Balikh and the Khabur, are both major rivers and also rise in Turkey. The right-bank tributaries of the Euphrates, however, are small seasonal streams called wadis. In 1973, Syria completed construction of the Euphrates Dam (also known as Tabaqah Dam or Thawra Dam) on the Euphrates River upstream from the town of Ar Raqqah. The dam created a reservoir named Lake Assad (Buhayrat al Assad), a body of water about eighty kilometers long and averaging eight kilometers in width.

Throughout the arid plateau region east of Damascus, oases, streams, and a few interior rivers that empty into swamps and small lakes provide water for local irrigation. Most important of these is the Barada, a river that rises in the Anti-Lebanon Mountains and disappears into the desert. The Barada creates the Al Ghutah Oasis, site of Damascus. This verdant area, some 370 kilometers square, has enabled Damascus to prosper since ancient times. In the mid-1980s, the size of Al Ghutah was gradually being eroded as suburban housing and light industry from Damascus encroached on the oasis.

Areas in the Jazirah have been brought under cultivation with the waters of the Khabur River. The Sinn, a minor river in Al Ladhiqiyah Province, is used to irrigate the area west of the Jabal an Nusayriyah, about thirty-two kilometers southwest of the port of Latakia. In the south, the springs that feed the upper Yarmuk River are diverted for irrigation of the Hawran. Underground water reservoirs that are mainly natural springs are tapped for both irrigation and drinking. The richest in underground water resources is the Al Ghab region, which contains about nineteen major springs and underground rivers that have a combined yield of thousands of liters per minute.

The most striking feature of the climate is the contrast of sea and desert. Between the humid Mediterranean coast and the arid desert regions lies a semiarid steppe zone extending across three-fourths of the country and bordered on the west by the Anti-Lebanon Mountains and the Jabal an Nusayriyah, on the north by the Turkish mountain region, and on the southeast by the Jabal al Arab, Jabal ar Ruwaq, Jabal Abu Rujmayn, and Jabal Bishri ranges.

Rainfall in this area is fairly abundant, annual precipitation ranging between seventy-five and one hundred centimeters. Most of the rain, carried by winds from the Mediterranean, falls between November and May. The annual mean temperatures range from 7.2° C in January to 26.6° C in August. Because the high ridges of the Jabal an Nusayriyah catch most of the rains from the Mediterranean, the Al Ghab depression, located east of these mountains, is in a relatively arid zone with warm, dry winds and scanty rainfall. Frost is unknown in any season, although the peaks of the Jabal an Nusayriyah are sometimes covered with snow.

Farther south, rain-bearing clouds from the Mediterranean pass through the gap between the Jabal an Nusayriyah and the Anti-Lebanon Mountains, reaching the area of Homs and, sometimes, the steppe region east of that city. Still farther to the south, however, the Anti-Lebanon Mountains bar the rains from the Mediterranean, and the area, including the capital city of Damascus, becomes part of the semiarid climatic zone of the steppe, with precipitation averaging less than 20 centimeters a year and with temperatures from 4.4° C in January to 37.7° C in July and August. The vicinity of the capital is, nevertheless, verdant and cultivable because of irrigation from the Barada River by aqueducts built during Roman times.

In the southeast, the humidity decreases, and annual precipitation falls below ten centimeters. The scanty amounts of rain, moreover, are highly variable from year to year, causing periodic droughts. In the barren stony desert south of the Jabal ar Ruwaq, Jabal Abu Rujmayn, and Jabal Bishri ranges, temperatures in July often exceed 43.3° C. Sandstorms, common during February and May, damage vegetation and prevent grazing. North of the desert ranges and east of the Al Ghab depression lie the vast steppes of the plateau, where cloudless skies and high daytime temperatures prevail during the summer, but frosts, at times severe, are common from November to March. Precipitation averages twenty-five centimeters a year but falls below twenty centimeters in a large belt along the southern desert area. In this belt, only the Euphrates and Khabur rivers provide sufficient water for settlement and cultivation.

Population

The 1981 census, the last official count for which full details were available in early 1987, showed a population of about 8,996,000, not including approximately 340,000 beduin and some 263,000 Palestinian refugees. The growth rate was calculated at about 3.4 percent a year. According to Syrian government reports available in 1987, the population in mid-1986 was about 10,612,000 and was growing at the same annual rate. Various international agencies and United States government sources, however, estimated the annual rate of population increase at between 3.7 and 3.8 percent, one of the highest in the world, and calculated the population at between approximately 10,310,000 and 10,500,000.

Both the 1970 and the 1981 censuses suggest that men outnumber women by over 4 percent, but this statistic must be viewed from the perspective of some sociological and biological factors characteristic of the area. Chief among these are the underreporting of women, particularly unmarried women, and the high mortality rate among women of childbearing age.

The 1970 census indicated that there were 104.6 men to every 100 women. The corresponding ratio in 1986 was estimated at 104.2 men to 100 women. A regional analysis of the sex ratio according to official 1986 population estimates shows that in the southern provinces of Al Qunaytirah, As Suwayda, and Dar'a, which are close to the Israeli border, the ratio of men to women is equal. These ratios illustrate the probable decline of males in refugee groups that have men involved in military operations or otherwise separated from their families. The ratio of males is higher in urban than in rural areas. In the cities of Damascus, Latakia, and Aleppo, there are, respectively, 197, 105, and 108 men per 100 women. However, women outnumber men in the rural areas of Halab, Al Hasakah,

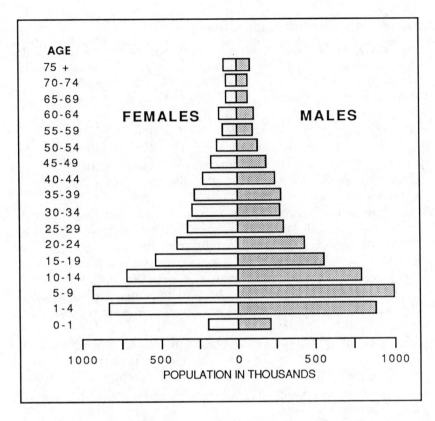

Source: Based on information from Syria, Central Bureau of Statistics, *Statistical Abstract 1986,* Damascus, 1986.

Figure 5. Population Distribution by Age and Sex, 1985

As Suwaydah, and Dar'a provinces. This imbalance occurs at least in part because males go to the cities in search of employment, leaving the women and children in the villages.

Syria's rapid population growth is reflected in the youthfulness of its population. Age-related data from Syria's 1985 population estimate indicated that about 49 percent of the population was under 15 years old, and 36 percent was under 10 years old (see fig. 5). An analysis of the same data showed that the proportion of people of working age (15 to 59 years) was just over 44 percent of the total. Therefore, the working population supported a large number of inactive youths, to which were added elderly dependents or retirees over the age of sixty, whose numbers were slowly rising because of improved health conditions.

Density, Distribution, and Settlement

Syria is one of the most densely populated countries in the Middle East and in 1986 had an overall average population density of approximately fifty-seven persons per square kilometer. There were considerable regional variations, however. Along Syria's Mediterranean coastline, the population density sometimes exceeded sixty-eight per square kilometer, but along the parallel inland axis between the Jordanian and Turkish borders, and in the vicinity of the Euphrates and Khabur river valleys, population density averaged only about twenty per square kilometer; desert areas were virtually uninhabited (see fig. 6).

Urbanization is progressing at a rapid rate, but the explosive urban growth of the 1960s had tapered off by the 1980s. Rural to urban migration, the lower mortality rates of urban groups, and the influx of refugees contributed to precipitous growth in the major cities. However, the administrative incorporation of rural areas adjacent to some urban centers has inflated some growth figures. Between 1960 and 1970, Syria's urban population increased by between 50 and 57 percent. Between 1970 and 1980, cities grew by approximately 40 percent. In 1981 an estimated 47 percent of the population lived in urban areas. Although nearly one in four Syrian citizens lived in either Damascus or Aleppo, a significant part of the urban population was distributed relatively evenly among a half dozen other major cities.

Damascus is growing at an annual rate of 5 percent. The last official census, in 1981, calculated its population at 1.1 million, and its 1986 population was estimated at 1.4 million, 13.2 percent of Syria's population. Aleppo, Syria's second largest city, had a population in 1986 of approximately 1.2 million. Between 1970 and 1981, the population of Damascus increased by 26 percent. However, during the same period, cities in eastern Syria and the coastal region grew at two to three times the rate of Damascus. For example, Ar Raqqah grew by 81 percent, Al Hasakah by 77 percent, and Tartus by 53 percent. Syria appears to have avoided the growth pattern of other developing nations in which the majority of the population is concentrated in one or two cities.

Vital Statistics

The most recent vital statistics, based on numbers of births and deaths per 1,000 population, varied according to source. According to Syrian government data, the crude birthrate in 1984 was 45.9 per 1,000. A 1986 estimate by an independent source calculated the crude birthrate at 47 per 1,000. Syrian sources estimated

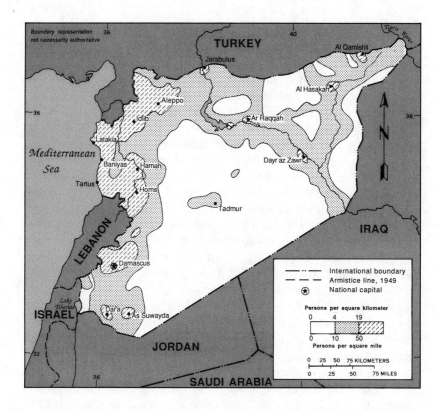

Figure 6. Population Distribution, 1981 Census

the 1984 crude death rate at 8.3 per 1,000, while a 1986 estimate by an independent source calculated the rate at 9 per 1,000, and another source estimated it at 13 per 1,000 in 1981. Life expectancy at birth was estimated in 1986 to be sixty-four years, a marked increase over the 1970 life expectancy of fifty-four years. The change in this figure was primarily a result of a much lower infant mortality rate, which was reduced from 105 per 1,000 to 59 per 1,000 in the same time period.

Vital statistics for Syria are incomplete and are regarded as unreliable by United Nations demographers. Because births and deaths in the countryside are rarely registered, estimates are based on deficient coverage. The recording of births in the cities is based on the date of registration rather than on the date of birth, which causes wide fluctuations from year to year.

61

The Peoples

The society is composed of a number of cohesive groups recognizing a common heritage and exhibiting great solidarity. Both linguistic and religious characteristics define these peoples; religious communities within the larger language groups function as separate quasi-ethnic entities and in many cases have developed distinctive cultural patterns. Ethnic and religious groups tend to be concentrated in certain geographic regions and certain social positions. For example, about 40 percent of the Sunnis are urban dwellers; of those, 80 percent live in the five largest cities. Alawis (also known as Alawites—see Glossary) are generally poor and live in rural areas. About 90 percent of the inhabitants of the Jabal al Arab are Druzes (see Glossary); the Jews and Armenians are largely urban traders.

The cultural differences distinguishing religious communities are far greater than would be expected to arise from strictly theological or religious sources. The differences arose during the lengthy social separation during which each of the various communities pursued an independent communal life. For example, in addition to the obvious difference of religious belief and ritual, differences in clothing, household architecture, etiquette, agricultural practice, and outlook characterize the cultures of Muslims, Christians, and Druzes (see Religious Life, this ch.).

Accurate statistical breakdowns by language and ethnic group were unavailable in 1986, and estimates by authorities varied. Arabs, or native speakers of Arabic, were thought to constitute nearly 90 percent of the population, but Kurdish, Armenian, Turkic, and Syriac were also spoken. Arabs are divided into a number of religious communities. Arabic-speaking Sunni Muslims, who constitute the largest single group, account for about two-thirds of the population (see fig. 7).

Arabs live in all parts of the country—in city and village, desert and mountain. Non-Arab groups generally live in partial isolation from each other, either in their own village or cluster of villages or in specific quarters of towns and cities, mostly in the area north of Aleppo or in the Jazirah region of the northeast. The Jazirah is particularly heterogeneous; among its settled population, the proportion of non-Arabs is much greater than in any other region. The concentration of non-Arab groups in Halab Province and in the Jazirah gives these areas a distinct character and has caused concern in the central government about the maintenance of order there.

Many city dwellers speak a Western language in addition to Arabic; French is by far the most common, and many educated

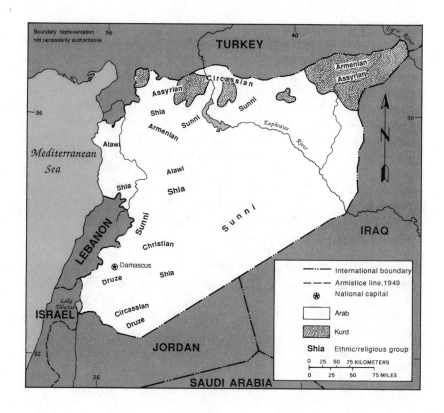

Figure 7. Distribution of Ethnic Groups

Syrians are as fluent in it as in Arabic. Although English is increasingly used, many Syrians do not know it as well as they do French, which has been the major channel for the exchange of learning between Syria and the West.

The consciousness of a Syrian nationality is not well developed. Among both Arabs and minority groups, primary individual loyalty is to the local ethnic or religious community. In effect, cooperation tends to be restricted to traditional family, ethnic, and religious groups. To protect themselves or to meet immediate needs, individuals cooperate with those personally known and trusted; impersonal cooperation for long-range programs with nonfamily or nonmembers of the same religious community is another matter. As one Syrian has noted, Syrians may want the government to do things for them, but will rarely cooperate in getting those things done.

Individuals have few obligations to their ethnic group at large.

Ethnic loyalties take shape only when one's group is under attack by another. For example, Kurds close ranks against Arabs if Arab landowners are raising land rents. Such action could be interpreted by Kurds as Arab persecution.

This extreme heterogeneity and lack of general coherence has led the government to attempt Arabization of the population. For example, it no longer refers to the Druze region as Jabal Druze (Mountain of the Druzes), but has renamed it Jabal al Arab (Mountain of the Arabs). Syrians are addressed in political speeches as "descendants of the Umayyads," "Arab citizens," "brother Arabs," and "descendants of Walid and of Saladin." "The blessed Syrian homeland" is "the land of Arabism." This deemphasis on ethnic differences has more and more equated the terms "Syrian" and "Arab."

The Syrian government deals with religious communities, not Arabs, Kurds, or Armenians. Census reports, for example, enumerate various Muslim groups, Druzes, Armenian Orthodox (Gregorian), Armenian Catholics, and Jews. There is no official listing of Arabs, Kurds, Armenians, or Jews, as such, as ethnic groups. Candidates for political office are named in government lists as members of religious communities only; the government lead is followed even in the press, which describes individuals as Arabs or as members of religious communities and does not identify them with ethnic minorities.

Arabs

The Arabs identify with speakers of their language throughout the Middle East. The majority of Syrian Arabs are Muslims; chiefly Sunni (see Glossary), they also include the Alawis, Ismailis (see Glossary), and Shias (see Glossary). All the Druzes are Arabic-speaking, as are the Jews and virtually all of the Christian population; most Christian Arabs are Greek Orthodox, Syrian Orthodox, or Greek Catholic (see Religious Life, this ch.). Being both Arab and Muslim leads many Syrians to feel that the two characteristics are natural companions and that one cannot be an Arab without being Muslim, and vice versa.

Syrian Arabs are highly conscious of the Islamic-Arab tradition. This is also true of Arab Christians, who follow Muslim customs in many of their daily activities and look with pride to the greatness of the Arab past.

Most Syrian Arabs think of the nomadic tribesman as the ideal Arab type. This attitude is common among both villagers and city dwellers, though the latter may also speak of the tribesman as quaint and backward. Arabs generally think of non-Arabs as inferior, but, because these groups are comparatively small and constitute no possible threat to the social position of the Arab majority, the feeling is not very strong.

Arabic, one of the most widely spoken languages in the world, is the mother tongue of about 200 million people, from Morocco to the Arabian Sea. One of the Semitic languages, it is related to Aramaic, Phoenician, Syriac, Hebrew, various Ethiopic languages, and the Akkadian of ancient Babylonia and Assyria.

Throughout the Arab world, the language exists in three forms: the Classical Arabic of the Quran; the literary language developed from the classical and referred to as Modern Standard Arabic, which has virtually the same structure wherever used; and the spoken language, which in Syria is Syrian Arabic. Educated Arabs, therefore, are bilingual, having knowledge of both Modern Standard Arabic and their own dialect of spoken Arabic. Even uneducated Arabic speakers, who in Syria consist of over 40 percent of the population, usually comprehend the meaning of something said in Modern Standard Arabic, although they are unable to speak it; however, they may have difficulty fully understanding radio and television programs, which are usually broadcast in Modern Standard Arabic. Because Classical Arabic is the language of the Quran and is regarded literally as the language of God, Arabs almost unanimously believe that the Arabic language is their greatest historical legacy.

Syrian Arabic is similar to Lebanese Arabic but differs significantly from colloquial Arabic in neighboring Iraq and Jordan. A Syrian would find colloquial Moroccan Arabic virtually incomprehensible. Like most people speaking dialects, Syrians proudly regard their dialect as the most refined. However, few Syrians believe that their dialect is actually correct Arabic. Although they converse in Syrian Arabic, there is general agreement that Modern Standard Arabic, the written language, is superior to the spoken form. Arabs generally believe that the speech of the beduin resembles Classical Arabic most closely and that the local dialects used by settled villagers and townspeople are unfortunate corruptions. To overcome these linguistic barriers, educated Arabs speak Modern Standard Arabic to one another. Uneducated and illiterate Arabs, if Muslim, can converse with other Arabs in Classical Arabic learned from oral recitation of the Quran.

Within Syria, regional differences in colloquial vocabulary, grammar, and accent are wide enough that a native speaker can readily identify another speaker's home province, tribe, city, and even neighborhood from the speaker's dialect. For example, Alawis from Al Ladhiqiyah Province are called ''Al Qaf'' because of their distinct pronunciation of this letter, the ''Q.''

Kurds

Estimates of the number of Kurds in Syria vary widely, but they are believed to constitute about 9 percent of the population. Although some Kurdish tribal groups have lived in the country for generations, many arrived from Turkey between 1924 and 1938, when Mustapha Kemal attempted to force his reform programs on the Kurds there.

The Kurds are a fiercely independent tribal people who speak their own language, Kirmanji. Living mainly in the broad, mountainous region of northwestern Iran, eastern Turkey, and northern Iraq, they are a cohesive people with intricate intertribal ties and a deep pride in their own history and traditions. Most Kurds are farmers; some are city dwellers; and others are nomads who drive their flocks far into the mountains in the summer and graze them on the lowlands in the winter.

Roughly 35 to 40 percent of the Kurds live in the foothills of the Taurus Mountains north of Aleppo. An equal number live in the Jazirah; about 10 percent, in the vicinity of Jarabulus northeast of Aleppo; and from 10 to 15 percent, in the Hayy al Akrad (Quarter of the Kurds) on the outskirts of Damascus.

Most Kurds are Sunni Muslims; a very small number are Christians and Alawis. In addition, the Syrian Yazidis (see Glossary), who speak Kirmanji, are sometimes considered Kurds. Numbering about 12,000, the Yazidis inhabit the Jabal Siman west of Aleppo; the Jabal al Akrad north of Aleppo; and a few villages south of Amuda and the Jabal Abd al Aziz in the Jazirah. Most of the Yazidis work the land for Muslim landowners.

Syria's Kurds are almost entirely settled, but they retain much of their tribal organization. Although some groups in the Jazirah are seminomadic, most are village dwellers who cultivate wheat, barley, cotton, and rice. Urban Kurds engage in a number of occupations, but not generally in commerce. Many are manual laborers; some are employed as supervisors and foremen, work that has come to be considered their specialty. There are some Kurds in the civil service and the army, and a few have attained high rank. Most of the small wealthy group of Kurds derive their income from urban real estate.

Kurds who have left the more isolated villages and entered Arab society have generally adopted the dress and customs of the community in which they live. In the Jazirah, for example, many have adopted beduin dress, live in tents, and are generally indistinguishable from the beduin, except in speech. Most Kurds speak both Kirmanji and Arabic, although others, particularly those in

A busy street in Dayr az Zawr
Courtesy Mona Yacoubian

Damascus, may speak only Arabic. Kurds who have entered the country in the present generation usually retain much of the language, dress, and customs of their native highlands.

For most Kurds, whether long established in Syria or recently arrived, tribal loyalty is stronger than national loyalty to either the Syrian state or a Kurdish nation. They are traditionally distrustful of any government, particularly that in Damascus. However, relatively peaceful residence in Syria and gradual assimilation have mitigated their distrust of Syrian authorities.

Armenians

The Armenians are descendants of a people who have existed continuously in Transcaucasia since about the sixth century B.C. Although a small number of Armenians have been settled in the country for several generations, the bulk of those in Syria arrived in successive waves as refugees from Turkey between 1925 and 1945.

Like Armenians throughout the Middle East, Armenians in Syria are city or town dwellers. About 150,000 Armenians lived in Syria in the mid-1980s. Roughly 75 percent live in Aleppo, where they are a large and commercially important element. About 15 percent live in the Hayy al Arman (Quarter of the Armenians), a new section of Damascus. The remaining approximately 10 percent are scattered in cities and towns throughout the country, especially in

67

the larger towns along the northern border of the Jazirah. Most Armenians belong to the Armenian Orthodox Church, but about 20,000 belong to the Armenian Catholic Church.

The Armenian language, which has its own alphabet, belongs to the Indo-European family at the same level as such other subfamilies as the Slavic and Italic languages. There is a classical form with an old, highly developed Christian literature, but modern Armenian differs essentially from the older form.

The Armenians work chiefly in trade, the professions, small industry, or crafts; a few are found in government service. In Aleppo, where some families have been traders for generations, their economic position is strong. Many of the technical and skilled workers of Damascus and Aleppo are Armenian; in the smaller towns, they are generally small traders or craftspeople.

Armenians are the largest unassimilated group in Syria. They retain many of their own customs, maintain their own schools, and read newspapers in their own language. Some leaders adamantly oppose assimilation and stress the maintenance of Armenian identity. As Arab nationalism and socialism have become more important in Syrian political life, Armenians have found themselves under some pressure and have felt increasingly alienated. As a result, they were reported in the 1960s and early 1970s to have emigrated in large numbers.

Others

Small groups of Turkomans, Circassians, Assyrians, and Jews retain ethnic identities in Syria. Although the last two are primarily religious groups, they may also be considered ethnic communities because of the cultural consciousness developed over a period of many years.

The Turkomans are a Turkic-speaking people who moved into Syria from Central Asia. Originally nomadic, they are now seminomadic herders in the Jazirah and along the lower reaches of the Euphrates River and are also settled agriculturists in the Aleppo area. Although most Turkomans have assumed Arab dress and speak some Arabic, others still speak Turkic and retain some ethnic customs. Because they are Sunni Muslims, the Turkomans are likely to become further assimilated and may eventually disappear as a distinct group.

Approximately 100,000 Circassians, descendants of Muslim nomads who emigrated to Syria from the Caucasus after its nineteenth-century conquest by the Russians, live in Syria. About half of them are concentrated in Al Qunaytirah Province. The provincial capital, Al Qunaytirah, destroyed in the October 1973

War, was regarded as the Circassian capital; after 1973 many Circassians moved to Damascus.

Circassian village dwellers, who are organized tribally, primarily cultivate grain crops. In addition to farming, they maintain herds of cattle, horses, sheep, and goats; some are blacksmiths and masons, passing on their skills from father to son.

Having resisted assimilation more successfully than the Turkomans, the Circassians retain many customs quite different from those of their Arab neighbors. Until recently, they spoke their own language exclusively, but most now speak Arabic as well. At times some Circassians, especially those in Al Qunaytirah, have demanded autonomy, but this is not an issue for most of them. Syrian Arabs still somewhat distrust Circassians because they served as troops for the French during the mandate period (see World War I, Arab Nationalism, and the French Mandate, ch. 1). In spite of these difficulties, the Circassians gradually are being assimilated into the Arab population, a process facilitated by their being Sunni Muslims.

The present-day Assyrians, of whom there are about 20,000 in Syria, are Nestorian Christians and speak Syriac, a form of Aramaic, the ancient language spoken throughout the region before the widespread adoption of Arabic. Fleeing persecution in Iraq in 1933, those in Syria settled in the Jazirah near Tall Tamir on the upper Khabur River. The French established this Assyrian settlement with the assistance of the League of Nations, and in 1942 it became an integral part of Syria.

The Assyrian settlement on the Khabur consists of about twenty villages, primarily agricultural. Although they own irrigated lands, the villagers barely make a living from their farming, possibly because they are former shepherds, not cultivators, and the lands granted to them are poor. Because of their difficult situation, some Assyrians have left the region.

Jews have been settled in Syria for centuries; at present most are concentrated in Aleppo and Damascus, and some are scattered in towns in the northern Jazirah. Of the estimated 29,000 Jews in Syria in 1943, some 3,000 remained in 1986, according to Israeli sources. Most had emigrated to Israel. Because Syria currently restricts emigration of Jews, Israel has had little success in negotiating with Syria through intermediaries for the relocation of the entire Jewish community to Israel.

The Jewish community of Aleppo was once fairly prosperous and an important element in the city's commercial life. However, most of the few Jews remaining in Aleppo live in the Bab al Faraj section, a dilapidated area in the center of the city. The Damascus

Jewish community lives primarily in the Hayy al Yahud (Quarter of the Jews) in the old city of Damascus, although it is not confined there and some Jews have taken up residence in other parts of the city. In the Hayy al Yahud, Jews are permitted to worship at synagogues and to operate their own private schools, where Hebrew is taught. Most Damascus Jews are peddlers, shopkeepers, money changers, or artisans; a few are important professional people, particularly physicians. Although most Syrian Jews publicly dissociate themselves from Zionism and Israel, most other Syrians distrust them, considering them real or potential traitors.

Structure of Society

In the mid-1980s, Syrian society was in a state of flux. The social, political, and economic developments of the preceding two decades had precipitated profound changes and realignments in the social structure, but the implications and probable outcomes of these changes were not entirely clear. This uncertainty arises from the division of Syrian society by vertical cleavages along religious and ethnic lines, as well as by horizontal cleavages along socioeconomic and class lines. Minority groups tend to segregate themselves in their own neighborhoods and villages. Although within a minority group there is a high degree of integration and homogeneity, the group as a whole is often ascribed a certain social status. Traditionally, Syrian society has been divided between landlords and tenants, between urban dwellers and rural peasants, and between a Sunni elite and minority groups.

Until the revolutions of the mid-1960s, a syndicate of several hundred Sunni Muslim extended families living in Damascus and Aleppo had dominated life in Syria. Some of these families were of the Sharifian nobility, which claims genealogical descent from the Prophet Muhammad. Most had accumulated great wealth and wielded virtual feudal power as landlords possessing vast agricultural and real estate holdings. Others made fortunes in industry and trade in the late nineteenth century. Another component of the ruling class was the ulama (sing., *alim*). This group consisted of religious scholars, Islamic judges (*qadis*), interpreters of law (muftis), and other persons concerned with the exposition of Sunni Islam. Prosperous Sunni bazaar merchants that were allied with the great families occupied the next level in the social hierarchy.

The Syrian elite was at the forefront of the anticolonial struggle against the Ottoman Empire in World War I and later against the French Mandate regime. At independence in 1946, Syria's first government was dominated by the old ruling class. However, the elite had never been a monolithic entity, and the new parliament was splintered by factionalism, feuding, and generational differences. These divisions provoked a military coup d'état in 1949 that ushered in a new era in Syrian society.

The armed services and the Baath Party were the mechanisms for the rise of a new ruling elite. Although military service traditionally had been disdained by the old Sunni elite, a military career was often the only avenue of upward mobility open to rural minority group members who could not afford an education. Such men enlisted in disproportionate numbers and came to dominate the officer corps and the enlisted ranks of Syria's armed forces. Likewise, disenfranchised elements of society joined the Baath Party. These dual trends culminated in the 1963 Baath Revolution and the 1970 takeover by the military of the Baath Party.

The land reform legislation of 1963 and the nationalization of larger financial, commercial, and industrial establishments virtually eliminated the economic and political power base of the old elite. At the same time, the new elite, comprised of the upper echelon of military and civilian leaders, consolidated its position by cultivating the support of peasants and the proletariat, who benefited from the new economic order. The regime's socialism eroded the position of the bazaar merchants while its secularism removed power from the ulama.

After coming to power in 1970, President Hafiz al Assad reversed or relaxed the more strident socialist economic measures instituted in 1963. His expansion of the role of the private sector led to the emergence of a relatively small, but highly visible, new class of entrepreneurs and businessmen who made fortunes in real estate, importing, and construction. This class, nicknamed in Syria "the velvet generation," includes higher ranking government bureaucrats and their relatives who have capitalized on their official positions to monopolize lucrative government contracts. It also has assimilated many members of the old Sunni elite, who have been co-opted by the Assad regime and have accommodated themselves to the new elite. To some extent, the old and new ruling classes have merged through business partnerships and marriages that combine the money and prestige of the old elite member and the power and prestige of the new elite member. Despite a well-publicized anticorruption campaign, patronage and favoritism have remained important forces in Syrian society.

Under Assad, rural peasants have reaped significant gains in their standard of living, primarily through government transfer payments and grants of land redistributed from the original upper-class owners. However, land reform has not been entirely successful in transforming the social structure of the countryside. In many cases, farmers who had previously depended upon their urban landlords to give credit for financing their crops until harvest and to deal with the government have drifted back into similar relationships with urban interests. The landlord's role as an influential advocate and local leader has not been filled by elected Baath Party representatives. In other cases, rich proprietors have begun to regain control over agricultural land and reconstitute large estates.

Since the 1963 Baath Revolution, the approximate middle of Syrian society has remained remarkably stable, both as a percentage of the work force and in terms of the standard of living and social mobility of its members. Because Syria has not yet developed a large industrial sector, it lacks a true proletariat of wage-earning factory workers. The number of persons employed by private and public sector industry in 1980 was 207,000, or 12 percent of the working population, according to statistics compiled by Syria's General Federation of Trade Unions. This approximates the size of Syria's "working class."

Syria compensates for its lack of a large proletarian class of industrial factory workers by a large and flourishing group of artisans and handicrafters who produce basic commodities such as soap, textiles, glassware, and shoes in small cottage industries. This group is a main component of Syria's traditional middle class, which also encompasses small proprietors, tradespeople, and white-collar employees and has remained at about 30 percent of the population.

Since the 1963 revolution, a new and upwardly mobile class of teachers, scientists, lawyers, technocrats, civil servants, doctors, and other professionals has slowly emerged. This new upper-middle class consists of men and women who rose from the old lower or middle classes by virtue of technical or secular higher education.

Even before the revolution of 1963, secular education had become a criterion of status among many ordinary Syrians, especially as higher education ensured a virtually automatic entry into admired and well-paying occupations. The importance of education in this context will probably grow.

Values taught in the schools and emphasized in the media reflect those of the group controlling the government and have gained some currency. Nevertheless, the traditional conservatism of the peasants as well as the economic problems of daily survival that have not been alleviated by changes in government policy militate against any sudden change in the values or way of life of the masses.

As in other Middle Eastern countries, Syrian society has for millennia been divided into three discrete systems of organization based on ecological factors; these are the town, the village, and the tribe. Although closely interrelated, each fosters a distinct and

A coppersmith plying his trade in a suq
Courtesy Mona Yacoubian

independent variation of Arab culture. The cities of the Middle East are among the most ancient in the world; urban life has been integral to the society of the region throughout recorded history. Therefore, the townsman and his role are well known to all segments of the population. The tribesman, or beduin, although suffering irreversible changes since the mid-twentieth century, has also been a widely known and admired figure throughout history. The peasant farmer, or fellah (pl., fellahin), although less admired than the townsman or the tribesman, also occupies a position of recognized value.

The members of each of the three structural segments of society look on the others as socially distinct. This social distance is symbolized by easily recognized differences in clothing, food, home furnishings, accent, and custom; intermarriage between village, town, and tribal families is usually considered irregular.

Traditionally, the cities have been an expression—at the highest level of sophistication and refinement—of the same Arab culture that animated the villages. As Western influence grew, however, during the late nineteenth and the twentieth centuries, the social distance between the city and village increased. Western customs, ideas, techniques, and languages were adopted first in the cities, especially by Christians, while the villages remained ignorant of them. The introduction and adoption of elements of a radically alien culture opened a gap between the city and the village that

73

has not narrowed with time. Only in recent years have modern transportation and mass communication begun to bring the countryside once again into the same cultural orbit as the cities.

Although the town, village, and tribe are socially distinct, they depend on each other for services and products and so are related by overall functional ties. The town supplies manufactured, specialty, and luxury products; administrative and governmental services; education and higher learning; sophisticated culture; law and justice; and financing. The village supplies agricultural products; and the tribe provides protection and navigation for caravans, travelers, and traders in the desert. As more and more villagers become educated and move to the cities, and as the beduin surrender their sole mastery of the desert to motor vehicles and the police power of the modern state and begin to adopt a sedentary life, the traditional distinctions will continue to blur.

Towns

Compared with many other developing nations, Syria is heavily urban, as approximately 50 percent of the population lives in cities. In addition, it is estimated that 70 percent of the townspeople live in the two largest urban centers.

Social structure in Syrian cities seems to be in a state of transition. The traditional city—built around a small, wealthy landowning and industrial elite, craft and artisan guilds, and small merchants—has been decisively undermined by political, economic, and technological changes. However, a cohesive structure based on modern secular education, technology, and class alignments has not yet developed. Many of the values associated with the traditional system endure and strongly influence the population, although admiration for modern values and techniques is increasing.

Cities are commonly composed of several architecturally distinct sections, which represent different periods of history and, to some extent, different ways of life. The very ancient core of a city, often of the pre-Greek or pre-Roman period, houses many of the groups longest settled there. Sections were added during Greek, Roman, and medieval times; these traditional sections also house both majority and minority groups oriented to traditional life. The *suq* (traditional market), with its small specialized artisan shops, is a prominent feature of the old city. In addition, cities have a relatively new section, often built on modern European lines by French architectural firms, that houses families and enterprises most closely identified with modern technology and values.

In keeping with the significance of the religious community in Syrian life, cities were traditionally organized into ethnic and religious residential quarters. Members of all faiths still tend to reside with their coreligionists, and a quarter functions as a small community within the larger urban environment.

A residential quarter traditionally had its own mosque or other religious structure, shops, and coffeehouses where the men met, as well as a *mukhtar* (mayor), who represented it to the outside society and was ordinarily a man of some importance in city politics. Families of all economic positions lived in the quarter appropriate to their religious or ethnic group. In relations within the quarter, family connections, personal reputation, and honor carried more weight than financial standing, although the latter was of course a factor. Individuals of varying financial positions dealt with one another on a personal basis, and wealthier and more prominent residents assumed leadership.

As new sections and suburbs with more spacious and modern residences were constructed, many of the wealthier families of the various quarters moved there, causing a breakdown in the struc-ture of the old quarters. In the new areas, residential segregation followed economic class rather than religion or ethnicity. As a con-sequence, the old quarters were robbed of much of their traditional leadership, and the estrangement developing between the tradition-minded masses and the modern-oriented new middle class was exacerbated. An additional factor in the breakdown of the old quar-ters was the large influx of rural migrants to cities and the result-ing tremendous demand for housing.

In the late 1980s, information on the urban upper and middle classes was inconclusive. The old elite appeared to have declined markedly in prestige, power, and influence. In addition, the emigra-tion of professional, commercial, and technical persons undoubt-edly had an effect on urban life. It is unlikely, however, that small trading or artisan establishments were greatly affected by the social changes of the 1960s, although future opportunities in these fields seemed to have contracted.

It appears that a middle class, based on education, profession, income, and style of life, is in the process of forming, but its for-mation is far from complete. The many disparate elements com-posing it, including government officials, technicians, clerks, professionals, merchants, and traders, come from a variety of social backgrounds and do not share a class consciousness or set of values. The traditional commercial classes had aspired to the life of the old elite; however, the new middle class of education and exper-tise seeks an entirely different way of life. This group values scien-tific rather than traditional knowledge, control of nature rather than passive reliance on the deity, modernity rather than tradition, individual initiative rather than family solidarity, and upward mobility rather than stability.

The urban lower class is also a mixed group, ranging from a comparatively small segment of skilled industrial workers to messengers, domestic workers, and others similarly employed. Industrial workers (skilled, semiskilled, and unskilled) have been located primarily in Damascus and Aleppo, although they are increasing in other towns, among them Latakia. Because of the comparative recency of industrialization in Syria, most industrial workers come from rural areas, and any expansion of industry under the revolutionary regime is likely, for a time, to bring other rural people into the cities. The development of Syria's oil resources in the extreme northeast should help, however, to diffuse the industrial working class over a wider area.

Villages

The effects of the changes of the 1960s, 1970s, and 1980s on the structure of village society are not entirely clear. The urban absentee landlord has been a figure of considerable importance in the life of some villages, and the redistribution of land among the peasants has undoubtedly altered social relations.

It is not possible to generalize about Syrian villages because ecological, ethnic, and other conditions vary. On the one hand, on the coast, where rainfall is regular, small farmers can operate successfully. On the other hand, in the interior, water supply is much less reliable; there, the small owner can easily be ruined by drought, and only large enterprises stand a reasonable chance of succeeding. For this reason, the peasant of the interior depends on financing from the cities in place of advances for crops and equipment previously supplied by urban absentee landlords.

The Syrian village traditionally was not a self-sufficient economic or social unit but was dependent on the nearest town or city for various services. This dependency increased in the 1970s and 1980s. Because of the development of a modern system of public transportation, peasants could visit the city with increasing frequency for reasons such as marketing, medical care, and entertainment. In addition, an increasing number of village youth attended urban secondary schools and in that manner gained a foothold in urban society, many remaining in the town after graduation. Increased migration to the city has to some extent lessened the isolation of the villagers from urban life, as many now have relatives or friends living in towns. Nevertheless, the village should remain a significant component of society.

The relatively homogeneous occupational structure of the village includes fewer status positions than exist in towns with less distinction between the positions. With one or two exceptions, every capable adult works in agriculture. There is a very general division of labor on the basis of sex—men doing the jobs connected with planting, harvesting, and processing of crops and women caring for young children, keeping house, preparing meals, and doing the more menial tasks connected with crops and the care of animals. Only two or three nonagricultural specialists are likely to be found in a village—a small storekeeper, a coffeehouse proprietor, and a barber—and they provide goods and services needed daily by the villagers. Such specialists, with the exception of the barber, are likely to be retired or part-time cultivators. Their occupations give them a degree of social distinction.

Villages are organized around families and their extensions. Often, a village consists of several lineages, or groups of descendants of the same ancestor; the lineages frequently form residential neighborhoods and political blocs within the village. An individual's primary social identity is as a member of a given lineage. The leaders of the various lineages, usually respected middle-aged and older men informally chosen and recognized, maintain stability and make necessary decisions on an informal basis. These leaders keep themselves informed of opinion within their own lineages and formulate policy in discussions with other leaders in the village coffeehouse or the guesthouse of a leading citizen. Those families not related to a lineage usually align themselves with the one in whose ward they live.

Whatever a man's economic situation, he reaches its full social status when he can abstain from direct agricultural labor. For the ordinary peasant, this abstention occurs when he is old enough to have sons to take over his work, allowing him to devote himself to religious matters and family and village affairs.

Traditionally, the nominal headman of the village was the *mukhtar*, who was not necessarily the man of highest prestige in the village. He was often chosen merely for his ability to read and write Arabic to the degree necessary to perform the functions of the office. If the *mukhtar* had a high standing in the community, it was because of his family background and personal qualities rather than his office. The *mukhtar* served primarily as a channel of communication from higher administrative officials.

In many, if not most, villages, ultimate power and status rested in the owners of village land, who frequently lived in town, although they might maintain a house in or near the village. In some cases, villages were mixed, in that a segment of a pastoral tribe had settled there. The head of such a segment (or of the tribe as a whole) had a good deal of status and authority in the village. This stemmed in part from a certain prestige accorded tribal Arabs but also occurred because such tribal heads had acquired large quantities of land.

Tribes

The precise size of Syria's beduin population is not known, although in the mid-1980s it was estimated at less than 7 percent. The number of actual nomads among the tribesmen is steadily decreasing because of government settlement policy and the extension of law to the desert. Nevertheless, the nomad remains a highly romantic and admired figure in folklore, and his pride, independence, sensitive honor, and disdain for agricultural or other manual labor are influential values among villagers, especially near the margins of the desert. However, the Baath Party views the nomadic way of life as primitive and hopes to settle all beduin. Ordinarily tribesmen settle in their own villages rather than merging with peasant communities.

In Syria, only eight wholly nomadic tribes remain, sometimes overlapping international boundaries. They are the Ruwala (by far the largest) and the Hassana of the Syrian Desert; the Butainat and the Abadah near Tadmur in central Hims Province; the Fadan Walad and the Fadan Kharsah of the Euphrates Desert; and the Shammar az Zur and the Shammar al Kharsah in Dayr az Zawr Province.

Tribal society consists of semiautonomous bands of kin moving their flocks within their respective territories. Each band is defined by its members' descent from a common male ancestor, and bands are grouped together according to their supposed descent from a more distant male. Each tribal group, from the smallest band to the largest confederation, ordinarily bears the name of the common ancestor who supposedly founded the particular kin-group.

The tribal community itself is defined in terms of kinship, and patterns of behavior, both within and between groups, are governed by kinship relations. The kinship system also serves to stabilize relations among different bands and groups of bands. The individual tribesman is placed in the center of ever-widening circles of kinship relations that, in theory at least, eventually link him with all other tribesmen within a particular region of the country, that is, with all tribesmen with whom he is likely to come into contact.

Within the basic tribal unit—the nomadic band—the individual's status is ascribed at birth in terms of the kinship relations existing between him and all other members of his band. He is considered subordinate to his elder kin and equal to his age-mates. However,

A settled beduin family living in Al Qamishli
Courtesy Susan Carter

a tribesman may gain prestige because of his special skills at riding horses, hunting, herding animals, or handling men—particularly in the settlement of disputes. His standing within the band will also be enhanced by his relative wealth in terms of the kind and number of animals and the special gear and equipment he owns. Beduin in Syria are not considered poor or underprivileged people; in fact, many beduin tribes are regarded as very wealthy by Syrian standards because of their ownership of large flocks of sheep—a valuable commodity.

High-prestige animals are horses, camels, sheep, and goats, in that order. A tribesman who owns a horse has more prestige than one who does not; one who has two horses is more esteemed than another who has only one. Otherwise, the relative social differences between tribesmen, other than for members of the lineage of the *mukhtars* and of the shaykh, are slight.

The *mukhtar* has a special, superior relationship to other tribesmen in that band; he is elected from among the adult male members of a specific lineage segment within the band. Generally the most prominent member of the lineage segment, he is selected by his close kin and approved by the tribesmen at large and by the leaders of the superordinate tribal group. Although the office of *mukhtar* does not necessarily pass from father to son, it tends to remain within the same lineage segment. This lineage segment is

79

likely to have a good deal of the band's wealth in terms of animals and gear and probably most of the money to be found within the band.

The *mukhtar* exerts most of his influence as the leader in the *majlis* (tribal council), which is composed of all adult males of the band, and the views of its most senior and respected members carry the most weight in council. The *mukhtar* holds open *majlis* daily in his guest tent, where the tribesmen discuss all matters of importance to the band. In addition, individual tribesmen appear before the *majlis* to air their own problems and to press grievances against fellow tribesmen. The *mukhtar* and his *majlis* try to solve all these problems and disputes within the tribal unit.

When settlement within the band is not reached or when the dispute involves members of two or more bands, the problem becomes a matter for consideration by the leaders of superordinate tribal groups, who stand in a senior position both to the *mukhtar* of the single band and to the parties to the dispute. Final appeal is to the paramount shaykh of the entire tribe. The Kurdish tribal groups have essentially the same structure as the Arab tribes but apply different titles to their leaders, and their political and economic tribal unit appears to be smaller than that common among Arabs.

The Individual, the Family, and the Sexes

Syrian life centers on the extended family. The individual's loyalty to family is nearly absolute and usually overrides all other obligations. Except in the more sophisticated urban circles, the individual's social standing depends on family background. Although status is changing within the emerging middle class, ascribed rather than achieved status still regulates the average Syrian's life. An individual's honor and dignity are tied to the good repute of the kin-group and, especially, to that of its women.

Gender is one of the most important determinants of social status in Arab society. Although the traditional seclusion of women is not strictly observed in most parts of the country, social contact between the sexes is limited. Among Muslims, men and women in effect constitute distinct social subgroups, intersecting only in the home. A strict division of labor by sex is observed in most social environments, with the exception of certain circumscribed professional activities performed by educated urban women. The roles of the sexes in family life differ markedly, as do the social expectations. The differences are expressed and fostered in child rearing, ideology, and daily life.

Because of the cohesiveness of religious and ethnic groups, they universally encourage endogamy, or the marriage of members within the group. Lineages, or groups of families tracing descent to a common ancestor, also strive for endogamy, although this is in fact less common, despite its theoretical desirability. Viewed as a practical bond between families, marriage often has political and economic overtones even among the poor.

Descent is traced through men, or patrilineally, in all groups. In addition, the individual household is based on blood ties between men. Syrians ideally and sentimentally prefer the three-generation household consisting of a senior couple; their married sons, daughters-in-law, and grandchildren; and their unmarried sons, daughters, and other miscellaneous patrilineal relatives. The latter might include a widowed mother or widowed or divorced sister of the household head or a widow of his brother along with her children. At the death of the household head, adult sons establish their own homes, each to repeat the pattern.

This ideal is realized in no more than a quarter of the households. Little reliable information is available about the size of households, but authorities believe that they average between five and seven persons and that city households are slightly smaller than rural; among Christians the difference between urban and rural household size is more marked than among Muslims. The relatively large size of the typical household probably results from a large number of children and the rarity of single adults living alone; children live at home until marriage, and the widowed tend to live with their children or other relatives.

Syrians highly value family solidarity and, consequently, obedience of children to the wishes of their parents. Young children, particularly boys, are often pampered and spoiled. When they become young adults, however, their independence and individuality are regarded as selfish traits, and young people are expected to work for the good of their families. Being a good family member includes automatic loyalty to kin as well. Syrians employed in modern bureaucratic positions, such as government officials, therefore find impersonal impartiality difficult because it conflicts with the deeply held value of family solidarity.

Syrians have no similar ingrained feelings of loyalty toward a job, an employer, a coworker, or even a friend. There is widespread conviction that the only reliable people are one's kin. An officeholder tends to select his kin as fellow workers or subordinates because he feels a sense of responsibility for them and trusts them. Commercial establishments are largely family operations staffed by the offspring and relatives of the owner. Cooperation among business firms may be determined by the presence or absence of kinship ties between the heads of firms. When two young men

A farming family from rural Muzayrib in southwestern Syria

become very close friends, they often enhance their relationship
by accepting one another as "brothers," thus placing each in a
position of special responsibility toward the other. There is no real
basis for a close relationship except ties of kinship.

Ideally one should marry within one's lineage. The son or daughter of one's father's brother, i.e., one's first cousin, is considered
the most appropriate mate. Particularly among the beduin, such
marriages occur frequently. In some communities, a male cousin
has a presumptive right to marry his female patrilineal first cousin
and may be paid by another suitor to release her from this obligation. In towns, marriage between cousins is common among both
the wealthiest and the poorest groups. In large metropolitan centers,
however, the custom is breaking down, especially among the middle class. Marriage between first cousins is common among Sunnis, including Kurds and Turkomans, although it is forbidden
among Circassians. Most Christians forbid marriage between first
cousins. Nevertheless, those groups that forbid marriage of cousins still value family endogamy and encourage the marriage of
more distant relatives.

Traditionally, in both Muslim and Christian marriages, the
groom or his family must pay a bride-price (*mahr*) to the bride or
her family. The bride-price can be extremely high; it is not unusual
for a middle-class family to demand of the groom the equivalent
of several years' salary as the price of marriage to their daughter.

However, this payment is often specified in prenuptial contracts to be payable only in the event of a divorce or separation. Therefore, the bride-price serves as an alimony fund. The wealthy marry within their families not only to preserve the presumed purity of their bloodlines but to keep the bride-price within the family, whereas the poor do so to avoid bride-price payments.

Therefore, marriage is customarily arranged. Among the members of the small urban, Westernized community, a man and woman participate in the decision making and usually can veto the family's choice; but, with rare exceptions, marriage is a familial as well as a personal matter. In rural areas, marriage remains a family matter, too important to be left to the whims and desires of the youthful participants. The preferred marriage is an endogamous one. Although, until recently, marriages were arranged for practical, i.e., nonromantic, reasons, there is a sizable folklore concerning passionate love affairs and elopements, but such actions rarely occur.

Endogamous marriage and high bride-prices serve as deterrents to divorce, counterbalancing the relative ease of divorce authorized in Islamic law and tradition. According to sharia, a man may summarily divorce his wife simply by pronouncing the *talaka*, or repudiation, three times, although it is far more difficult for a wife to divorce her husband. Currently in Syria, a sharia court adjudicates divorce. Incompatibility is cited most often as justification.

Seven percent of marriages end in divorce, according to Syrian statistics from 1984. The rate varied from a high of 16 percent in urban Damascus to a low of 2 percent in rural Al Hasakah.

If a woman marries within her own lineage, she has the security of living among her people, and the demands upon her loyalty are simple and direct. If she marries into a different lineage, she is among comparative strangers and may also be torn between loyalty to her husband's family and lineage and loyalty to her paternal kin, particularly if trouble should develop between the two. As a wife, she is expected to support her husband and his family, but as a daughter—still dependent on the moral support of her father and brothers—she may feel compelled to advocate their interest. Her father's household always remains open to her, and, in case of a dispute with her husband, she may return to her father's house.

Except in the small, urban, Westernized segment of society, the spheres of men and women tend to be strictly separated, and little friendship or companionship exists between the sexes. People seek friendship, amusement, and entertainment with their own sex, and contact between the two sexes takes place primarily within the home.

Women are viewed as weaker than men in mind, body, and spirit and therefore in need of male protection, particularly protection from nonrelated men. The honor of men depends largely on that of their women, especially on that of their sisters; consequently, the conduct of women is expected to be circumspect, modest, and decorous, their virtue above reproach. Veiling is rarely practiced in villages or tribes, but in towns and cities keeping one's women secluded and veiled was traditionally considered a sign of elevated status. In the mid-1980s, the practice of wearing the veil was quite rare among young women in cities; however, the wearing of the *hijab* (a scarf covering the hair) was much more common. Wearing the *hijab* was sometimes more a symbol of Islamic affiliation than a token of modesty, and the garment underwent a revival in the 1980s as a subtle protest against the secular Baath regime. For this reason, the government discouraged the wearing of such Islamic apparel.

The traditional code invests men as members of family groups with a highly valuable but easily damaged honor (*ird*). The slightest implication of unavenged impropriety on the part of the women in his family or of male infractions of the code of honesty and hospitality could irreparably destroy the honor of a family. In particular, female virginity before marriage and sexual fidelity afterward are essential to the maintenance of honor. In the case of a discovered transgression, the men of a family were traditionally bound to kill the offending woman, although in modern times she is more likely to be banished to a town or city where she is not known.

There is no evidence that urbanization per se has lessened the importance of the concept of honor to the Syrian. The fact that town life is still concentrated in the face-to-face context of the quarter ensures the survival of the traditional notion of honor as personal repute in the community. Some authorities have suggested, however, that although urbanization in itself does not threaten the concept, increased modern secular education will probably do so.

In common with most traditional societies, traditional Arab society tended—and to an unknown extent continues—to put a different and higher value on sons than on daughters. The birth of a boy is an occasion for great celebration, whereas that of a girl is not necessarily so observed. Failure to produce sons may be used as grounds for divorcing a wife or taking a second. Barren women, therefore, are often desperately eager to bear sons and frequently patronize quack healers and medicine men and women.

Religious Life

Islam, in addition to being a system of religious beliefs and practices, is an all-encompassing way of life. Muslims believe that

Allah revealed to the Prophet Muhammad the rules governing proper life of the individual and society; therefore, it is incumbent upon the individual to live in the manner prescribed by the revealed law and upon the community to build the perfect human society on earth according to holy injunctions. Ideally, life for a Muslim should take place within a religious community. As a consequence, in Muslim countries religion has an importance in daily life far greater than it has in the West.

The Prophet enjoined his followers to convert the infidel to the true faith. However, he specifically exempted the "people of the book," Christians and Jews, whose religions he recognized as forming the historical basis of Islam; these peoples were to be permitted to continue their religious observances unimpeded so long as they recognized the temporal rule of Muslim authorities, paid their taxes, and did not proselytize or otherwise interfere with the practice of Islam.

The Ottoman Empire organized the society of present-day Syria around the *millet,* or autonomous religious community (see Ottoman Empire, ch. 1). The non-Muslim people of the book living under Muslim occupation were called *dhimmis.* They paid taxes to the government and, in return, were permitted to govern themselves according to their own religious law in matters that did not concern Muslims. The religious communities were therefore able to preserve a large measure of identity and autonomy. The French Mandate continued this system, tending to favor the Christians.

In matters of personal status, such as birth, marriage, and inheritance, the Christian, Jewish, and Druze minorities follow their own legal systems. All other groups, in such matters, come under the jurisdiction of the Muslim code.

Although the faiths theoretically enjoy equal legal status, to some extent Islam is favored. Despite guarantees of religious freedom, some observers maintain that the conditions of the non-Muslim minorities have been steadily deteriorating, especially since the June 1967 War. An instance of this deterioration was the nationalization of over 300 Christian schools, together with approximately 75 private Muslim schools, in the autumn of 1967. Since the early 1960s, heavy emigration of Christians has been noted; in fact, some authorities state that at least 50 percent of the 600,000 people who left during the decade ending in 1968 were Christians. Many Christians remaining in the country, fearing that they were viewed with suspicion, have attempted to demonstrate their loyalty to and solidarity with the state.

Membership in a religious community is ordinarily determined by birth. Because statistics on the size of the various religious communities were unavailable in 1987, only rough estimates can be made. Muslims were estimated as constituting 85 percent of the population, although their proportion was possibly greater and was certainly growing. The Muslim birthrate reportedly was higher than that of the minorities, and proportionately fewer Muslims were emigrating abroad. Of the Muslims, 80 to 85 percent were members of the Sunni sect, some 13 to 15 percent were Alawis, and approximately 1 percent were Ismailis; Shia groups constituted less than 1 percent of the population.

A striking feature of religious life in Syria is the geographic distribution of the religious minorities. Most Christians live in Damascus and Aleppo, although significant numbers live in Al Hasakah Province in northeastern Syria. Nearly 90 percent of the Alawis, also known as Nusayris, live in Al Ladhiqiyah Province in the rural areas of the Jabal an Nusayriyah; they constitute over 80 percent of the rural population of the province. The Jabal al Arab, a rugged and mountainous region in the southwest of the country, is more than 90 percent Druze inhabited; some 120 villages are exclusively so. The Imamis, a Shia sect, are concentrated between Homs and Aleppo; they constitute nearly 15 percent of Hamah Province. The Ismailis are concentrated in the Salamiyah region of Hamah Province; approximately 10,000 more inhabit the mountains of Al Ladhiqiyah Province. Most of the remaining Shias live in the vicinity of Aleppo. The Jewish community is centered in the Damascus and Aleppo areas, as are the Yazidis, many of whom inhabit the Jabal Siman and about half of whom live in the vicinity of Amuda in the Jazirah.

In addition to the beliefs taught by the organized religions, many people believe strongly in powers of good and evil and in the efficacy of local saints. The former beliefs are especially marked among the beduin, who use amulets, charms, and incantations as protective devices against the evil power of jinns (spirits) and the evil eye. Belief in saints is widespread among nonbeduin populations. Most villages contain a saint's shrine, often the grave of a local person considered to have led a particularly exemplary life. Believers, especially women, visit these shrines to pray for help, good fortune, and protection. Although the identification of the individual with his religious community is strong, belief in saints is not limited to one religious group. Persons routinely revere saints who were members of other religious communities, and, in many cases, members of various faiths pray at the same shrine.

Unorthodox religious beliefs of this kind are probably more common among women than men. Because they are excluded by the social separation of the sexes from much of the formal religious life of the community, women attempt to meet their own spiritual needs through informal and unorthodox religious beliefs and practices, which are passed on from generation to generation.

Religion permeates life in all but the most sophisticated social groups. The Syrian tends to view religion instrumentally, depending on the deity and subsidiary powers to aid in times of trouble, solve problems, and ensure success. The terms *bismallah* (in the name of Allah) and *inshallah* (if Allah is willing) are commonly heard, expressing the individual's literal dependence on divine powers for his well-being.

Muslims

In A.D. 610, Muhammad (later known as the Prophet), a merchant belonging to the Hashimite branch of the ruling Quraysh tribe in the Arabian town of Mecca, began to preach the first of a series of revelations granted him by God through the angel Gabriel. A fervent monotheist, Muhammad denounced the polytheistic paganism of his fellow Meccans. However, because the town's economy was based in part on a thriving pilgrimage business to the shrine called the Kaabah and numerous other pagan religious sites located there, his vigorous and continuing censure eventually earned him the bitter enmity of the town's leaders. In 622 he and a group of followers accepted an invitation to settle in the town of Yathrib, later known as Medina (meaning the city) because it was the center of Muhammad's activities. The move, or *hijra*, known in the West as the Hegira, marks the beginning of the Islamic era and of Islam as a historical force. The Muslim calendar, based on the lunar year, thus begins in 622. In Medina, Muhammad continued to preach, eventually defeated his detractors in battle, and consolidated both the temporal and the spiritual leadership of all Arabia in his hands before his death in 632.

The *shahada* (testimony, creed) succinctly states the central belief of Islam: "There is no god but God (Allah), and Muhammad is his Prophet." Muslims repeat this simple profession of faith on many ritual occasions, and a recital in full and unquestioning sincerity designates one a Muslim. The God depicted by Muhammad was not previously unknown to his countrymen, for Allah is Arabic for "God" rather than a particular name. Rather than introducing a new deity, Muhammad denied the existence of the many minor gods and spirits worshiped before his ministry and declared the omnipotence of the unique creator, God. According to Islam, God is invisible and omnipresent; to represent him in any visual symbol is a sin. Events in the world flow ineluctably from his will; to resist it is both futile and sinful.

*One of the many mosques
found throughout Syria
Courtesy Michael Eisenstadt*

Islam means submission (to God), and he who submits is a Muslim. According to its doctrine, Muhammad is the "seal of the prophets"; his revelation is said to complete for all time the series of biblical revelations received by Jews and Christians. God is believed to have remained one and the same throughout time, but men had strayed from his true teachings until set right by Muhammad. Prophets and sages of the biblical tradition, such as Abraham, Moses, and Jesus (known in Arabic as Ibrahim, Musa, and Isa, respectively) are recognized as inspired vehicles of God's will. Islam, however, reveres as sacred only the message, rejecting Christianity's deification of the messenger, Jesus. It accepts the concepts of guardian angels, the Day of Judgment (or last day), general resurrection, heaven and hell, and eternal life of the soul.

The duties of the Muslim form the five pillars of the faith. These are the recitation of the *shahada*; daily prayer (*salat*); almsgiving (*zakat*); fasting (*sawm*); and *hajj*, or pilgrimage. After purification through ritual ablutions, the believer is to pray in a prescribed manner each day at dawn, midday, midafternoon, sunset, and nightfall. Prescribed genuflections and prostrations accompany the prayers, which the worshiper recites facing toward Mecca. Whenever possible, men pray in congregation at the mosque with the imam (see Glossary) and on Fridays make a special effort to do so. The Friday noon prayers provide the occasion for weekly sermons by religious leaders. Women may also attend public worship at the mosque, where they are segregated from the men, although more frequently women pray at home. A special functionary, the muezzin, intones a call to prayer to the entire community at the appropriate hour; those out of earshot determine the proper time by the sun. Public prayer is a conspicuous and widely practiced aspect of Islam in Syria, particularly in rural areas.

In the early days of Islam, a Muslim's obligation to give alms was fulfilled through the tax on personal property proportionate to one's wealth imposed by the authorities; this tax was distributed to the mosques and to the needy. Today, however, almsgiving has become a more private matter. Many pious individuals have contributed properties to support religious and charitable activities or institutions, which traditionally were administered as inalienable *waqfs* (foundations, or religious endowments).

The ninth month of the Muslim lunar calendar is Ramadan, a period of obligatory fasting in commemoration of Muhammad's receipt of God's revelation, the Quran. Throughout the month, all but the sick, the weak, pregnant or lactating women, soldiers on duty, travelers on necessary journeys, and young children are enjoined from eating, drinking, smoking, and sexual intercourse during the daylight hours. Those adults excused are obligated to undertake an equivalent fast at their earliest opportunity. A festive meal breaks the daily fast and inaugurates a night of feasting and celebration. Owing to the lunar calendar, Ramadan falls at various seasons in different years; when it falls in summer, it imposes severe hardships on manual laborers.

Finally, at least once in their lifetime all Muslims should, if possible, make the hajj to Mecca to participate in special rites during the twelfth month of the lunar calendar. The Prophet instituted this requirement, modifying pre-Islamic custom to emphasize sites associated with Allah and Abraham, founder of monotheism and father of the Arabs through his son Ishmael.

Once in Mecca, pilgrims, dressed in the white seamless *ihram*, abstain from sexual relations, shaving, haircutting, and nail paring for the duration of the hajj. Highlights of the pilgrimage include kissing the sacred black stone; circumambulating the Kaabah, the sacred structure reputedly built by Abraham that houses the stone; running seven times between the mountains Safa and Marwa in imitation of Hagar, Ishmael's mother, during her travail in the desert; and standing in prayer on Mount Arafat. The returning pilgrim is entitled to the honorific "hajj" before his name. Id al Adha, a major festival celebrated worldwide, marks the end of the hajj month.

Jihad, the permanent struggle for the triumph of the word of God on earth, represents an additional general duty for all Muslims and is construed by some as a sixth pillar of the faith. Although in the past this concept has been used to justify holy wars, modern Muslims see it in the broader context of civic and personal action. In addition to specific duties, Islam imposes an ethical code encouraging generosity, fairness, honesty, respect for the elderly and those in authority, and forbidding adultery, gambling, usury, and the consumption of carrion, blood, pork, and alcohol.

A Muslim stands in a personal relationship to God; there are neither intermediaries nor clergy in orthodox Islam. Those who lead prayers, preach sermons, and interpret the law do so by virtue of their superior knowledge and scholarship rather than because of any special powers or prerogatives conferred by ordination.

During his lifetime, Muhammad held both spiritual and temporal leadership of the Muslim community and established the concept of Islam as a total and all-encompassing way of life. Islam traditionally has recognized no distinction between religion and state. Religious and secular life merged, as did religious and secular law. In keeping with this concept of society, all Muslims have been traditionally subject to sharia, or religious law. A comprehensive legal system, sharia developed gradually during the first four centuries of Islam, primarily through the accretion of precedent and interpretation by various judges and scholars. During the tenth century, legal opinion began to harden into authoritative doctrine, and the figurative *bab al ijtihad* (gate of interpretation) gradually closed. Thenceforth, rather than encouraging flexibility, Islamic law emphasized maintenance of the status quo.

In 632, after Muhammad's death, the leaders of the Muslim community consensually chose Abu Bakr, the Prophet's father-in-law and one of his earliest followers, to succeed him. At that time, some persons favored Ali, the Prophet's cousin and husband of his favorite daughter, Fatima, but Ali and his supporters (the so-called Shiat Ali, or party of Ali) eventually recognized the community's choice. The next two caliphs (from the Arabic word *khalifa*; literally, successor)—Umar, who succeeded in 634, and Uthman, who took power in 644—enjoyed the recognition of the entire community. When Ali finally succeeded to the caliphate in 656, Muawiyah, governor of Syria, rebelled in the name of his murdered kinsman Uthman. After the ensuing civil war, Ali moved his capital to Mesopotamia, where in a short time he was murdered (see Muslim Empires, ch. 1).

Ali's was the last of the so-called four orthodox caliphates, the period during which the entire community of Islam recognized a single caliph. In Damascus, Muawiyah then proclaimed himself caliph. The Shiat Ali, however, refused to recognize Muawiyah or his line, the Umayyad caliphs. In the first great schism, the Shiat Ali withdrew and established a dissident sect known as the Shias (also known as Shiites), supporting the claims of Ali's line to a presumptive right to the caliphate based on descent from the Prophet. The major faction of Islam, the Sunni, adhered to the position of election of the caliph; over the centuries the Sunnis have represented themselves, and have come to be identified, as the more orthodox of the two branches.

Originally political, the differences between the Sunni and Shia interpretations rapidly took on theological and metaphysical overtones. Ali's two sons, Hasan and Husayn, killed after the schism, became martyred heroes to the Shias and thus repositories of the claim of Ali's line to mystical preeminence among Muslims. The Sunnis retained the doctrine of leadership by consensus, although Arabs and members of the Quraysh, Muhammad's tribe, predominated in the early years. (Reputed descent from the Prophet still carries great social and religious prestige throughout the Muslim world.) Meanwhile, the Shia doctrine of rule by divine right became more and more firmly established, and disagreements over which of several pretenders had the truer claim to the mystical power of Ali precipitated further schisms. Some Shia groups developed doctrines of divine leadership far removed from the strict monotheism of early Islam, including beliefs in hidden but divinely chosen leaders and in spiritual powers that equaled or surpassed those of the Prophet himself.

Fueled both by fervor for the new faith and by economic and social factors, the early Islamic polity was intensely expansionist. Conquering armies and migrating tribes swept out of Arabia, spreading Islam with the sword as much as by persuasion, and by the end of Islam's first century, Islamic armies had reached far into North Africa and eastward and northward into Asia. Syria was among the first countries to come under the sway of Islam; by 635 Muslim armies had conquered Damascus.

In Islam, the Quran is the principal source of religious law, supplemented by the Sunna, which sets forth the perfect example of the Prophet as represented by his deeds, his teachings and decisions, and his unspoken approval as reported by witnesses. In addition to "Allah's Quran and the Prophet's Sunna," the hadith records the deeds, teachings, legal interpretations, and consensual decisions by the Prophet's companions in the period immediately after his death.

Sunnis

The largest religious group in Syria is the Sunni Muslims, of whom about 80 percent are native Syrian Arabs, the remainder being Kurds, Turkomans, Circassians, and Palestinians. Sunni Islam sets the religious tone for Syria and provides the country's basic values.

Sunnis follow nearly all occupations, belong to all social groups and nearly every political party, and live in all parts of the country. There are only two provinces in which they are not a majority: As Suwayda, where Druzes predominate, and Al Ladhiqiyah, where Alawis are a majority. In Al Hasakah, Sunnis form a majority, but most of them are Kurds rather than Arabs.

In theory, a Sunni approaches God directly because the religion provides no intercession of saints, no holy orders, no organized clerical hierarchy, and no true liturgy. In practice, however, there are duly appointed religious figures, some of whom exert considerable social and political power. Among them are men of importance in the community who lead prayers and give sermons at Friday services. Although in the larger mosques the imams are generally well-educated men who are informed about political and social affairs, an imam need not have any formal training. Among beduin, for example, any literate member of the tribe may read prayers from the Quran. Committees of socially prominent worshipers usually run the major mosques and administer mosque-owned land and gifts.

The Muslim year has two canonical festivals—the Id al Adha, or "sacrificial" festival on the tenth of Dhu al Hijjah, the twelfth Muslim month; and the Id al Fitr, or "festival of breaking the fast," which celebrates the end of the fast of Ramadan on the first of Shawwal, the tenth month. Both festivals last three or four days, during which people wear their best clothes, visit and congratulate each other, and give gifts. People visit cemeteries, often remaining for some hours, even throughout the night. The festival of the Id al Fitr is celebrated more joyfully than the Id al Adha because it marks the end of the hardships of Ramadan. Lesser celebrations take place on the Prophet's birthday, which falls on the twelfth of Rabia al Awwal, the third month, and on the first of Muharram, the beginning of the Muslim new year.

Islamic law provides direction in all aspects of life. There are four major schools of Islamic law—the Hanafi, the Hanbali, the Shafii, and the Maliki—each named after its founder and all held to be officially valid. Any Muslim may belong to any one of them, although one school usually dominates a given geographical area.

The schools agree on the four recognized sources of law—the Quran, the Sunna, the consensus of the faithful (*ijma*), and analogy (*qiyas*)—but differ in the degree of emphasis they give to each source. Represented in Syria are the Shafii school and the more liberal Hanafi school, which places greater emphasis on analogical deduction and bases decisions more on precedents set in previous cases than on literal interpretation of the Quran or Sunna.

Conservative Sunni leaders look to the ancient days of Islam for secular guidance. Only since the first quarter of the twentieth century have Syrian Sunnis become acutely aware of the need for modern education. Therefore, secularization is spreading among Sunnis, especially the younger ones in urban areas and in the military services. After the first coup d'état in 1949, the *waqfs* were taken out of private religious hands and put under government control. Civil codes have greatly modified the authority of Islamic laws, and the educational role of Muslim religious leaders is declining with the gradual disappearance of *kuttabs*, the traditional mosque-affiliated schools.

Despite civil codes introduced in the past years, Syria maintains a dual system of sharia and civil courts (see The Judiciary, ch. 4). Hanafi law applies in sharia courts, and non-Muslim communities have their own religious courts using their own religious law.

Shias

Shia Islam is often viewed as a deviant or heretical form of orthodox Islam. However, Shia Islam is the result of schism, and, as scholars correctly observe, the elements for a Shia interpretation of Islam are present in the Quran as well as in the hadith. The catalyst for Shia Islam's development was the political turmoil over a temporal successor to Muhammad and the ensuing murders of Ali and his sons. Shias maintain, however, that Sunni-Shia polemics are not as much about who should have succeeded the Prophet as about the function of the office of the successor and the qualifications of the man to hold it.

Shia Islam's distinctive institution is the Imamate, which holds that the successor of the Prophet is more than a political leader. He must have *walayat*, the ability to interpret the inner mysteries of the Quran and sharia; only those who are free from error and sin (*masum*) and have been chosen by God (*nass*) through the Prophet possess *walayat*.

The five Shia principles of religion consist of the following: belief in divine unity (*tawhid*); prophecy (*nubuwwah*); resurrection (*maad*); divine justice (*adl*); and the belief in the Imams (see Glossary) as successors of the Prophet (*imamah*). The latter principle is not accepted by Sunnis.

Implied in the Shia principle of the *imamah* is that imams are imbued with a redemptive quality as a result of their sufferings and martyrdoms. And, although imams are not divine, they are sinless and infallible in matters of faith and morals, principles very similar to the notion of papal infallibility in the Roman Catholic Church. That an individual needs an intermediary with God is an Iranian idea that long predates Islam, as is the idea of a savior or messiah (*mahdi*) who will come to redeem man and cleanse the world. To expect that the *mahdi*, who is the last (twelfth) Imam, really will come is a religious virtue (*intizar*).

The Imamate began with Ali, because it is his descendants who are the Imams. To justify their beliefs, Shias emphasize the close lifetime association of the Prophet and Ali. When Ali was six years old, the Prophet invited Ali to live with him, and he is considered by Shias to be the first to make the declaration of faith to Islam. He also slept in the Prophet's bed on the night of the *hijra*, when it was assumed that the house would be attacked by unbelievers and the Prophet stabbed to death. Ali fought in all except one battle with the Prophet, and the Prophet chose Ali as the husband of his favorite daughter. Also regarded as especially significant is a hadith that records the Prophet as saying: "God placed the children of all the prophets in their backbone but placed my children in the backbone of Ali."

Most Shia religious practices are comparable to those of Sunni Islam. There are, however, two distinctive and frequently misunderstood Shia practices: *mutah*, temporary marriage, and *taqiyah*, religious dissimulation. *Mutah*, that is, marriage with a fixed termination contract subject to renewal, was practiced by Muslims as early as the formation of the first Muslim community at Medina. Banned by the second caliph, it has since been unacceptable to Sunnis, but Shias insist that if it were against Islamic law, it would not have been practiced in early Islam. *Mutah* differs from permanent marriage in that it does not require divorce proceedings for termination because the contractual parties have agreed on its span, which can be as short as an evening or as long as a lifetime. By making the *mutah*, a couple places the sexual act within the context of sharia; the act then is not considered adulterous, and offspring are considered legitimate heirs of the man.

Taqiyah is another practice condemned by the Sunni as cowardly and irreligious but encouraged by Shia Islam and also practiced by Alawis and Ismailis. One resorts to *taqiyah* either to hide one's religion or disavow certain religious practices to escape danger from opponents of one's beliefs. *Taqiyah* can also be practiced when not to do so would bring danger to the honor of the female members of a household or when a man could be made destitute as a result of his beliefs. Because of the persecution frequently experienced by Shia imams, particularly during the period of the Umayyad and Abbasid caliphates, *taqiyah* has been continually reinforced.

Shias play only a minor role in Syrian politics. They are among the least educated religious groups, and their members are more resistant to change. In religious affairs, they look to Shia centers in Iraq, especially Karbala and An Najaf, and to Iran. However, Iran's 1979 Islamic Revolution and Syria's alliance with Iran in its war with Iraq have elevated the prestige of Syria's Shia minority. As hundreds of Iranian tourists began to visit Damascus each week, the Shia shrine of the tomb of Sitt az Zaynab, daughter of the Prophet Muhammad, located in the Al Ghutah region outside Damascus, became a major pilgrimage destination, replacing those areas no longer accessible in Iraq. However, the government of Syria has viewed with caution the resurgence of Shia Islamic fervor in Syria and has taken steps to dampen it.

Ismailis

The Ismailis are an offshoot of Shia Islam, the split having occurred over the recognition of the Seventh Imam. Shia Twelvers, those who accept the first Twelve Imams, believe that Jafar, the Sixth Imam, passed over his eldest son, Ismail, in favor of Ismail's brother Musa al Kazim. Ismailis, however, believe that Jafar appointed Ismail to be the Seventh Imam—hence Ismailis are often called Seveners. Little is known of the early history of the sect, but it was firmly established by the end of the ninth century. From 969 to 1171, an Ismaili dynasty, the Fatimids, ruled as caliphs in Egypt.

Ismailis are divided into two major groups, the Mustafians and the Misaris. The Ismailis of Syria, numbering about 200,000, are predominantly Misaris; this group gained prominence during the Crusades when a mystical society of Misaris, called Assassins, harassed both the Crusaders and Saladin (Salah ad Din al Ayyubi). The Misari Ismaili community has continued in Syria to the present day and recognizes the Aga Khan as its head. The Mirzahs are the leading family in the community.

Originally clustered in Al Ladhiqiyah Province, most of the Syrian Ismailis have resettled south of Salamiyah on land granted to the Ismaili community by Abdul Hamid II, sultan of the Ottoman Empire from 1876 to 1909. A few thousand Ismailis live in the mountains west of Hamah, and about 5,000 are in Al Ladhiqiyah.

The western mountain group is poor and suffers from overpopulation and limited land—resulting in a drift toward the wealthier eastern areas as well as seasonal migration to the Salamiyah area, where many of them find employment at harvest-time. The wealthier Ismailis of Salamiyah have fertile and well-watered land and are regarded as clannish, proud, and tough.

Ismailis accept many Shia doctrines, such as the esoteric nature of truth and the inspiration of the Imams. Although holding their Imams to be of divine origin, as the Shias do, Ismailis have a dual Imamate. They believe the succession of visible Imams has continued to the present. There are, however, two imams, the visible and the hidden, the speaker and the silent. The identity of the hidden imam is not known to the community, but it is believed he will return to lead the faithful. Ismailis generally follow the religious practice of the Shia Twelvers in prayers, fasts, and Quranic prescriptions, but in their conservatism they resemble Sunnis on some points. For example, they do not observe the tenth of Muharram in the impassioned way of the Shias.

Alawis

The Alawis, or Nusayris, who number about 1.4 million, constitute Syria's largest religious minority. They live chiefly along the coast in Al Ladhiqiyah Province, where they form over 60 percent of the rural population; the city of Latakia itself is largely Sunni. The Alawis appear to be descendants of people who lived in this region at the time of Alexander the Great. When Christianity flourished in the Fertile Crescent, the Alawis, isolated in their little communities, clung to their own pre-Islamic religion. After hundreds of years of Ismaili influence, the Alawis moved closer to Islam. However, contacts with the Byzantines and the Crusaders added Christian elements to the Alawis' new creeds and practices. For example, Alawis celebrate Christmas, Easter, and Epiphany and use sacramental wine in some ceremonies. For several centuries, the Alawis enjoyed autonomy within the Ottoman Empire, but, in the mid-nineteenth century, the Ottomans imposed direct rule. Regarding the Alawis as infidels, the Ottomans consistently persecuted them and imposed heavy taxation. During the French Mandate, the Alawis briefly gained territorial autonomy, but direct rule was reimposed in 1936.

For centuries, the Alawis constituted Syria's most repressed and exploited minority. Most were indentured servants and tenant farmers or sharecroppers working for Sunni landowners. However, after President Assad, an Alawi, and his retinue came to power in 1970, the well-being of the Alawis improved considerably.

Split by sectional rivalries, the Alawis have no single, powerful ruling family, but since independence many individual Alawis have attained power and prestige as military officers. Although they are settled cultivators, Alawis gather into kin-groups much like those of pastoral nomads. The four Alawi confederations, each divided into tribes, are Kalbiyah, Khaiyatin, Haddadin, and Matawirah.

Alawis claim they are Muslims, but conservative Sunnis do not always recognize them as such. Like Ismaili Shias, Alawis believe in a system of divine incarnation. Unlike Ismailis, Alawis regard Ali as the incarnation of the deity in the divine triad. As such, Ali is the ''Meaning''; Muhammad, whom Ali created of his own light, is the ''Name''; and Salman the Persian is the ''Gate.'' Alawi catechesis is expressed in the formula: ''I turn to the Gate; I bow before the Name; I adore the Meaning.'' An Alawi prays in a manner patterned after the *shahada:* ''I testify that there is no God but Ali.''

According to Alawi belief, all persons at first were stars in the world of light but fell from the firmament through disobedience. Faithful Alawis believe they must be transformed seven times before returning to take a place among the stars, where Ali is the prince. If blameworthy, they are sometimes reborn as Christians, among whom they remain until atonement is complete. Infidels are reborn as animals.

Because many of the tenets of the faith are secret, Alawis have refused to discuss their faith with outsiders. Only an elect few learn the religion after a lengthy process of initiation; youths are initiated into the secrets of the faith in stages. Their prayer book, the source of religious instruction, is the Kitab al Majmu, believed to be derived from Ismaili writings. Alawis study the Quran and recognize the five pillars of Islam, which they interpret in a wholly allegorical sense to fit community tenets.

Alawis do not set aside a particular building for worship. In the past, Sunni government officials forced them to build mosques, but these were invariably abandoned. Only the men take part in worship.

Druzes

In 1987 the Druze community, at 3 percent of the population the country's third largest religious minority, continued to be the overwhelming majority in the Jabal al Arab, a rugged and mountainous region in southwestern Syria.

The Druze religion is a tenth-century offshoot of Islam, but Muslims view Druzes as heretical for accepting the divinity of Hakim, the third Fatimid caliph of Egypt. The group takes its names from

Muhammad ibn Ismail ad Darazi, an Iranian mystic. Druzes regard Jethro, father-in-law of Moses, as their chief prophet and make annual pilgrimages to his tomb in lower Galilee. They also revere Moses, Jesus, and Muhammad, the three most important prophets of Islam.

The Druzes have always kept their doctrine and ritual a secret to avoid persecution. Only those who demonstrate extreme piety and devotion and the correct demeanor are initiated into the mysteries. The initiated (*uqqal*; sing., *aqil*) are a very small minority and may include women. Most Druzes are *juhhal*, ignorant ones. Apparently the religion is complex, involving neo-Platonic thought, Sufi mysticism, and Iranian religious traditions.

Endogamy and monogamy are the rule among the Druzes. Until recently, most girls were married between the ages of twelve and fifteen, and most men at the age of sixteen or seventeen. Women are veiled in public, but, in contrast to Muslim Arab custom, they can and do participate in the councils of elders.

Christians

The Christian communities of Syria, which comprise about ten percent of the population, spring from two great traditions. Because both Roman Catholicism and Protestantism were introduced by missionaries, a small number of Syrians are members of Western denominations. The vast majority, however, belong to the Eastern communions, which have existed in Syria since the earliest days of Christianity. The main Eastern groups are the autonomous Orthodox churches; the Uniate churches, which are in communion with Rome; and the independent Nestorian church. Even though each group forms a separate community, Christians nevertheless cooperate increasingly, largely because of their fear of the Muslim majority.

The schisms that brought about the many sects resulted from political and doctrinal disagreements. The doctrine most commonly at issue was the nature of Christ. In 431 the Nestorians broke away because of their belief in the dual character of Christ, i.e., that he had two separate but equal natures, the human Jesus and the divine Christ. Therefore, Mary was not the mother of God but only of the man Jesus. The Council of Chalcedon, representing the mainstream of Christianity, in 451 confirmed the dual nature of Christ in one person; Mary was therefore the mother of a single person, mystically and simultaneously both human and divine.

The Monophysites, another schismatic group, taught that Christ's divinity overpowered his humanity, resulting in a single divine nature. They were the precursors of the present-day Syrian

98

and Armenian Orthodox churches. The Monothelites tried to evolve a compromise by postulating that Christ had two natures, human and divine, but only a single divine will.

By the thirteenth century, Eastern (or Greek) Christianity had irrevocably separated from Western (or Latin) Christianity. In the following centuries, however, especially during the Crusades, some offshoots of the Eastern churches accepted the authority of the pope in Rome and entered into communion with Roman Catholic Christianity. Today called the Uniate churches, they retain a distinctive language and liturgy.

The largest Christian denomination in Syria is the Greek Orthodox, the Syrian branch being known as the Greek Orthodox Patriarchate of Antioch and All the East. The principal language of the liturgy is Arabic. The members of the Syrian Orthodox (or Jacobite) Church, whose liturgy is in Syriac, are Monophysites. Syrians of Armenian origin tend to belong to the Armenian Apostolic Church, the orthodox national church of Armenia. It uses an Armenian liturgy, and its doctrine is Monophysite.

Of the Uniate churches, the oldest is the Maronite, which has ties to Rome dating to the twelfth century. This group originally held to the Monothelite heresy but in 1215 renounced it. The liturgy is in Syriac.

The largest Uniate church in Syria is the Greek Catholic Church, sometimes called the Melchite, and is an offshoot of the Greek Orthodox Church. It uses the Byzantine liturgy in Arabic. The Syrian Catholic Church is a Uniate offshoot of the Syrian Orthodox Church and uses the seventeenth-century liturgy of Saint James and some readings in Arabic. In contrast to the Uniate Chaldean Catholics, who derive from the Nestorian church, the Nestorians, descendants of the ancient Nestorian schismatics, have their own very ancient liturgy and maintain a special relationship with the Anglican Communion.

With the exception of the Armenians and Assyrians, most Christians are Arab, sharing the pride of Muslims in the Islamic-Arabic tradition and in Syria's special role in that tradition. Many Christians, particularly the Eastern Orthodox, have joined in the Arab nationalist movement. More Syrian Arab Christians participate in proportion to their number in political and administrative affairs than do Muslims. Especially among the young, relations between Christians and Muslims are improving.

There are several social differences between Christians and Muslims. For example, Syrian Christians are more highly urbanized than Muslims; many live either in or around Damascus, Aleppo, Hamah, and Latakia, and there are relatively fewer of them in the lower income groups. Proportionately more Christians than Muslims are educated beyond the primary level, and there are relatively more of them in white-collar and professional occupations. The education that Christians receive has differed in kind from that of Muslims in the sense that many more Christian children have attended Western-oriented foreign and private schools.

Other Minorities

Jews

Most Jews now living in the Arab world belong to communities dating back to Old Testament times or originating as colonies of refugees fleeing the Spanish Inquisition. In Syria, Jews of both origins, numbering altogether about 3,000 in 1987, are found. A Syrian Jew is Arabic-speaking and is barely distinguishable from the Arabs around him. In Syria, as elsewhere, the degree to which Jews submit to the disciplines of their religion varies.

The government treats the Jews as a religious community and not as an ethnic group. Official documents refer to them as *musawiyin* (followers of Moses) and not *yahudin* (Jews). The government's translation into English of *musawiyin* is "Judists."

Although the Jewish community continues to exercise a certain amount of authority over the personal status of its members, as a whole it is under considerable restriction, more because of political factors than religious ones. The economic freedom of Jews is limited, and they are under continual surveillance by the police. Their situation, although not good before the June 1967 War, has reportedly deteriorated considerably since then.

Yazidis

In 1964 there were about 10,000 Yazidis in Syria, primarily in the Jazirah region and in Aleppo; reliable population data were not available in 1987. Once seminomadic, most Yazidis now are settled; they have no great chiefs and, although Kurdish speaking, gradually are being assimilated into the surrounding Arab population.

The Yazidis are believed to be of Kurdish ethnic stock. Yazidis, however, believe themselves to be a people apart from the human race, not descended from Adam and Eve. According to their own tradition, the Yazidis originated in southern Iraq and migrated to their present-day mountainous stronghold—Jabal Sinjar in northern Iraq—at the end of fourteenth century, where they adopted the Kurdish language. Although some 70,000 Yazidis are scattered in Iraq, Turkey, Iran, the Caucasus Mountains of the Soviet Union, and Syria, Iraq remains the center of their religious life, the home of their amir, and the site (north of Al Mawsil) of their most revered saint, Shaykh Adi.

The etymology of the name *Yazidi* is obscure. According to some sources, it derives from the name of the Umayyad Caliph Yazid ibn Muawiyah (died 683), who is regarded as a historical patron of the religion. Other sources ascribe the name to the modern Farsi word *izes*, meaning angel or deity. Yazidis are referred to in Syria, and call themselves, Dawasin, after the old geographic name of a region in northern Iraq.

The Yazidi faith is secret and contains elements of Judaism, Christianity, and Islam, as well as paganism and occultism; Yazidis consider the Bible and the Quran sacred. Yazidis are often called, somewhat inaccurately, "devil worshipers" by other Syrians. Yazidi rites involve placating an angel, called Malik Taus and symbolized as a sacred peacock, who fell from grace and after repentance in hell was restored to God's favor. This central Yazidi belief probably derived in part from the Christian concept of Satan. However, it was also influenced by notions of redemption, resurrection, and immortality, of which the peacock, like the phoenix, is an ancient Middle Eastern pagan symbol.

Education

Since 1967 all Syrian schools, colleges, and universities have been under close government supervision. The Ministry of Education and the Ministry of Higher Education are primarily responsible for all aspects of administration, including curriculum development.

Schooling is divided into six years of compulsory primary education, three years of lower secondary education, and three years of upper secondary education. General secondary education offers academic courses and prepares students for university entrance; the last two years of this stage are divided into literary and scientific streams. Vocational secondary training offers courses in industry, agriculture, commerce, and primary-school-teacher training. The usual entrance age for secondary schooling is fifteen but is fourteen for teacher training institutions. This system was established in 1967, when the country signed the Arab Cultural Unity Agreement with Jordan and Egypt, introducing a uniform school ladder in the three countries and determining curriculum examination procedures and teacher training requirements for each level.

In the mid-1980s, Syrian education policies reflected the official intention of the Baath Party to use the schools to indoctrinate the masses with its ideology and to make school training responsive to the nation's manpower needs (see Political Dynamics, ch. 4).

A University of Damascus building on the old campus
Courtesy Susan Carter

The Fourth Five-Year Plan (1976–80) established a target of full enrollment of boys of primary school age by 1980 and of girls by 1990. By the early 1980s, Syria had achieved full primary school enrollment of males of the relevant age; the comparable figure for females was about 85 percent. Enrollment in secondary school dropped to 67 percent for boys and 35 percent for girls, reflecting a high drop-out rate. Enrollments in remote rural areas were frequently far below the national average. In some villages of Dayr az Zawr Province, for example, only about 8 percent of the girls attended primary school, whereas in Damascus about 49 percent of the girls completed the six-year primary system.

The demand for education has increased sharply. Between 1970 and 1976, enrollment in the primary, lower secondary, and upper secondary levels increased by 43 percent, 52 percent, and 65 percent, respectively. During the same period, enrollments in the various institutes of higher learning increased by over 66 percent. In 1985 about 1 million boys and 873,000 girls attended primary schools, which numbered 8,747. About 1,700 secondary schools enrolled over 200,000 students (see table 2, Appendix).

In 1984 the Ministry of Higher Education supervised four universities, in Damascus, Aleppo, Latakia, and Homs. The University of Damascus, founded in 1923, had faculties of law, medicine, pharmacology, letters, dentistry, Islamic jurisprudence, agriculture, architecture, engineering, science, fine arts, commerce, and education. The Higher Institute for Social Work, established in 1962 to conduct research into social and economic problems, also was affiliated with the university. Syria's ruling Baath Party operated an institute of political science at the university that conducted mandatory classes in political orientation and current Syrian history. The University of Aleppo, opened in 1958, had faculties of engineering and sciences, agriculture, and literature. Tishrin University in Latakia had a similar curriculum. Al Baath University in Homs, opened in 1979, was Syria's only university with departments of petroleum engineering and veterinary medicine.

In the 1980s, the Syrian government was attempting to expand enrollment in its university faculties of science. In 1984 Syrian universities graduated 948 physicians and 1,693 engineers. However, over 3,100 students graduated from the faculties of arts and literature.

A second major thrust of Syrian educational planning was eliminating illiteracy. In 1981 an estimated 2 million Syrians—42 percent of the population over 12 years of age—were illiterate. In accordance with the government's drive to eliminate illiteracy by 1991, in 1984 approximately 57,000 Syrians attended literacy classes sponsored by the Ministry of Education and the Ministry of Social Affairs and Labor. Public demand for education has remained strong, reflecting the importance of education as a channel of upward mobility. The government has continued to expect the system to provide trained citizens to meet the economic and political needs of the society. In the mid-1980s, however, the educational system was still inadequately funded and, even within its funding restrictions, was viewed by impartial observers as failing to achieve its limited objectives and goals.

In the Syrian education system of the mid-1980s, the concept of examining a "truth" in an effort to confirm or refute it was largely unknown and, in any event, was often viewed as an unacceptable challenge to authority. If the teacher's instructions and assertions are questioned and refuted, other centers of authority—the family and the government—might then be asked to submit their truths to objective examination and testing. Because research possesses limited intrinsic value, the inadequate research and laboratory facilities were infrequently used.

In 1977 one observer stated that although the Syrian government has been seeking to improve the situation, the task is formidable because of the "many shortcomings and defects" in the educational system and because the society and government have been unable to agree on a modernizing, energizing social role for the system. The assessment was largely valid in the mid-1980s.

A technical training school laboratory
Courtesy Embassy of Syria

Health

Because of the increasing use of vaccinations and various preventive measures, health conditions in Syria generally improved in the 1980s. Malaria, and to a lesser extent tuberculosis, declined, but trachoma and gastrointestinal and parasitic diseases were endemic, particularly among the rural population. Diphtheria and tetanus also plagued rural communities, and there was a high rate of infectious diseases, heart disease, and cancer in urban areas.

Syria's Ministry of Health had a budget of approximately LS187 million in 1985. As a socialist government, Syria provided virtually free medical care to its citizens and imposed a ceiling on charges by private hospitals.

In 1984 there were 41 state-run hospitals and 139 private hospitals in Syria. The state hospitals averaged 200 beds each, while the private hospitals averaged only 20 beds each. As of 1980, Syria had established state hospitals in every province except Al Qunaytirah; however, these public facilities were concentrated in Damascus, which had 15 public hospitals with a total of 3,801 beds, and Aleppo, which had 8 state hospitals with a total of 1,870 beds. Private hospitals were likewise concentrated in Damascus and Aleppo. Syria also had established 503 public health clinics throughout the country.

Syria's public health program was augmented by programs administered by the Ministry of Social Affairs and Labor and the Ministry of Education. The Ministry of Social Affairs and Labor provided vaccinations, medicine, and maternity care at rural community development centers throughout the nation. The Ministry of Education administered a preventive medicine and dentistry program for schoolchildren. In 1981 this program operated with a staff of 62 physicians, 22 dentists, and 110 nurses in 160 schools, and Syria was implementing plans to double the size of the program.

Syria had 6,163 physicians in 1985, about one for every 1,666 people. There were 1,975 dentists, one for every 5,198 people. Syria had 8,326 nurses and 2,201 midwives (see table 3, Appendix).

Syria's socialist government provided extensive welfare services to citizens. Most welfare programs were administered by the Ministry of Social Affairs and Labor, which in 1985 had a budget of LS265 million. This ministry controlled labor unions, set minimum wages, was in charge of occupational safety, paid social security premiums, and operated orphanages, institutions for the handicapped, and rural community development centers. Many citizens had access to subsidized public housing.

*   *   *

The scholarly literature on religion in the Middle East is vast, expanding, and subject to constant revision and analysis. For a comprehensive and challenging history of the founding of Islam and its subsequent development and meaning, Marshall G.S. Hodgson's three-volume *The Venture of Islam* is highly recommended. *Islam and the Arab World,* edited by Bernard Lewis, is a well-regarded collection of monographs by numerous specialists in the field, as are *The Cambridge History of Islam,* edited by P.M. Holt, Ann K.S. Lambton, and Bernard Lewis, and *Religion in the Middle East: Three Religions in Concord and Conflict,* edited by A.J. Arberry.

In contrast, literature on Syrian social systems written by trained social scientists remained scanty in 1987. Because of the vital importance of sectarian differences and disputes within the society, such studies as Robert M. Haddad's *Syrian Christians in Muslim Society: An Interpretation,* which contains valuable insights into religious life in both communities, are among the more useful sources for further reading. The articles by A.R. George, Donald M. Reid, and Gordon Roberts present material on some of the minority communities, and Frederick Jones Bliss's *The Religions of Modern Syria and Palestine* contains observations on contemporary society. (For further information and complete citations, see Bibliography.)

Chapter 3. The Economy

Marble relief of a goblet and leaves from door frame of a palace bath, ca. A.D. 727, Qasr al Hayr al Gharbi

SINCE SYRIA BECAME independent in 1946, the economy has undergone widespread structural change. Although the presence of the Allied forces during World War II stimulated commerce by providing markets for agriculture, textiles, and other locally manufactured goods, Syria lacked both the infrastructure and the resources to promote economic prosperity. Agriculture controlled the country's economy and determined the pace of industrial expansion as large landowners channeled profits from agricultural exports into agroindustrial and related urban enterprises. Syria's predominantly rural population, working under land tenure and sharecropping arrangements, derived few benefits from the agriculturally induced economic growth of the 1950s. However, Syria's union with Egypt (1958–61) and the rise of the Baath (Arab Socialist Resurrection) Party as the major political force in the country in the 1960s, transformed Syria's economic orientation and development strategy.

By the mid-1960s, government-sponsored land reform and nationalization of major industries and foreign investments had confirmed the new socialist direction of Syria's economic policy. As the state assumed greater control over economic decision-making by adopting centralized planning and strictly regulating commercial transactions, Syria experienced a substantial loss of skilled workers, administrators, and their capital. Despite the political upheavals, which undermined the confidence of landowners, merchants, and industrialists, the state successfully implemented large-scale development projects to expand industry, agriculture, and infrastructure.

During the 1970s, Syria achieved high rates of economic growth. The dramatic rise of world oil prices from 1973 to 1974 led to increased production from domestic refineries. Moreover, higher prices for agricultural and oil exports, as well as the state's limited economic liberalization policy, encouraged growth. Also, Syria's economic boom was furthered by increased remittances from Syrians working in the oil-rich Arab states and higher levels of Arab and other foreign aid. By the end of the decade, the Syrian economy had shifted from its traditional agrarian base to an economy dominated by the service, industrial, and commercial sectors. Massive expenditures for development of irrigation, electricity, water, road building projects, and expansion of health services and education to rural areas contributed to prosperity. However, the economy remained dependent on foreign aid and grants to finance the growing deficits both in the budget and in trade. Syria, as a front-line state in the Arab-Israeli conflict, was also vulnerable to the vagaries of Middle East politics, relying on Arab aid transfers and Soviet assistance to support mounting defense expenditures.

By the mid-1980s, the country's economic climate had shifted from prosperity to austerity. Syria's economic boom collapsed as a result of the rapid fall of world oil prices, lower export revenues, drought affecting agricultural production, and falling worker remittances. Also, Arab aid levels decreased because of economic retrenchment in the oil-producing states and Syrian support for Iran in the Iran-Iraq War. To restore the economy, the government sharply reduced spending, cut back imports, encouraged more private sector and foreign investment, and launched an anticorruption campaign against smugglers and black-market money changers. However, massive defense outlays continued to divert resources from productive investments.

By the late 1980s, spot shortages of basic commodities occurred frequently, and industry operated far below capacity because of routine power outages. Foreign exchange reserves plummeted, the trade deficit widened, and real gross domestic product growth fell as economic difficulties compounded. Although the government instituted limited reforms to respond to the burgeoning crisis, Syria's pressing economic problems required a radically restructured economic policy to improve future economic performance.

Growth and Structure of the Economy

At independence Syria had a relatively well-developed economic base. Rapid economic growth began in the 1930s, accelerated in the 1940s, and lasted until the late 1950s. Growth was based primarily on the opening of new land to cultivation and financed largely by wealthy urban merchants, particularly from Aleppo. The new farms, which grew wheat, barley, and cotton as main crops, were large, using mechanization and irrigation as much as possible. Industry also expanded rapidly, stimulated by the needs of Allied forces in the area during World War II and domestic shortages of goods. Most industries were small, consisting of powered flour mills, bakeries, laundries, and repair shops, but also including larger facilities, in particular textile mills.

In the mid-1950s, a group of economists from the World Bank (see Glossary) concluded that the period of rapid growth based on private sector investment was ending. The slowdown occurred partly because the supply of new land that could easily be cultivated was nearly exhausted. Further expansion of arable land would require large public sector investments in irrigation, drainage, and reclamation. Large public sector investments were also needed in electric power, ports, and the transportation system. Thus, economic conditions required an expanded role for government at about the same time that socialist-oriented political leaders became more influential.

Only the waning portion of this period of rapid growth is reflected in contemporary official statistics because statistical services developed late and reliability of data was uncertain. Although statistics improved slowly over the years, problems remained in the late 1980s. Many economic measurements were best viewed as indicative rather than precise. Moreover, sharp yearly fluctuations in agricultural output caused by variations in rainfall further compounded economic analysis. Although agriculture's share in the economy had declined over the years, even in the late 1980s the wide swings in annual harvests had pronounced effects on such sectors as trade, transportation, finance, and industry.

Specific data concerning the growth of the economy extend back to 1953. Such data, measured by the gross domestic product (GDP) at market prices in terms of constant 1963 prices, indicate that growth averaged 6.3 percent a year between 1953 and 1976. The period of rapid growth led by the agricultural and industrial sectors ended in 1957 because of a prolonged, four-year drought that severely curtailed agricultural output. In the 1960s, land reform, nationalization of key industries, and the socialist transformation of the economy affected the pace and scope of economic development. Growth of the economy, measured by GDP at market prices in terms of constant 1980 prices, averaged 9.7 percent a year during the 1970s. Real growth peaked at 10.2 percent in 1981 but declined sharply to 3.2 percent in 1982 and –2.1 percent in 1984.

The pattern of growth by sectors was uneven. Between 1953 and 1976, the value of agricultural output (in constant 1963 prices) increased by only 3.2 percent a year, slower growth than in other sectors of the economy. In the late 1970s, the value of agricultural output (in constant 1980 prices) increased by an average of 9.3 percent a year, despite large weather-induced fluctuations in output. From 1981 to 1984, output fell each year, although 1985 levels surged to approximate 1983 yields (see table 4, Appendix).

Although agricultural output remained relatively fixed, industry and construction rapidly increased in the mid-1970s, stimulated in large part by the oil boom in the Persian Gulf states. Construction grew 16.3 percent a year during the 1970s, while output of the mining and manufacturing sectors increased 7.1 percent a year. In the early 1980s, average yearly growth in these sectors was

5.6 percent and 7.9 percent, respectively. The growth of electric power and the extractive industries, particularly crude oil and phosphates, aided industrial expansion.

The expansion of government services in the 1970s and 1980s helped sustain economic growth. In the 1970s, government services grew at an average of 12.4 percent, contributing 14.1 percent to GDP in 1976 and rising to 19.6 percent in 1984. Contributing to this high rate of growth was state commitment to expanding the educational system, health care, and social services; extending public sector enterprises as part of the nationalization program; constructing new commercial, industrial, and residential facilities; and increasing defense expenditures.

As a result of the varying sectoral growth rates, the economy gradually shifted from an agrarian-based structure prior to 1970 to an economy based on services and the commercial sector in the 1980s (see fig. 8). In 1953 agriculture contributed nearly 40 percent of GDP compared with 30 percent in 1963 and approximately 20 percent in 1984 (at constant 1980 prices), according to the figures published by the International Bank for Reconstruction and Development (IBRD). Official Syrian government sources placed agriculture's share of GDP at 16.9 percent in 1984. From 1953 to 1976, industry, including extractive industries and electric power, increased from about 10 to 22 percent of GDP. In 1984 industry contributed 15.1 percent of GDP. Construction, trade, and transportation retained approximately the same relative importance as they had in the mid-1970s. By 1976 government services contributed over one-half of GDP. In 1984 the GDP share from government services increased to 61 percent, according to official Syrian statistics, while the IBRD ranked that sector's 1984 contribution at 57 percent.

Labor Force

Historically, agriculture was the most important source of employment in the economy. However, the share of the labor force engaged in agriculture declined significantly from 1965 to 1984. According to the World Bank, the percentage of the work force engaged in agriculture fell from 53 percent in 1965 to 48 percent in 1976 and to 30 percent in 1984. Manufacturing, construction, trade, and services were the other major sources of employment, providing opportunities for advancement and economic security for unskilled workers migrating from underdeveloped rural areas to the larger cities. From 1965 to 1981, the industrial labor force expanded from 20 to 31 percent. The service sector continued to be the largest employer in the 1980s, employing about 35 percent of the labor force.

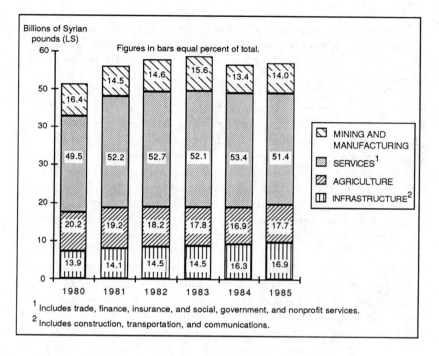

Source: Based on information from Syria, Central Bureau of Statistics, *Statistical Abstract 1986*, Damascus, 1986.

Figure 8. Growth and Structure of Gross Domestic Product, 1980-85

The government, including public sector enterprises but excluding defense, employed some 473,000 workers in 1983, about 21 percent of the employed labor force and 32 percent of nonfarm workers. These figures represented a substantial increase in the number of workers employed by the government—up from the 1975 figure of some 280,000, which was about 16 percent of the work force (see table 5, Appendix). Although Syria did not guarantee jobs to all college graduates, the government absorbed many new graduates into the state bureaucracy. Government organizations were thus overstaffed, reducing profitability and efficiency in public sector enterprises and causing bureaucratic delays. In addition, new graduates and unskilled workers frequently took jobs with the government to gain experience and training but subsequently switched to higher paying jobs in the private sector. Moreover, surveys suggested that many government employees worked outside their area of expertise. Government workers also took second jobs in business and services to supplement their incomes.

The economy suffered a lack of skilled workers and trained professionals in a wide variety of fields. In 1983 professionals, technicians, administrators, and managers made up only 10 percent of the work force, although their number was double the percentage in 1970. Both the shortage of skilled labor and the low wage policy in the public sector constrained the mid-1970s investment boom. Skilled workers and professionals headed to the oil-rich, labor-poor states of the Arabian Peninsula for higher wages. Although the government adopted various measures to curtail the "brain drain" from both the public and the private sectors, Syrians continued to migrate. In the 1980s, following the collapse of world oil prices and the subsequent economic downturn of the oil-producing states, many Syrian workers began returning home, and their industrial management skills and expertise therefore became available to the state.

In the 1970s, planners and government organizations gave greater attention to increasing the skills of the labor force. Vocational schools and specialized training facilities, including one for administrators and managers, became more active, and new industrial plants and other projects often included job training by foreign suppliers. The government made greater efforts to identify and plan for the economy's manpower needs. As a result, public sector employees received wage increases, but it was not clear that the raises were sufficient to make public sector employment more attractive than private enterprise. How fast the level of the work force would rise and how the low level of skilled manpower would affect economic development were still uncertain.

Officially, unemployment remained a relatively minor problem into the 1980s. In 1983 registered unemployed totaled 2 percent. However, actual unemployment may have been higher because much of the population depended on seasonal agricultural employment. Many urban workers were also underemployed, further complicating employment statistics. United States government observers estimate that in 1984 unemployment may actually have reached 20 percent. Although government programs to stimulate cottage industry and local processing in rural areas helped provide additional income for seasonal workers, the dramatic increase in the number of beggars appearing in large cities in the mid-1980s indicated a sharp decline in the urban standard of living.

As of 1983, about 15 percent of nonfarm labor was unionized (222,203 members in 179 unions). Union membership was largest among government, construction, textile, and land transportation workers. The government encouraged and supported labor organizations but closely supervised their activities, restricted their political influence and economic power, and minimized labor disputes. Labor achieved a voice in management of public enterprises through the participation of workers' representatives in committees at each plant, but the managers headed the committees. In an effort to increase production and productivity, in the late 1970s public businesses established production councils consisting of the business manager and representatives of the Baath Party, the union, and plant workers.

Role of Government

During the rapid economic development preceding and following independence, government played a minor role. Expansion resulted primarily from private sector investment in agriculture and industry. Although the economy grew rapidly, benefits were not shared equally. Many people's incomes were very low, and most of the rural population lacked amenities; electricity, education, health care, and an adequate diet were available almost exclusively in cities and a few towns. In the 1950s, disparities of income and social inequality contributed to the rise of political leaders favoring a much stronger economic role for the government, including some leaders who demanded state ownership of the means of production. Economic conditions, primarily the need for large investments in roads, ports, and irrigation, also required more active government participation (see Radical Political Influence, ch. 1).

Between 1958, after the union with Egypt, and 1965, a series of laws were enacted that resulted in progressive socialization of the economy. By 1961 the state had acquired control of the development of natural resources, and land reform measures had been introduced, although not effectively implemented. Also, a new economic plan that emphasized large public sector investments had been formulated, and the banking system had been moved toward nationalization through what Syrians called "Arabization." In 1961, while Syria was still the junior partner with Egypt in the United Arab Republic, widespread nationalization was decreed, but Syria withdrew from the republic before completion of the nationalization measures (see United Arab Republic, ch. 1). Not until March 1963 did the socialist transformation make headway.

Between 1963 and 1965, a socialist economy was erected, although some laws enacted later extended and refined the public sector. In 1963 agrarian reform stripped large landowners of their estates and much of their political power, provided some land to landless farmers, and improved conditions for farm tenants and sharecroppers (see Agriculture, this ch.). In 1963 commercial banking and insurance were completely nationalized, and in 1965 most

115

A suspension footbridge over the Euphrates River at Dayr az Zawr

large businesses were nationalized wholly or partially. By 1966 the public sector included development of natural resources, electric power, and water; the bulk of industrial plants, banking, and insurance; part of transportation; and most international commerce and domestic wholesale trade. In addition, the government was responsible for the bulk of investments, the flow of credit, and pricing for many commodities and services, including a substantial part of wages.

By 1986 the situation remained essentially unchanged. As a result of these earlier measures, the government dominated the economy—accounting for three-fifths of GDP—and exerted considerable influence over the private sector. However, President Hafiz al Assad had liberalized the structure somewhat to encourage more private sector activity and investment. For example, the government relaxed exchange controls and permitted private traders to import more goods, although over 100 of the most important foreign commodities were still exclusively imported by state trading organizations. In addition, the government established six free-trade zones, where local traders and manufacturers could import, process, and reexport commodities freely. Also, private investment (domestic and foreign) in portions of manufacturing and tourist facilities was encouraged through such measures as tax exemptions and cheap credit. The post-1970 measures were more a rationalization of the economy to promote greater private sector development than a dismantling of government controls and ownership. As a result of these measures, the private sector dominated agriculture and retail trade and was important in light industry—particularly fabrics and clothing—and construction, transportation, and tourist facilities.

Cotton, the country's most important export before 1974, provided an extreme example of government involvement in the economy. Areas put into cotton cultivation were controlled by government licensing of individual farmers. A government bank supplied the credit, most of which went to cotton farmers; much of the credit was in kind, and the bank would purchase, store, and distribute the approved seeds, fertilizers, and other items. Government organizations purchased and graded the cotton, operated the gins and spinning mills, and marketed the products internally and abroad. The government established the price for cotton at all stages and subsidized prices for such inputs as credits, seeds, fertilizers, and fuel to run the irrigation pumps.

The effect on Syria's economy of the socialist measures of the 1960s was significant. First, there was a substantial exodus of trained personnel and capital from the private sector, a trend that continued in the 1970s, although the exodus was of a smaller magnitude and occurred for different reasons (see Industry, this ch.). The other major consequence was a rapid expansion of government responsibilities, even though the government had few trained people, limited funds, and inadequate organization and procedures. The political instability of the 1960s and the small number of trained people in the country further hampered development of effective organizations. Government services, including defense, became the main growth sector of the economy in the 1960s as people were added to the payroll, but effective expansion was slow.

In the mid-1980s, observers characterized the government and its activities as inefficient and excessively bureaucratic. Much of the criticism was caused by the continuing shortage of trained and competent officials. Part of the criticism reflected continuing deficiencies in organizations and practices. Government organizations were still trying to catch up with the huge additional responsibilities that had been imposed on inexperienced government personnel. By 1986 budgetary procedures and financial controls had steadily improved, but they were not as good as the situation required or as officials desired. Proposals for evaluations and implementation of projects were deficient, but progress had been made, and the government sought advice and help from outside experts for more improvements.

When the socialist transformation was taking place in the 1960s, the rationale was to promote economic development for the benefit of all. Although some direct redistribution of income occurred, redistribution was effected largely by way of pricing, subsidies, and tenancy legislation rather than by taxation. However, in 1986 data were insufficient for a conclusive opinion. Growth afforded job opportunities at higher incomes, but it had the negative effect of attracting even more workers to already crowded urban areas. However, economic development did provide gradual improvement of living standards; considerable investments were made in roads, ports, schools, irrigation, and the Euphrates Dam (also known as Tabaqah Dam or Thawra Dam) that would facilitate future growth. Nonetheless, the economic wrenching of the 1980s restrained development; incomes of most Syrians remained low by world standards, and substantial income gaps between various groups persisted.

Budget

As economic power was progressively transferred from private enterprise to the state, public finance became a major economic determinant. Even though the government's fiscal responsibilities increased during the early 1960s, budgetary practices changed little until 1967, when legislation established a single, consolidated, and centralized annual budget that covered all spending units of the public sector. This budget was closely geared to development plans and complemented a reorganization of the banking system. Under the law, each budgeted outlay was to be matched by the funds required to finance it.

The budget legislation was accompanied by a reorganization of the Ministry of Finance and of auditing and statistical services. An annual foreign exchange budget was instituted to preview probable foreign exchange receipts and expenditures, thus allowing the Ministry of Finance and the State Planning Organization (SPO) to anticipate the government's needs in foreign and local currencies.

The new law required that budget accounts be closed thirty days after the end of the fiscal year. Unused funds were to be returned to the treasury, although those already committed were to be placed in special, segregated accounts in the treasury. This stopped the previous practice whereby transactions continued to be recorded on budget accounts for several years after the end of a fiscal year.

Since 1967, when the state introduced the consolidated budget, all expenditures and receipts of the ministries, the central public sector administrative agencies, the public sector economic enterprises, and the local, municipal, and religious administrative units have been combined into one budget. Expenditures and receipts of the ministries and central government administrative units were included in the general budget in full; other units were represented by inclusion of the net total surplus or deficit of their respective budgets. Economic units financed almost none of their own expansion. Instead, they turned any surplus (profit) back to the government and received funds via budget expenditures for investments.

Although budgetary practices improved and the budget became a more useful tool for officials, published budget data in the late 1980s remained a difficult source from which to interpret developments in the economy. Expenditures and receipts continued to be published as proposals only. Actual expenditures and receipts were not available, although fragmentary data gave indications of shortfalls. Although Ministry of Finance statistics generally depicted balanced budgets, there were many accounting errors, and such important balancing items as proposed domestic borrowing and anticipated foreign aid were not clearly designated. Thus it was impossible to determine how effective the government was in implementing programs, whether deficits were incurred and, if so, their size, and how dependent the government was on external assistance. The uncertainties may have been intentional for security reasons.

The budget gave few clues about the extent of Syria's economic malaise in the mid-1980s. For example, it did not reflect the rapid depreciation of the Syrian pound, the steep rise in prices, the shortages of basic commodities, or the acute foreign exchange crisis that compelled the government to reduce imports. However, budget data during the mid-1980s clearly depicted the mood of austerity underlying economic policy as well as the government's commitment to reducing expenditures. The 1986 budget revealed a major decrease in expenditure in real terms for the third consecutive year, as inflation—estimated at between 20 to 30 percent—negated the 2 percent increase in spending.

Defense spending towered above all other budgetary allocations in the 1980s (see The Armed Forces and Society, ch. 5). The cost of Syria's military presence in Lebanon since 1976, coupled with the government's desire to reach strategic parity with Israel, accounted for the level of spending. Defense spending averaged over 50 percent of current expenditures in the mid-1980s, accounting for about 30 percent of total spending.

Agricultural development also benefited from high allocations in the mid-1980s designed to counteract the governmental neglect of the 1970s. In 1985 allocations rose 22 percent above 1984 figures, amounting to 20 percent of total spending. In 1986 figures indicated a 5 percent investment increase for the agricultural sector.

Allocations for the mining industry (including petroleum) increased substantially in the 1986 investment budget. The 1986 allocations rose 46 percent above 1985 levels as government officials targeted increased petroleum and phosphate production and export in the Sixth Five-Year Plan (1986–90).

However, budget deficits continued in the 1980s because of the rapid increase in defense expenditures and falling revenues from exports. The government financed the deficit through domestic borrowing and foreign aid. But, in the mid-1980s, budgeted foreign aid grants greatly exceeded actual disbursements by donors because of depressed economic conditions in the Arab oil-exporting states. Although Syria budgeted about LS2 billion (for value of the Syrian pound—see Glossary) in foreign aid grants in 1986, the country expected to receive only about one-fifth of this figure and to incur a substantial budget deficit. However, the country's internal and external public debt remained moderate and did not impose an oppressive annual repayment burden.

Revenues

The growth rate of proposed government revenues (in current prices) averaged 14.3 percent a year from 1964 to 1970, 26 percent a year in the 1970s, and 8.3 percent a year from 1980 to 1985. Growth in government revenues in the 1970s reflected higher levels of foreign aid because of Syria's key role in inter-Arab politics and increased internal borrowing for development. Government receipts included part of expected foreign financial assistance as well as anticipated domestic borrowing. Actual receipts for various revenue headings were not available, but many economists believed that actual receipts were substantially less than those shown in proposed budgets. Proposed government revenues increased from LS1.2 billion in 1964 to LS2.8 billion in 1970, LS10.4 billion in 1975, LS1.2 billion in 1978, and LS43 billion in 1985 (see table 6, Appendix).

Syrian revenues were a much higher ratio of GDP than in most countries because budget receipts incorporated the funds, including foreign aid and internal borrowing, used for the bulk of the country's investments. In fact, Syrian revenue structure differed from that of most countries in a number of ways. Personal income taxes have traditionally been low, amounting to only LS550 million, or 1.3 percent of total revenues, in 1985. Reluctance to tax income stemmed from generally low incomes combined with high tax-collection costs. Furthermore, tax rates were low, and had numerous exemptions for special interests, despite a 1982 law enacted to close loopholes for certain public sector ventures. Tax evasion also was common among all social classes. Business income taxes were relatively small as well, amounting to 10 percent (LS4.3 billion) of total revenues in 1985. Even so, this amount was a significant increase over the LS510 million (3 percent of total revenues) collected in 1977.

In addition, taxes on capital, real estate, and inheritance yielded small sums. In 1985 taxes on capital brought in LS50 million, real estate taxes produced LS400 million, and inheritance taxes LS40 million, equivalent to about 1 percent of the total. Direct taxes and duties totaled LS6.2 billion in 1985.

Because they were easy to collect, levies on production and consumption (including taxes on imports) were the primary form of taxation. Like many other developing countries, Syria relied on indirect taxes, which in 1985 amounted to LS4.2 billion, 10 percent of total revenues, equal to two-thirds the amount of direct taxes and duties. Customs duties and other fees on foreign trade, including duties on cotton exports, amounted to LS2 billion in 1985. Excise taxes on several commodities (e.g., cement, fuel, livestock, sugar, and salt) made up the remainder of indirect taxes.

Transfer of surpluses (after taxes and profits) from public sector enterprises served as the main source of domestic revenue. The share of these transfers (excluding foreign aid and internal credits) reached 32 percent in 1970, 50 percent in 1976, and 31 percent in 1985 (LS13.1 billion). In the 1960s, banking-financial and industrial public sector businesses together provided the bulk of the surpluses. In the 1970s, in industrial concerns alone accounted for 75 percent of the surpluses transferred to the budget; this figure declined slightly to 70 percent in 1985. In the 1970s and 1980s, the government increasingly relied on the pricing of commodities and services rather than taxes to finance expenditures. In an effort to expand future budget revenues, officials intended to increase efficiency, productivity, and profits of public sector business.

Foreign credits and grants and domestic borrowing also provided supplemental funding for key development projects. The 1984 budget projected LS1.9 billion in foreign loans and LS7.7 billion in "support funds" from Arab states (see Balance of Payments, this ch.). After 1982 grants in oil aid from Iran also significantly contributed to the growth of revenues. However, when external aid declined in the 1980s, domestic borrowing levels increased. Although the banking system provided most of the internal credits, reserves of public enterprises also provided some funds.

Until 1977 transit fees for crude oil pumped through international pipelines across Syrian territory were an important source of revenue. Pipeline payments, which averaged about 25 percent of total domestic revenues in the early 1970s, fell to zero in 1977. The pipeline reopened briefly in 1979, was shut down in the early stages of the Iran-Iraq War, and then reopened again in 1981 before Syria closed down the pipeline from Iraq in 1982 as a show of support for Iran in the war (see Industry, this ch.).

Expenditures

Proposed expenditures matched proposed revenues because budgets submitted for approval were balanced. However, actual expenditures usually fell considerably short of those planned, although the fragmentary data available in 1987 generally precluded measurement of the amount of difference. In the 1980s, budgets began including planned deficits, and investment spending repeatedly trailed allocations. Only 70 percent of Syria's 1984 investment budget of LS17.9 million was actually spent. Expenditures fell under two headings—the ordinary budget covering current (recurring) expenditures and the development (capital) budget. Beginning in the early 1960s, capital investments had become a much more important part of the budget. Development expenditures amounted to 42 percent of total expenditures in 1964, increased to 50 percent in 1970, and peaked at 64 percent in 1976. However, by 1980 development expenditures had fallen back to 50 percent and in 1985 fell to 45 percent of total expenditures.

In the 1980s, normal proposed revenues (taxes, duties, fees, and surpluses of public sector enterprises) usually financed proposed current expenditures, and there was a small remainder to help with capital investments. Foreign aid and domestic borrowing financed the rest of the development budget.

Throughout the 1970s and 1980s, defense spending dominated current expenditures. Some observers maintained that in the 1970s defense spending accounted for approximately three-fifths of current expenditures, although such amounts were not reflected in official statistics (see fig. 9). Officially, defense spending rose from LS675 million in 1970 to LS4.6 billion in 1978, increasing at an average rate of 27 percent a year during this period. In the 1985 budget, defense spending again accounted for the greatest portion of current expenditures. However, the LS13 billion defense budget in 1985 reflected only a 9 percent rate of growth, slower than that in previous years, but a related item, internal security expenditures, accounted for a further LS672 million in the 1985 budget. Most of the remainder of current expenditures covered operating expenses of ministries and agencies—largely personnel costs (see table 7, Appendix).

Identifiable payments on the public debt amounted to LS135 million in 1976 and 1977, less than 1 percent of total expenditures.

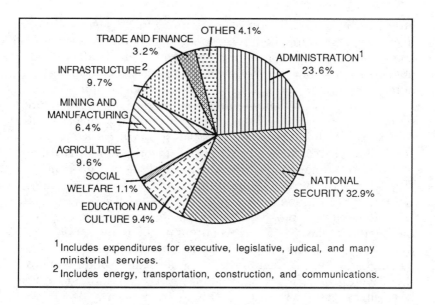

Source: Based on information from Syria, Central Bureau of Statistics, *Statistical Abstract 1986*, Damascus, 1986.

Figure 9. Government Expenditures by Sector, 1985

The 1984 budget allocated LS1.8 billion to the public debt, equal to 7.6 percent of current expenditures.

Identifiable price subsidies amounted to LS600 million in 1977 and LS1.4 billion in 1985, accounting for 9 percent and 6 percent of current expenditures, respectively. Subsidies rose rapidly in the mid-1970s as a result of higher rates of internal and international inflation. The government attempted to keep meat, bread, coffee, sugar, diesel fuel (for irrigation pumps), and other essential items within reach of the poor; the subsidized prices for sugar and diesel fuel, for example, were about one-quarter of the regular market price in the 1980s.

In the 1970s, the government demonstrated its commitment to economic development through sizable increases in the development budget by increasing investment expenditures an average of 26 percent a year. Although they increased substantially from LS1.4 billion in 1970 to LS14 billion in 1980, growth of investment expenditures slowed to just 6 percent a year in the 1980s.

Development Planning

Development planning began in 1947, when a British firm was

hired to survey the Syrian economy and make suggestions for investments. Presumably, the report guided the government's limited development expenditures for several years. In 1955 an economic mission from the World Bank suggested a six-year, LS1.9 billion development program and formation of a planning agency. In the same year, a planning organization that immediately presented a seven-year, LS660-million development plan was established. Although this plan was adopted, it was discarded in 1956. In 1958 a ten-year plan was prepared, incorporating the results of the 1957 aid agreement with the Soviet Union. This plan was also discarded in order to mesh plans with Egypt.

After Syria's union with Egypt, Syria's First Five-Year Plan (1960–65) within a broader ten-year program was adopted. As in the Egyptian plan, Syria's gross output of goods and services was to double in 10 years, requiring a yearly increase of 7.2 percent. Total planned investment in the five-year plan, including that by the private sector, was LS2.7 billion. Irrigation and agriculture were allocated 20 percent of the investments; transportation and communications, 20 percent; and industry—particularly the oil and electric power industries—19 percent. Foreign aid was to supply nearly one-quarter of the financing (nearly 40 percent of public sector investments), supplemented by a small amount of internal borrowing. However, withdrawal from the union with Egypt, political instability, private investors' fear of nationalization, and inadequacies of the government structure combined to keep actual investment to less than 60 percent of the plan.

The Second Five-Year Plan (1966–70) maintained the same growth target (an annual average increase of 7.2 percent for GDP) but substantially increased planned public sector investments to achieve the socialist economy envisioned by Syria's leaders. Planned development expenditures were LS5 billion, of which the public sector was to contribute LS3.5 billion and the private sector LS1.5 billion. Dependence on foreign aid increased, amounting to a planned LS1.9 billion, or 56 percent of public sector investments (4 percent of total investments). Planned allocations included LS1.4 billion to irrigation and agriculture (primarily the Euphrates Dam and other irrigation projects), LS612 million to fuel and electric power, LS894 million to transportation and communications, LS399 million to manufacturing and mining, and LS1.3 billion to housing, construction, and public works. More than two-thirds of private investments were to be in housing, construction, and agriculture.

Implementation of the second plan fell short of goals, partly because of the June 1967 War and the resources devoted to national security. Economic growth was about two-thirds of that projected under the plan, and investments were about 70 percent. Public sector development expenditures lagged considerably during the first three years, and only large investment in 1969 and 1970 partially salvaged the situation. Private sector investment (largely in housing and construction) appeared to be closer to what was planned than public sector investment. Export growth exceeded the plan but was less than import growth, causing a deterioration in the balance of payments.

The Third Five-Year Plan (1971–75) aimed at an 8.2 percent growth rate for GDP (in constant prices) and investments totaling LS8 billion, of which LS6.4 billion was planned for the public sector and LS1.6 billion for the cooperative and private sectors. Public sector allocations were 25 percent for completion of the Euphrates Dam; 10 percent for agricultural and other irrigation projects; 18 percent for industry and mining; 16 percent for fuel and electric power; 12 percent for transportation and communications; 9 percent for housing, water, and other public works, and 10 percent for miscellaneous, including debt service. Private sector investments were scheduled primarily for housing and construction (LS903 million); much smaller amounts were scheduled for other sectors. Domestic savings were expected to increase sharply to finance investments. Surpluses of public enterprises alone were expected to finance over three-quarters of public investments.

Implementation of the third plan started slowly; development expenditures were far less than planned by the outbreak of the October 1973 War. The war damaged key industrial facilities, particularly power stations and the oil refinery at Homs. The plan was modified for necessary repairs and for additional projects because substantial new aid became available. Over 50 percent of investments were concentrated in the last two years of the plan.

The results of the third plan were mixed. GDP (in constant prices) increased over the five years by 10.7 percent a year, considerably more than planned because of relatively good weather for crops, increasing production of and higher prices for crude oil, and the high level of construction, particularly after 1973. Some large projects were completed during the Second Five-Year Plan, such as the Euphrates Dam, a fertilizer plant, and the beginning of a steel industry that added to and diversified the industrial strength of the country. Public investments, however, reached only about 70 percent of the target in spite of heavy development expenditures in the final two years, and the pattern by sectors was irregular. Even with the large expenditures in the Euphrates basin, investment in agriculture and irrigation stagnated in real terms.

Public savings and surpluses of public enterprises fell considerably short of goals. Without new and unplanned foreign aid, public investments would not have even approached targets as closely as they did. However, the high level of investment after 1973 contributed to shortages of goods and skilled workers and to serious inflation.

Aware of deficiencies, the government attempted to remedy problems in planning and implementation. In 1968 the planning structure was reorganized; as of 1986 it retained the same form. The Supreme Planning Council, consisting of the prime minister and the highest officials concerned with the economy, determined broad strategy and general objectives from which the SPO drew up detailed guidelines. Planning units in ministries developed sectoral plans in collaboration with appropriate SPO officials. The process then was reversed—the sectoral plans passing the SPO for final formulation, with subsequent approval by the Supreme Planning Council. The SPO prepared the annual development budget for inclusion with the government's current budget expenditures and shared responsibilities with another organization under the prime minister's office in the follow up of the plan. The Central Bureau of Statistics also supported the prime minister in providing data for planning and implementation. Statistical services had improved considerably by the mid-1980s, but collection and processing still needed improvement to meet the requirements of officials and planners.

The reforms made failed to raise the government's management of the economy to the level outlined in the Third Five-Year Plan. Deficiencies remained in project identification, preparation, implementation, and coordination. Management of public sector businesses was generally weak, reducing the profits available to the government for development expenditures and often leaving industrial capacity underutilized. In spite of efforts by the Ministry of Finance to reform the tax system and increase efficiency of domestic resource mobilization, deficiencies in labor, wage, and price policies hampered development. Corruption became so widespread that the government initiated a program against it. Some economists viewed the government's administrative problems as so complex that many years of serious reform would be required to achieve satisfactory efficiency.

Preparation of the Fourth Five-Year Plan (1976–80) required a reassessment by the country's economic leaders. In particular, the reduced availability of economic resources (caused in part by a slowing of foreign aid, loss of pipeline transit fees and concessionary crude oil supplies from Iraq, military expenditures for

126

peacekeeping in Lebanon, and care for the large number of refugees from Lebanon) forced a program of austerity. The reassessment contributed to a cabinet change in August 1976, in which the new cabinet was charged with improving economic management and particularly with strengthening public sector performance.

The original draft of the fourth plan, completed by 1975, was overly optimistic. A drastically revised draft was finished in June 1976 but was further revised downward during the year. Because of the shortages of agricultural workers in the northeast and technicians and managers in industry, the new cabinet reportedly viewed the revised plan as still too optimistic about GDP growth, expansion of irrigation, and production increases from manufacturing and extractive industries. The revised plan was approved and became law in April 1977, although as a tentative plan subject to further revision.

The approved Fourth Five-Year Plan anticipated an increase in real terms of 12 percent a year in agricultural output, 15.4 percent a year in mining, manufacturing, and electric-power production, and 16 percent a year in construction. Total planned investments were LS54.2 billion, of which LS44.8 billion was to be generated by the public sector. Agriculture and irrigation received the largest allocation, LS12.9 billion, of which LS10.4 billion was generated by the public sector, including LS7.4 billion for irrigation in the Euphrates basin and LS1.1 billion for fifty-eight small dams and irrigation and drainage projects elsewhere. Mining and manufacturing were allocated LS11.3 billion, of which public sector investments were LS9.9 billion. Fuel and electric power, all in the public sector, received LS7.9 billion. Housing was allocated LS8.1 billion, almost evenly divided between public and private investments. The transportation and communication systems, primarily public sector, were allocated LS5.6 billion. Investments in public works, local government, trade, and other services (largely public sector) made up the remainder.

Despite the infusion of funds from Arab oil-producing states, Syrian officials had concluded that the targets set for the Fourth Five-Year Plan were unrealistic and that the plan contained too many large and overly ambitious projects. Consequently, the Fifth Five-Year Plan (1981–85) sought more modest goals than its predecessors. The plan, announced only in mid-1981 and published in 1982, called for few new major projects, indicating the return of realism to Syrian development planning. Although planners concentrated on completing projects begun under the fourth plan, emphasis shifted from industry to agriculture in an effort to achieve self-sufficiency in food. The large increase in food imports since the late 1970s and the general neglect of the agricultural sector in that decade produced a renewed commitment to agricultural development. The Fifth Five-Year Plan sought a reduction in both public and private consumption while continuing to increase investment. In addition, the plan targeted a decrease in the trade deficit and a reduction in the growth of public spending. Under the Fifth Five-Year Plan, total planned investment was LS101.5 billion, with LS9.4 billion derived from foreign loans and aid. The private sector was slated to provide LS23.3 billion. Agriculture received LS17.2 billion, and mining and manufacturing's allocation was LS27 billion, including LS4.6 billion for the extractive industries and LS10.1 billion for electricity, gas, and water. The transportation and communication sector received LS12.8 billion, the financial sector LS18.4 billion, and the service sector LS20.6 billion.

Although the Fifth Five-Year Plan's goals were more realistic than goals of previous plans, targets proved unattainable. In fact, the fifth plan achieved only 50 percent of its goals in key areas. Factors largely beyond the control of the government contributed to this failure. The oil crisis of the 1980s, which lowered the price and demand for petroleum, reduced the value of Syria's crude oil exports. The crisis also produced depressed economic conditions in the Arab oil-producing states, leading to a marked decrease of workers' remittances and foreign aid and grants from the Persian Gulf states in the mid-1980s. In addition, the 1983–84 drought damaged not only the production of key crops but also adversely affected agriculturally dependent sectors of the economy. Mounting defense expenditures and government policies, including price controls and marketing restrictions on agricultural production, also accounted for the failure to achieve the projected goals of the plan. In general, less than 70 percent of the amount allocated for investment budgets in the early 1980s actually was spent. The Fifth Five-Year Plan projected a 44.7 percent growth in real GDP (in 1980 prices), equivalent to an average annual increase of 7.7 percent, but real GDP fell from 1982 to 1985.

Individual sectors clearly failed to meet or even approach the targets. The value of agricultural production was slated to grow an average of 7.8 percent a year under the plan. Despite the state's renewed emphasis on agricultural development, production decreased in the early 1980s as a result of drought conditions. Increased production levels in 1985 occurred more as a response to good weather than as an emerging trend toward increased agricultural output. Structural changes in the economy and the movement of the labor force away from the agricultural sector weakened attempts to increase production. The mining and manufacturing sector, targeted to rise 42.7 percent over the five-year period, grew only about 8.5 percent in the early 1980s. The sector experienced an overall decrease in the real value of production from 1980 to 1985, despite increases in electric power generation and manufacturing output.

The plan also anticipated an 8.9 percent per year rise in investment and a 6.4 percent per year increase in current expenditures. Allocated development expenditure actually declined in real terms from the 1980 to the 1985 budget. Gross domestic investment, both public and private, grew about 2.9 percent per year. Current expenditure grew 9 percent per year in real terms during the period of the Fifth Five-Year Plan. The planned yearly increases for imports and exports were 3.4 and 6.5 percent, respectively, yet both actually fell. The trade deficit and food imports, however, continued to grow.

In early 1987, the Sixth Five-Year Plan (1986–90) had still not been published. However, Syrian government officials had revealed the general goals of the plan in statements to the international media. Like its immediate predecessor, the Sixth Five-Year Plan stressed completion of existing projects and increased productivity in ongoing ones, rather than the implementation of major new development projects in a period of economic retrenchment. Officials anticipated that total investment in the Sixth Five-Year Plan would barely exceed the LS101.5 billion allocated for the fifth plan. The government continued to emphasize agriculture, including land reclamation and water resource exploitation. Agriculture's share of investment was expected to increase from 16.9 percent in the fifth plan to about 19 percent in the sixth plan. Industry's allocation was also slated to rise slightly from 12.2 percent in the fifth plan to 13.7 percent in the sixth plan.

Agriculture

Until the mid-1970s, agriculture had been Syria's primary economic activity. At independence in 1946, agriculture (including forestry and fishing) was the most important sector of the economy, and in the 1940s and early 1950s, agriculture was the fastest growing sector. Wealthy merchants from such urban centers as Aleppo invested in land development and irrigation. Rapid expansion of the cultivated area and increased output stimulated the rest of the economy. However, by the late 1950s, little land that could easily be brought under cultivation remained. During the 1960s, agricultural output stagnated because of political instability and land reform. Between 1953 and 1976, agriculture's contribution to GDP increased (in constant prices) by only 3.2 percent, approximately the rate of population growth. From 1976 to 1984, growth declined to 2 percent a year. Thus, agriculture's importance in the economy declined as other sectors grew more rapidly.

In 1981 (the year of the latest census), as in the 1970s, 53 percent of the population was still classified as rural, although movement to the cities continued to accelerate. However, in contrast to the 1970s, when 50 percent of the labor force was employed in agriculture, by 1983 agriculture employed only 30 percent of the labor force. Furthermore, by the mid-1980s, unprocessed farm products accounted for only 4 percent of exports, equivalent to 7 percent of nonpetroleum exports. Industry, commerce, and transportation still depended on farm produce and related agrobusiness, but agriculture's preeminent position had clearly eroded. By 1985 agriculture (including forestry and fishing) contributed only 17.7 percent to GDP, down from 22.1 percent in 1976.

By the mid-1980s, the Syrian government had taken measures to revitalize agriculture. The 1985 investment budget saw a sharp rise in allocations for agriculture, including land reclamation and irrigation. The government's renewed commitment to agricultural development in the 1980s, by expanding cultivation and extending irrigation, promised brighter prospects for Syrian agriculture in the 1990s.

Water Resources

Water is a scarce resource in Syria as it is throughout the Middle East, but Syria is more fortunate than many other countries. Sufficient rainfall supports cultivation in an arc from the southwest, near the border with Israel and Lebanon, extending northward to the Turkish border and eastward along that border to Iraq. The other main area of cultivation, although dependent on irrigation, is along the Euphrates River and its major tributaries (see Land, Water, and Climate, ch. 2).

Rainfall is highest along the Mediterranean coast and in the mountains just inland; Syria's limited forestry activities are concentrated in the higher elevations of these mountains. Rainfall diminishes sharply as one moves eastward of the mountains paralleling the coast and southward from the Turkish border. The arc of cultivation from the southwest (and east of the coastal mountains) to the northeast is largely semiarid, having an annual rainfall between 300 and 600 millimeters. Areas south and east of the arc receive less than 300 millimeters of rain annually, classifying the land as arid. Grass and coarse vegetation suitable for limited grazing grow in part of this arid belt, and the rest is desert of little agricultural value.

Rainfall is concentrated between October and May. Without irrigation, cropping is finished by summer, when the climate is very hot and dry. Moreover, the amount of rainfall and its timing vary considerably from year to year, making rain-fed farming extremely risky. When rains are late or inadequate, farmers do not even plant a crop. Successive years of drought are not uncommon and cause havoc not only for farmers but for the rest of the economy. In the mid-1980s, about two-thirds of agricultural output (plant and animal production) depended on rainfall.

Extension and improvement of irrigation systems could substantially raise agricultural output. For example, in 1985, because of the expansion of irrigation systems, Syria's agricultural output rose 10 percent above the drought-plagued yield of 1984. Yields from irrigated fields have been several times higher than from rain-fed fields, and many irrigated areas could grow more than a single crop a year. Development of irrigation systems, however, is both costly and time-consuming.

Syria's major irrigation potential lies in the Euphrates River valley and its two major tributaries, the Balikh and Khabur rivers in the northeast portion of the country. The Euphrates is the third largest river in the Middle East (after the Nile in Egypt and the Tigris in Iraq) and its headwaters rise in Turkey, where relatively heavy rainfall and snowpack provide runoff much of the year. The river flows southeastward across the arid Syrian plateau into Iraq. It joins the Tigris River shortly before emptying into the Persian Gulf. In addition to Syria, both Turkey and Iraq use dams on the Euphrates for hydroelectric power, water control, storage, and irrigation. In the mid-1980s, about one-half of the annual Euphrates River flow was used by the three nations.

Syrians have long used the Euphrates for irrigation, but, because the major systems were destroyed centuries ago, they make only limited use of the river's flow. In the mid-1980s, the Euphrates River accounted for over 85 percent of the country's surface water resources, but its water was used for only about two-fifths (200,000 hectares) of the land then under irrigated cultivation. In 1984 about 44 percent of irrigated land still used water from wells.

Several project studies were conducted after World War II. In the 1960s, the Soviet Union agreed to provide financial and technical assistance for the Euphrates Dam, a large hydroelectrical power station, and portions of the major Euphrates irrigation project. The dam, located at Tabaqah, a short distance upriver from the town of Ar Raqqah, is earth fill, sixty meters high and four and one-half kilometers long. Construction began in 1968, and work was essentially completed by 1978. The dam was closed in 1978, when Lake Assad, the artificial lake behind the dam, began filling. About eighty kilometers long, Lake Assad averages about eight kilometers in width and holds nearly 12 billion cubic meters of water. The power plant has eight 100-megawatt turbines for power generation and transmission lines to Aleppo. Until 1983 the power station operated at 65 percent of capacity, generating 2,500 megawatts a year, or about 45 percent of Syria's electricity. In 1986 the power station operated at only 30 to 40 percent of capacity because of the low water level in Lake Assad. Provisions were made, however, for future construction to raise the height of the dam, increase the capacity of Lake Assad by about 10 percent, and increase the number of turbines. In 1984, as a result of the disappointing performance of the dam, the government studied the possibility of building a second dam upstream from Tabaqah between Ash Shajarah, situated on the northern edge of Lake Assad, and Jarabulus, located near the Turkish border.

The ultimate goal of the Euphrates irrigation project is to provide 640,000 cultivable hectares by the year 2000, in effect doubling the area of Syria's irrigated land in the mid-1970s. In 1978 observers believed that 20,000 to 30,000 hectares of land had been irrigated and that new housing, roads, and farms had been completed for the 8,000 farmers displaced by the creation of Lake Assad. In the early 1980s, Syrian officials had anticipated the completion of irrigation on about 50,000 to 100,000 hectares in the Euphrates basin; about 20,000 hectares were planned for completion each year after that. The Fourth Five-Year Plan actually called for irrigating an additional 240,000 hectares by the end of the plan. In 1984, however, Syrian government statistics revealed that only 60,000 hectares were actually being irrigated. Ten years after its inception, the Euphrates irrigation project irrigated only about 10 percent of its long-term goal.

A variety of complex, interrelated problems frustrated realization of targeted irrigation goals. Technical problems with gypsum subsoil, which caused irrigation canals to collapse, proved more troublesome than at first anticipated. Large cost overruns on some of the irrigation projects made them much more expensive than planned and created difficulties in financing additional projects. Moreover, these large irrigation projects required several years before returns on the investments began. There was also doubt about whether farmers could be attracted back from urban areas or enticed from more crowded agricultural areas to the sparsely populated Euphrates River valley.

Another complication is that the Euphrates flow is insufficient for the irrigation needs of the three countries—Turkey, Iraq, and

Syria—that share the river. In 1962 talks on allotment of Euphrates water began and continued sporadically throughout the 1970s and early 1980s, but acrimonious relations between Syria and Iraq hampered final agreements. In fact, in 1978 when Syria began filling Lake Assad and water to Iraq was greatly reduced, the two countries almost went to war. In addition, Turkey's use of the waters of the Euphrates River for its Keban Dam ensures that water levels in Lake Assad will remain low. This problem will undoubtedly continue into the 1990s, when Turkey completes construction of the Ataturk Dam.

By 1987 numerous Euphrates irrigation projects and additional irrigation projects throughout the country were proceeding, but what had been accomplished was not clear. Projects initiated in the 1980s included irrigation of 21,000 hectares in the Ar Raqqah area pilot project, 27,000 hectares reclaimed in the Euphrates middle-stage project, and about half of a 21,000-hectare plot reclaimed with Soviet assistance in the Meskanah region. There were also major irrigation schemes involving 130,000 hectares in the Meskanah, Al Ghab, and Aleppo plains project. In addition, Syria completed a small regulatory dam with three seventy-milliwatt turbines approximately twenty-five kilometers downstream from Tabaqah. In the mid-1980s, work continued on the Baath Dam, located twenty-seven kilometers from the Euphrates Dam, and work on the Tishrin Dam on the Kabir ash Shamali River near Latakia evolved from the planning to implementation stage. The government also planned to construct as many as three dams on the Khabur River in northeast Syria and more effectively use the waters of the Yarmuk River in southwest Syria. Foreign contractors carried out most of these major development projects. The Soviets and Romanians were particularly active in irrigation schemes as part of their economic aid programs. French, British, Italian, and Japanese firms, the World Bank, and Saudi Arabian and Kuwaiti development assistance funds were deeply involved in financing and implementing these projects.

In the 1980s, there was good potential for expanding and refining irrigation in the western portion of Syria. The government obtained economical results using small impoundments that held winter runoffs to supplement rain-fed cultivation and to provide some summer irrigation. Small storage areas for water from wells and springs permitted additional irrigation. Farmers, however, had not yet turned to sprinkler systems or trickle irrigation, which would considerably reduce the amount of water needed for cultivation.

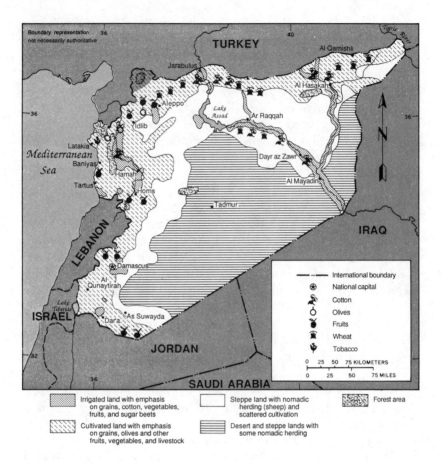

Figure 10. Land Use

Land Use

The bulk of the country is arid, and has little vegetation. In 1984, nearly 20 percent was classified as desert (see fig. 10). Another 45 percent of the land was classified as steppe and pasture, although its grazing capacity was very limited—much like land in the American Southwest. Less than 3 percent of the land was forested, and only part of it was commercially useful. Cultivable land amounted to about 32 percent of the total area. In 1984, about 92 percent of the total cultivable area of 6.2 million hectares was cultivated (see table 8, Appendix).

Major expansion of the cultivated area occurred in the 1940s and 1950s. Much of the expansion was the result of investment

134

by wealthy urban merchants, many of whom were from the country's religious minorities. Their innovations included large-scale use of farm machinery, pumps, and irrigation where possible and different tenure arrangements for farm operators than were used in other parts of the country. But the efforts of the merchants of Aleppo and other commercial centers largely exhausted the potential for bringing new land under cultivation. The area of cultivation (6.9 million hectares) and land irrigated (760,000 hectares) peaked in 1963 and has been appreciably smaller since then. By 1984 approximately 5.7 million hectares were under cultivation, 618,000 of them irrigated.

Opinions differ as to the causes of the decline of cultivated and irrigated areas after 1963. Some observers say that marginal lands brought under cultivation proved uneconomical after a few years and were abandoned. Others claim that the merchant-developers used exploitive techniques that eventually reduced the productivity of the soil. Still other observers blame land reform measures, which coincided with the decline of the cultivated and irrigated areas. Each view is probably somewhat valid.

In the future, expansion of the cultivated area will be slow and costly. Although the Euphrates irrigation projects will provide water to bring additional land under cultivation, growth will be partly offset by the loss of arable land to urban expansion, roads, and other facilities for a growing population. After the disappointing results of the Euphrates irrigation projects through the mid-1980s, the government began to develop rain-fed agriculture to offset potential setbacks in the Euphrates scheme. Drainage investments also will be required to maintain cultivation on some irrigated areas that currently suffer from waterlogging or excessive salinity.

Land Reform

The dynamism of the agricultural sector caused by the opening of new farmland in the north and northeast through investments of wealthy merchants worsened the situation for the poor and often landless rural population. In 1950 the first Syrian constitution placed a limit on the size of landholdings, but the necessary implementing legislation was not passed until 1958, after the union of Syria and Egypt.

The 1958 agrarian reform laws were similar to those in Egypt and not only limited the size of landholdings but also provided sharecroppers and farm laborers with greater economic and legal security and a more equitable share of crops. The Agricultural Relations Law laid down principles to be observed in administering tenancy leases, protected tenants against arbitrary eviction, and reduced, under a fixed schedule, the share of crops taken by landlords. It also authorized agricultural laborers to organize unions and established commissions to review and fix minimum wages for agricultural workers.

However, by the time Syria withdrew from the merger with Egypt in 1961, opposition from large landowners, administrative difficulties, and severe crop failures during the prolonged 1958–61 drought had effectively curtailed movement toward land reform. The conservative regime in power from 1961 until March 1963 blocked implementation of the land reform program in practice by enacting a number of amendments to the original law that substantially raised the ceilings on ownership and opened loopholes.

Shortly after the Baath Party seized power in March 1963, Decree Law 88 of 1963 was promulgated, canceling the actions of the previous regime and reinstating the original agrarian reform laws with important modifications. One of the most significant modifications was lowering the limit on the size of holdings and providing flexibility in accordance with the productivity of the land. The new ceilings on landownership were set at between 15 and 55 hectares on irrigated land and between 80 and 300 hectares on rain-fed land, depending on the area and rainfall. Land in excess of the ceilings was to be expropriated within five years. The compensation payable to the former owners was fixed at 10 times the average 3-year rental value of the expropriated land, plus interest on the principal at the rate of 1.5 percent for 40 years.

The expropriated land was to be redistributed to tenants, landless farmers, and farm laborers in holdings of up to a maximum of eight hectares of irrigated land or thirty to forty-five hectares of rain-fed land per family. Beneficiaries of the redistribution program were required to form state-supervised cooperatives. The 1963 law reduced the price of redistributed land to the beneficiaries to the equivalent of one-fourth of the compensation for expropriation. The land recipients paid this amount in equal installments to their cooperatives over a twenty-year period to finance such cooperative activities as development, dispensaries, schools, and cultural centers.

By 1975 (the latest available data in early 1987) 1.4 million hectares (68,000 hectares of irrigated land) had been expropriated, primarily in the early years of the program. Distribution moved much more slowly. By 1975, redistributed land had amounted to 466,000 hectares (61,000 hectares of irrigated land) and undistributed land to 351,000 hectares. In addition, there were 254,000 hectares of land that had been allocated to cooperatives, ministries, and other organizations and 330,000 hectares that were categorized as excluded and sold land. Although it was far from clear what the disposition was in the latter two categories, the statistical data gave the impression that land reform had not transformed the former numerous farm sharecroppers and laborers into landowners. This impression was supported by government data indicating that slightly more than 50,000 family heads (over 300,000 people) had received land under the reform program. In addition, at various times the government offered state farmland for sale to the landless on the same terms as expropriated land, but reported sales were relatively small; farmers apparently chose to lease the land.

Most observers credited land reform measures with liquidating concentration of very large estates and weakening political power of landowners. Some government data of uncertain coverage and reliability indicated that before land reform more than half of agricultural holdings consisted of 100 hectares or more, but after reform such large holdings amounted to less than 1 percent. The same data showed that smallholdings (7 hectares or less) had increased from about one-eighth before land reform to just over one-half of total holdings after reform and that 42 percent of holdings were between 8 and 25 hectares. Other government statistics indicated that holdings of 25 hectares or less, representing 30 percent of all land under cultivation before 1959, represented 93 percent in 1975. A May 1980 order mandated additional expropriations and further reduced the size of agricultural holdings. Data from the 1970 census revealed that the average landholding was about ten hectares and that one-fifth of the rural population remained landless. Despite the Baath Party's commitment to land reform, the private sector controlled 74 percent of Syria's arable land in 1984.

Role of Government in Agriculture

Government involvement in agriculture was minimal prior to Syria's union with Egypt. Although state intervention in the agricultural sector increased following the union, the government avoided playing a direct role in cultivation. In 1984 private farmers tilled 74 percent of the cultivated land, cooperatives 25 percent, and public organizations (essentially state farms) 1 percent.

Government involvement arose indirectly from socialist transformation measures in various parts of the economy and directly from government efforts to fill the void in the countryside caused by land reform. As an example of the former, the Agricultural Cooperative Bank, a private bank established in the eighteenth century but inherited by the socialist regime, in the mid-1960s became the single source for direct production credits to farmers (see

Apricot paste drying in the Al Ghutah Oasis near Damascus

Banking and Monetary Policy, this ch.). The bank had limited funds and confined itself almost completely to short-term financing, the bulk of which went to cotton growers. Part of its lending was in kind—primarily seeds, pesticides, and fertilizers at subsidized prices. Although the bank appeared effective, there was insufficient credit through the 1960s and early 1970s for farmers who did not grow cotton and for long-term loans for such needs as machinery or capital improvements. In the mid-1970s, the flow of funds to the bank increased, thus allowing it to expand its lending to the agricultural sector. The bank became an important influence in shaping farmers' production decisions, particularly concerning cotton.

In the 1960s, government marketing organizations for the major agricultural commodities were established. The Cotton Marketing Organization had a complete monopoly. Organizations for tobacco and sugar beets had purchasing monopolies, set the farm purchase prices, and supervised the processing and marketing of their respective commodities. An organization for grains set prices, purchased some of the farmers' surplus, and supervised the marketing of the remainder through private dealers. The government also set prices for several other agricultural commodities, most imports, and many consumer items.

Some economists attributed part of the stagnation in agriculture to the government's pricing of farm produce. Farm prices remained unchanged over long periods and by the 1970s and 1980s were quite low relative to world prices. Some smuggling out of farm products for sale in Turkey, Iraq, and Lebanon resulted as well as some black marketing in controlled commodities. Pricing also was not coordinated to achieve agricultural goals. Although the Ministry of Agriculture and Agrarian Reform attempted to get farmers to increase wheat production, the government's desire to keep basic food costs low for urban consumers imposed low grain prices for farmers. The ministry also urged farmers to shift irrigated areas from cotton to wheat at the same time that the farm price of cotton was raised relative to that of wheat.

Aware of the problems, officials made efforts to improve pricing policy. By 1977 prices paid to farmers had risen substantially and favored grains and some industrial crops over cotton. In fact, the 1977 prices (when converted to United States dollars at the official exchange rate) paid to farmers for wheat, soybeans, and sugar beets were substantially higher (more than 100 percent for wheat) than the prices paid to American farmers for those products. In 1985 the government again raised procurement prices for a variety of crops. Prices for hard wheat rose by 9 percent, soft wheat by 14 percent, red lentils by 13 percent, white lentils by 18 percent, and barley by 22 percent from the preceding year.

When land reform was introduced, those receiving expropriated or government land were required to join farm cooperatives. Cooperatives were expected to furnish the organization, techniques, credit, and joint use of machinery to replace and expand the functions supplied by the landowners and managers of the large estates. Syrian farmers' individualism and aversion to cooperatives may explain their apparent preference for renting land from the government rather than buying the land and having to join a cooperative. Whether the cause was aversion by farmers or an inability by the government to organize and staff cooperatives, as some economists suggest, the cooperative movement grew slowly until the early 1970s but accelerated thereafter. In 1976 there were 3,385 agricultural cooperatives with 256,000 members—more than double the number and membership in 1972. By 1984 there were 4,050 agricultural cooperatives with 440,347 members. Statistics do not distinguish between cooperatives for farmers receiving expropriated or government land and voluntary cooperatives of established landowners.

Officials expected cooperatives eventually to mitigate, if not eliminate, two serious agricultural problems. First, farmers tended to specialize in certain crops without practicing crop rotation. Second, substantial amounts of arable land were left fallow each year. In the 1970s, government extension workers and cooperatives strongly urged farmers to rotate cropping in a pattern that would maintain the fertility of the soil and avoid having cultivable fields left fallow. Cooperatives were also expected to facilitate the use of machinery after land reform reduced the average size of farms, partly by cooperative ownership of equipment and partly by pooling small plots into an economically sized bloc that would then be cultivated as a single unit in the cropping rotation. By 1986 it was not clear how much success cooperatives had achieved in crop rotation or mechanization, but statistics showed an accelerated use of farm equipment by the agricultural sector after the October 1973 War.

Cropping and Production

Because only about 16 percent of the cropped area was irrigated, the output of agriculture (both plant and animal) was heavily dependent on rainfall. The great variation in the amounts and timing of rainfall can immediately cause very substantial shifts in areas planted, yields, and production, but the effect on livestock is less predictable. When drought is unusually severe or prolonged, loss of animals may depress livestock production for several years.

In 1984 crop production accounted for 72 percent of the value of agricultural output; livestock and animal products, 28 percent. Livestock alone, not counting products such as milk, wool, and eggs, amounted to 11 percent of the total.

In 1984 crop production amounted to LS13.6 billion. The United States Department of Agriculture (USDA) valued Syrian 1985 production at US$1.1 billion. Grains contributed 15 percent to the value of total crop production in 1984, in contrast to 41 percent in 1974. Industrial crops remained 20 percent of the total. Fruits rose from 15 to 25 percent of the total, and vegetables rose from 16 to 35 percent. In 1984 grain continued to be planted on 66 percent of the cultivated land, consistent with the mid-1970s percentage.

Fluctuations in rainfall resulted in major variations in crop production throughout the 1980s. In 1980 wheat was planted on 1.4 million hectares, yielding 2.2 million tons—the largest wheat harvest since the early 1960s. In 1984 wheat planted on 1.1 million hectares produced only 1.1 million tons (see table 9, Appendix). In 1980 and 1984, barley was planted on 1.2 million hectares, but production fell from 1.6 million tons in 1980, the peak year, to 303,500 tons in 1984, revealing the impact of the drought on rain-dependent crops. In 1985 wheat and barley crops rebounded to 1.7 million tons and 740,000 tons, respectively. In 1984 Syria grew a record 60,000 tons of corn.

Earlier stagnation of agricultural output meant primarily stagnation of grain production. Instead of exporting wheat, in the 1980s, Syria became a net importer. In 1985 Syria imported 1.4 million tons of wheat, worth more than LS800 million. In addition, cereal imports rose from LS368 million in 1982 to LS1.6 billion in 1984, amounting to 56 percent of the LS2.9 billion spent on food imports that year.

During the 1970s and 1980s, the government encouraged greater grain production by providing improved high-yield seeds, raising prices paid to farmers, and urging shifts toward wheat growing on some irrigated land formerly planted in cotton. Its intent was to raise grain output at least to self-sufficiency to ease the pressure on the balance of payments.

Beginning in the late 1970s, the government showed increased interest in improving rain-fed agriculture and acquired funding from the World Bank, the International Fund for Agricultural Development, and the United Nations Development Program for a US$76.3 million project to expand food production and raise the standard of living in Dar'a and As Suwayda provinces. In addition, Syrian agriculture benefited from research projects undertaken by the International Center for Agricultural Research in the Dry Areas (ICARDA) branch office located near Aleppo. ICARDA helped develop the Sham-1 durum wheat and Sham-2 bread wheat used by Syrian farmers in the mid-1980s and demonstrated through its research the positive effect of phosphate fertilizers on barley crops in dry areas, encouraging the government to consider a change in agricultural strategy.

In the 1980s, vegetables and fruits exhibited the fastest growth rates of the various crops, although they started from a low base. Urbanization and rising incomes spurred cultivation of these products, which were also generally exempt from official price control. Fruits and vegetables were grown primarily in the northwest and the coastal plain in irrigated fields and in areas where rainfall and groundwater were greatest. However, Syria lagged considerably behind Lebanon in cultivation of fruits and vegetables in similar terrain, and seasonal fruits were consistently smuggled in from Lebanon in the 1980s.

Syria has produced cotton since ancient times, and its cultivation increased in importance in the 1950s and 1960s. Until superseded by petroleum in 1974, cotton was Syria's most important industrial and cash crop and the country's most important foreign exchange earner, accounting for about one-third of Syria's export earnings. In 1976 the country was the tenth largest cotton producer in the world and the fourth largest exporter.

Harvesting cotton in Al Ladhiqiyah Province
Courtesy Embassy of Syria

Almost all the cotton was grown on irrigated land, largely in the area northeast of Aleppo. Syrian cotton was medium staple, similar to cotton produced in other developing countries but of lower quality than the extra-long staple variety produced in Egypt. The cotton was handpicked, although mechanical pickers were tried unsuccessfully in the 1970s in an attempt to hold down rising labor costs.

Cotton production (cotton lint) rose from 13,000 tons in 1949 to 180,000 tons in 1965. However, land reform and nationalization of the cotton gins precipitated a sharp decline in output in the next few years. Beginning in 1968 and during the 1970s, annual lint production hovered around 150,000 tons. However, in 1983 Syria enjoyed a record cotton crop of 526,000 tons, the third highest yield in the world, estimated at 3 tons per hectare. To a large measure, this increase was attributable to the government's raising cotton procurement prices by 44 percent in 1981–82 and by another 20 percent in 1982–83.

Although the area under cotton cultivation has declined since the early 1960s, yields have increased as a result of improved varieties of seed and increasing amounts of fertilizer. The area planted dropped from over 250,000 hectares in the early 1960s to 140,000 hectares in 1980. In response to the jump in procurement prices by 1984, it increased to 178,000 hectares.

As domestic consumption of cotton increased in the 1960s and 1970s, the government built several textile mills to gain the value added from exports of fabrics and clothes compared with exports of raw cotton. In the 1980s, cotton exports averaged 120,000 tons, ranging from a low of 72,800 tons to a record of 151,000 tons in 1983. Syria's seed cotton harvest was 462,000 tons in 1985, about 3 percent higher than in 1984. Approximately 110,000 tons of the 1985 harvest were destined for export markets. Major foreign customers in 1985 included the Soviet Union (18,000 tons), Algeria (14,672 tons), Italy (13,813 tons), and Spain (10,655 tons).

The government's goal of expanding and diversifying food production created intense competition for irrigated land and encouraged the practice of double cropping. Because cotton did not lend itself to double cropping, the area devoted to cotton was declining in real terms. However, the total area under cultivation and the significance of other industrial crops substantially increased during the 1980s.

For example, the government initiated policies designed to stimulate sugar beet cultivation to supply the sugar factories built in the 1970s and 1980s. The area under cultivation for sugar beets rose from 22,000 hectares in 1980 to 35,700 hectares in 1984. Sugar beet harvests totaled about 1.3 million tons in 1984, but Syria still imported LS287 million worth of sugar that year. The USDA estimated that Syria would achieve self-sufficiency in tobacco in 1985 and have harvests of 12.3 million tons (dry weight) compared with 12.2 million tons in 1984. Although yields per hectare fell slightly in 1985, the USDA expected imports to match exports. In 1984 Syria imported 559 tons of tobacco and exported 225 tons. Other important commercial crops included olives and tomatoes.

Animal Products

During the 1960s, the output of animal products stagnated along with crop production. The majority of Syria's livestock population consisted of sheep and goats of mainly indigenous breeds— multipurpose animals raised for meat, milk, and wool or hair. Although the private sector continued to dominate livestock farming, the government marshaled considerable resources, raising output in the mid-1970s. Between 1976 and 1984, the number of sheep almost doubled from 6.5 to 12.7 million. Goats numbered 950,000 in 1976 and increased to 1.1 million in 1985. Sheep raising accounted for about 65 percent of all meat produced and about one-third of the milk and milk products. In 1984 sheep produced 353,000 tons of milk, cows produced 579,000 tons, and goats produced 73,000 tons. About 35,000 beduin families, largely located in arid and semiarid regions, took about three-fifths of the sheep on annual migrations into the desert and steppe for grazing after the winter rainy season. When the sparse natural vegetation dried up, the flocks returned to cultivated areas, where they fed on crop stubble and grass and weeds growing on fallow land. Many of the animals became diseased, and the migrations were difficult, particularly when rainfall was light. The beduin primarily depended on sheep raising for their income, and they were part of the poorest segment of the population, having incomes generally less than half the national average.

About two-fifths of the sheep were raised by farm families to supplement cash income and food production. Because most sheep raising occurred in western Syria where rainfall was heaviest, these sheep obtained a large share of their feed from crop residue and even some regular fodder and concentrated feed mixes. Sheep fattening in feed yards has been long-established in western Syria.

In the early 1970s, a serious shortage of milk, meat, and eggs had developed for a population that already averaged a low level of meat consumption and had a deficiency of protein in the diet. In response, the government intensified efforts to increase production of animal products and particularly to improve conditions for beduin sheep raisers. A number of small dams were constructed and wells sunk to provide water for nomadic flocks, the area planted in fodder was enlarged, veterinarian field clinics providing free animal vaccinations were established (although they were chronically short of staff and medicines), and shelters were built and stocked with feed in migratory areas.

The establishment of cooperatives in the mid-1970s improved range management, extension services, availability of reasonable credit, and supply and marketing activities for families engaged in sheep raising, whose incomes had been smaller than those of the beduin. In the mid-1970s, there were fourteen sheep-breeding and thirty-seven sheep-fattening cooperatives. By the mid-1980s, the number of sheep-breeding cooperatives had grown to 318, and sheep-fattening cooperatives totaled 66. In 1974 the government established a state-run organization responsible for the supply, storage, distribution, and marketing of animal feed. Although the number of sheep increased substantially from 1976 to 1984, it was not clear whether the increase was a direct response to the government's program or a result of periods of good rainfall that occurred before the 1984 drought. In spite of increased sheep raising, in the mid-1980s, Syria remained a net importer of meat. Syria imported 4,550 tons of meat in 1984 valued at LS23 million, compared with 12,176 tons of meat in 1983 valued at LS90 million.

Shortages of milk, meat, and eggs encouraged large investments in poultry and dairy production. Poultry production expanded rapidly in the 1970s because of the establishment of several large-scale, commercial-style chicken farms. In the mid-1980s, Syria became self-sufficient in poultry, meat, and eggs. In 1984 annual poultry production reached 1.5 million chickens, 80,000 tons of poultry meat, and 1.8 billion eggs, an increase of approximately half a billion eggs above 1979 levels. Syria's private sector was responsible for 91 percent of this output.

In 1984 cattle totaled 736,000, including 501,000 dairy cows that produced 579,000 tons of milk. Cattle were located primarily in western Syria and in areas with substantial irrigation. In the mid-1970s, several large farms were constructed to accommodate imported high-yield dairy cows. Cattle were imported from Turkey and Eastern Europe for fattening to provide meat to domestic markets in the mid-1980s. The government also established two artificial insemination centers, encouraged the formation of dairy cooperatives, and expanded extension services. Despite these measures, in the mid-1980s Syria remained a net importer of milk and milk products, importing LS255 million worth of milk and milk products in 1984.

Agricultural Potential

In the mid-1980s, the government redirected its energies toward revitalizing the agricultural sector. Despite substantial increases in the 1985 investment budget allocations for agriculture, there was no quick solution to the problem of sustaining agricultural growth. Although since the 1950s farmers had steadily expanded use of fertilizers and new seeds and had adopted new techniques, which improved productivity in cotton, fruit, and vegetable cultivation, agricultural development had stagnated. Socialist transformation of the economy and the expanded role of the state in all aspects of economic life combined with the political instability of the 1960s to disrupt agriculture. Although the state drew up plans to use Syria's water resources more efficiently by expanding irrigation systems in the 1970s and 1980s, the government failed to devise an agricultural policy with appropriate incentives and pricing mechanisms to stimulate output. Although low rainfall in the early 1980s and the prolonged drought of 1984 had an impact on agricultural output, economists linked agriculture's poor performance in the 1970s and early 1980s to government policy. The government's renewed interest in agricultural development in the mid-1980s signaled guarded optimism for the future; economists questioned, however, whether Syria could raise future animal and crop

Manufacturing cotton yarn
Courtesy Embassy of Syria

production above its astoundingly high 3.7 percent annual population growth rate.

Industry

Manufacturing, other than that represented by traditional handicrafts, textiles, and animal-powered flour mills, is a post-World War II addition to the Syrian economy. Requirements of Allied forces stationed in Syria during the war and shortages of imported goods for local consumption stimulated industrial development, and wealthy merchants and landowners channeled resources into industrial expansion. Factories established in the 1950s and 1960s processed local agricultural goods and manufactured a wide range of light consumer products. Although the nationalization measures of the 1960s disrupted privately financed industrial expansion, in the 1970s the state embarked on a major industrial development program stressing heavy industry. Between 1953 and the mid-1970s, the growth rate of the industrial sector was 8.3 percent (in constant prices)—a major factor in the rise in incomes and in the improvement in standards of living. Manufacturing (including extractive industries and power generation) contributed 22.4 percent of GDP in 1976 but only about 13.4 percent in 1984 as the state committed scarce resources to completing existing projects rather than to initiating new ones. The public sector dominated

146

the chemical, cement and other construction materials, engineering, sugar, food, and various textile-manufacturing industries. The private sector, stymied by government restrictions, concentrated on certain textiles, electrical and paper products, leather goods, and machinery.

Energy and Natural Resources

Although Syria's crude oil reserves were small and production minor by Arab and international standards, in the 1970s and 1980s petroleum extraction played a vital role in Syria's economy, generating much-needed foreign exchange. However, the size of Syria's proven crude oil reserves remained secret. In 1977 United States government figures placed Syria's proven oil reserves at 2.2 billion barrels. International sources estimated that Syria's crude oil reserves had fallen to 1.5 billion barrels by the end of 1983, indicating a life span of no more than 20 years at 1984 production levels. Some publications listed substantially higher reserves (perhaps reflecting total rather than recoverable reserves) that appeared large in relation to Syrian production data in the 1980s.

Although Syria awarded its first oil concession to foreign firms in the 1930s, it did not emerge as an oil producer until the late 1960s. In 1956 an American company discovered oil at Qarah Shuk (also known as Karachuk) in the northeast near the Iraqi border. In 1959 a West German firm discovered the Suwaydiyah field, located about fifteen kilometers south of the first oil discovery. The Syrian government nationalized the oil industry in 1964, and in the late 1960s the Syrian General Petroleum Company (SGPC), the national oil company, brought the two fields on stream with Soviet assistance. Although Suwaydiyah initially averaged 20,000 barrels per day (bpd—see Glossary) and Qarah Shuk produced 30,000 bpd, the oil from both fields carried American Petroleum Institute (API) quality ratings of 25.5 and 19, respectively. Both had high sulfur contents, confirming the poor quality of Syrian oil. Syria became an oil exporter in 1968 with the completion of a 663-kilometer pipeline to transport oil to a terminal at Tartus on the Mediterranean coast. Both the Qarah Shuk and the Suwaydiyah fields continued to produce oil into the 1980s (see fig. 11).

Oil exploration intensified in the 1970s. The SGPC discovered the Rumaylan field, about 10 kilometers southwest of Qarah Shuk, which had produced over 39 million barrels of oil by mid-1984. Smaller fields also produced minor amounts of heavy crude in the 1970s. The Jubaysah field, located about 150 kilometers southwest of Qarah Shuk, came on stream in 1975. It had a 40.2 API crude oil rating but a 0.6 percent sulfur content, suggesting that Syria

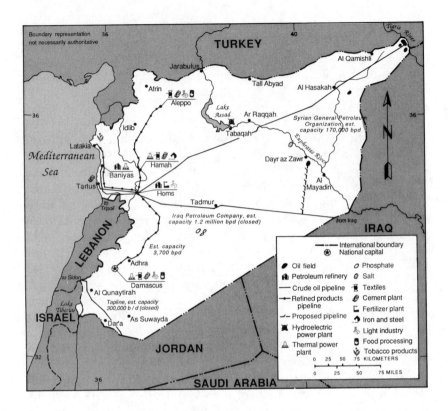

Boundary representation not necessarily authoritative

TURKEY

Al Qamishli

Jarabulus

Afrin

Tall Abyad

Al Hasakah

Aleppo

Lake Assad

Ar Raqqah

Idlib

Tabaqah

Syrian General Petroleum Organization est. capacity 170,000 bpd

Euphrates River

Latakia

Mediterranean Sea

Hamah

Dayr az Zawr

Baniyas

Tartus

Homs

Al Mayadin

Tadmur

Iraq Petroleum Company, est. capacity 1.2 million bpd (closed)

from Iraq

to Tripoli

IRAQ

Est. capacity 3,700 bpd

Adhra

LEBANON

to Sidon

Damascus

Al Qunaytirah

Lake Tiberias

Tapline, est. capacity 300,000 b/d (closed)

ISRAEL

Dar'a

As Suwayda

JORDAN

Legend	
--- International boundary	
⊛ National capital	
Oil field	Phosphate
Petroleum refinery	Salt
Crude oil pipeline	Textiles
Refined products pipeline	Cement plant
Proposed pipeline	Fertilizer plant
Hydroelectric power plant	Iron and steel
Thermal power plant	Light industry
	Food processing
	Tobacco products

0 25 50 75 KILOMETERS

0 25 50 75 MILES

SAUDI ARABIA

Figure 11. Economic Activity

might look forward to discovering major quantities of light crude. In 1974 the government eased the way for the return of foreign contractors, granting a Romanian company a production-sharing concession. Western companies returned in 1977 when Pecten, a Royal Dutch Shell subsidiary, won a 20,000-square-kilometer exploration concession in north central Syria. The Syrian American Oil Company and Samoco, a subsidiary of the American-based Coastal States Gas Corporation, won the 15,570-square-kilometer concession to exploit the resources of Dayr az Zawr Province in 1977. Deminex, a West German company, joined the group in 1979. In 1983, after Samoco dropped out, Deminex joined Pecten in an expanded concession of 21,800 square kilometers. Pecten held 31.25 percent, Royal Dutch Shell 31.25 percent, and Deminex the remaining 37.5 percent. Chevron, Pennzoil, and Marathon Oil also won exploration concessions in the 1980s. Marathon's two wells at Sharifah, near Homs, produced promising results for gas exploitation from 1983 to 1985. The SGPC also continued exploration and drilling to bring the small, newly discovered Qayrik, Wahab, Said, and As Safih fields on stream by the mid-1980s. The 1984 discovery of large quantities of light, sweet crude oil at the Pecten consortium's Thayim field near Dayr az Zawr gave a much-needed boost to the Syrian oil industry and economy. The Dayr az Zawr oil, ranked at 36 API with a low sulfur content, offered the prospect that Syria could cut by up to US$200 million its own imports of light crude oil required for use in domestic refineries in the 1990s. Early production estimates confirmed an initial output of 50,000 bpd when the Thayim field came on stream in late 1986. In 1985 the SGPC and Pecten formed the Furat Oil Company to operate the concession with the state. In 1986 Czechoslovakia's Technoexport completed a ninety-two-kilometer spur line linking the Thayim field to the Iraqi-Syrian pipeline, unused since 1982. Syrian government officials estimated that production levels at Dayr az Zawr would rise to 100,000 bpd in 1988.

Syria's oil production remained virtually static in the mid-1980s. The International Monetary Fund (IMF) put production at 162,000 bpd for 1985 (see table 10, Appendix). Excluding the new Dayr az Zawr discovery, however, Syria claimed production of approximately 170,000 bpd in 1985, blending one-third of its heavy sulfurous domestic crude with two-thirds imported light oil. Domestic consumption of oil products averaged around 190,000 bpd in the mid-1980s; up to 120,000 bpd of this total came from Iran in 1985.

Oil contributed about 10 percent to Syria's GDP through the 1980s. Following the rapid rise of world oil prices in 1973, oil became Syria's chief source of foreign exchange. The value of Syria's oil exports rose from LS291 million in 1973 to LS1.6 billion in 1974 and almost doubled to LS2.6 billion in 1976, accounting for 63 percent of total exports. In 1979 the total export value of oil reached 68.9 percent before declining to 51.4 percent in 1982 and rising slightly to about 55 percent in 1984 and 1985. However, Syria's oil and petroleum products' trade surplus of the late 1970s (and 1980) turned into a deficit in the 1980s. The 1980 surplus of LS2.4 billion fell to a deficit of LS767 million in 1984, making Syria's ability to boost domestic production and reduce oil imports an economic imperative of the 1990s.

Since 1982, when Syria closed its oil pipeline from Iraq and stopped purchasing Iraqi oil as a show of support for Iran in the Iran-Iraq War (see Regional Foreign Relations, ch. 4), Iran has supplied large quantities of oil to Syria on concessionary terms and as outright gifts. In 1984 Iran provided Syria with 6.4 million tons of oil, discounted by US$2.50 per barrel, and 1.6 million tons free, for a total of 8 million tons. In 1985 Iran supplied Syria with 6 million tons of oil, including a 1-million ton gift. However, Iran interrupted supplies in October 1985 because of Syria's estimated US$1.5 billion payment arrears and price disagreements. Syria turned briefly to Arab suppliers on the spot market, further depleting foreign exchange reserves, before Iran negotiated a new agreement with Syria in July 1986, guaranteeing the supply of 2.5 million tons of oil between October 1986 and March 1987.

Until oil prices jumped in the early 1970s, Syria earned more from the international pipelines that crossed its territory than from domestic oil production. In the early 1950s, Tapline (Trans-Arabian Pipeline)—running from the oil fields in Saudi Arabia across Jordan and the southwest corner of Syria to the terminal of Sidon on the Lebanese coast—was completed. Capacity was 25 million tons of crude oil a year. Syria earned small amounts of foreign exchange from transit fees (reportedly US$2.8 million in the mid-1970s) for the oil crossing the country via Tapline. Various interruptions of pipeline operations, escalating transit fees, and the reopening of the Suez Canal in June 1975 reduced the use of Tapline in the 1970s. Pumping via Tapline was suspended in 1977 while Syria negotiated a new arrangement with Lebanon. In 1987 observers were pessimistic about the future uses of Tapline.

The larger and more important pipeline carried crude oil from the former Iraq Petroleum Company (IPC) fields across Syria via Homs, after which the pipeline branched, with one spur leading to Tripoli in Lebanon and the other spur leading to the Syrian terminal at Baniyas. The IPC pipeline (actually three separate lines) had a capacity of about 55 million tons a year in the 1970s. The pipeline began operation in the early 1950s, providing transit fees as well as the crude oil that was refined at the Homs refinery into products for Syrian consumption. In the 1960s, Syria frequently used its control of the pipeline for political leverage over Iraq, which depended on the pipeline across Syria until the late 1970s, when its pipeline through Turkey began operation.

Transit rates increased substantially after 1966. In the early 1970s, earnings from the pipelines were more important than direct taxes and one of the most important sources of budget revenue. These earnings peaked in 1974 at LS608 million and were estimated at LS575 million in the 1975 budget. In April 1976, however, Iraq canceled the transit agreement because of price disputes and cut off oil supplies to Syria. Saudi Arabia supplied oil for the Homs refinery until February 1979, when Iraq and Syria negotiated a new agreement, setting transit fees at US$0.35 per barrel compared with US$0.45 when the pumping stopped. In 1979 Iraq pumped

10 million tons of oil through the pipeline, approximately two-thirds less than the average amount pumped between 1971 and 1976. The outbreak of the Iran-Iraq War in September 1980 again interrupted pumping, but it put Syria in a stronger position vis-à-vis the pipeline, given Iraq's need for revenues to finance the war. Although pumping resumed in February 1981, Syria argued that the pipeline cost more to operate (US$31 million in 1981) than it generated in transit fees (US$25.7 million in 1981). In April 1982, after negotiating an agreement to purchase oil from Iran, Syria closed the pipeline to Iraqi petroleum exports.

By the mid-1980s, Syria had two domestic pipeline systems and two refineries. A crude oil line, with a capacity of 15 million tons a year in 1977, led from the fields in the northeast to a sea terminal at Tartus, with a spur to the refinery at Homs. Three pipelines for refined products from Homs (each with a capacity of 350,000 tons a year) led to the major consumption centers of Damascus, Aleppo, and Latakia. In 1984 the state-owned Syrian Company for Oil and Transport carried 9.5 million tons of crude through its pipeline, up from 8.9 million tons in 1983. In 1979 the new Baniyas refinery was also connected to the domestic crude oil and products pipeline system.

The refinery at Homs was completed in 1959 and began processing Iraqi crude oil for local consumption. In 1977 the refinery's capacity stood at about 2.7 million tons, but after the sixth planned expansion in 1985, its capacity doubled to 5.4 million tons per year. The US$143 million project contracted to Czechoslovakia's Technoexport included the construction of a 480,000-ton-per-year hydrogenation unit, a 380,000-ton-per-year catalytic reformer, and two steam- and power-generating units. Four hundred Syrian workers received training in Czechoslovakia in 1985 in connection with the sixth expansion of the refinery. The seventh expansion of the refinery, scheduled to be completed in the late 1980s, involved the construction of a 100,000-ton-per-year base lubrication oil complex located at the Homs refinery. The Homs refinery used a blend of crude oil in the 1970s, mixing light Iraqi oil with heavy Syrian crude. Israeli bombing raids on Syria during the October 1973 War severely damaged the operating capacity of the Homs refinery, and the desulfurization unit was not fully repaired until 1976. After 1982 Syria used imported Iranian oil with domestic products at the Homs refinery. In 1985 it processed 5,064,000 tons, down from 5,197,000 tons in 1984.

The Baniyas refinery was completed in 1979 at a cost of LS1.1 billion. The refinery's maximum capacity was 6 million tons. In its first year of production, the refinery produced only 1.7 million tons, but this figure more than doubled in 1982 to 4.4 million tons. In 1984 and 1985, the refinery operated at 95 percent of capacity, refining approximately 5.7 million tons of crude oil for an annual production value of LS4 billion. Principal products included high octane and regular gasoline, butane gas, jet fuel, asphalt, and sulfur. The plant employed 2,250 workers in 1984, including 73 Romanian technicians—a sharp decline from the 450 Romanian technical advisers who assisted operations at the Baniyas refinery in 1982.

Syria's natural gas was discovered in conjunction with oil-exploration operations in the northeast part of the country. In 1984 proven gas reserves were estimated at 98.8 billion cubic meters and associated gas reserves at 33.3 billion cubic meters. Although into the 1980s most natural gas was flared, Syria began exporting small quantities of liquefied petroleum gas in late 1981. Marathon Oil made two promising gas discoveries in 1982 and 1985, finding a gas potential of 450 million cubic meters a day in 1982 at Sharif-2 and 400 million cubic meters a day at Ash Shair 1. The economic viability of Marathon's gas discoveries combined with uncertain market forces to cloud future exploitation of these resources. In 1982 Syria awarded major contracts to Technoexport of Czechoslovakia to build a gas treatment plant at Jubaysah and a gas transmission line to Homs for use in the Homs ammonia-urea plant. France also began construction on a gas treatment plant at Rumaylan.

Phosphate was the country's other major mineral resource. The government claimed reserves of 1 billion tons. The first government-operated mine, near Tadmur, began producing in 1971, and two others began operating in 1974. Syrian phosphate was low grade (about 30 percent concentration) and high in moisture. Installation of a drying plant in one government-run mine in 1978 helped improve the quality and quantity of output. Production grew from 800,000 tons in 1978 to 1.5 million tons in 1984 but fell slightly to 1.3 million tons in 1985. Syria exported about two-thirds of its phosphate in the 1980s, largely to East European countries as part of barter arrangements concluded between the governments. Although Syrian government officials anticipated that output would triple by 1988 to 5 million tons and by 2000 equal the output of Morocco, the world's largest producer, production levels have remained well below projected targets. In 1981 Syria's giant triple super phosphate plant, built by Romanian contractors at Homs, began production with a capacity of 450,000 tons of triple super phosphate and 800,000 tons of phosphate and phosphoric acid. Syria's production of phosphatic fertilizer more than doubled from 1981 to 1984, rising from 68,333 tons to 191,176 tons.

The other products of the extraction industries were minor. Natural asphalt was extracted at a coastal site and in the central part of the country. In 1976 production amounted to 125,000 tons—a tremendous jump from the 31,000 tons or less produced in 1975; however, by 1984 production had declined to 52,000 tons.

Pure rock salt deposits, totaling over 100 million tons, existed northwest of Dayr az Zawr. Expansion of the mine facilities in the early 1970s raised the potential capacity to over 250,000 tons a year, but production hovered around 50,000 tons through the mid-1970s. Production peaked at 102,000 tons in 1982 but fell back to 38,000 tons in 1984.

In addition, construction materials (sand, gravel, stone, and gypsum) were mined in various parts of the country. In 1986 Syria signed an agreement with Turkey establishing joint ventures for mineral exploration, and Soviet and Polish scientific missions discovered sizable iron ore deposits near Az Zabadani and Tadmur. In late 1986, the government also announced the discovery of significant quantities of diamonds.

Electric Power

At independence, only a small part of the population in the larger urban centers had access to electricity, and per capita consumption ranked among the lowest in the world. Small separate, local companies owned by private domestic or foreign interests supplied electricity. During the 1950s, capacity increased, and production expanded by an average of 12.4 percent a year. Rapid expansion continued, and during the 1960s, the state began a national grid. In 1976 electric power generation amounted to 1.7 billion kilowatt-hours, an average annual increase of over 14 percent since 1966.

According to the Ministry of Electricity, electricity production rose from 3.7 billion kilowatt-hours in 1980 to 7.3 billion kilowatt-hours in 1984 and 7.6 billion kilowatt-hours in 1985. Annual production growth, however, fell from an average of 19 percent in 1980 to only 10 percent in 1984 and 1985. By 1986 electricity consumption outstripped production, forcing power cutbacks of four hours a day throughout the country. Industry consumed 52 percent of total electricity in 1984, but some factories reported operational capacity of only 60 percent because of power shortages.

In May 1986, the People's Council debated the electricity crisis, urging renewed efforts to ration electricity consumption and to devise new projects to increase power generation and distribution. Although the electric power industry was one of the fastest growing sectors of the economy in the 1960s and 1970s (Syria even exported electricity to Lebanon and Jordan in the late 1970s), the state's success in providing electricity to ever greater numbers of the population in a remarkably short time paradoxically precipitated the crisis.

Although the state nationalized electric power generation in 1951, the industry remained fragmented under local administration until a single national company emerged in 1965. In 1974, when the state created the Ministry of Electricity to supervise the development of the electric power supply, the national electrical company became an agency of the ministry. By 1976 nearly all of the country's generating units were under the national electrical company and linked in a grid. At the end of 1984, the national system had an installed capacity of 2,834 megawatts, compared with 1,779 megawatts in 1976.

However, the 1980s witnessed a shocking and somewhat unanticipated decline in hydroelectric power production, the dominant source in the state's plan to increase electricity output. In 1979 hydroelectric power generated 73 percent of the country's electricity, up from 55.6 percent in 1975. Hydroelectric power accounted for 59 percent of installed nominal capacity in 1979. But by 1984, hydroelectric capacity produced only 820 megawatts (29 percent of total megawatts) and 1.9 billion kilowatt-hours of electricity, or 26 percent of the total. Thermal capacity generated 2,014 megawatts, 71 percent of the total produced in 1984, and produced 5.4 billion kilowatt-hours of electricity, or 74 percent of the total.

The precipitous decline of hydroelectric power generation resulted from technical and operational problems inherent in the Euphrates Dam. In the mid-1980s, the dam's 800-megawatt turbines operated below capacity, often producing only one-third of projected output. The low level of water in Lake Assad, caused by poor rainfall and Turkey's use of the Euphrates waters for its Keban and Ataturk dams, also contributed to the difficulties. Although the Euphrates Dam was the most important component in the state's plan to expand the national power system in the late 1960s and 1970s, it failed to produce the expected 80 percent of the country's electric power between 1977 and the early 1980s.

In the early 1980s, Syria implemented few new projects to meet the growing demand for energy, but it planned extensions of existing power stations to expand production and new projects for the end of the decade. The Baniyas station, completed in 1981 for US$140 million, anticipated a two-turbine, 165-megawatt extension in the late 1980s. The Suwaydiyah power station also expected to benefit from a 150-megawatt extension and four new turbines. At the Muhradah power station, located west of Hamah and completed in 1979, a major extension totaling US$195 million and financed largely by Persian Gulf development agencies was planned. The US$97 million Soviet-assisted Tishrin power plant (formerly known as Widan ar Rabih station) and another power station near Homs were under construction in the mid-1980s.

In addition, the government considered constructing a nuclear power plant with Soviet assistance. In mid-1983 Syria signed a protocol with the Soviet Union to conduct feasibility studies and select an appropriate location for the country's first reactor. Although Syrian and Soviet officials had originally intended that a 1,200-megawatt nuclear plant come on line in 1990, the project had advanced little beyond the design stage by the mid-1980s. Although nuclear energy promised a solution to Syria's pressing electricity shortage, the political and military obstacles to Syria's developing nuclear energy were formidable, especially in the wake of Israel's bombing of Iraq's nuclear reactor in 1981. As nuclear power became a more costly alternative energy source in the context of volatile Middle East politics, in the late 1980s the government explored the prospects for solar energy.

By 1978 a national grid linked nearly all of the country's generating units and most of the larger towns; distribution extended to rural areas only in the west around such major cities as Damascus and Aleppo. In 1970, based on a housing census, about 85 percent of the urban population had access to electricity, but only about 10 percent of the rural population did. According to government statistics, 40 percent of the population remained without electricity in 1980. However, by the middle of the decade, almost all of the urban population had received electricity. Rural electrification projects, a top priority of the Ministry of Electricity in the 1970s, had also achieved widespread success. The government planned extending electricity to all villages with over 100 inhabitants by 1990. The number of villages receiving electricity grew from 424 prior to 1975 to 1,581 in 1979 and had reached 5,894 in 1984. In Ar Raqqah Province alone, the number of electrified villages increased from 47 in the period from 1953 to 1979 to 405 in 1984, indicating the dramatic extension of electricity to rural areas. The number of subscribers in rural areas tripled between 1970 and 1984, increasing from 442,307 to 1,564,625.

In the mid-1980s, there was an electricity crisis caused by expansion of electric power distribution and usage in the 1970s, sectoral mismanagement, lack of spare parts for power plants, technical impediments, and declining water levels in Lake Assad. Syrian official statistics and Ministry of Electricity data projected that consumption, growing at an annual rate of 20 to 22 percent in the mid-1980s, would outstrip production until the mid-1990s. Syria could meet the surging demand for electricity in the mid-1980s only by producing 300 to 400 additional megawatts a year. However, with only one 25-megawatt unit at the Baath Dam scheduled to come on line in late 1986, ambiguous plans for 1987, a 320-megawatt increase projected for 1988, and a 400-megawatt increase expected when the Tishrin station begins production in 1989, Ministry of Electricity plans fell far short of satisfying demand. The ministry's plans for the 1989–95 period projected a production increase to 2,970 megawatts to meet an anticipated demand ranging from 1,800 to 2,400 megawatts. The theoretical excess production, however, would barely meet the accumulated shortages of the mid-1980s. Electricity shortages, blackouts, power cuts, and rationing remained a prominent feature of Syrian life in the late 1980s, frustrating industrial development and impeding economic growth.

Industrial Development Policy

Through most of the 1950s, private investment primarily fueled industrial development while the government protected public order and fostered a climate suitable for economic growth. After Syria withdrew from a customs union with Lebanon in 1950, domestic manufacturing received considerable protection from competition by imports. The government also provided investment incentives through tax exemptions and cheap credit. Although data for the 1950s were sparse and of questionable reliability, they indicated that the growth rate of industrial production was about 12 percent a year between 1950 and 1958, substantially higher growth than for the economy as a whole.

Between 1958 and 1965, Syria experienced an almost complete reversal of development policy. The government assumed a greater role in economic planning and by 1965 had nationalized most of the larger manufacturing concerns. Prior to nationalization in 1965, land reform, talk of socialism, and the 1961 nationalization decrees during the union with Egypt frightened private investors. In addition, the government was unable to implement the investments included in the First Five-Year Plan. Consequently, the rate of increase of value added by industry amounted to an annual average of 4 percent in constant prices between 1958 and 1965, although other factors, particularly a severe, prolonged drought (1958–61), contributed to the slower growth of industrial output.

Through the complete or partial nationalization of 108 large and medium-sized enterprises, the state created the nucleus of the public industrial sector in January 1965. Thirty-seven firms were completely nationalized, and the other seventy-one firms were nationalized to an extent varying between 75 and 90 percent; however, these semipublic firms were fully nationalized in 1970, retroactive to 1965.

After nationalization, most public sector industry was located under the Ministry of Industry and organized under four broad holding companies called unions—food, textiles, chemicals, and engineering unions. Separate ministries controlled the national electric power and petroleum companies. In the mid-1970s, the SGPC was divided into several separate companies responsible for such particular functions as exploration and production, transport and terminals, refining, and domestic sales and distribution.

After the 1965 nationalizations, the government dominated the economy and controlled most elements affecting industrial development, including planning, investments, foreign trade, pricing, and training. The planners avoided the temptation, succumbed to by many developing countries, of constructing large, expensive prestigious industrial projects that provided only small or distant returns. Most projects were geared to the size and needs of the Syrian economy. Development emphasized natural resources (essentially oil and phosphates for export), additional capacity for processing local materials (textiles, sugar refining, and cement), and import substitution (fertilizers, iron and steel, and consumer durables).

In the late 1970s and the 1980s, however, observers questioned government priorities that resulted in creation of large industries relying on import substitution. An example of domestic questioning of the government's economic management occurred at the Eighth Baath Party Regional Congress in 1985. The issue of a planned sugar refinery—a prominent symbol of public sector domination of an industrial sphere—generated significant debate. Critics challenged the wisdom of the project because the cost per kilogram of processed sugar would be several times the price of imported sugar. Completed in the late 1970s with a capacity of 1.6 million tons of sugar beets a year, the plant produced an average of only 500,000 tons of sugar per year from 1980 to 1983.

Since the late 1960s, economists generally have characterized Syrian public sector industry as inefficient, having underused capacity and high production costs. A number of factors contributed to inefficiency. For example, during the political instability of the 1960s, rapid turnover of key personnel and selection of high officials and managers on the basis of loyalty rather than qualifications contributed to inefficiency. Wide swings in agricultural output because of variation in rainfall was another factor. In addition, government pricing created distortions and even undermined the basis for judging efficiency; subsidies to plants were sometimes required because retail prices were kept low for consumers.

Planning was also poor. For example, a US$100 million paper mill using straw for raw material went into production at Dayr az Zawr in 1979 but operated far below capacity, as officials realized that Syria barely produced enough straw to operate the mill. Furthermore, the cement works at Tartus were forced to cut production in half, falling from 5,000 to 2,500 tons a day in 1984, as a result of construction delays in the completion of a special unit to package the cement for export. However, the Eighth Baath Party Regional Congress endorsed a series of measures to correct public sector mismanagement, upgrade administrative capabilities, and revitalize the industrial sector as a stimulator of economic growth.

The shortage of skilled workers and capable managers also plagued public sector manufacturing. Because of the nationalization drive and political instability of the 1960s, Syria experienced tremendous capital flight and a substantial exodus of administrators, engineers, physicians, and other technically skilled professionals. The shortage of skilled labor intensified in the 1970s, as Syrian professionals found higher paying jobs and increased opportunities in the Persian Gulf states. In addition, many Syrians entered government service to gain experience and soon after went to work for private industries offering much higher salaries. Moreover, vocational training institutes could not keep pace with the needs of the economy. However, the shortage of skilled workers began to improve in the mid-1980s as Syrian workers came home to escape depressed economic conditions in the Persian Gulf states and invested accumulated capital in new enterprises.

When Assad took control of the government in 1970, he introduced important modifications of economic policy. Although commitment to state socialism, central planning, and a large public sector remained firm, Assad liberalized controls and encouraged greater private sector industry. Encouragement to the private sector that extended to both domestic and foreign investors included decreased difficulty in obtaining construction permits and licenses for machinery imports plus various tax concessions. Although private investments in industry increased in the 1970s, domestic investors remained hesitant and foreign companies even more so, despite conclusion of bilateral investment guarantee agreements with the United States and some West European countries. Observers expected private investors gradually to increase their industrial activity if the government continued its liberalization policies.

The government attempted to introduce growth in the industrial sector by ensuring the private sector a greater economic role.

*Syrian students receiving training
in the operation of a bench lathe
Courtesy Embassy of Syria*

Between 1965 and 1970, the growth rate of the index of manufacturing (excluding extractive industries and public utilities) remained at 4 percent a year, revealing the largely static condition of manufacturing. The general index for all industrial production increased by 7.8 percent a year over the same period, reflecting the importance of the expansion of oil production after 1967.

Although the results of the government initiative to stimulate private sector investment after 1970 could not be distinguished in available data from a rise in public sector industrial growth, the index for the combined output of public and private manufacturing (excluding extractive industries and public power) showed remarkable improvement between 1970 and 1976, averaging 9 percent a year. The increase in 1976 alone was 17 percent. Increased production by manufacturing derived from public sector investments and reflected increasing government development expenditures since the mid-1960s. The increase also resulted from Syria's miniversion of the oil boom in 1974 and 1975, when industrial investments rose sharply as a result of increased aid from oil-rich Arab countries. Between 1980 and 1984, however, the general index for all industrial production increased only 6.8 percent a year, while the index for the combined output of public and private manufacturing grew 13 percent per year.

In 1985 the government embarked on another liberalization campaign to encourage increased private sector investment in the productive sectors, as detailed in the fifth and sixth five-year development plans (see Development Planning, this ch.). Although the public sector continued to dominate the economy, the private sector's role grew in the 1980s, accounting for over 30 percent of GDP by 1984. The government hoped that its liberalization campaign would further boost the private sector's contribution to GDP in the 1990s. This hope was reflected in the final communique of the Eighth Baath Regional Congress, which recommended a more market-oriented approach to solving Syria's pressing economic problems. Accordingly, the government eased restrictions on the private sector and encouraged exports by establishing more competitive exchange rates for imports (see Banking and Monetary Policy, this ch.). The April 1985 reappointment of Muhammad Imadi, architect of Syria's economic opening in the 1970s, as minister of the economy and foreign trade, confirmed the government's desire to proceed with its liberalization program. Imadi, who had served as chairman of the Kuwait-based Arab Fund for Economic and Social Development in the early 1980s, urged widespread economic reforms to improve Syria's economic performance through private sector initiatives and joint ventures between the state and the private sector.

In September 1985 President Assad approved Decree Law 356, which permitted importers for the first time to pay for raw materials, spare parts, and other industrial inputs with foreign currency earned through employment or investment outside the country. The severe foreign-exchange shortage of the 1980s, exacerbated by declining worker remittances from the Persian Gulf states and shrinking oil revenues, frustrated industry's efforts to acquire much-needed raw materials and forced factories to shut down or significantly reduce production. The state's tight currency controls and restrictions on imports caused businesses to channel imports illegally into Syria via Lebanon and produced a drastic decrease in officially recorded imports in the 1980s. However, even the thriving "parallel economy" (or black market) did not meet industry's demands. The government continued the crackdown on smugglers, begun in 1984, and introduced reforms to decrease the time and capital expenditure required to obtain official import permits and letters of credit. Another major component of the government's mid-1980s liberalization drive involved an attempt to attract Arab and other foreign investment in Syria's tourism industry by offering a seven-year tax deferment and exemption from most foreign exchange and import restrictions.

Foreign Trade

Since the early 1950s, the value of imports has been close to double the value of exports. The two exhibited similar growth patterns, both growing slowly until the 1970s. Between 1951 and 1970, imports increased an average of 6.2 percent and exports 5.6 percent a year, and the trade balance slowly worsened. In the 1970s, the value of imports and exports increased much more rapidly. For example, the average rate of growth of imports increased 28 percent a year and that of exports 23 percent a year. In the 1980s, the trade imbalance widened further. Syria instituted austerity budgets to reduce imports drastically and to conserve foreign exchange. As a result, by the mid-1980s the trade deficit had declined from LS11.6 billion in 1981 to LS10.3 billion in 1983 and LS8.9 billion in 1984, still large but offering the hope of continued future reductions.

Imports

Syria experienced considerable growth in imports in the 1970s, fueled by the increased flow of foreign aid, the investment and construction boom that followed the October 1973 War, and the oil-price rise stemming from Organization of Petroleum Exporting Countries (OPEC) policies of the mid-1970s. Machinery and equipment emerged as the most rapidly growing import segment (see table 11, Appendix). Increased construction necessitated more imported semiprocessed goods, such as cement, iron and steel rods, and other raw materials. Private consumption also increased, requiring ever greater imports of sugar, cereals, dairy products, foodstuffs, pharmaceuticals, and other products.

Public sector trading firms imported most of these commodities. In 1976 public sector enterprises accounted for 72 percent of total imports. In 1984 public sector enterprises retained the lion's share of imports, accounting for about 79 percent of the total, excluding military matériel.

In the 1980s, the government implemented a policy to curb public and private sector imports. The policy was part of the general austerity pervading economic planning and a way of maintaining rapidly depleting foreign currency reserves. Because of the large volume of consumer goods and industrial inputs that entered Syria via the black market in the 1980s, official import statistics must be treated as rough indicators of actual import figures. Informed estimates placed the value of black market trade at about US$1 billion in 1985. Officially recorded imports fell from LS19.8 billion in 1981 to LS17.8 billion in 1983 and to LS16.2 billion in 1984. In February 1983, the government called for a partial suspension of industrial imports to ease balance of payments problems. Officially recorded private sector imports fell from LS2.1 billion in 1983 to LS1.3 billion in 1984, reflecting industry's increased resort to the black market, the impact of government austerity programs, and long waiting periods for import permits and letters of credit. In 1986 the government reformed letter-of-credit regulations to ease bureaucratic delays for private sector imports (see Banking and Monetary Policy, this ch.).

In the 1970s, Syria diversified its sources of imports. Western Europe became Syria's most important supplier, accounting for 49 percent of total imports in 1975 and 56 percent in 1976. By the 1980s, the direction of Syria's imports had changed drastically. Between 1980 and 1984, the European Economic Community's (EEC) share of exports to Syria fell sharply, ranging between only 25 to 32 percent of the total. Since 1982 Syria has experienced a tremendous increase in imports from Iran and Libya, largely in the form of oil shipments. The percentage of Syria's imports from Iran in 1983 was 26.1, but the figure fell to 22.7 percent in 1984 as a result of decreased shipments of Iranian oil. Imports from Libya climbed from LS37.6 million in 1983 to LS1.2 billion in 1984, or 75 percent of Syria's total imports from Arab states that year. The Federal Republic of Germany (West Germany), France, Italy, Japan, the German Democratic Republic (East Germany), and the Soviet Union were Syria's most important suppliers in 1984. Oil, machinery, transportation equipment, iron and steel, cereals, sugar, and produce were the main imports.

Exports

Syria's growing exports of crude oil and the sharp rise of world oil prices in 1973–74 produced a steep increase in the value of exports in the 1970s. The value of petroleum exports rose from LS129 million in 1970 to LS2.7 billion in 1976; crude oil exports alone increased from LS291 million to LS1.6 billion from 1973 to 1974. In the 1980s, however, Syria experienced a steep decline in the value of exports because of falling world oil prices and reduced oil exports. Syrian statistics claim that the value of oil exports shrank from LS6.5 billion in 1980 to LS4.6 billion in 1984; other sources state that the drop was from LS5.2 billion to LS3.6 billion. Crude oil and oil products exported fell to 7.8 million tons in 1980, peaked at 8.1 million tons in 1982, and nosedived to 6.8 million tons in 1984. In 1980 exports totaled LS8.3 billion and fell to LS7.4 billion in 1984. The overall index in the volume of exports fell from 100 to 95 in 1983.

The value of cotton exports totaled LS310 million in 1970, LS664 million in 1980, and over LS1 billion in 1984, the record harvest year. The value of cotton exports in 1984 equaled 14.8 percent of Syria's total exports and 29.3 percent of nonpetroleum exports. In 1984 petroleum and cotton exports together accounted for 64 percent of the country's total exports. In 1985 the figures for cotton exports fell by nearly 30 percent, and the price of cotton on the world market dropped from US$1,800 a ton in 1984 to about US$1,400 a ton in 1985. Major buyers in the 1980s included the Soviet Union, Algeria, Italy, and Spain.

In addition to cotton and petroleum, Syria exported phosphates and small quantities of diverse goods. Phosphates generated LS106.3 million of export revenues in 1983. The Fifth Five-Year Plan envisioned an increase in phosphate production to 5 million tons by 1985, generating LS580 million in export earnings. Targets fell far short of the goal, but preliminary 1986 figures reflected a record increase in production (see Energy and Natural Resources, this ch.). Export of textiles, chemicals, glassware, and a variety of agricultural products also earned small amounts of foreign exchange.

In the 1960s, Syria's major trading partners were East European states, but in the 1970s the direction of trade shifted to Western Europe, as the government pursued limited economic liberalization policies. In 1976 Western Europe (primarily the EEC) provided the main markets for Syrian exports, accounting for 57 percent. East European and Arab countries accounted for 25 and 11 percent of total exports, respectively.

In the 1980s, Syria experienced another shift in the direction of trade. Exports to Western Europe had risen to 61.6 percent by 1980 but fell to 35.7 percent in 1984. In 1980 the East European share of Syrian exports totaled only 16.1 percent but rose to 43.8 percent in 1984, clearly indicating the return to those markets. However, in contrast to the 1960s, when East European states served as the main export market for Syrian goods on a cash basis, in the 1980s much of Syria's East European trade occurred as countertrade or barter deals as a result of Syria's severe shortage of foreign exchange. In 1985 Syria concluded barter deals with Czechoslovakia and Yugoslavia, exporting phosphates in exchange for engineering and construction equipment and industrial raw materials.

To boost trade, Syria also signed important treaties of friendship and cooperation with East European states in the 1980s. Syria renewed its 1980 Treaty of Friendship and Cooperation with the Soviet Union in 1985 and signed a similar agreement with Bulgaria in May 1985. In 1984 the most important export markets were Romania (LS2 billion), Italy (LS1.4 billion), France (LS877 million), the Soviet Union (LS838 million), Spain (LS240 million), Algeria (LS164 million), and Iran (LS164 million).

Balance of Payments

In most of the years before 1970, remittances from Syrian workers in Lebanon and other places, tourism receipts, some grants, and pipeline transit fees usually covered a large part of the trade imbalance. Borrowing from foreign sources, primarily for large development projects, balanced the country's international payments. In exceptional years, part of the country's modest international financial reserves were drawn down to meet emergencies and subsequently built up again.

In the 1970s, the same pattern continued, but after 1976, Syria faced considerable balance of payments problems, including large trade deficits. The trade deficit was US$130 million in 1970, US$1 billion in 1976, US$1.8 billion in 1980, and US$1.9 billion in 1984 (see table 12, Appendix). By early 1977, foreign exchange reserves, down to about US$220 million, were sufficient to pay for about one month's worth of imports. Only grant aid, largely from Arab oil-producing states, totaling US$1.1 billion in 1977, averted an economic crisis. Although grant aid cushioned the economy, foreign exchange reserves continued to dwindle. At the end of 1983, foreign exchange reserves totaled US$43 million, down from US$185 million in 1982. Estimates in 1984 placed Syria's foreign exchange reserves at about US$100 million.

Decreased oil exports, increased oil imports, recession in the Persian Gulf states, declining worker remittances, and lower world prices for phosphate and cotton in the 1980s contributed to the state's shrinking foreign exchange reserves. Decreased agricultural production and Western aid transfers also adversely affected Syria's reserves. Total international reserves were valued at US$257 million in 1983, enough to cover about half a month's imports.

In addition, balance of payments problems intensified because of increased defense spending and development expenditures. The June 1967 War, the October 1973 War, Syria's participation in the Arab Deterrent Force and subsequent involvement in Lebanon following the 1982 Israeli invasion, and President Assad's commitment to achieving strategic parity with Israel by expanding force levels and acquiring more sophisticated weapons systems, rapidly accelerated national security costs. In the budgets of the mid-1980s, defense spending represented more than 50 percent of current spending and 30 percent of total expenditure. Development expenditures also rose quickly after 1973, increasing from LS5.9 billion in 1975 and LS14.3 billion in 1981 to LS19.4 billion in 1985.

Syria had extremely limited opportunities to earn foreign exchange other than by exporting goods. Pipeline transit fees for crude oil, a primary service activity in the 1970s, largely ceased after 1976. Although the government built new hotels and holiday villages with foreign companies, tourism did not generate sufficient foreign exchange in the mid-1980s to affect the foreign liquidity crisis. For example, tourism earned only LS451 million in 1984. Consequently, Syria turned to outside sources to offset the trade deficit, relying on foreign grant aid, worker remittances, and foreign lending from banks and development funds to ease balance of payments pressures.

Syria received little foreign grant aid until after the June 1967 War when Kuwait, Libya, and Saudi Arabia agreed to provide financial assistance to the confrontation states—Syria, Egypt, and Jordan. Except for 1967, the published amounts given Syria remained small until 1971, when they reached US$21 million. Grant aid for balance of payments amounted to US$364 million in 1973 and US$654 million in 1975. To purchase military equipment, Syria reportedly received large additional transfers not included in the statistics. Arab grant aid decreased in 1976 because of uncertainty over Syria's intentions in Lebanon, but it jumped sharply to US$1.1 billion in 1977.

At the 1978 Baghdad summit conference, the Arab oil-producing states pledged US$1.8 billion a year in financial support to Syria. However, most observers agreed that actual cash transfers amounted to far less than official allocation levels. Syria's political relations with Middle East neighbors and the mid-1980s economic downturn in the Persian Gulf states tended to determine the flow of Arab aid. Organization for Economic Cooperation and Development (OECD) figures valued OPEC aid to Syria at US$1.4 billion in 1981, dropping to US$799.7 million in 1983. The highest estimates for 1983 placed Arab aid to Syria at US$1.2 billion, but most observers considered US$1 billion a more accurate figure. Only Saudi Arabia and Kuwait, the wealthiest Arab oil-producing states, provided regular aid installments as stipulated under the Baghdad summit agreement. In 1983 Saudi Arabia contributed roughly US$800 million and Kuwait provided US$200 million in aid. By 1985 Syria had suffered a marked decrease in financial support from the Arab states, reportedly receiving only US$700 million in Baghdad summit money that year. To protest Syrian support of Iran in the Iran-Iraq War and Syrian policies in Lebanon, the Kuwaiti parliament voted to suspend its annual contribution, but the amir moved quickly to restore aid levels. In 1986 Saudi Arabia reportedly gave Syria US$700 million, including a US$176 million cash grant in July, as part of its Baghdad summit commitments. Official grant aid cited in Syria's balance of payments peaked in 1981 at US$1.8 billion and declined to US$1.2 billion by 1984.

Apart from "official" Baghdad summit aid, Syria received additional support from Arab states. Unconfirmed reports revealed that Libya paid about US$1 billion to the Soviet Union in 1979-80 to cover Syria's mounting military debt. In the aftermath of the Israeli invasion of Lebanon in 1982, reports also suggested a major transfer of funds, perhaps up to US$2 billion, from Saudi Arabia to Syria for immediate arms resupply. Since 1982 Iran has channeled aid to Syria (including oil), valued at its peak in the 1983-84 period at US$1 billion.

The government also relied partially on workers' remittances to alleviate balance of payments pressures. Officially recorded remittances peaked at US$901 million in 1979. However, by 1983 the propensity of workers to invest remittances outside Syria because of worsening economic conditions decreased their impact on the balance of payments. As the economic downturn in the Persian Gulf states became more pronounced in 1984 and 1985, remittances dropped further—from US$327 million in 1984 to US$300 million in 1985. Economists expected the downward trend to continue as long as world oil prices remained at their low 1986 levels.

In the 1970s, Syria increasingly turned to private and government financial institutions to finance part of its economic development. Before 1973, drawing rights on available credits were only slightly higher than repayments of earlier loans. Since 1972 government drawings on long-term loans have increased, reaching US$340 million in 1976. This rapid rise of available credits (excluding military) was even more striking, amounting to US$340 million in 1970, US$650 million in 1973, and US$2.8 billion at the beginning of 1977. Into the 1980s, other governments continued to provide the bulk of the credits, supplemented by loans from World Bank organizations and international development funds. Syria's stature as a borrower in international commercial credit circles remained weak in the 1980s.

The increase of the external public debt (over one year and excluding military loans) also occurred rapidly but was slower than available credits because of Syria's deficiencies in implementing projects. The external public debt amounted to US$232 million in 1970, US$411 million in 1973, US$1.2 billion in 1977, and US$2.5 billion at the end of 1984. Debt service costs barely exceeded US$100 million in 1975 but tripled by 1984, representing 13 percent of the exports of goods and services. Syrian officials appeared relatively prudent in the use of foreign loans, cutting back plans rather than going deeply in debt. The debt service ratio stood at 11.2 percent in 1983, a relatively low rate as a result of Syria's reliance on grant aid and workers' remittances to finance the trade deficit.

National and international economic development funds, the World Bank, the European Investment Bank, and agencies affiliated with the United Nations (UN) conducted and financed aid programs. World Bank loan commitments increased substantially in the 1970s, exceeding US$250 million in 1978. World Bank missions to Syria occurred more frequently through the mid-1980s, and project loans continued to rise. The World Bank joined other international lenders, including the Arab Fund for Economic and Social Development, the Kuwait Fund for Arab Economic Development, the Saudi Fund for Development, and other Arab development funds, to finance projects in electric power, rural electrification, highway construction, telecommunications, irrigation, education, livestock, water resources, and other areas.

Since the late 1950s, East European states have provided substantial economic development loans to Syria. In the 1960s, Soviet technical and financial assistance was instrumental in constructing the Euphrates Dam, including the hydroelectric power station. The Soviet Union provided a US$185 million loan at concessional rates to finance the dam, Syria's largest development project of the decade. After completion, the Soviets and several East European countries helped construct parts of the dam's irrigation and drainage facilities.

In the late 1970s and 1980s, the Soviet Union, Czechoslovakia, and Romania continued to be particularly active in developing Syria's infrastructure. For example, Czechoslovakia played a major role in developing Syria's crude oil and refinery facilities. In 1986 Technoexport completed work on a ninety-two kilometer spur linking Syria's new oil field at Dayr az Zawr with the old Iraqi-Syrian pipeline. Further, Syrian refinery workers underwent training in Romania. The Soviet Union continued to lend assistance for power plant projects, including the US$97-million Tishrin plant, a joint venture undertaken by the Soviet Union's Technopromexport and Syria's Milihouse. Throughout the 1980s, economic and technical cooperation agreements with the Soviet Union and East European states generated new aid commitments, but in 1987 the exact amounts remained unknown. Total Syrian indebtedness to East European states (including military assistance) was estimated at about US$12 billion to US$13 billion in the mid-1980s. In 1984 there were over 5,000 Soviet and East European technicians working in Syria, in addition to over 2,000 military advisers.

Beginning in the 1970s, Syria also received considerable amounts of aid from Western Europe and the United States. Members of the EEC agreed to provide nearly US$70 million to finance Syrian development projects. Individual states, including West Germany and France, also provided bilateral aid, but in 1979–80, as relations deteriorated, West Germany stopped all funding for Syrian development projects. In 1985 West Germany decided to restore project funding but withdrew all development assistance to protest Syria's alleged role in the 1986 bombing of the German-Arab Friendship Society Office in West Berlin. In 1986 the West European countries and Britain endorsed a series of economic sanctions to demonstrate their disapproval of Syria's alleged role in terrorist operations (see Sponsorship of Terrorism, ch. 5).

Between 1945 and the end of 1976, the United States channeled US$103 million in economic aid to Syria. In the years shortly after independence, the United States provided nearly half of this aid, primarily in the form of grants. After Syria and the United States resumed diplomatic relations in 1974, United States project aid to Syria increased dramatically. In 1981, however, the United States Congress froze about 60 percent of a US$227.8 million allocation of development aid, bringing United States Agency for International Development financed water, electricity, highway, and other infrastructure projects to a halt. All United States government economic assistance to Syria was canceled in 1983, and in 1986 the United States adopted diplomatic and economic sanctions in support of those of its West European allies against Syria.

Banking and Monetary Policy

When first issued in 1920, the Syrian pound was linked to the French franc. At independence French- and British-owned banks dominated banking activity. The largest bank, the French-owned Bank of Syria and Lebanon, became the bank of currency issue and assumed other central bank functions, in addition to its commercial operations. In 1947 Syria joined the IMF and established a par value of LS2.19 equivalent to US$1. In 1949 Syria broke the link to the franc.

The primary legislation establishing a central bank and control of the banking system was passed in 1953, but the Central Bank was not formed until 1956. Its functions included issuing notes, controlling the money supply, acting as fiscal agent for the government, and controlling credit and commercial banks. It was also to act as the country's development bank until specialized banks were established for various sectors. The Central Bank had considerable discretionary powers over the banking system but was itself responsible to and under the control of the Council on Money and Credit, a policy group of high-ranking officials.

The banking system has exhibited resilience in the wake of widespread political change since independence. Before independence, Syria was the junior partner in terms of banking facilities in a customs union with Lebanon. Dissolution of that relationship in 1950 stimulated the establishment of foreign banks, especially Arab, and expansion of some already operating there. After the 1956 Suez War, French and British banking interests were sequestered as enemy assets. In 1958 and after the union with Egypt, the state began to Arabize the commercial banking system and in 1961 implemented a policy of limited nationalization.

In 1966 the state achieved complete ownership of commercial banking by merging all existing commercial banks into the single consolidated Commercial Bank of Syria. In addition, the government created specialized banks to promote economic development. It extended the charter of the Agricultural Cooperative Bank from the preindependence period and established the Industrial Bank in 1959, the Real Estate Bank in April 1966, and the Popular Credit Bank in July 1966.

In 1986 the banking system consisted of those five banks in addition to the Central Bank. Legislation in 1966 largely limited each bank's lending to the sector in its title. All five banks could extend short- to long-term credit and accept deposits. The Commercial Bank of Syria was by far the largest and most active.

The total assets of the specialized banks reached LS44.9 billion at the end of 1984, and total deposits amounted to LS28 billion. The Commercial Bank of Syria, the largest of the five specialized banks, had assets of LS33.7 billion in over 40 branches in 1984. Deposits totaled LS19.3 billion in 1985. The specialized banks extended credits of LS26.1 billion in 1984. Banking authorities allocated credit primarily to commerce (51 percent), industry (27 percent), and construction (15 percent). The public sector received 75 percent of the credit.

The Council on Money and Credit established monetary policy and supervised banking, subject to review by a ministerial committee responsible for the whole economy. The general philosophy was that the banking system should be an agent of government economic policy. Direct controls were used more often than indirect ones; credit, for example, was regulated by setting limits for each sector and each bank.

Although the money supply increased rapidly, it consisted primarily of money in circulation. In the 1960s, demand deposits generally were less than one-third of the money supply and, by the late 1960s, about one-fifth. Banking activity increased in the 1970s, and currency in circulation slowly decreased from 77 percent of the money supply in 1970 to 61 percent in 1980 and 56 percent in 1984.

Bank accounts were predominantly demand deposits; use of time and savings accounts grew slowly. For example, in 1984 time and savings deposits were only 40 percent the size of demand deposits.

In fact, banking played a rather limited role in the economy. There were several possible reasons for the limited use of banks, including distrust of or unfamiliarity with banks, low incomes and limited savings, low interest on savings accounts, lack of more convenient branches, and especially the increased resort to the black market for currency transactions and imported goods in the mid-1970s.

Bank lending was mainly for short-term commercial transactions. Bank financing of trade was 53 percent of total lending in 1964, 67 percent in 1970, 79 percent in 1976, 46 percent in 1980, and 50 percent in 1984. The value of loans to the commercial sector nearly tripled from 1975 to 1984. Loans to other sectors of the economy, especially to industry and construction, diverted bank lending from commerce in the late 1970s. The value of loans to the industrial sector increased more than twentyfold from 1975 to 1984, to become 27 percent of total lending. The value of construction loans grew seventeenfold, and agricultural loans tripled.

The sources of bank funds, largely borrowing from the Central Bank and demand deposits, contributed to the short-term nature of most lending. In general, the banks were undercapitalized. In the 1970s and 1980s, more medium-term loans and a few long-term loans (in agriculture and housing) were made. Long-term loans constituted 15 percent of agricultural loans and 71 percent of housing loans.

Short-term commercial credits, however, increased faster. The Industrial Bank appeared to invest equity capital in both public and private plants instead of making long-term loans. Public sector enterprises received most bank lending, but the percentage fell from 84 percent in 1976 to 75 percent in 1984.

Monetary expansion in the 1960s largely resulted from financing government budget deficits. The growth of the economy, extension of the use of money, and government price controls minimized the impact of deficit financing on prices. Monetary expansion accelerated in the 1970s, particularly after 1972. The large inflows of foreign funds, plus the sharp increase in Syria's own oil revenues, facilitated rapid growth of government expenditures while building up government deposits with the banking system. A high rate of credit expansion, primarily to public sector enterprises, followed, and private sector borrowing also increased substantially. After 1976 the expansion of the money supply continued in tandem with the need to finance chronic budget deficits.

The money supply grew 21.3 percent during the 1970s and 22.8 percent a year during the early 1980s, a rate much higher than the growth of GDP.

Monetary expansion, along with shortages of goods and labor, caused a period of high inflation. Inflation was also fueled by steep rises in world prices of imported commodities. The wholesale price index increased an average of 18.2 percent a year between 1972 and 1976; from 1977 to 1984, wholesale prices more than doubled. This period was Syria's miniboom—a smaller version of the high level of investment and construction activity, rapidly rising prices, shortages of goods and labor, and overtaxed storage and transportation facilities that characterized the nearby Arab and Iranian oil economies.

In addition to setting a great number of prices directly, the government controlled many more. Limited markups (generally between 5 and 10 percent) were applied to a wide range of commodities produced or imported by the private sector. Essential commodities were supplied at low, subsidized prices. When the price discrepancy of an item became too great, encouraging smuggling, the government rationed the amount that could be bought at subsidized prices. Rationed commodities included rice, sugar, and cottonseed oil. A person wanting more than the ration could buy as much as he wanted at the much higher open-market price.

The government's rationing policy directly contributed to black market growth in the early 1970s. The black market flourished during Syria's miniboom of the mid-1970s and substantially increased as the Syrian presence in Lebanon facilitated the transfer of consumer goods, raw materials, and industrial spare parts across the border. Frustrated by bureaucratic delays in obtaining import permits and letters of credit, the private sector increasingly turned to the underground economy to acquire essential imports. The public sector, also suffering from strict government control over imports and from shortages of foreign exchange, resorted to similar means to import spare parts for state-run factories. Observers estimated black-market trade at about US$1 billion per year in the mid-1980s, almost one-quarter the size of officially recorded imports.

The black market in foreign exchange also played a more active role in the economy, as Syrians working abroad sought higher exchange rates for their currency. In mid-1986 Syrian pounds traded for about thirty to the United States dollar in contrast to the official exchange rate LS3.92 to the United States dollar.

Government responses to increased resort to the black market for imported goods and currency exchange varied. In 1984 and 1985, as part of its efforts to alleviate the foreign exchange crisis, the state launched a campaign against black-market money changing and currency smuggling. Syria decreed heavy sentences for black marketing, including up to twenty-five years' imprisonment for currency smuggling and one- to five-year sentences for Syrians who failed to repatriate funds earned overseas from business inside Syria. Widespread but brief arrests of money changers signaled the government's intention to limit the black market, rather than eradicate it; in the late 1980s, the official economy still remained heavily dependent on underground transactions for foreign exchange. In addition, the government issued new regulations severely limiting the amount of foreign exchange allowed out of the country and requiring tourists to change US$100 upon entry.

In 1986 the Commercial Bank of Syria issued a new regulation to facilitate private sector imports through official channels and reduce black market activity. The regulation permitted any importer with an official import license and source of foreign currency to pay the Commercial Bank of Syria 105 percent of the total amount required in the letter of credit and receive a letter of credit immediately. The regulation was designed to reduce the waiting period for letters of credit, which had reached up to two years for some private sector firms in the mid-1980s. However, private businessmen initially reacted cautiously to the reform measure, fearing retribution from state tax collectors or the police by admitting they held large amounts of foreign currency outside the system.

In the 1980s, the government also revised exchange rates in an attempt to attract workers' remittances to official channels, make government rates more competitive with the black market, and stop the depreciation of the Syrian pound. In 1981 Syria reverted to a multitier exchange rate, in which the government established a "parallel" rate for private sector imports that floated against major international currencies. In 1986 the parallel rate was LS5.40 to US$1. The official rate of LS3.92 to US$1 remained in use for public sector imports. In 1982 the government established a tourist rate for Syrians working abroad; this rate was LS9.75 to US$1 in 1986. By 1986 many commercial activities were calculated at the tourist rate to encourage a return to official banking channels. In addition, government regulations instituted in 1984 permitted Syrians working abroad and foreigners doing business in Syria to maintain hard currency accounts of up to 75 percent of the value of agricultural and industrial imports. After September 1985, the government permitted resident Syrians to open hard currency, interest-bearing accounts at the Commercial Bank of Syria specifically to finance imports.

Transportation, Telecommunications, and Construction

Since antiquity, Syria has served as a major crossroads for international trade. Syrian merchants traditionally have prospered from the east-west and north-south movement of goods and people. In the early twentieth century, Syrian transportation links continued to be more provincial than national. The boundaries preceding independence further fragmented the country's transportation system. Splitting off Lebanon from Greater Syria (see Glossary) deprived the country of its main port, Beirut, and placed part of the rail network connecting Syria's main cities in Lebanon. The French cession of Syria's northwest corner to Turkey before World War II took away the country's other port, Iskenderun (formerly known as Alexandretta), and important rail and road segments. At independence the country lacked a port; adequate links between the main cities of Damascus, Homs, and Aleppo; and transportation arteries to the important northeast agricultural area and the fertile coastal plain. Moreover, the traditional east-west and north-south transit trade had diminished considerably.

After independence the state began a major effort to develop a national transportation system of roads, railroads, and (later) pipelines. Three ports (Tartus, Latakia, and Baniyas) served domestic and transit trade. Two international airports (Damascus and Aleppo) and several secondary airports provided international and internal connections for freight and passengers. By the mid-1970s, the main population and economic areas were connected by the various forms of transportation (see fig. 12).

In 1986 about one-half of the roads, one-half of the railroads, and two-fifths of port capacity had been added during the previous sixteen years. However, the transportation system remained overtaxed as a result of the country's development boom and the increase of transit goods destined for the Persian Gulf states. Under the Fourth Five-Year Plan, a high level of investment in transportation infrastructure was planned to remove constraints on economic development caused by inadequate transportation.

In the mid-1980s, over 95 percent of freight and passenger traffic moved by truck or bus on the highways. The main arteries were north-south between the Turkish and Jordanian borders (but primarily between the major west-central cities of Damascus, Homs, Hamah, and Aleppo) and north-south along the coastal plain; east-west traffic also was heavy between the main west-central cities and towns and the port cities of the coast. Important corridors, although less heavily used, extended from Damascus eastward to the border

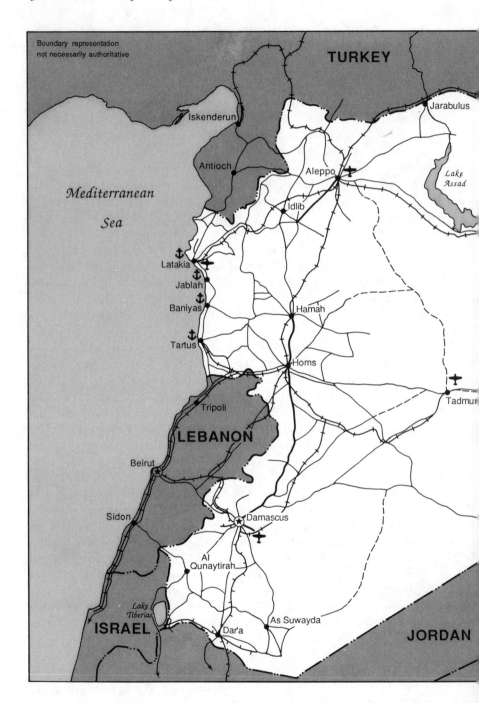

Figure 12. Transportation System

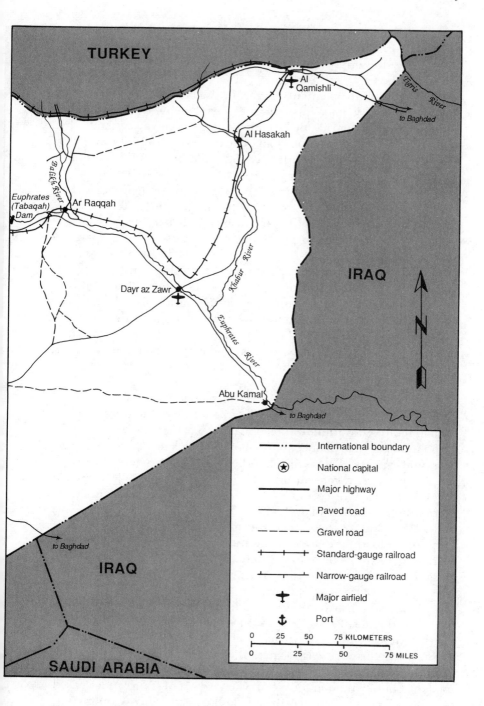

(the primary road to Baghdad), from Homs eastward to Tadmur for the export of phosphates via the port of Tartus, and from Aleppo eastward to the important northeast economic area and continuing to Baghdad.

Major road improvements began in the late 1960s. The paved highway network had approximately tripled by 1985, reaching 18,000 kilometers or, about 72 percent of the highway system. The state spent LS598 million on road construction in 1984. From 1980 to 1984, major roads grew from 4,527 kilometers to 5,230 kilometers.

About 99 percent of the paved roads were two-lane, inadequate for the north-south traffic between the major cities, towns, and coastal ports. By the late 1970s, overuse of particular arteries caused congestion, maintenance problems, and shortened life span of trucks. In the mid-1980s, the government studied a number of plans to ease congestion in the capital; plans included construction of a southern ring road, a ring road along the city wall, and more bridges. The state also continued plans to upgrade four-lane highways in some heavily populated western portions of the country and to complete a new 104-kilometer highway to the Jordanian border by 1988. The 1980s also witnessed an expansion of the rural road network, which grew from 16,290 kilometers in 1980 to 21,796 kilometers in 1984.

After independence the country developed three major ports. By 1984 the port of Tartus, opened in 1965, was the most important, handling 8.8 million tons of cargo. Tartus handled general-cargo imports, phosphate exports (857,000 tons in 1984), and large crude-oil exports. Tartus also handled 8,000 passengers. The port of Latakia handled general cargo (1.7 million tons in 1984), including 147,000 tons of cotton exports. The government planned to increase the capacity of Latakia to 3.5 million tons a year in the late 1980s. Both of these general-cargo ports experienced congestion and unloading delays in the mid-1970s because of the rapid increase (up to 50 percent between 1974 and 1976) of seaborne cargo destined for Syria and transit trade to Persian Gulf countries. Closing of the port of Beirut in 1976 as a result of the Lebanese Civil War temporarily diverted additional transit cargo to Syrian ports. In the late 1970s, Syrian port congestion diminished, and waiting time in the 1980s was minimal.

Syria's other port was located at Baniyas, the terminal for the crude-oil pipeline from Iraq. In 1975 crude exports from Baniyas totaled about 27 million tons, but when export of Iraqi crude ceased in 1982, activity in Baniyas dropped off considerably. Completion of the 6-million-ton-capacity oil refinery at Baniyas in 1978 maintained some activity at the oil port. In 1984 Baniyas exported 1,520 tons of petroleum.

At independence the country inherited two separate railroads. The narrow-gauge (1.05 meters) Hijaz Railway served Damascus and the southwest, with connections to Lebanon and Jordan. In 1984 it had 327 kilometers of track. The standard-gauge (1.4 meters) Northern Railway had 757 kilometers of track from the port of Latakia to the northeast corner of the country and Iraq via Aleppo, Ar Raqqah, Dayr az Zawr, and Al Hasakah. The link between Latakia and the northeast was completed in the mid-1970s, and it resulted in a substantial rise in freight, primarily shipments of cotton, wheat, and barley.

By the late 1970s, the railroads required considerable rehabilitation in order to make an important contribution to the economy. Transportation policy needed attention and equipment needed upgrading. The government had long-term plans to add equipment and trackage, link the two systems, and make the railroads much more important carriers of passengers and traffic. In 1978 work began on lines linking the phosphate mines near Tadmur to Tartus. In 1981 the Soviet Union provided Syria with US$49.5 million in development aid, including funding for the 150-kilometer railroad from Dayr az Zawr to Abu Kamal and an 80-kilometer line between Tartus and Latakia, with a 10-kilometer spur to the Tartus cement plant. The 209-kilometer line from Damascus to Homs opened for freight in 1983. The opening of the Homs to Tadmur and Homs to Tartus routes, coupled with other expansions of the railroad network, connected Syria's main towns and industrial centers in the mid-1980s. By 1984 total standard extended gauge track stood at 1,686 kilometers.

Syria's civil aviation sector experienced considerable growth in the 1980s. Syrian Arab Airlines (SAA), the state-owned carrier established in 1961 as a successor to Syrian Airways, provided domestic service from Damascus to Aleppo, Latakia, Al Qamishli, and Dayr az Zawr. SAA's service included thirty-three overseas routes to major Middle Eastern, European, and South Asian capitals. In 1986 the airline added biweekly flights to Tehran and Riyadh. The airline had a total of twenty-three major transport aircraft.

The General Directorate of Civil Aviation reported a steady increase in the number of arrivals and departures at Damascus International Airport, Syria's major air terminal in the 1980s. The number of passengers rose from 1.3 million in 1983 to 1.5 million in 1984 and 1985, an increase of approximately 16 percent. About 95 percent of Syrian air traffic went via Damascus; about 3.3 percent went via the Aleppo airport. In 1985 the number of airplanes arriving at Damascus International Airport totaled 10,997; an additional 607 arrived at Aleppo and 539 at Dayr az Zawr. In 1985 freight unloaded at Damascus International Airport totaled 2.8 million tons; freight loaded amounted to 2.2 million tons.

Not until the 1980s did the country's telecommunications facilities experience significant growth. The ratio of telephones to people remained extremely low throughout the 1960s and 1970s, numbering 13.5 telephones per 1,000 people in 1963 and 17.5 telephones per 1,000 people in 1970. In 1979 Syria embarked upon a major expansion of the country's telecommunications infrastructure. The Public Telecommunications Establishment, Syria's state-owned agency responsible for overseeing and developing the country's telecommunications, signed a major contract with a Japanese firm to install two 40,000-line electronic switching systems in Damascus and Aleppo, a project that placed Syria's local telephone exchanges among the largest in the world. By autumn 1983, Syria possessed an improved network of microwave links and digital systems. In 1983 the number of telephones per 1,000 people increased to 43, and by 1985 the country had 512,600 telephones, an increase to 53 telephones per 1,000 inhabitants. Dimashq Province accounted for about 40 percent of the country's telephones, followed by Halab Province with 15 percent, and then by Hims, Hamah, and Al Ladhaqiyah provinces.

In the late 1980s, Syria's international links depended on its participation in the International Telecommunications Satellite Organization (INTELSAT), a coaxial cable to Crete, and radio relay to neighboring countries. Furthermore, plans to link Syria with the Soviet-sponsored Intersputnik network and the regional Arab Satellite Organization (ARABSAT) system would significantly contribute to Syria's telecommunications capabilities, as would the new telecommunications network slated to link Damascus, Ash Shaykh Miskin, and Dar'a in Syria with towns in Jordan and Saudi Arabia in the 1990s.

Radiobroadcast transmissions were made from six AM stations for domestic service and from a high-frequency station located at Sabburah for international service. Television was broadcast from 13 transmitters, including a 350-kilowatt transmitter that broadcast into Israel, and 27 low-power relay stations.

In the mid-1970s, construction became a major growth sector of the economy and, because it is labor intensive, an important employer, particularly of unskilled labor. The construction industry helped absorb the large flow of agricultural workers who moved to urban areas seeking a better living. Construction expanded an

A portion of the Beirut-Damascus highway
Courtesy Murhaf Jouejati

average of 8.2 percent a year (in constant prices) between 1953 and 1976, but there were great variations in growth. From 1977 to 1984, construction expanded a total of 160 percent. The sector expanded in terms of value added (at constant prices) by nearly 20 percent a year between 1970 and 1976. Between 1978 and 1984 the sector expanded 7.5 percent a year in terms of value added at constant prices.

Housing construction had fallen considerably behind the needs of the population in the mid-1970s. From 1975 to 1978, the number of residential building licenses issued by the government grew from 12,388 to 22,626, but in 1984 the state issued only 14,666 new residential building licenses—a signal that the mid-1970s construction boom was winding down. The high rate of population increase, the rural to urban migration, and the desire of Syrians to invest in secure areas like housing put severe pressures on housing and services such as water, sewerage, electricity, and telephones in most cities and towns. Figures to measure the housing shortages were lacking in 1987, but soaring real estate prices in the major cities in the 1980s confirmed the shortage. Young couples and those with limited incomes experienced particular difficulties as a result of sharply rising land and construction costs that priced moderate wage earners out of the market. By 1986 government efforts to curb

179

urban land speculation and to ease the supply of building material had only limited success. The average price of ordinary apartments in Damascus topped LS1 million in the mid-1980s, and there was little hope for relief.

Period of Economic Retrenchment, 1986–90

In 1987 Syria's economy had a well-developed agricultural and industrial base, unlike some of its Arab neighbors that depended almost exclusively on oil. Although agriculture remained nearly as dependent on rainfall as at independence, the government's renewed commitment to agricultural development, expansion and extension of irrigation systems throughout the country, and application of new cultivation technologies provided incentives to stimulate agricultural output. Industry, too, had expanded considerably in terms of value, both in the range of products and in their sophistication. During the Assad years, Syria's infrastructure grew rapidly, as the state channeled resources into the building of new electric, water, telecommunications, and other development projects.

Nevertheless, in the late 1980s, the Syrian economy faced a number of serious difficulties. The collapse of world oil prices, weak markets for Syrian exports, large trade deficits, foreign exchange shortages, declining workers' remittances, unreliable sources and amounts of donor aid from the Persian Gulf states and Iran, rapid depreciation of the Syrian pound, and massive defense expenditures forced Syria into a period of economic retrenchment. A mood of austerity pervaded the economy as the state struggled to adjust to lower rates of economic growth.

The Syrian economy faced a long and difficult road to recovery despite the government's adoption of measures designed to forestall an economic crisis by sharply reducing imports, cutting spending, stabilizing local currency and foreign exchange markets, encouraging the private sector by introducing more market-oriented mechanisms into the economy, and limiting black market activity. Observers agreed that in the 1990s, economic recovery would depend in part upon the state's ability to initiate and implement major economic reform programs, improve public sector management, and overcome bureaucratic inertia and corruption. Continued internal stability and external elements, such as the outbreak of an Arab-Israeli war or a severe world depression, would also affect Syria's prospects for economic recovery. However, through the end of the 1980s, only the discovery of sizable quantities of high-grade oil at Dayr az Zawr—by generating much-needed foreign exchange and reducing expenditures for oil imports in the balance of payments—offered the possibility of economic relief.

* * *

The Syrian government publishes a variety of statistics; the one most frequently available in the United States and adequate for most purposes is the annual *Statistical Abstract,* published by the Central Bureau of Statistics. *The Quarterly Bulletin,* published by the Central Bank of Syria, and *Syrie et Monde Arabe,* published by Office Arabe de Presse et de Documentation in Damascus, contain useful information. International Monetary Fund publications, such as the *International Financial Statistics* and the *Balance of Payments Yearbook,* usually include considerable statistics for Syria. The UN and affiliated agencies issue a variety of publications that include statistics for Syria. The World Bank's annual *World Development Report* also contains useful statistics. The United States government publishes a number of reports containing information about the Syrian economy. Most useful are the Department of Commerce's *Foreign Economic Trends* series on Syria and the Department of Agriculture's *Middle East and North Africa Situation and Outlook Report.* Several broad surveys, such as *The Middle East and North Africa* and the *Middle East Annual Review,* cover Syria's economic development. *Middle East Economic Digest* and the Economist Intelligence Unit's *Quarterly Economic Review of Syria* provide detailed descriptions of key economic events. Much of the information on aspects of Syria's economy is in small, fragmented bits published in a variety of forms. (For further information and more complete citations, see Bibliography.)

Chapter 4. Government and Politics

Assyrian court officials from wall painting,
c.a. 750 B.C., Tall Hariri

IN EARLY 1987, President Hafiz al Assad, in power since his November 1970 takeover in a bloodless military coup d'état, continued to lead Syria. His regime appeared to be resilient, if not altogether stable. Only a few years earlier, the regime had encountered several major threats. In 1982 the government of Syria endured nearly simultaneous major domestic and external challenges: the uprising of Muslim fundamentalist rebels and the Israeli attack on Syrian forces in Lebanon. Then, in late 1983 and early 1984, Assad became seriously ill, leading to splits within the regime as factions maneuvered to succeed him. These machinations proved to be premature, however, because Assad subsequently recovered and reasserted his power. Nonetheless, the domestic political infighting and external military clashes that occurred while Assad was incapacitated reminded Syrians of their nation's chronic instability of the 1950s and 1960s and foreshadowed the return of such instability after Assad. The crises also reinforced the perception that the strength of the Syrian government was not only vested in the president but derived from him personally. Consequently, although Assad had transformed Syria into a regional power in the Levant and had created domestic stability, his accomplishments could prove ephemeral because they were not buttressed by legitimate and viable institutions. Even more unsettling, in 1987 the question of a successor to President Assad was still unresolved.

Since 1970 Assad's pragmatism, ambition, and patience have helped transform Syria into a regional power. Syrian development has been motivated and hastened by the threat posed by Israel. In fact, in 1984 Assad announced Syria's determination to attain "strategic parity" with Israel and further stated that Syria would strive to match Israel's level of modernization across the wide spectrum of "political, demographic, social, educational, economic, and military aspects of life."

However, Syria's status as a regional power imposed costs and liabilities. For instance, in 1987 Syria was relatively isolated in the Arab world, primarily because of its maverick support for Iran in the Iran-Iraq War and its involvement in Lebanon. Also, its economy staggered under the weight of its military budget, and it depended heavily on the Soviet Union for military equipment.

Despite the outward appearance of radicalism and dogmatic rigidity, Syrian diplomacy was conducted on the basis of hardheaded and pragmatic calculation of perceived costs and benefits to the national interest. Its position on the Arab-Israeli conflict, once believed to be immutably rigid, changed not only in style but in substance. In the years after the October 1973 War, Syria modified its categorical refusal to negotiate directly with Israel. After 1973 it indicated its intention to negotiate, in return for Israel's withdrawal from all occupied territories and for a form of Palestinian self-determination.

The political effectiveness of Assad's leadership depended heavily on firm control of the pervasive military and internal security and intelligence apparatus—the only countercoup forces available to an incumbent regime. The officially sanctioned Baath (Arab Socialist Resurrection) Party, also played an increasingly important role in maintaining the regime.

Syria was a socialist state under the political influence of the Baath Party, which provided ideological legitimation and continuity to Assad's rule. However, Assad's implementation of Baath Party doctrines has been more pragmatic than ideological. To broaden the government's base, in 1972 Assad incorporated non-Baathist parties into the National Progressive Front. Although the front theoretically ruled Syria, the Baath Party remained the real power.

The authorities closely monitored political activities and dealt sternly with expressions of organized dissent or opposition—a source of grievance for the nation's intellectuals, students, some conservative Sunni religious leaders, and labor groups. Absence of open political channels other than through the Baathist-controlled framework made estimating the extent of popular support for Assad's regime difficult. Clearly, sectarian tensions persisted because the centers of power in 1987 remained in Alawi hands, whereas the majority of the population were Sunni Muslims who had traditionally held power until the Assad regime was installed in 1970.

In 1987 Syrian popular opinion was split between those who supported and those who opposed President Assad's regime. However, those who opposed the regime did so vehemently, while those who supported Assad appeared ambivalent. The charismatic Assad continued to enjoy considerable personal popularity among the latter group, but its approval did not extend to his regime as a whole. Even many of Assad's supporters feared and loathed the draconian security measures that ensured the Assad regime's survival, and they were shocked at the regime's brutal repression of the Hamah insurrection in 1982. Yet this fear was mitigated by the feeling that any successor regime would be worse than Assad's, and his strong authoritarian and paternalistic management of political affairs was endorsed because it had provided Syria with its first uninterrupted period of stability since independence in 1946.

Constitutional Framework

Between the collapse of the Ottoman Empire in 1916 and promulgation of a permanent constitution in 1973, Syria adopted several constitutions, all reflecting an amalgam of West European (chiefly French), Arab, and Islamic political cultures. The initial impetus to constitutionalism came from Syrian nationalist leaders of the post–World War I era who had been educated in the West during the late nineteenth century. These leaders proposed a Western-style parliament and a separate, independent judiciary as a counterbalance to the untrammeled power of Ottoman and later French Mandate administrators. The system of government envisioned by Syrian nationalists and legal scholars was to provide for popular participation in the political process and constitutional safeguards of personal and political rights.

Constitutionalism failed to take hold, however, because of unremitting postindependence instability. A change in government leadership through a coup or a countercoup was almost always followed by a constitutional change intended to buttress the new political order.

In 1987 the governmental structure was based on the Permanent Constitution of March 13, 1973. This charter is similar to the provisional constitution of May 1, 1969, as amended in February and June 1971. The Constitution provides for a republican form of government in what it calls "a democratic, popular, socialist, and sovereign state" and stipulates that the people are the ultimate source of national sovereignty.

The Constitution reaffirms the long-held ideological premise that Syria is only a part of the one and indivisible "Arab nation" that is struggling for complete Arab unity. Syria is constitutionally declared still to be a member of the Federation of Arab Republics (FAR), which was inaugurated in April 1971 by Egypt, Syria, and Libya. Although the FAR was short lived, its constitutional formula provides a framework for ongoing Syrian efforts at unity with other Arab nations.

Among the principles in the Constitution is the stipulation that the president be a Muslim, that the main source of legislation be Islamic *fikh* (doctrine and jurisprudence), and that the Baath Party be "the vanguard party in the society and the state." In addition, the state is directed to safeguard the fundamental rights of citizens to enjoy freedom and to participate in political, economic, social, and cultural life within the limits of the law. Free exercise of religious belief is guaranteed as long as such exercise does not affect public order. In keeping with the Arab character of the nation,

187

the purpose of the educational system is described as creation of "an Arab national socialist generation with scientific training"—a generation committed to establishment of a united Arab socialist nation.

The Constitution's economic principles not only set forth a planned socialist economy that should take into account "economic complementarity in the Arab homeland" but also recognize three categories of property. The three kinds are property of the people, including all natural resources, public domains, nationalized enterprises, and establishments created by the state; collective property, such as assets owned by popular and professional organizations; and private property. The Constitution states that the social function of private property shall be subordinated, under law, to the national economy and public interests. However, expropriation may occur only with just compensation.

Governmental powers are divided by the Constitution into executive, legislative, and judicial categories (see fig. 13). The Constitution is notable for strengthening the already formidable role of the presidency; the framers of the Constitution were clearly more concerned with the supremacy and stability of presidential powers than with the issue of checks and balances among the three branches of government. Official concern for political and governmental stability is reflected in the relatively difficult procedures for amending the Constitution. A bill to amend the Constitution may be introduced by the president or one-third of the members of the People's Council (parliament), but its passage requires approval by a majority of three-fourths of the People's Council as well as by the president.

Government

The President and the Cabinet

The president is elected for a seven-year term by universal suffrage. A candidate to the office must be a Syrian Arab Muslim, at least forty years of age, proposed by the Baath Party, and nominated by the People's Council. The nominee is submitted to a national referendum. To be elected, the candidate must receive an absolute majority of votes cast. If not, a new candidate must be selected by the Baath Party for formal nomination by the People's Council.

The Constitution states that in the case of the president's temporary disablement, the vice president becomes acting president. However, in 1982 Assad named three vice presidents—Foreign Minister Abd al Halim Khaddam, Rifaat al Assad, and Baath Party

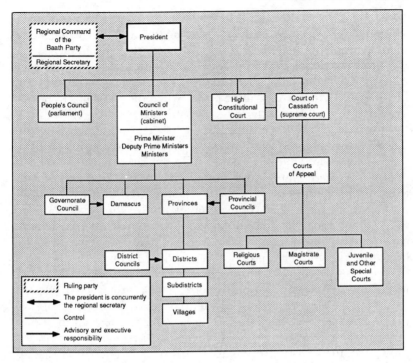

Source: *Syrian Statistical Yearbook*, 1986.

Figure 13. Governmental System, 1987

deputy director Zuhayr Mashariqa—but none of the three was specifically designated as successor. If the presidency falls vacant by resignation or death, a referendum must be held within ninety days to elect a new president. Under certain circumstances, the prime minister may exercise presidential functions for up to ninety days.

The president cannot be removed except for high treason. Impeachment proceedings may be initiated through a petition signed by one-third of the members of the People's Council voting openly or by a petition of two-thirds of the council members voting at a special closed session. The president can be tried only by the High Constitutional Court, of which he is a member.

The president is both the head of state and the chief executive officer of the government. He is vested with sweeping powers that may be delegated, at his sole discretion, to his vice presidents. The president is also commander in chief of the armed forces. He appoints and dismisses the prime minister and other members of the Council of Ministers (the cabinet) and military officers.

Apart from executive authority relating to a wide range of governmental functions including foreign affairs, the president has the right to dissolve the People's Council, in which case a new council must be elected within ninety days from the date of dissolution. He may also exercise legislative power when the council is in recess, provided that all legislative acts promulgated by him are submitted to the legislature for approval at its first subsequent session. The Constitution also empowers the president to preempt legislative power even while the People's Council is in session "in case of absolute need relating to national security." It states, however, that all presidential decrees must be presented to the legislature for its endorsement. The council may, by a two-thirds vote, amend or rescind presidential decrees, provided that the two-thirds majority constitutes no fewer than the absolute majority of the council membership. The council's power to amend or nullify a presidential decree is only nominal, inasmuch as the council's action, whether for amendment or abrogation, is not to have a "retroactive effect."

Under the Constitution, presidential authority extends also to the broadly phrased "right to submit to popular referendum important matters relating to the higher interests of the country." However, the question of what constitutes "higher interests" is left undefined. The results of such a referendum are "binding and executory with effect from the date of their promulgation" by the president. The presidential emergency power granted under Article 113 provides a mandate that is beyond any legal challenge: "In case of grave danger threatening national unity or the security and independence of the national territory or impeding the government's exercise of its constitutional prerogatives, the President of the Republic has the right to take appropriate emergency measures." This article has been in effect since the late 1960s (see Crime and Punishment, ch. 5).

The Council of Ministers, headed by the prime minister, is responsible to the president and serves collectively as the executive and administrative arm of the president and of the state. A cabinet member can also be a member of the People's Council and, if so, is not answerable to the legislature for his official conduct while acting as a cabinet member.

As of 1987, the Council of Ministers had last been reshuffled in April 1985. The council was headed by Prime Minister Abd ar Rauf al Kassim, who had served as prime minister since 1980, and three deputy prime ministers, who also held the portfolios of defense, services, and economic affairs. Ministers were in charge of the following portfolios: agriculture and agrarian reform, communications, construction, culture and national guidance, defense, economy and foreign trade, education, electricity, finance, foreign affairs, health, higher education, housing and utilities, industry, information, interior, irrigation, justice, local administration, oil and mineral wealth, religious trusts (*waqfs*), social affairs and labor, supply and internal trade, tourism, and transportation. In addition, the Council of Ministers included ministers of state for cabinet affairs, foreign affairs, planning affairs, People's Council affairs, and presidential affairs and three newly elected ministers of state without portfolio.

The People's Council

The members of the People's Council are elected for four-year terms by universal suffrage of citizens eighteen years of age or older in direct and secret ballot. The members, the number of which is determined by law, are chosen on the basis of single-member electoral districts. The Constitution requires that at least half of the council seats be set aside for "workers and peasants." The 195° members of the People's Council serving in 1987 were elected in 1986.

The People's Council sits in three regular sessions annually and may be called into special session by the speaker, by the president, or at the request of one-third of the council members. The lawmakers are granted parliamentary immunity, and even when they are charged with criminal offenses, prior consent of the speaker is required before any prosecution against a member may proceed.

The functions of the council include the nomination of a presidential candidate, enactment of laws, discussion of government policy, approval of the general budget and development plans, and ratification of treaties. In addition, as part of its monitoring of the executive branch, the People's Council is authorized to act on a motion of no-confidence in the Council of Ministers as a whole or in an individual minister. Such a motion must be initiated by at least one-fifth of the members and, to become effective, must be approved by the majority of the People's Council. If the motion is carried, the Council of Ministers or the individual minister concerned must resign. The president can dissolve the People's Council, although the Constitution does not specify grounds for dissolution. It does say that the council may not be dissolved more than once for the same cause.

The Judiciary

In the 1980s, the Syrian judicial system remained a synthesis of Ottoman, French, and Islamic laws. The civil, commercial, and criminal codes in effect were, with some amendments, those promulgated in 1949 and were based primarily on French legal practices. In addition, special provisions sanctioned limited application of customary law among beduin and religious minorities. Islamic religious courts based on sharia (Muslim law) continued to function in some parts of the country, but their jurisdiction was limited to issues of personal status, such as marriage, divorce, paternity, custody of children, and inheritance. In 1955 a personal code pertaining to many aspects of personal status was developed. This law modified and modernized sharia by improving the status of women and clarifying the laws of inheritance.

The High Judicial Council is composed of senior civil judges and is charged with the appointment, transfer, and dismissal of judges. Article 131 of the Constitution states that the independence of the judiciary is to be guaranteed by the president in his role as chairman of the High Judicial Council. Article 133 stipulates that judges be autonomous and subject to no authority other than the law. Although the concept of an independent judiciary is enshrined in the Constitution, the president clearly exercises considerable power in the execution, as well as the formulation, of law.

In 1987 Syria had a three-tiered court system, in addition to the state security courts. The Court of Cassation, sitting in Damascus, was the supreme court and the highest court of appeals. It had the authority to resolve both jurisdictional and judicial issues. Below the Court of Cassation were courts of appeal, and at the lowest level were courts of first instance, designated variously as magistrate courts, summary courts, and peace courts. Also at the basic level were juvenile and other special courts and an administrative tribunal known as the Council of State.

Under the 1973 Constitution, the High Constitutional Court was established to adjudicate electoral disputes, to rule on the constitutionality of a law or decree challenged by the president or People's Council, and to render opinions on the constitutionality of bills, decrees, and regulations when requested to do so by the president. The High Constitutional Court is forbidden, however, to question the validity of the popularly approved "laws submitted by the President of the Republic to popular referendums." The court consists of the president and four judges he appoints to serve a renewable term of four years.

Local Administration

In 1987 Syria was divided into thirteen provinces: Halab, Dimashq, Dar'a, Dayr az Zawr, Hamah, Al Hasakah, Hims, Idlib, Al Ladhiqiyah, Al Qunaytirah (which includes the Golan Heights),

The water tower is often a symbol of government services in rural areas.

Ar Raqqah, As Suwayda, and Tartus (see fig. 1). Damascus, as the national capital, was administered separately as a governorate until 1987, when it was designated as a province; the areas outside the city, which had constituted the separate Dimashq Province, were brought under the jurisdiction of the capital and were referred to as the "Province of Damascus rural area." In addition, Syrian maps included the Turkish province of Hatay, which the Syrians call Iskenderun. Each province is divided into districts, which in turn have subdistricts. Under Assad, government power remained highly centralized in Damascus, giving provincial governments little autonomy.

Each province is headed by a governor nominated by the minister of the interior and appointed by the central government. The governor is responsible for administration, health, social services, education, tourism, public works, transportation, domestic trade, agriculture, industry, civil defense, and maintenance of law and order in the province. The minister of local administration works closely with each governor to coordinate and supervise local development projects.

The governor is assisted by a provincial council, three-quarters of whose members are popularly elected for a term of four years, the remainder being appointed by the minister of the interior and the governor. In addition, each council has an executive arm consisting of six to ten officers appointed by the central government from among the council's elected members. Each executive officer is charged with specific functions.

Districts and subdistricts are administered by officials appointed by the governor, subject to the approval of the minister of the interior. These officials work with elected district councils to attend to assorted local needs and serve as intermediaries between central government authority and traditional local leaders, such as village chiefs, clan leaders, and councils of elders.

Since Assad's 1970 Corrective Movement, the government has sought systematically to strengthen its control over local politics. The central government's firmer grasp on power has eroded the autonomy of both nomadic beduin and settled villagers who have until recently been allowed to practice self-government according to their own traditions and customs.

In urban areas, local municipal councils license businesses, control public services and utilities, and levy taxes. Some members of these councils are elected and some appointed. The councils are headed by mayors, who, in small towns, are responsible to the central government's district officer. If the town is the seat of the provincial government, the council is answerable directly to the governor of the province.

Political Dynamics

In early 1987, Syria remained under the effective control of the Assad regime. The country's stability contrasted sharply with the instability of earlier years, which had been punctuated by coups and countercoups and a bewildering succession of cabinets (see Coups and Countercoups, 1961–70, ch. 1).

Background

After independence in 1946, Syrian leaders established a parliamentary democracy, which failed because politics remained centered on personalities and because factional, sectarian, and tribal rivalries persisted. Such a situation was not conducive to domestic unity, much less to national consensus or political momentum. The multiparty political system gave way to a series of military dictatorships, then to Syria's subordination to Egypt in the short-lived United Arab Republic (UAR) from February 1958 to September 1961 (see United Arab Republic, ch. 1). Since 1963, when the Baath Party came to full power in Syria, political competition has evolved and shifted within the party. Under the party, the role of the military has been especially significant.

At independence, power was concentrated in the hands of a wealthy oligarchy of landlords, industrialists, merchants, and lawyers. Most of this aristocracy were urban Sunni (see Glossary) Muslims who derived their influence from inherited wealth and social position, as well as from their early involvement in the Arab nationalist movement (see World War I, Arab Nationalism, and the French Mandate, ch. 1). Their political experience, however, was entirely based on opposition, first to Ottoman Turkey and then to France and Zionism. They had no precedent for a more positive platform of national reconciliation and integration, mass mobilization, and popular welfare.

The most prominent political organization in 1946 was the National Bloc, a loose alliance originally formed in 1928 by leading members of landowning families and other well-known individuals. This group was wealthy and well educated, chiefly at French and Turkish universities or at French- and American-operated colleges in Lebanon and Egypt. Their priority was eliminating the French while maintaining their personal power. They had little contact with the masses and did not seek to bridge the traditional gap separating the upper classes from the rest of society.

Of the various political parties forming in Syria, two had risen to prominence by mid-1947: the National Party and the People's Party. The National Party, which dominated the government until 1949, represented the industrialists of Damascus, leading businessmen, and prominent landlords. It was dedicated to continuing the power of men who had long worked together not only for independence but against union with Jordan and Iraq.

Until 1949 the People's Party was the principal opposition. It represented the interests of the merchants and landlords of Aleppo against domination by Damascus. The party had a strong interest in agricultural issues—in contrast to the National Party's focus on industry—and close ties with Iraq, with which many of the members had strong commercial and trade relationships. The two parties therefore embodied the major traditional political divisions within Syria: the rivalry between Aleppo and Damascus and that between those who favored unity with the Levant (Palestine, Lebanon, and Syria) as opposed to those who favored unity with the Fertile Crescent (Iraq, Jordan and Syria).

Along with these parties, a new party was evolving. The Baath Party can be traced to 1940, when two Damascene secondary schoolteachers, Michel Aflaq and Salah ad Din al Bitar, were inspired by the Arab renaissance movement. In 1943 the term *Baath* (meaning resurrection) became associated with the movement, and in 1944 the movement was transformed into a party. In April 1947, the Baath Party held its first congress, which was attended by around

250 members. Most were Syrians, but Jordanian, Lebanese, and Iraqi students in Syrian schools were also present. Most of the original members were students, teachers, professionals, and public employees—the kernel of Syria's emerging new middle class. The congress elected Aflaq, the party's philosopher and ideologue, as "dean," the equivalent of secretary general. Bitar became the organizational and administrative leader.

In 1947 the Baath Party was a marginal political force. It was organizationally weak and unprepared to assert itself effectively. Gradually, it broadened its constituency beyond the narrow circle of students and intellectuals to include the urban lower middle class, which was attracted to the party's proposed program of social and economic reform. At the same time, the party's unflagging emphasis on Arab nationalism evoked considerable support from the military's officer corps.

The constitution adopted by the Baath founding congress of 1947 extolled the motto of "Unity, Freedom, and Socialism" as an integrated concept, in which no one element could be attained without the other two. Of the three, however, Arab unity was considered first among equals as the primary catalyst of Arab resurrection. Socialism was not an end in itself but a means to achieve the higher ends of freedom, unity, and socioeconomic justice.

Aflaq rejected a doctrinaire definition of socialism. He maintained that his socialism aimed at more than merely equalizing wealth and providing food, shelter, and clothing; instead, it aimed at the higher goal of freeing an individual's talents and abilities. This higher goal was to be attained not through evolution but revolution, which he described as a "violent wrenching away" and an awakening and self-purification. Baath dogma exalted the individual, who was to be free in action, thought, and opportunity in a democratic, parliamentary, constitutional state.

The doctrine of a single, indivisible Arab nation was central to Baathist ideology, and statehood was regarded as parochial, negative, and doomed to failure (see Political Orientations, this ch.). Baathist doctrine condemned colonialist imperialism, which was and is held to include Zionism, negativism, restrictive state nationalism, sectarianism, and racial and ethnic prejudice. The Arab superstate envisioned by the Baathists was to be founded on a secular, rather than Islamic, framework. However, Christians and other religious minorities were admonished to regard Islam as a "beloved cultural heritage." Furthermore, religious life and values were to endure in an atmosphere of religious toleration. In foreign policy, the party advocated nonalignment with the superpowers and espoused neutrality. Aflaq and Bitar were impressed by Marxist visions of a utopian society free of exploitation but were not won over to communism, which they regarded as subservient to Soviet interests and therefore detrimental to Arab national self-determination.

In 1949 popular dissatisfaction with the performance of the conservative ruling elite reached a peak, giving the Baath Party an opportunity to play a more prominent role in Syrian politics. Army officers were angered by what they perceived as civilian bungling of the 1948 Arab-Israeli War. This anger paved the way for Brigadier General Husni az Zaim to stage Syria's first army coup d'état, an event that presaged the rise of the military as the controlling force in Syrian politics. The bloodless takeover, which was widely applauded by the press, opposition politicians, and much of the public, marked the permanent transfer of political power from the traditional landowning elite to a new coalition of young intellectuals, army officers, and the small but growing middle class. The Baath Party welcomed the coup and hoped the Zaim regime would stamp out the government's endemic corruption and usher in parliamentary politics.

However, the Zaim government did not bring stability. Rather, four more military coups were staged prior to Syria's unification with Egypt in 1958. Beneath the facade of dictatorial rule, proliferating Syrian political parties were locked in chaotic competition with the Baath Party for dominance of Syrian politics. Partisan rivalry was particularly intense for the allegiance of the armed forces, which party organizers realized would control the government. The conservative National Party and People's Party waned in influence, while the semifascist Syrian Socialist Nationalist Party (SSNP), founded in 1933 by a Lebanese Christian, Antun Saadeh, gained numerous adherents. The SSNP called for the creation of a "Greater Syria" encompassing Lebanon, Palestine, Jordan, and Cyprus. The Syrian Communist Party (SCP), headed by Khalid Bakdash, was small, but its tight organization and disciplined following gave it far greater importance than its size alone would have merited. Another party, the Arab Socialist Party (ASP), was a serious contender for the allegiance of the middle class. The ASP was founded in 1950 by Akram Hawrani as an outgrowth of the Youth Party he had established in 1939. His doctrine followed closely that of Aflaq and Bitar. Hawrani's followers were drawn mostly from Hamah and Homs; they included teachers, students, urban workers, and numerous associates organized by his relatives. In addition, he cultivated many followers in the armed forces.

In early 1953, the ASP merged with the Baath Party, combining the well-developed ideological framework of the Baath Party with Hawrani's grass-roots organizational base. No substantial changes were required in the merger except the insertion of the word *socialist* (*ishtiraki*) in the new party's name. Hawrani also found no difficulty in accepting Aflaq's 1947 constitution, which continued in toto as the scripture of Baathism, and the founding year of the Baath Party is still considered 1947.

The new Baath Party quickly became a serious challenge to all existing parties. The intense rivalry between the Baath Party and the SSNP climaxed in the April 1955 assassination of Colonel Adnan Malki, the deputy chief of staff and a leading Baathist, by a sergeant in the SSNP. Following the assassination, the SSNP was accused of plotting to overthrow the government, and its leaders either fled the country or were convicted of conspiracy. Consequently, the SSNP disappeared as an effective political force in Syria.

In 1957 the Baathists entered into a partnership with their erstwhile adversaries, the Communists, in order to crush the residual power of conservative parties. This left-wing alliance succeeded in eliminating the right wing. However, in the last months of 1957, the Communists and other radicals came to dominate the left-wing alliance, while the Baath Party's power eroded.

Fearing the Communists' growing power, the Baath Party drafted a bill in December 1957 for union between Syria and Egypt. Because Arab unity is a sacred aspiration, the Baathists knew that neither the Communists nor any other politicians could openly oppose it. In February 1958, Syria joined Egypt to form the UAR. The Baath Party realized that President Gamal Abdul Nasser's declared hostility to political parties would mean the end of its legal existence but gambled that the communist movement, which was being ruthlessly persecuted in Egypt at the time, would be damaged disproportionately.

The Baathists were partially correct. Hawrani, titular head of the Baath Party, was appointed vice president of the new republic. However, all real power resided in Nasser's hands, and Syria was governed as a virtual colony of Egypt. On September 28, 1961, a military coup took Syria out of the UAR, and in December 1961, a general election for the constituent assembly was held; Communists and Nasserites were banned from running for office. Although a few Baathists were elected, the majority of the new assembly consisted of members of the conservative People's Party and National Party. People's Party leader Nazim al Qudsi was elected president.

From 1961 to 1963, Syria was in a state of near anarchy. Coups and countercoups, street fighting between Nasserites, Communists, and Baathists, and battles between rival army factions plunged the nation into chaos.

Early in 1963, a group of senior officers conspired to stage yet another coup. To build their alliance within the military, they joined forces with a group of Baathist majors and lieutenant colonels, who turned out to be more formidable than they or anyone else realized. The original group of officers had been transferred to Egypt during the union as a form of internal exile because of their suspected opposition to the UAR. Irritated at Egyptian dominance of the union, they organized the secret Military Committee, which was dedicated to seizing power. They deviated from the Baath Party's pan-Arabism in championing Syrian nationalism. Having grown up for the most part in relatively poor rural areas of Syria, these men strongly advocated land reform and other socialist measures. Most of the committee belonged to minority groups. For example, the original core of conspirators consisted of three Alawis (see Glossary) and two Ismailis (see Glossary). Later, the Military Committee was enlarged to include fifteen members. Only six of these members were Sunni Muslims; the remainder consisted of five Alawis, two Druzes (see Glossary), and two Ismailis.

The coup, subsequently called the Baath Revolution, occurred on March 8, 1963. Baath Party cofounder Bitar was installed as prime minister, and, within several months, the Baathists had maneuvered their non-Baathist associates out of power. The Baath Party, especially its military component and its "Regional Command" as opposed to its National Command, has dominated Syria since (see The Baath Party Apparatus, this ch.).

Although the Baath Revolution was bracketed chronologically by prior and subsequent coups, countercoups, and power struggles, it was far more than another convulsion in the body politic. Rather, it marked a crucial turning point in Syria's postindependence history. Because of the coup, the focus of Syrian politics shifted markedly to the left, where it has remained since. However, just as the Baath Party became ascendant, the military officers who had commandeered it as a vehicle for their own rise to power abandoned its original egalitarian ideology by establishing a military dictatorship. In 1966 the party's cofounders, Aflaq and Bitar, were expelled from the party and exiled from Syria. Bitar, in an interview conducted several weeks before he was assassinated in Paris in July 1980, reportedly at the hands of Syrian intelligence, said "The major deviation of the Baath is having renounced democracy . . . the two real bases of the regime are dictatorship and confessionalism. The Baath Party, as a party, does not exist." Assad's November 1970 takeover of Syria in a bloodless coup—the

Syrian President
Hafiz al Assad
Courtesy Embassy of Syria

Corrective Movement—cemented Baath Party dominance in Syrian politics. Yet, as Assad created the political institutions through which he would rule, he sought to liberalize the political situation, albeit within carefully circumscribed limits, to diversify support for his new regime. For example, in February 1971 he established the People's Council as an appointed deliberative body; following adoption of the Permanent Constitution in 1973, it became an elected body.

In 1972 Assad instituted a multiparty system by creating the National Progressive Front (NPF), a coalition of the Baath Party, the SCP, and three small left-wing parties—the ASP, the Nasserite Syrian Arab Socialist Union, and the Socialist Union Movement. In 1987 this coalition continued to govern Syria with its seventeen-member Central Command, which coordinated the activities of the five parties. Although the Baath Party was unquestionably the dominant party in the coalition, and the other parties were nearly invisible, Syria remained one of the few Arab nations with multiple legal political parties.

In 1978 Assad pledged to implement a "new formula" that would rehabilitate and incorporate some of the old conservative political parties from the pre-Baath regime under the NPF umbrella. Although the new formula was never implemented because Syria was beset with internal security problems, in 1987 the NPF retained an open-ended framework that could expand to include diverse elements. Assad appeared committed to broadening his regime's support, so long as broadening did not diminish his power.

The Baath Party Apparatus

The Baath Party has never been a mass party. Although party membership has expanded considerably beyond the several hundred activists of the 1963 revolution, regime policy has kept membership relatively small. Although Aflaq and Bitar rejected communism, they intentionally emulated the Leninist organizational model of a vanguard elite. Party admission has been highly selective, particularly at higher echelons. Recruits must be nominated by a member and pass through a rigorous initiation period of at least two years before becoming members. The Baath Party has attempted to limit membership to the ideologically committed, believing that indiscriminate recruitment would dilute the party's effectiveness. In the late 1960s, for example, class origin was a determining criterion, and anyone from a class judged hostile to the party's goals, regardless of his or her personal political beliefs, was excluded.

In the Assad era, however, membership criteria were relaxed. In 1987 the Baath Party had approximately 50,000 full members and a further 200,000 candidate members in probationary status. The Baath Party administered a panoply of "popular organizations" whose membership was not exclusively, or even primarily, Baathist. Thus the party incorporated many Syrian citizens while restricting full-fledged membership.

Nominally, the highest body within the Baath Party was the National Command, whose status dated from before the party split in 1966. This twenty-one-member body was composed of about half Syrians and half Arabs from other countries, such as Lebanon, Jordan, and Iraq, as well as Palestinians. Theoretically, the National Command was the embryonic government of a future unified Arab nation, and it embodied the fiction that Syria continued to place priority on pan-Arabism. Although Syria in 1987 still paid lip service to the pan-Arab slogans that were a driving force in the party in the 1940s and 1950s, the National Command's power was more symbolic than real. Although the National Command potentially could play an evangelical role in creating new Baath Party branches in Arab countries and could support existing branches, Syrian policymakers have de-emphasized such a role. In actuality, the National Command, headed by Assad in 1987, provided honorary posts for some figures who had been retired from active Syrian political life and for others waiting in the wings to assume greater responsibility.

The actual executive core of the Baath Party was the twenty-one-member Regional Command, also headed by Assad, which directed Baath activities in Syria. Its name referred to the Baath consideration of Syria as one region within the larger Arab nation. In 1987 Syria's three vice presidents, prime minister, minister of defense, armed forces chief of staff, and speaker of the People's Council held positions on the Regional Command. The other Regional Command members were solely Baath Party functionaries, including the party secretaries of Aleppo and Hamah, and the party representatives who headed the party bureaus of higher education, trade unions, and economy.

Below the Regional Command was the Central Committee, created in January 1980 at the seventh Baath Party regional congress as a conduit for consultation and communication between the Regional Command and its subordinate local branches. At the eighth Baath Party regional congress in January 1985, the Central Committee's membership was increased from seventy-five to ninety-five. Its most important task was to elect the Regional Command, a task that had previously been the responsibility of the delegates to the regional congress meeting in plenary session. The Central Committee was also intended to represent the regional congress when the latter was not in session.

Subordinate to the Regional Command was a layer of nineteen branch commands: one in each of the thirteen provinces, one each in Damascus and Aleppo, and one in each of the country's four universities. Typically, the provincial governor, chief of police, mayor, and other local officials were members of the Branch Command, but the branch secretary and other executive posts were held by full-time party functionaries. Farther down the organizational chart, each provincial district or quarter of a city had a party organization commensurate with its size. At the grass-roots level, the party was organized into circles or cells of three to seven members, a remnant from the party's past as a secret organization. Three to seven circles in turn comprised a division, and several divisions formed a section. Each section represented a village or neighborhood.

The Regional Command and the Central Committee were elected every four years at the regional congress. Delegates of the branch organizations elected the Central Committee, which in turn elected the Regional Command. Although Assad and his intimates set the agenda and controlled results of the regional congresses, the rank and file nevertheless had an opportunity to complain and voice opinions about important national issues. During the eighth regional congress in January 1985, the 771 branch delegates expressed remarkably candid criticism of corruption and economic stagnation.

Baath Party presence in the armed forces was separate but parallel to that in the civilian apparatus. The two wings of the Baath Party joined only at the Regional Command, where both military and civilian members belonged to the Regional Command and where delegates from party organizations in military units met at regional congresses. The military wing of the Baath Party has established branches down to the battalion level. The leader of such a branch was called a *tawjihi* (political guide). Not all military officers were party members, but it was almost a prerequisite for advancement to flag rank (see Manpower, Recruitment, and Conscription, ch. 5).

Baath Party appointees included a five-member Inspection and Control Committee, selected in 1980 and charged with enforcing the statutes of the Baath Party and monitoring internal affairs, discipline, and deviation from party norms. "Deviation" was defined in the Party Security Law, passed in 1979, which imposed a prison term of between five and ten years for any party member joining another political organization or anyone infiltrating the Baath Party to work for the interests of another party. Prison terms were also set for such offenses as attacking party offices, obstructing party activities, and attempting to obtain classified party documents or confidential information. If carried out at the instigation of foreign interests, such infractions carried the death penalty.

Through its People's Organizations Bureau, the Baath Party administered a number of organizations, including its own militia, the People's Army. Other organizations were the Revolutionary Youth Organization, Union of Students, Women's Organization, Peasants' Federation, and General Federation of Trade Unions. Each organization was supervised by a member of the Regional Command; a popular organization with a large membership in a given province might have a provincial branch command responsible for its activities. These organizations inculcated Baath values in their members, provided new recruits, and extended services to various social groups.

The coming generation was carefully cultivated by the party. Indoctrination began with membership in the Vanguards, an organization for grade-school boys and girls. Vanguard members attended summer paramilitary training camps operated by the armed forces. Later, youth joined the Revolutionary Youth Organization, Union of Students, or General Federation of Trade Unions.

As befitted a party founded by teachers and that for many years recruited its members from secondary schools and universities, the

Baath Party still catered to the intellectual and educated elite. The organizational parity of party branches in universities, having student bodies of only several thousands, with party branches in provinces, having populations of hundreds of thousands, testified to this partiality. Furthermore, the Baath Party operated its own school system, the apex of which was the Higher Political Institute, which was the graduate department of political science at the University of Damascus.

Nevertheless, the party has been working assiduously for years to increase the number of peasants and workers in its ranks. In the mid-1970s, the Baath Party instituted a special mobilization campaign throughout rural agricultural areas of Syria to swell enlistment in the Peasants' Federation. It was claimed that union membership was growing by 30,000 people per year.

The Syrian Communist Party

The Syrian Communist Party (SCP), the bitter adversary of the Baath Party in the late 1950s, was in 1987 the second largest legal political party in Syria and an important constituent element of the NPF. The venerable Khalid Bakdash, a Kurd from Damascus who has been called the "dean of Arab communism," remained the SCP's secretary general. Politburo member Daniel Nimah represented the party on the Central Command of the NPF and accompanied Assad on his state visits to Moscow. In the early 1980s, the SCP was temporarily banned by Assad; however, in 1986 it was restored to favor, partially as a concession to the Soviet Union. Nine SCP members were elected to the People's Council in early 1986 elections, and the SCP held its sixth party congress in Damascus in July. During the congress, SCP Central Committee members who had precipitated the rift with Assad through strident criticism of the regime were purged from the party.

The SCP was organized like other communist parties and had a Politburo, Secretariat, Central Committee, and official publication, a magazine entitled *Nidal ash Shaab* (The People's Struggle). In the mid-1980s, the SCP stressed its political and ideological independence from the Syrian regime and operated to a limited extent as a genuine opposition party. It criticized Baath Party economic policies, refereed regime relations with the Soviet Union, and, through its Committee for Solidarity with African and Asian Nations, acted as a conduit for Syrian relations with some Third World nations.

SCP criticism of the Syrian government has been surprisingly candid. Politburo member Khalid Hammami wrote in 1984 that "Syria has abandoned its progressive socioeconomic policy" and stated that the "ruling quarters are suspicious and fearful of the masses" and curtail democratic freedoms. SCP deputy secretary general Yusuf Faysal has excoriated the "parasitic and bureaucratic bourgeoisie" in the Syrian government. However, the SCP is careful to limit its criticism to lower level Syrian politicians and more often acts as a silent partner to the Baath Party in Syrian politics.

The Power Elite

In early 1987, the Syrian government remained an autocracy in which power was concentrated in the hands of President Assad. Assad (the name means "lion" in Arabic and was chosen by Assad to replace his actual family name of Al Wahash, which means "beast") had tightened his grip in sixteen years as chief of state. Assad's leadership was legitimized through such governmental structures as the Baath Party apparatus, the People's Council, and the Council of Ministers. These institutions, however, were a veneer for military rule, and the holders of nominally important political posts rarely wielded independent power. Assad's true base of support lay in his control of key military units, various praetorian guards, and the intelligence and security services. The commando forces, bodyguards, and secret police—referred to generically by Syrian citizens as the *mukhabarat*—were instrumental in maintaining the Assad regime's power. The men Assad entrusted with command of these forces often exerted political influence disproportionate to their official positions and had a greater political voice than civilian politicians. Ultimately, however, Assad was more inclined to designate responsibility to his underlings than to delegate authority to them.

Until the mid-1980s, the Syrian power elite was composed of Assad and his family. The president's younger brother, Rifaat, commanded a division-sized praetorian guard called the Defense Companies (Saraya ad Difa), which was stationed in Damascus as a countercoup force. His older brother, Jamil al Assad, commanded a militia called the Murtada. A nephew, Adnan al Assad, commanded the Struggle Companies (Saraya as Sira), while another nephew, Fawwaz, led a security force stationed in Latakia. These commando forces were not under the command of the regular armed forces; rather, they were constructed as counterweights to the power of the regular military. Jamil was put under house arrest in 1981 after an unsuccessful challenge to his brother, and in 1984 Rifaat was exiled to Europe and his Defense Companies incorporated into the army when he likewise sought to attain power. Assad was therefore compelled to dilute the power of his family members because they posed a threat to him.

In 1987 Assad was not the apex of a pyramid of power nor had he created a hierarchical power elite below him. Rather, he relied on a coterie of about a dozen men with approximately equal power who commanded key military units or security services. In competing to protect their positions, they counterbalanced and neutralized each other. Their areas of responsibility were compartmentalized and overlapping, and they reported directly to the president rather than coordinating with their counterparts. Consequently, they could not easily build their own power bases or form coalitions that might pose a threat to Assad's rule.

This cell structure allowed Assad to retain power in Syria for an unprecedented period of time. Most of the elite group belonged to Assad's Alawi minority, and many belonged to Assad's own Numaylatillah clan and Matawirah tribe within the Alawi minority. Some were related to the president and to each other by blood or marriage, further ensuring their loyalty. Moreover, Assad reportedly had been assiduous in paying homage to the Alawi traditional tribal elders to reinforce this minority power base.

In theory, the most important men in Syria after the president were the vice presidents. However, Assad's appointment of three vice presidents in 1985 reflected the divide-and-rule strategy he applied elsewhere in the government. In order to maintain family solidarity, Rifaat al Assad was made vice president for security affairs, but by 1987, stripped of his military command, he had no real power. As a matter of protocol to symbolize the continued importance of the party, Baath Party functionary Zuhayr Mashariqa, a Sunni Muslim, was appointed vice president for party affairs. Abd al Halim Khaddam, the former foreign minister, was promoted to vice president for political and foreign affairs. Of the three vice presidents, Khaddam acted as the true deputy to Assad and was firmly ensconced in the president's inner circle. In early 1987, foreign observers tended to view Khaddam as a candidate to succeed Assad as a compromise leader.

Non-Alawis were also influential in the Assad regime. Khaddam, for example, was a Sunni Muslim (athough his wife was a Matawirah Alawi). Prime Minister Abd ar Rauf al Kassim, Speaker of the People's Council Mahmud az Zubi, Baath Party assistant secretary general Abdallah al Ahmar, and Armed Forces Chief of Staff Hikmat Shihabi were other Sunni Muslims holding high government positions in 1987. Minister of Defense Mustafa Tlas was also a Sunni Muslim, although his mother was an Alawi. Most Sunnis who had risen to prominence in the military since the Baath Revolution, including Shihabi and Tlas, had a similar background: they were born in and grew up in rural villages, rather than in

A panoramic view of the Al Mazzah district of Damascus; the presidential palace is to the right of the divided highway

Damascus or other large cities. Such men, although belonging to the nation's Sunni majority, were never members of the old privileged Sunni elite and shared a common socioeconomic class origin with the new minority elite. Assad's refusal to designate a successor was typical of his refusal to share political power. His mysterious demeanor seemed to justify his nickname, "the sphinx," which he earned while a member of the secret officers' conspiracy in Egypt in the late 1950s.

In 1980, however, Assad began to cultivate the support of members of the old Sunni Damascene elite, a class that contained many of Syria's influential technocrats, intellectuals, and merchants. He propelled some of these people into high-profile (if not powerful) positions in his government. Assad's patronage gave the Sunni elite a vested interest in accommodating itself to the new order, which helped legitimize and stabilize his regime. For example, Prime Minister Kassim is from an old Damascene family. Minister of Culture Najah al Attar is the sister of exiled Muslim Brotherhood opposition leader Issam al Attar. Because the Attar family is respected by Damascene Sunni Muslims, her appointment served to discourage the Muslim fundamentalist opposition from operating in Damascus.

Another less-known pillar of regime support was the tacit coalition of minorities that Assad had constructed. Non-Muslims such

207

as Christians and Druzes, heterodox Muslims such as Ismailis and Yazidis, and non-Arab Muslims such as Kurds and Circassians had made common cause with the Alawi minority because of the shared fear that they would be persecuted under an orthodox Sunni government. Consequently, members of such minority groups were appointed to important posts in the Assad government.

In addition to these groups, several important and influential military figures supported Assad in 1987. Major General Muhammad Khawli, chief of air force intelligence and head of the National Security Council, was Assad's right-hand man. Khawli was a Matawirah Alawi and a long-time trusted friend of Assad. His position was especially sensitive because Assad rose to power through the air force, and this service has been the breeding ground for several abortive coup attempts. Khawli's deputy, Lieutenant Colonel Haitham Sayid, was allegedly involved in sponsorship of terrorism in Europe (see Sponsorship of Terrorism, ch. 5). Ali Aslan, also a Matawirah Alawi, was deputy chief of staff of the armed forces. Aslan, a rising political star, was promoted to army corps general in 1984, a rank shared only by the minister of defense and the armed forces chief of staff. Both Khawli and Aslan were elected to the Baath Party Central Committee in 1984. Adnan Makhluf, the president's brother-in-law, commanded the Republican Guard, a presidential protection force. Other core members of the Syrian power elite in 1987 included Air Defense Commander Ali Salih and Army Intelligence Chief Ali Duba, both Alawis of the Matawirah tribe. In 1987 Duba reportedly was leader of a clique that included Army First Division Commander Ibrahim Safi and Syria's intelligence chief in Lebanon, Ghazi Kanaan; this coterie was competing for influence with a group led by Khawli and Aslan.

Members of the power elite occasionally fall from grace. After the 1984 power struggle, General Intelligence Directorate Chief Ahmad Diab, a staunch supporter of Rifaat's bid for succession, was demoted. However, Assad, pursuing his evenhanded policy, also chastised Rifaat's rivals for power; Ali Haydar, commander of the Special Forces, and commander of the army's Third Division Shafiq al Fayyad were removed from their commands as well. Rifaat al Assad was exiled to Western Europe once again in early 1986, where he remained in early 1987. These men probably could be rehabilitated and restored to rank if they proved their renewed loyalty to Assad.

In 1987 the power elite remained in a state of flux in which people were rising to power, being demoted, being rehabilitated, and forming and breaking alliances. Assad permitted and manipulated much of this maneuvering because it both revealed and dissipated the ambitions of potential rivals.

In 1987 the question of who will eventually succeed Assad as president remained open. In a 1984 interview, Assad stated that his successor would be nominated by the Baath Party and the People's Council, which constituted the "supreme legitimate authority in the country," and elected by public referendum. Although Assad has governed Syria through a power elite, his answer expressed his desire for Syria to be governed in the future by institutions rather than personalities.

Post-1982 Political Developments

In 1982 Syria neutralized nearly simultaneous foreign and domestic challenges: it maintained its dominance in Lebanon in the face of the Israeli invasion through strategic, if not tactical, victory, and it crushed the internal insurrection of Muslim Brotherhood rebels. Although the victories may have been Pyrrhic, the regime emerged in an apparently strong position.

However, just as Syria was poised to exploit its new strength and assert greater regional dominance, a new crisis threatened to topple the government. In November 1983, Assad, a diabetic, suffered a severe heart attack, complicated by phlebitis. He was hospitalized for a protracted time, and the government was essentially paralyzed. Then, fissures began to appear within the regime. The president's younger brother, Rifaat, plastered public places in Damascus with his own photograph, bearing the caption "the commander," along with photographs of the eldest Assad brother, Jamil, bearing the caption "the spiritual father." In February 1984 Rifaat, in a premature attempt to succeed his ailing brother, dispatched his Defense Companies to positions around Damascus. The Defense Companies were confronted by other military units loyal to the president: the Special Forces under the command of Haydar, the army's Third Division commanded by Fayyad, and the Republican Guard commanded by Makhluf. The two sides engaged in skirmishes, and shots were fired near the presidential palace.

In March the president recovered sufficiently to regain control of the situation. He demobilized the army units, and on March 11 he shuffled his cabinet and appointed the three vice presidents. Syria had not had a vice president since the resignation of Mahmud al Ayyubi in 1974, and the appointments were clearly aimed at defusing the struggle for succession. The vice presidents were announced in the following order: Khaddam, former minister of foreign affairs; Rifaat; and Mashariqa, deputy secretary of the Baath Party Regional Command. The minister of state for foreign affairs, Faruq Sharaa, was named minister of foreign affairs, and the governor of Damascus, Yassin Rajjuh, was appointed minister of information to replace Ahmad Iskander Ahmad, who had died. Tlas, who retained his portfolio as minister of defense, was also named deputy prime minister. The president's actions were stop-gap measures designed to disperse power among the rival contenders and to dilute his work load.

In early May, Assad suffered a relapse, and Rifaat once again attempted to seize power, surrounding radio and television broadcasting stations in Damascus and stationing surface-to-air missiles atop Mount Qasiyun overlooking the capital. Fierce street fighting broke out in the northern city of Latakia between Rifaat's Defense Companies and the Special Forces. In a week of combat, nine officers and and about 200 soldiers died. The repercussions of the clash far outweighed the number of casualties, for a miniature civil war between Alawi military units in the Alawis' home province of Al Ladhiqiyah posed a grave danger to the minority regime. Syrian opposition leaders, exiled in Western Europe and the Middle East, applauded what they believed to be the imminent downfall of the Assad regime, but, lacking a base within Syria, they were powerless to take advantage of the factional fighting.

Assad acted at first tentatively, and then more boldly, to reassert his power and restore public confidence in his regime. First, the Alawi clans held a reconciliation meeting. Then, at the end of May, Rifaat and his two chief competitors, General Haydar and General Fayyad, were dispatched first to Moscow and then to Western Europe on lengthy ''diplomatic missions.'' Around 150 lower ranking officers and officials who had played a part in the power struggle were also sent to Western Europe. On July 1, the day a semiannual round of military retirements and rotations traditionally occurs, Assad transferred to administrative positions military figures who had sided too aggressively with either camp. Also in July, *Rabitah,* Rifaat's public relations organ, was disbanded and his newspaper, *Al Fursan,* was suppressed. A month later, the Baath Party's National Command was purged of seven members loyal to Rifaat, including Suhayl Suhayl, head of the People's Organizations Bureau; foreign relations head Muhammad Haydar, head of the foreign relations section; Naji Jamil, former air force commander, who joined Rifaat's camp in Switzerland.

The president also acted to discipline the armed forces as a whole by conducting an anticorruption and antismuggling campaign. The public had long been irritated by the apparent immunity from the law of many military officers. The rampant and open smuggling across the Lebanese border was particularly visible. Assad first

A busy street in Damascus

closed down the smugglers' market in downtown Damascus, where contraband was unloaded from military trucks and sold by men in uniform. Next, several army commanders were court-martialed. Then, in another military reform, Assad began to organize a new corps structure in the armed services, a move that added a protective layer of bureaucratic insulation between the troops in the field and national-level politics (see The Regular Armed Forces, ch. 5).

Internal stability remained precarious, however, and on July 10, 1984, newly appointed Vice President Khaddam narrowly escaped an assassination attempt when a car bomb exploded near his entourage. Khaddam publicly implied that Rifaat was to blame for the attempt, and in a September interview Minister of Defense Tlas claimed that Rifaat was "persona non grata forever" in Syria, and that if he returned, he would be "shorter by a head."

Nonetheless, the president felt secure enough to invite his prodigal brother back to Syria, ending his six-month-long banishment. To bolster his reputation as a statesman, Rifaat, who had moved to Paris and established an antiregime newspaper, timed his arrival on November 26, 1984, to coincide with a visit of French president François Mitterrand. Although Rifaat returned to great fanfare, his wings had been clipped; he was stripped of command of the powerful Defense Companies. In addition, Rifaat's efforts to delegate the command to his brother-in-law, Muayyin Nassif, were blocked by President Assad, who instead appointed loyalist Hikmat

211

Ibrahim to the post. Furthermore, the Defense Companies were stripped of their organic air defense elements and several of their commando units and were eventually absorbed into the regular army as Unit 569 (see Special and Irregular Armed Forces, ch. 5).

In the wake of these chaotic events, in 1985 President Assad acted decisively to restore public faith in his government, to reassert his personal leadership, and to dispel the popular perception that he was an ailing figurehead. For example, Assad raised his public profile with a series of inspirational speeches to various university, military, and Baath Party audiences. Whereas Syria had pursued a policy of attempting to match unilaterally Israel's military capability since the 1978 Camp David Agreements between Israel and Egypt, Assad ambitiously expanded the concept of strategic parity with Israel to include the political, demographic, social, educational, economic, and military spheres.

Simultaneously, for the first time in his presidency, Assad began to promote a personality cult. Praise and panegyric for his presidency dominated the media, which compared him to President Nasser and called Assad the "new Saladin." Also, the government organized massive demonstrations in Assad's support. In one such rally, enthusiastic crowds carried his limousine through the streets of Damascus. Assad's twenty-six-year-old son, Basil, who had previously been hidden from the public spotlight, suddenly was given a higher public profile and started training to become an air force officer, leading to speculation that he was being groomed to inherit the presidency and that an Assad dynasty would be established.

To prove to Syrian citizens that the government was functioning normally, in January 1985 (after a two-year delay), the Baath Party convened its first congress since 1980. The most important item on the agenda was the election of a new Regional Command. Assad retained his position at the helm of the party, party Assistant Secretary General Abdallah al Ahmar and Vice President for Party Affairs Zuhayr Mashariqa kept the second and third slots in the hierarchy, and Vice President Abd al Halim Khaddam was put in the fourth position. Rifaat al Assad was put in the fifth position; however, three of his principal allies—one-time Interior Minister Nasir ad Din Nasir, Security Chief Ahmad Diab, and party official Ilyas al Lati—were banished from the inner circle of power; in fact, these men were the only Regional Command members not re-elected. Armed Forces Chief of Staff Hikmat Shihabi, the front man in the military's confrontation with Rifaat in 1984, remained in sixteenth place.

At the congress, Assad's keynote speech set the tone when he adhered to a hard line on Syria's regional aspirations, the

Palestinian issue, the military balance with Israel, and the Lebanese situation. Assad's emphasis on foreign affairs deflected attention from the still-turbulent domestic situation, focusing instead on undeniable Syrian successes in using its military power to attain regional political goals (see National Security Doctrine and Concerns, ch. 5). Syria's ascendant regional power was underlined by visits by regional clients, proxies, and allies, who came to Damascus to pay homage to President Assad. At the congress, George Habash, leader of the Popular Front for the Liberation of Palestine, and Khalid al Fahoum of the Palestine National Council represented the pro-Syria Palestinians. Lebanese leaders Walid Jumblatt, Nabih Berri, and Mahdi Shams ad Din were also in attendance, as was Libyan vice premier Abdul Salam Jallud.

The delegates to the congress endorsed Syria's continued military buildup, but in doing so, they faced the classic choice between guns and butter. Syria's economy was faltering under a staggering burden of military expenditure that consumed at least one-third of the budget (see Budget, ch. 3). To deal with the problem, the delegates rubber-stamped Assad's controversial initiative to modify Syria's statist approach to economic planning and liberalize the private sector. Taking their cue from Assad's crackdown on military smuggling, the delegates also voiced blunt criticism of the widespread high-level government corruption, patronage, and bribery, which hampered economic development. Such corruption was so pervasive that the Syrian government was described as a "kleptocracy." Many delegates confessed to being guilty of corruption, and a number of officials were dismissed from their posts.

There had been speculation that Assad would withdraw his candidacy or postpone his re-election when his second seven-year term expired in March. However, Assad felt enough confidence in his position to hold a referendum on February 10, 1985. Assad won approval in the yes-or-no vote by the predictable nearly unanimous total of over 99.97 percent.

In a further display of confidence, Assad announced that as a result of contacts with the Muslim Brotherhood's "vanguard organization" in Western Europe, the government had decided to pardon and grant amnesty to former members of the opposition. Accordingly, over 500 Muslim Brotherhood members were freed from Syrian prisons.

On April 8, Assad formed a new cabinet. Perhaps the most significant appointment was that of Muhammad Imadi as minister of economy and foreign trade. Because Imadi was a recognized proponent of free market economics, the Syrian private sector regarded his appointment as heralding a liberalization of Syria's planned socialist economy.

As a whole, Assad's shake-up of the Syrian power elite and his rearrangement of the military and the Baath Party effected significant changes in Syria's domestic political apparatus. Some editorials exuberantly referred to the new changes as representing a revolutionary "second corrective movement," a sequel to the Corrective Movement in 1970 when Assad first took power.

The government tried to conduct business as usual in 1986. Elections were held for the People's Council, with approximately 2 million of the 5.3 million eligible voters participating. The Baath Party won 129 of the 195 seats. The other parties in the NPF won fifty-seven seats. The SCP, which had not been represented in the previous People's Council, won nine seats. The number of women in the assembly grew from twelve to eighteen.

However, in March and April 1986, terrorist bombings in Syria shattered the tranquillity that the Assad regime had been trying to restore. These attacks, and other recurrent internal and external threats, revealed the permeability of Syria's borders and the inextricable link between Syria's internal security and its foreign policy. The relative stability in Damascus in early 1987 appeared to many Syrians to be no more than the calm at the eye of the storm.

Political Orientations

Attitudes Toward Politics, Political Parties, and Government

At gatherings in Syria, politics is often the chief topic of conversation; the Middle Eastern stereotype of fervent political coffeehouse discussions applies in part to Syria. Politics absorbs much of the active energy of the Syrian male. Most Syrians have strong opinions about what is wrong in Damascus or in their subdistrict centers and about what should be done. Urban Syrians, whether wealthy or poor, educated or illiterate, talk of political personalities and the central government. Rural Syrians talk of local political personalities, agricultural problems, and local politics. However, public criticism of the regime is muted and circumspect. Among the tribes and in more isolated villages, political discussion exists, but primarily on the basis of relations between villagers or tribes.

Political energy generally has been channeled toward clandestine opposition to the government in power and surreptitious criticism of other political forces and even other members of one's own political group, rather than toward active party participation. There are two reasons for this. First, few political parties have attempted to gain broad membership; many have been mere collections of prominent personalities without organization below the top central committees. Second, most citizens have questioned the efficacy of party activity as a means to political ends and personal advancement. The fortunes of political parties have been uncertain; some party members have been exiled or have gone to jail if the party has lost power. Consequently, persons with political ambitions often preferred to operate as independents rather than affiliate with a party.

Popular awareness of broader issues has expanded substantially in recent years as a result of radio broadcasts and the expanding press, both of which have remained under the jurisdiction of the Ministry of Information. Headed in 1987 by Yassin Rajjuh, the ministry played a key role in the dissemination of information and, through editorials, the formulation of public opinion. The ministry censored the domestic and foreign press, controlled radio and television networks, and published newspapers and magazines. It supervised the Syrian Arab News Agency (SANA), the country's only domestic news service, and the Al Baath publishing house, which printed *Al Baath,* the organ of the ruling Baath Party and the nation's most widely circulated daily newspaper, and *At Talia* (The Vanguard), the fortnightly magazine of the Baath Party. Other major dailies included *Ath Thawrah* (The Revolution), and *Tishrin* (October, named after the October 1973 Arab-Israeli War) in Damascus; *Al Jamahir al Arabiyya* (The Arab Masses) in Aleppo; and *Al Fida'* (The Sacrificer) in Hamah. The Ministry of Defense published the magazine *Jaysh ash Shaab* (The People's Army).

In Syria, individuals interested in politics have historically had limited means of expressing opinion. Often frustrated, they have seized upon the most direct means available of registering opposition: strikes, demonstrations, personal conflicts with politicians, and even, at times, violence and assassination. The method used most frequently is the demonstration, which has often led to rioting.

Industrial workers, merchants, farmers, and other groups have all used demonstrations to demand or protest government actions. Although demonstrations have not always been successful in achieving the aims of the instigators, they have served as useful barometers of public opinion. The skill of the Baath Party in initiating demonstrations was an important factor in the party's rise to power. The government has tolerated spontaneous public demonstrations, but more often it has stage-managed large public rallies in support of its policies.

Most Syrians have a strong libertarian streak and are wary of any government. This suspicion has been most pronounced in rural areas, where authority has been represented in the person of a tax

215

collector or policeman. Moreover, government officials were usually townspeople, and members of villages and tribes felt that urban officials did not understand their problems and were condescending. Government officials often contributed to this attitude by posing as patrons or masters of the rural population. Indeed, urban officials still refer to prosperous peasants as "kulaks." As a result, any government effort to assist villagers or tribesmen was apt to be met, at least initially, with an uncooperative attitude.

Although distrust of the government has been less intense in urban centers, it has existed there as well. Regional jealousies have played a part in the lack of trust. People of Aleppo, Homs, and Hamah have felt that politicians in Damascus were primarily interested in maintaining the ascendancy of the national capital over the provincial capitals. Nevertheless, townspeople attach considerable prestige to holding a government position.

After 1958 the negative attitude of townspeople and villagers toward government began to diminish as people became increasingly aware that government could be an instrument for satisfying some of their needs. Successive governments attempted to bolster this process with a constant barrage of propaganda aimed at creating trust and building loyalty, not only to the government as a social institution but to the particular regime in Damascus. The regimes appealed to citizens on the basis of economic self-interest, as well as on the broader and more emotional grounds of Arab and Syrian nationalism. The appeals found a wide and enthusiastic response, although the individual citizen incurred few obligations or duties that would test the sincerity of the response.

Concepts of Nationalism, Unity, and the Arab Nation

Because it entails definition of where the national boundaries should be drawn, nationalism is a controversial concept for Syrians. Shortly after independence, most Syrians retained a strong ethnocentrism based on the city or region where they were born and grew up; they owed their first allegiance to their tribe, clan, or ethnic group, rather than to the new nation-state. Over the years, these forces have diminished, but not disappeared, and now nearly all Syrians manifest an intense patriotism, coupled with a strong desire for the recovery of what they feel are integral areas of Syria split off from the nation by French Mandate authorities. A small minority of Syrians, however, have not been assimilated into the Syrian identity. For example, beduin in eastern Syria feel a strong affinity for their neighbors in Iraq and Jordan, and some Christians and Druzes look for guidance to their coreligionists in Lebanon.

The Syrian government has never recognized the legality of Turkey's possession of Hatay Province, which was the Syrian province of Iskenderun until it was ceded to Turkey by France in 1939. Syrian maps still describe the Syrian-Turkish frontier at Iskenderun as a "temporary border." The Syrian attitude toward Lebanon is more ambivalent: Syria officially recognizes Lebanon's de jure existence but has refused to open formal diplomatic relations. Syria feels justified in exerting hegemony over Lebanon and ensuring that it remains a Syrian satellite. In fact, since 1976 Syria has virtually annexed parts of Lebanon. Finally, Syria views the recovery of the Israeli-annexed Golan Heights as a national priority. Syrian citizens support their government's policy toward these three areas almost unanimously.

Many Syrians advocate the more far-reaching goal of restoring Greater Syria. Adherents of this concept believe Syria should encompass the entire Levant, including Lebanon, Jordan, and Israel or Palestine. The Greater Syria concept was formulated in response to a centuries-old, and now quiescent, Middle Eastern dynamic in which Iraq and Egypt traditionally vied for dominance over the Arab heartland between the Euphrates and the Nile rivers. The Syrian Socialist Nationalist Party (SSNP), which is banned in Syria but has numerous surreptitious supporters, has made the quest for a Greater Syria the cornerstone of its ideology; the SSNP also includes Cyprus as a part of Greater Syria. Although it bears the word *Syrian* in its title, the SSNP was, ironically, actually established in Lebanon and has become a Syrian proxy force in that country.

At a broader level, Baath Party ideology reflects the viewpoint of many Syrian citizens in championing pan-Arab nationalism and proposing unification of all Arab countries into one Arab nation stretching from the Atlantic Ocean to the Arabian Sea, transcending what are regarded as arbitrary and artificial borders drawn by Ottoman or European colonial rulers. However, this vision of Arab unity has not been limited to Baathists. Arab unity was the clarion call of most Arab nationalists during the struggles against European colonialism after World War I. Baathist ideology differs from this older sentiment in making socialism an integral element of pan-Arab nationalism.

Although most Syrians support pan-Arabism, some view it negatively. In many respects, the notion of pan-Arab nationalism contradicts Syrian nationalism because Syria would be subsumed in the larger entity and its identity subordinated to that of the new superstate. Aware of this paradox, Syrian officials reserve for Syria a special place in their utopian ideal as the "beating heart" of the Arab nation. However, Syrian religious minorities fear that extreme pan-Arab nationalism would entail Islamic fundamentalism because Islam is an important common denominator of many Arabs and a potential vehicle for uniting the Arab countries. Therefore, religious minorities, particularly Christians, have stridently resisted proposed unification with other Arab nations, while at the same time supporting the notion of a Greater Syria, which includes Lebanon and other areas with a large Christian population. Some minorities oppose unification; for example, Kurds and Assyrians in northeastern Syria have vivid memories of persecution in Iraq, from which they sought refuge in Syria, and naturally oppose being brought again under Iraqi jurisdiction.

Because using Islam as the defining criterion of Arabism is prejudicial to minorities, Syrians have instead emphasized the common cultural heritage of all Arabs. Specifically, the Arabic language is perceived as the root of Arab nationalism. Additionally, the nearly universal antipathy toward Zionism is another factor around which Arabs can rally, regardless of their ethnicity or religion.

This secular rather than religious emphasis has succeeded to the extent that religious minorities have often been in the forefront of Arab nationalist drives. Nevertheless, much of the appeal of Arab nationalism among uneducated or rural citizens has a strong Islamic component. Such people look to an Arab nation that re-creates the Islamic empire, or Dar al Islam, prescribed by the Quran and achieved under the Umayyad dynasty based in Damascus.

In any case, pan-Arab unity is a moot issue in Syria, an ideal rather than a practical policy. Syria's unification with Egypt in the UAR proved unpalatable to Syrian politicians. Although since 1980 Syria has been officially united with Libya and has studied merger with Jordan and Iraq, unification in these cases is simply a euphemism for what would be a regular alliance between autonomous nations elsewhere in the world. However, Syria has also been adept at wielding Arab unity as a propaganda weapon. When other Arab countries pressured Syria to improve relations with its enemy Iraq in 1986, it acquiesced in conducting negotiations but demanded complete and total unification. Iraq, as expected, rejected this proposal, giving Syria the moral high ground of appearing to favor pan-Arab unity.

Attitudes Toward Foreign Ideologies and Systems

Whatever their background, Syrians generally distrust foreigners on initial contact, although this wariness wanes over time. Syrian rejection of foreign ideologies and systems, especially those of the West, has deep historical roots. Muslim scholars divide the world into two realms: the Dar al Islam, the realm of Islam, and the Dar al Harb, the realm of warfare inhabited by infidels. It is in theory incumbent upon Muslims to convert the latter into the former, by persuasion if possible, by conquest if necessary (see Muslims, ch. 2). Moreover, Islam stipulates that Muslim nations cannot enter into peace agreements with nations of the Dar al Harb, only temporary truces, a distinction that causes disputes in translating peace treaties. Although few contemporary Syrians espouse such a categorical worldview, Syrian politicians do invoke the medieval Crusaders' invasion of the Dar al Islam to arouse nationalism and compare it to more modern European intervention in the area. Furthermore, the long periods of colonial control and exploitation of Syria by Ottoman Turks and the French are well remembered.

Indignation and a deep-seated sense of injustice are common among Syrians, who feel their country has been betrayed by European powers, which Syria, to its chagrin, must nevertheless emulate or solicit for development aid. Added to this sense of betrayal is an acute realization of Syrian's economic and social underdevelopment in comparison with modern industrialized nations, to which underdevelopment the Syrians attribute the succession of military defeats by Israel since 1948. Syrians find their country's underdevelopment is especially painful because they are aware that Syria was the ancient cradle of civilization and, during the Umayyad era, the world's preeminent empire.

These sentiments gave birth to a new, indigenous ideology of Arab renaissance and resurrection and the rejection of foreign ideologies. Although Syrian political parties were influenced by Western models, the first generation of Syrian political leaders sought to establish their nationalist credentials by dissociating themselves from French colonialism. Therefore, they avoided or denied the similarities between their new political parties and those of the West. In addition, although communism has a distinct political constituency in Syria, it is not popular among radical nationalists because of its non-Arab origin and its atheism, which offends traditionalists. However, the Soviet Union, having played little or no part in the historic reasons for the rejection of the West and having actively supported Syria and the Arab cause against Israel, is accepted as friendly, as are the East European states and China. However, Syria has attempted to adhere to a nonaligned foreign policy with regard to the East-West confrontation, and in recent years it has tempered its strident anti-Westernism with growing tolerance and pragmatic adaptation.

Foreign Policy

Regional Foreign Relations

In 1987 Syria's policy toward the superpowers and its Middle Eastern neighbors, as well as much of its domestic politics, continued to be affected profoundly by the Arab-Israeli conflict. Because of the Egyptian-Israeli Camp David Agreements, periodic Jordanian-Israeli mutual accommodation, and Israeli domination of southern Lebanon, Syria perceived itself as the last Arab confrontation state to share a border with Israel. Syria believed that the Arab-Israeli conflict had been reduced to a bilateral Syrian-Israeli conflict, in which other parties, including the Palestinians, were marginal.

Recovering the Golan Heights from Israel was the specific motive of Syria's policy, but it was only a part of a broader ambition of regional hegemony. Therefore, Syria's goal was to prevent Jordan, the Palestine Liberation Organization (PLO), or Lebanon from formalizing Syria's isolation by entering into piecemeal settlements with Israel, while Syria simultaneously undermined Egypt's separate peace with Israel. Syria has declared that the Arab nations could extract maximum concessions from Israel only by acting in concert, a policy some regional observers refer to as the "Assad Doctrine." Implicit in the Assad Doctrine is the assumption that Damascus will orchestrate Arab negotiations. Syria's central role in the Arab-Israeli conflict, therefore, is predicated to some extent on the older ideology of Greater Syria, the notion that Syria should dominate its Arab neighbors.

Syria perceived regional politics in bipolar terms, dividing the Arab world into two camps: the rejectionist front of Syrian allies, and the capitulationists who advocated concessions to Israel. However, Syria's categorical classification of the Arab world seemed only to highlight its regional isolation. Syria's only partners in the "Arab Steadfastness and Confrontation Front" were Libya, Algeria, and the People's Democratic Republic of Yemen (South Yemen).

Israel

As of 1987, Syria had successfully vetoed its neighbors' peace initiatives and constructed a credible unilateral military deterrent to Israel. It had also outlined its position on potential multilateral negotiated solutions to the Arab-Israeli conflict. Syria had accepted United Nations Security Council Resolution 338 of October 22, 1973, and indicated that such acceptance implied acceptance of Resolution 242, which was adopted after the June 1967 War. However, in 1986 Damascus suggested a willingness to negotiate only a state of "nonbelligerency" with Israel, not a comprehensive peace treaty. Whereas Resolution 242 specifically requires Arab recognition of Israel in return for Israeli withdrawal from occupied territories, Resolution 338 more generally calls for negotiations between the parties concerned "under appropriate auspices aimed at establishing a just and durable peace in the Middle East." Although Resolution 338 does, in fact, call on the parties to start implementation of Resolution 242, it does not spell out in its text Arab recognition of Israel's right to exist. Although the distinction appears to be semantic, Syria's refusal to endorse Resolution 242 without reservation remained a block to Syrian participation in Middle East peace negotiations. Syria has indicated that it would accept Resolution 242 only if Israel first withdrew from occupied Arab territory and guaranteed Palestinian rights. At the same time, some Syrian propagandists have maintained the more intransigent definition of the entire state of Israel, rather than the areas seized by Israel in the June 1967 War only, as occupied Arab territory. When the Israeli Knesset voted in December 1981 to permanently annex the Golan Heights, Syria perceived the action as a renunciation of Resolution 242 and the "land for peace" formula for resolution of the Middle East conflict. In 1987 Syria viewed Resolution 242 as a virtually obsolete framework for a settlement.

Instead, Syria advocated the implementation of the Fez Resolutions that were sponsored by Saudi Arabia at the Arab Summit at Fez, Morocco, in 1982. The Fez Resolutions demand settlement of the Arab-Israeli dispute at an international conference to be attended by representatives of all Arab governments, Israel, the PLO, and both superpowers.

Although Syria wants involvement in such diplomatic initiatives, it has increasingly less faith that a negotiated, peaceful resolution of the Middle East conflict will fulfill its demands. Accordingly, Syria has come to rely more heavily on the hope that its military will ultimately secure its objectives or, at the least, act as a credible deterrent to future Israeli aggression. The Syrian-Israeli combat in Lebanon in 1982 increased Syrian confidence in confronting Israel on the battlefield. Although the Syrian armed forces lost men and military matériel, they performed well in several crucial engagements (see Syria and the Lebanese Crisis, 1975–87, ch. 5).

Throughout 1985 and 1986, Syria and Israel engaged in brinkmanship and saber rattling, as Syria brandished its new military strength. For example, Syria deployed some of the troops it had withdrawn from Lebanon to the Golan Heights. Then, on November 19, 1985, Israel shot down two Syrian MiG-23 jets inside Syrian airspace. In December Syria retaliated by deploying mobile air defense missiles to Lebanon. Although the missiles posed an identical tactical threat to Israeli reconnaissance flights over Lebanon whether they were stationed in Syria or just across the border, Israel regarded the move as a challenge to a long-standing tacit understanding that such missiles, if located in Lebanon, would be subject to Israeli attack. Syria withdrew the missiles within several weeks after the United States interceded and mediated the dispute. On February 4, 1986, Israel intercepted and forced down a Libyan executive jet, en route from Tripoli to Damascus, which was carrying Baath Party assistant secretary general Abdallah al Ahmar and other senior Syrian politicians. Israel had ostensibly been searching for Palestinian terrorists, but Syria viewed the interception as a deliberate provocation and an act of air piracy. Finally, in May 1986, it was revealed that Syria had built revetments and entrenched fortifications in Lebanon that faced Israel. Although the construction was defensive, Israel viewed it as enhancing Syria's potentially offensive position on the Golan Heights.

To underscore Syria's increasing belligerence, in an important speech delivered to the People's Council in February 1986, Assad departed from his usually calm demeanor by declaring that Syria would work to put the Golan Heights "in the middle of Syria and not on its borders." Assad was engaging in hyperbole and exaggerating Syria's true intentions. Nevertheless, in 1987 most Syrian and Israeli officials believed that, because of the two countries' irreconcilable conflicts, the outbreak of war was inevitable in the future; some felt it to be in the distant future, while a minority, cognizant of the escalation of tensions in 1985 and 1986, believed it to be imminent.

Lebanon

Consistent with the Assad Doctrine, Syria stridently and successfully opposed the May 17, 1983, accord between Israel and Lebanon that would have normalized relations between the two countries. The February 26, 1984, withdrawal of United States Marines from Beirut, the June 1985 phased Israeli retreat from Lebanon, and the abrogation by the Lebanese government of the accord left Syria the dominant foreign power in Lebanon.

Emboldened by these victories, Syria attempted to capitalize on its position and impose a "Pax Syriana" on Lebanon. On December 28, 1985, it summoned representatives of three of Lebanon's factions—the Christians, Shias, and Druzes—to Damascus to sign the Tripartite Accord. The Tripartite Accord was essentially a new Lebanese constitution, drafted by Syria, that called for the elimination of the old confessional formula and replaced it with a new system of majority rule and minority representation. The Tripartite Accord guaranteed Lebanese sovereignty and independence. However, Chapter 4 of the accord stressed that Lebanon "must not allow itself to be the gateway through which Israel can deliver any blow to Syria" and called for "strategic integration" between Syria and Lebanon. The Syrian blueprint for Lebanon's future thus sustained Syrian suzerainty over Lebanese security affairs and sanctioned the continued deployment of Syrian troops in Lebanon. However, Syria's ambitious initiative failed when the Lebanese Christian community rebelled against the agreement and ousted Elie Hobeika, the Christian signatory.

As a result, Syria reverted to its previous policy toward Lebanon, a balancing act that it had pursued since its 1976 intervention in the civil war. The reinfiltration of PLO guerrillas into southern Lebanon and the reappearance of Israeli advisers in Christian East Beirut indicated that Lebanon was reverting to a situation similar to that before the 1982 Israeli invasion, and battle lines were being drawn for a rematch.

Jordan

The February 1985 agreement between King Hussein of Jordan and Yasir Arafat of the PLO to form a joint delegation to negotiate with Israel was anathema to Syrian policy as outlined in the Assad Doctrine. Consequently, Syria exerted strong political pressure on Jordan to change its stance. For example, observers accused Syria of unleashing dissident Palestinian terrorists of the Abu Nidal organization, which it controlled, against Jordanian targets in retaliation for Jordan's pursuit of an independent policy. Syria also spread propaganda to persuade Jordanians that their king was giving in to Israeli demands without getting concessions from Israel. Syria also convinced other Arab rulers that Jordan was treacherously dealing with Israel. Within a year, Syria seemed to have succeeded in weaning Jordan from the moderate camp and bringing it into the Syrian sphere.

The December 30, 1985, visit by King Hussein to Damascus marked the end of seven years of unremitting hostility between the two nations. In conformity with the Assad Doctrine, Jordan renounced "partial, separate, and direct talks with Israel" and issued an abject apology and admission of guilt for having harbored and supported anti-Syrian Muslim Brotherhood terrorists in the early 1980s (see Ethnic and Religious Opposition Movements, ch. 5).

223

A Palestinian refugee camp in Syria Courtesy UNRWA, photo by Sue Herrick Cranmer

The Palestinians

In another move consistent with the Assad Doctrine, Syria continued its attempts to control the Palestinian movement and to prevent any Palestinian-Israeli agreement. Accordingly, Syria sponsored the creation of the Palestine National Salvation Front, headquartered in Damascus, an umbrella organization comprising Palestinian splinter organizations that rejected any compromise with Israel. Syria supported these groups as proxy forces against Arafat's more moderate PLO, which had joined with Jordan to explore possible negotiations with Israel. In mid-1986 Syrian and PLO leaders met with inconclusive results to negotiate a reconciliation; such a rapprochement, however, would necessarily entail a return of the PLO to the rejectionist camp and its subservience to Syrian control.

Iran and Iraq

Syrian support of Iran in the Iran-Iraq War and its enmity toward Iraq was modified in 1986. The Syrian-Iranian alliance had been cemented with a March 1982 economic accord that provided for shipments of subsidized Iranian oil to Syria, at which time Syria closed Iraq's oil pipeline through Syrian territory. Syria's support for Iran was not a reflection of any ideological affinity between Assad's regime and Ayatollah Ruhollah Khomeini's Islamic fundamentalism but rather an instance of pragmatic politics. It seemed to illustrate the Arab saying that "the enemy of my enemy is my friend." Syria supported Iran because Iraq had been Syria's implacable foe for decades. Moreover, Syria's alliance with Iran allowed it to exert control over pro-Iranian Shia forces in Lebanon and use them as a proxy force to impose Syrian designs there. In supporting Iran, Syria broke ranks once again with a nearly unanimous Arab opinion favoring Iraq.

However, although Syria wanted Iraq weakened and neutralized, it did not envision the installation in Baghdad of a pro-Iranian fundamentalist Shia regime. As the beleaguered Iraqi regime lost ground to advancing Iranian forces, Assad stated in October 1986 that Syria could not accept the occupation of Iraqi land by anyone. Subsequently, Syrian and Iraqi officials met to explore the possibility of restoring relations. Assad's statement may have prompted the temporary kidnapping, the following day, of the Syrian chargé d'affaires in Tehran. Later in October, Assad met in Damascus with Iranian minister of the Revolutionary Guards Muhsin Rafiq-Dost to repair Syrian-Iranian relations. Rafiq-Dost stated that the Syrians had announced their resolute support of Iran until the downfall of the Iraqi regime and the "liberation of Iraq." However, Syria did not affirm the Iranian statement, and in early 1987, Syrian support for Iran appeared to be qualified.

Syrian–United States Relations

Over the years, United States–Syrian bilateral relations ranged between grudging mutual accommodation and outright mutual hostility. But even when the relationship was strained severely, the fundamental United States policy toward Syria with regard to the broader Arab-Israeli conflict has remained consistent. The United States endorses United Nations Security Council Resolution 242, the implementation of which would entail the return of the Israeli-annexed Golan Heights to Syrian control.

For its part, Syria has often vehemently criticized American policy in the Middle East. At the same time, however, it has recognized that Resolution 242 contains provisions in its favor. Syria has been willing to negotiate with the United States over the Arab-Israeli conflict and other regional issues, as long as the diplomacy is conducted quietly and behind the scenes. Syria has also adhered scrupulously to the commitments and promises it has made to American negotiators.

Since the administration of President Dwight D. Eisenhower in the 1950s, the United States has strongly supported Israel but has simultaneously indicated, particularly after the October 1973 War, that it acknowledges the legitimacy of some of Syria's grievances against Israel. In the aftermath of Israel's attack on Syrian forces in Lebanon in 1982, the United States was forced to choose between irreconcilable Israeli and Syrian ambitions in Lebanon; the administration of Ronald Reagan chose to endorse the Israeli position. President Reagan supported the May 17, 1983, Lebanese-Israeli accords and linked this peace treaty to his attempts to revive the Arab-Israeli peace process. However, Syria stymied the Reagan initiative, in part by inciting opposition to American policies among its surrogates and proxies in Lebanon. The United States also suspected Syria of having played a role in attacks on the United States Embassy and on the Marine barracks in Beirut. Although the degree of Syrian complicity was never determined, American officials believed that Syria at least had foreknowledge of and acquiesced in the attacks (see Sponsorship of Terrorism, ch. 5). Syrian–United States relations reached their nadir in December 1983, when the two nations engaged in near warfare. On December 4, United States carrier-based warplanes attacked Syrian antiaircraft installations in Lebanon's Biqa Valley (two were shot down), and on December 13 and 14, United States battleships shelled Syrian positions. From a military viewpoint, the clashes were not highly significant. However, they marked the first American-Syrian armed conflict and reinforced Syria's view of the United States regional policy as gunboat diplomacy.

In June 1985, Syrian–United States relations improved dramatically when Syria interceded on behalf of the United States after the hijacking to Beirut of Trans World Airlines flight 847. Reagan expressed his appreciation of Syria's role in securing release of the hostages, albeit in guarded language. Yet to some observers Syria's ability to impose its will on the hijackers confirmed Syrian links to terrorism. Although Syria had been accused repeatedly of supporting Palestinian terrorism against American, West European, and Israeli targets in the Middle East and in Western Europe, there had been little evidence, much less proof, of direct Syrian complicity in terrorist attacks against Western targets.

However, when a Jordanian, Nizar Hindawi, was apprehended on April 17, 1986, after attempting to smuggle a bomb aboard an Israeli El Al Airlines plane in London, he confessed that Syrian intelligence officers had masterminded the abortive attack and that Syria had provided him with the training, logistical support, and explosives to carry out the plot. Britain reportedly collected evidence that corroborated Hindawi's story. As a consequence, on May 6, 1986, Vice President George Bush said of Syria, ''We are convinced their fingerprints have been on international terrorist acts,'' and on November 14, 1986, the United States imposed sanctions on Syria ''in response to Syria's continued support for international terrorism.'' The White House, however, also stated that ''Syria can play an important role in a key region of the world, but it cannot expect to be accepted as a responsible power or treated as one as long as it continues to use terrorism as an instrument of its foreign policy.''

In these statements, the United States censured Syria for sponsoring terrorism but also implied recognition of Syria's potentially central role in the Middle East. Ever since Secretary of State Henry Kissinger's first visit to Damascus in December 1973, Assad has attempted to persuade successive American administrations of the truth of the old adage ''There can be no war in the Middle East without Egypt, but there can be no peace in the Middle East without Syria.'' Assad sought to convince the United States that Syria, however intransigent its negotiating stance, should not be ignored in any comprehensive Middle East peace treaty because it could resume war with Israel and therefore exert veto power over an Arab-Israeli settlement. At the same time, however, Assad was convinced that the United States was indispensable in any Middle East peace because only the United States could force Israel to make concessions to the Arabs.

Syrian-Soviet Relations

In 1987 the relationship between Syria and the Soviet Union appeared to be close and deep. Syria was clearly favored among Soviet client states in the Third World. For over twenty years, Syria had obtained most of its military equipment from the Soviet Union. In addition, there was a large Soviet military presence in Syria; by mid-1984 there were an estimated 13,000 Soviet and East European advisers in Syria. However, many of these advisers were withdrawn in 1985 during a dispute so that in 1986 between 2,000 and 5,000 remained.

Syrian-Soviet relations were upgraded and formalized in the Treaty of Friendship and Cooperation signed by Assad in Moscow in October 1980. The treaty runs for twenty years and has automatic five-year extensions, unless one of the parties terminates the agreement. It provides for regular consultations on bilateral and multilateral issues of interest, coordination of responses in the event of a crisis, and military cooperation.

A secret protocol to the treaty reputedly details Soviet military obligations to Syria and may mandate the dispatch of Soviet troops to Syria in case of an Israeli invasion. Syrian defense minister Tlas warned in 1984 that the Soviet Union would dispatch two Soviet airborne divisions to Syria within eight hours in the event of a conflict with Israel. Tlas has also stated that the Soviet Union would use nuclear weapons to protect Syria. Tlas' statements, however, were not endorsed by the Soviet Union. Syrian-Soviet nuclear cooperation is limited to a February 1983 agreement for cooperation and exchange for peaceful purposes.

Although the Syrian-Soviet relationship is close, Syria is not a Soviet proxy, and the Soviet Union has gained little leverage over Syrian domestic and regional policy in return for its military support. Although Syria may be aligned with the Soviet Union, its basic orientation is toward the West. Syrian leaders have little affinity with communism, and Moscow has been powerless to prevent Syrian repression of the SCP. Syria's pursuit of independent policies has caused considerable friction with the Soviet Union. Examples of Syrian intransigence include its 1983 rebuff of Soviet requests for a naval base at the port of Tartus and its deviation from Moscow with regard to the Palestinian issue.

Former Soviet leader Yuri Andropov appeared to be a staunch advocate of Syria, and the Soviet Union acquiesced to many of Syria's demands. However, after Mikhail Gorbachev succeeded Konstantin Chernenko in March 1985, the Soviet Union reassessed its relationship with Syria. Assad made a brief visit to Moscow in May 1985 and restated Syria's plea for a stronger Soviet military commitment. However, the Soviet leadership reprimanded him for Syria's hostility toward the PLO and Iraq and reminded him that Syria was not its only Middle Eastern ally. In June 1985, Assad again met Gorbachev in Moscow to debate the Palestinian issue, but there was no resolution. Shortly thereafter, the Soviets withdrew a significant number of their military advisers from Syria. In early 1987, it was not known whether Assad expelled the Soviet advisers in retaliation for his cold reception in Moscow or whether the withdrawal occurred at Soviet behest; however, the strain in relations was clear. Syria's persistent refusal to accede to Soviet desires regarding the PLO was becoming a test case of the relative power of the patron state and its client. At the same time, the Soviet Union could not afford to appear to abandon Syria.

In May 1986, Gorbachev renewed Soviet promises to supply Syria with military equipment and excoriated Israeli and American pressure on Syria. Yet Gorbachev, unlike his predecessors, appeared prepared to pressure Syria for concessions in return for Soviet military aid. Gorbachev expected Syria to support his embryonic new agenda for the Middle East, which revived the

long-standing Soviet plan for an international Middle East peace
conference attended by all parties, including Israel.

*   *   *

Most information on Syria is fragmentary or impressionistic.
Moreover, primary source material is in Arabic, although much
of it has been translated by the United States Joint Publications
Research Service. Scholarly books on Syrian internal politics are
few, and although journalistic accounts are more numerous, they
generally focus on Syrian foreign policy. However, published
materials have increased in the 1980s and provide an adequate basis
for an informed understanding of the country. Because Syria's high
profile in Middle Eastern events has sparked renewed scholarly
interest in the country, a considerable number of new books about
Syria are due for publication in 1987 and 1988. For those interested
in gaining further insight into Syria politics, the following works
offer varied and broad perspectives: *Syria: Modern State in an Ancient
Land* by John F. Devlin; *Syria under Assad,* an anthology edited by
Moshe Ma'oz and Avner Yaniv; *The Islamic Struggle in Syria* by Umar
F. Abd-Allah; *Linkage Politics in the Middle East: Syria Between Domestic
and External Conflict, 1961–1970* by Yaacov Bar-Simon-Tov; *The
Ba'ath and Syria, 1947–1982: The Evolution of Ideology, Party, and State*
by Robert W. Olson; and the chapter on Syria by Yosef Olmert
in the annual *Middle East Contemporary Survey.* Also of interest are
*The Struggle for Power in Syria: Sectarianism, Regionalism, and Tribal-
ism in Politics, 1961–1978* by Nikolaos Van Dam; *Political Participation under Military Regimes* by Gabriel Ben-Dor; "Domestic/External
Linkages: Syria, 1961–1967" by Robert Burrowes and Gerald
DeMaio; "Syria under Asad, 1970–78: The Centers of Power,"
both by Adeed I. Dawisha; *The Ba'th Party: A History from Its Origins to 1966* by John F. Devlin; "Syria and the Baath Party" by
John Galvani; the Syria section in George M. Haddad's *Revolutions and Military Rule in the Middle East: The Arab States, II, Part I.
Iraq, Syria, Lebanon, and Jordan; Political Organization in Syria: A Case
of Mobilization Politics* by Raymond A. Hinnebusch; *Arab Politics:
The Search for Legitimacy* by Michael C. Hudson; and "Society and
State in Modern Syria" by Moshe Ma'oz.

In addition, readers are referred to Ted Morgan's "The Wild
Men Become a Nation"; Tabitha Petran's seminal work *Syria*;
Itamar Rabinovitch's insightful *Syria under the Baath, 1963–66: The
Army-Party Symbiosis*; Gordon H. Torrey's informed observations
on "Aspects of the Political Elites in Syria," as well as his "The
Ba'th—Ideology and Practice"; P. J. Vatikiotis's analysis of "The

Politics of the Fertile Crescent''; and Labib Zuwiyya Yamak's highly regarded *The Syrian Social Nationalist Party: An Ideological Analysis.* (For further information and complete citations, see Bibliography.)

Chapter 5. National Security

Lion-headed eagle pendant, Tall Hariri

IN EARLY 1987, Syrian national security encompassed a wide range of issues. Military and political problems were created by the deployment of around 25,000 troops to Lebanon and by Syria's ambitious attempt to attain strategic parity with Israel. Whether President Hafiz al Assad and his primarily Alawi civilian and military advisers would be able to maintain Syria's unprecedented period of continuous political rule was a further consideration. During the 1980s, the Syrian armed forces gained greater manpower, equipment, and operational capability, but this improvement in quantity was not matched in quality. The quality of Syria's forces remained an important national security consideration because the Syrian military, after having suffered defeat and loss to Israel of the Golan Heights in the June 1967 War, had faced difficult battles in the October 1973 War and in the 1982 Lebanon War. As of 1987, prospects for future Syrian-Israeli hostility had not lessened.

As part of Syria's quest to improve its armed forces, in 1987 the Soviet Union continued large shipments of military equipment, including some of the most modern items in the Soviet arsenal. However, financial and military aid from traditional Arab sources declined, primarily because of the fall in Arab oil revenues. Decreased aid was also caused by Syria's increasingly confrontational role in regional affairs, including its support of Iran in the Iran-Iraq War and its association with the radical Shia groups that have emerged as a threat to the stability of Muslim Arab regimes. Syria's continued presence in the Lebanese quagmire further contributed to diminished Arab assistance. Moreover, Syria's "peace-keeping mission" in Lebanon, to which the Arab states had agreed, had grown detrimental to the morale of its armed forces and had weakened Syria's defensive and offensive capability vis-à-vis its principal enemy, Israel.

However, in early 1987, Syria's perception of threats to its national security extended beyond Israel. To the east, Iraq remained a rival for ideological leadership and political power within the Baath movement. For many years, the two countries had been embroiled in vitriolic propaganda warfare and internal subversion, and, with the outbreak of the Iran-Iraq War in 1980, Syria actively supported Iran. To the west, the government perceived as a threat the emergence in Lebanon of either a radical Muslim state or a Christian-dominated state aligned with Israel.

Major internal threats included sectarian rivalry within Syria's many communities. Syria's long history of coups d'état also caused concern to a government that had itself achieved power in November 1970 through a military coup. Fear of a coup was demonstrated by maintenance of powerful internal security services and a praetorian guard.

Because of the ever-present threats to Syria's national security, both domestic and external, and its ties to the Soviet Union, information about Syria's military and police affairs was severely limited. However, national security concerns, which have played a central role since Syrian independence in 1946, clearly pervaded the society and its economic and political activities.

National Security Doctrine and Concerns

Under Assad, Syria has sought to be a leading Arab and regional power, capable of controlling or influencing Lebanon, Jordan, and the Palestinians. Syria seeks to participate in every issue in the region and to further policies that substantiate its claim to an effective regional role. In pursuing these objectives, Syria is striving for regional hegemony—a goal that ultimately is likely to go beyond Syria's capabilities and resources. In fact, according to various analysts, Syria's pursuit of this goal will undermine its precarious stability.

Syria also has striven to lead the Arab resistance to Israel and to oppose, both militarily and politically, the path leading to diplomatic recognition of Israel's legitimacy, to which Egypt agreed through the Camp David Agreements (see Foreign Policy, ch. 4). In pursuit of its goals, the Syrian regime formulated the doctrine of "strategic parity" with Israel, which involved upgrading the country's military capability and matériel to give it an edge in a future confrontation.

Regionally, Syria was intent on achieving a number of military and political objectives. These included the reconquest of the Golan Heights (in early 1987 it had deployed a force of about six divisions in the Damascus-Golan Heights region) and opposition to the establishment of an Israeli-dominated "security zone" (manned largely by the Christian forces of the pro-Israel South Lebanon Army) in southern Lebanon. Syria also sought to control Lebanese affairs and to restrict the presence of the Palestine Liberation Organization (PLO) military forces in Lebanon without formally annexing territory or having to maintain a large military presence there.

As part of its national security doctrine, Syria has sought to expand its relationship with the Soviet Union, as embodied in the

1980 Treaty of Friendship and Cooperation. Specifically, Syria endeavored to formalize the relationship with a "strategic cooperation" agreement comparable to the treaty between the United States and Israel.

Syria also employed terrorism in pursuit of its security objectives. In the mid-1980s, Syria was accused—primarily by the United States and the United Kingdom—of playing an active role in international terrorist activities through sponsorship of Palestinian, Lebanese, and other Arab terrorist groups. Furthermore, Syria had been directly implicated in a series of terrorist attacks on American, West European, Israeli, Jewish, Palestinian, Jordanian, and Turkish targets outside the Middle East.

Syria and the Middle East Conflict
Historical Background

For more than 4,000 years, the area known as Syria has been populated by successive waves of Semitic peoples, including nomadic tribes. It has also been a battleground for myriad conquerors, including Akkadians, Assyrians, Hittites, Babylonians, Egyptians, Persians, Macedonian Greeks, Romans, Byzantines, Arabs, European Crusaders, Kurds, Ottomans, and the French. Countless dynasties, whether local or foreign, have ruled the area. From the time of the Arab conquest in the seventh century A.D. until it became part of the Ottoman Empire in the sixteenth century, the region was repeatedly invaded, occupied, merged, and fragmented. Syrian armed units were formed under the Umayyad caliphate during the eighth century A.D. and for the next years played an important role in the Arab campaign against the Byzantine Empire.

Under Ottoman rule, which ended in 1916, Syrians were regularly conscripted into the empire's forces or pressed into service in the armies of contending local chieftains (see Ottoman Empire, ch. 1). Syrians fought on one side or the other, but without a sense of national purpose. These centuries of foreign subjugation, combined with political and social fragmentation, provided scant grounds for the development of a national military tradition; new generations learned regional consciousness or gave their allegiance to tribe, clan, or village.

The Arab inhabitants of the provinces of historical Greater Syria (see Glossary) took part in World War I. When the Ottoman Empire allied itself with Germany and Austria-Hungary, new opportunities opened up for the Arabs, and some came to the defense of the Ottoman Empire. Others, as in the case of the small semisecret societies operating in Syria, which advocated various forms of Arab nationalism, and the Arabs from the Hejaz, opposed the Ottomans.

The Arab revolt in the Hejaz, headed by the ruling Hashimite family of Mecca, occurred in 1916. A number of Syrians served in the forces advised by T.E. Lawrence and other Britons during the revolt and also in the Eastern Legion (La Legion d'Orient), a French-organized unit. The revolt did not lead to a major uprising in Syria, but, in 1916, when the Ottoman Empire collapsed and Syria was conquered by the Allies, Arab troops commanded by Prince Faysal, son of Sharif Husayn of Mecca, entered Damascus and were greeted warmly by the local population. Prince Faysal proclaimed himself king of Syria in 1918, but his reign was short (1918–20). Faysal had been supported by officers of the Arab Army from the Hejaz, former Ottoman officers, and local Syrian nationalists. However, there were many conflicts among these diverse groups. Following their defeat by the French (and the intervention of Britain, which compensated the Hashimites for their loss of Syria by giving them Transjordan and Iraq), the French Mandate was established in Syria (and Lebanon) in April 1920, and a volunteer Arab force was formed to maintain internal order (see World War I, Arab Nationalism, and the French Mandate, ch. 1).

Development of the Syrian Military

The French Mandate volunteer force formed in 1920 was established with the threat of Syrian-Arab nationalism in mind. Although the unit's officers were originally all French, it was, in effect, the first indigenous modern Syrian army. In 1925 the unit was designated the Levantine Special Forces (Troupes Spéciales du Levant). In 1941 the force participated in a futile resistance to the British and Free French invasion that ousted the Vichy French from Syria. After the Allied takeover, the army came under the control of the Free French and was designated the Levantine Forces (Troupes du Levant).

French Mandate authorities maintained a gendarmerie to police Syria's vast rural areas. This paramilitary force was used to combat criminals and political foes of the French Mandate government. As with the Levantine Special Forces, French officers held the top posts, but as Syrian independence approached, the ranks below major were gradually filled by Syrian officers who had graduated from the Military Academy at Homs, which had been established by the French during the 1930s. In 1938 the Levantine Special Forces numbered around 10,000 men and 306 officers (of whom 88 were French, mainly in the higher ranks). A majority of the

Syrian troops were of rural background and minority ethnic origin, mainly Alawis (see Glossary), Druzes (see Glossary), Kurds, and Circassians. By the end of 1945, the army numbered about 5,000 and the gendarmerie some 3,500. In April 1946, the last French officers left Syria; the Levantine Forces then became the regular armed forces of the newly independent state and grew rapidly to about 12,000 by the time of the 1948 Arab-Israeli War, the first of four Arab-Israeli wars between 1948 and 1986 (not counting the 1982 Israeli invasion of Lebanon).

The air force was formed in 1948 on the graduation of the first class of Syrian pilots from British flight schools. Two years later, with the procurement of a few naval craft from France, a small navy was established, using army personnel that had been sent to French academies for naval training.

French Mandate authorities were thus responsible for the initial development of Syria's armed forces, but by the mid-1940s, for a variety of reasons, Syrians had developed a profound distrust of the French in particular and Western Europeans in general. The growth of pan-Arabism throughout much of the Arab world, including Syria, during the interwar years paralleled the feelings of anti-Westernism that were growing in the region.

Syrian-Israeli Hostility

Support for Greater Syria, opposition to Jewish settlement in Palestine, and the 1917 Balfour Declaration in which Britain promised Jews a "national home" in Palestine (as part of the World War I promises to the Arabs and Jews) contributed to the growth of pan-Arabism as well as to the opposition to recognizing Israel as a legitimate Middle Eastern nation (see World War II and Independence, ch. 1). The November 1947 United Nations (UN) declaration calling for partition of Palestine into Jewish and Arab states provoked a general strike in Damascus and major rioting throughout Syria. In addition, armed bands of irregulars from Syria's fledgling armed forces began to raid Jewish settlements near the Syrian border.

In February 1948, Syria signed the League of Arab States (Arab League) political and military alliance, under which King Abdullah of Transjordan was appointed commander in chief of the invading armies. On May 16, 1948, one day after the declaration of Israeli independence, Syrian armed forces, as part of the Arab forces, attacked Israel near Lake Tiberias (Sea of Galilee) from the Golan Heights. Syria's leaders, as well as the leaders of other Arab League states that simultaneously invaded Israel, expected a swift Arab victory. The Syrian forces numbered 8,000 troops, in two

A war memorial in a cemetery near As Suwayda

infantry brigades with a mechanized battalion of French-built tanks, and a small air force. Although General Taha al Hashimi of Iraq was the figurehead leader of the Arab Liberation Army, its real leader was a former Syrian officer of the Ottoman Turkish Army, Fawzi al Kaukji (who had been a leader of the Arab irregulars during the 1936 revolt in Palestine and had led the Arab guerrilla forces based around Nablus). Arab forces were equipped with modern weapons (such as tanks, armored cars, artillery, and aircraft support) and trained by European instructors attached to Transjordan's Arab Legion, but they lacked an effective central command. The Israeli forces, on the other hand, became a coordinated fighting force under their outstanding and committed leadership.

By October 31, following its defeat, Syria's war along Israel's northern borders had ended, although the war continued along Israel's southern front. The Arab forces were stunned by the effective Israeli resistance and the incompetence of the Arab armies, both factors having become apparent after only ten days' fighting. By June 11, when the UN imposed a truce, the Syrians had been pushed back across their frontier in all but two small border areas. Sporadic fighting continued, however, until the Syrian-Israeli armistice agreement, signed on July 20, 1949.

Although Syria lost no territory in its first confrontation with Israel, the war had a profound effect on newly independent Syria. Revelations of corruption and profiteering and the incompetence of Syria's civilian political leaders were seized upon by military officers as an excuse for Syria's debacle in the war. In addition, the presence in Syria of around 100,000 Palestinian Arabs who had fled Israel during and after the war compounded the country's economic and social problems and initiated what would remain, four decades later, one of the central exacerbating issues in the Middle East and the Arab-Israeli conflict.

Political and economic discontent led to widespread rioting. On March 30, 1949, Husni az Zaim, commander in chief of the army, led the first of many Syrian coups d'état to restore political order and the supremacy of the armed forces. Such coups would punctuate Syrian politics for over two decades.

The 1949 Syrian-Israeli armistice agreement contained numerous clauses that were interpreted differently by Israel and Syria, leading to ambiguities over such issues as administrative rights within the demilitarized zone that had been created from areas evacuated by the Syrian Army in 1949, fishing rights in Lake Tiberias, and access to the waters of the Jordan River. These and other issues were constant sources of tension between the two countries, leading to localized exchanges of artillery and rocket fire, which escalated on December 11, 1955, into an Israeli raid on Syrian forces in which fifty Syrian troops were killed. Syria did not fight in the 1956 Sinai campaign, although it was a member of the Unified Military Command established in October 1956 among Egypt, Syria, and Jordan. Israel's victory in that war intensified Syria's determination to confront Israel militarily and was a factor in establishing the Syrian-Egyptian union of 1958-61. The stationing of the United Nations Emergency Force (UNEF) in Gaza and Sharm ash Shaykh following Israel's withdrawal in 1957 meant that the Syrian-Israeli front now became the most important source of confrontation between the Arab states and Israel, leading to armed skirmishes, such as the Tawafiq raid by Israel of February 1, 1960.

On May 17, 1967, President Gamal Abdul Nasser of Egypt forced the UNEF to withdraw from the Sinai Peninsula and the Gaza Strip, where it had been engaged in peacekeeping functions since the 1956 Suez War. Then, on May 22, Egypt announced a blockade against Israeli shipping in the Strait of Tiran (at the southern tip of the Sinai Peninsula). Contingents arrived in Syria from other Arab countries, including Kuwait and Algeria, and Israel was soon surrounded by an Arab force of 250,000 troops, over 2,000 tanks, and some 700 fighter and bomber aircraft. Strategically, Israel faced a military offensive on its border with Egypt, Jordan, and Syria.

Against this background of mobilization, Israeli leaders began planning a preemptive strike against the Arabs. The attack came on the morning of June 5 as the Israeli Air Force bombed military airfields and engaged in aerial battles with Egypt, Jordan, and Syria. In the fight, Syria lost thirty-two MiG-21s, twenty-three MiG-15 and MiG-17 fighters, and two Ilyushin Il-28 bombers—two-thirds of its total air inventory. To Egyptian dismay, no major move of Syrian ground forces occurred, although Syrian cooperation had been a major consideration in Egypt's mobilization and deployment in the Sinai. Although it issued belligerent communiqués, the Syrian leadership's behavior was very restrained. At the beginning of the war, the Syrian Air Force mounted an attack against Israeli oil refineries in Haifa, but the Israeli Air Force retaliated and destroyed the bulk of what remained of Syria's aircraft. Syrian artillery kept up a steady bombardment of the Israeli forces in eastern Galilee, while the rest of the Israeli forces were deployed along the Egyptian and Jordanian fronts. Despite Jordanian pleas for reinforcements, no Syrian troops had been deployed in Jordan by the end of the war.

After defeating the Egyptian and Jordanian armies, Israel turned to the Syrian front to end Syrian harassment of Israeli border settlements from the Golan Heights. The Israeli Northern Command attack came on June 9 in an armored and infantry assault following Israeli Air Force strikes that systematically reduced Syrian forward positions. On June 10, the Syrian forces collapsed and, despite their previous geographic and tactical advantages, fled, abandoning tanks. After about thirty hours of fighting, the Israeli armed forces occupied about 1,150 square kilometers of Syrian territory on the Golan Heights. An estimated 2,500 Syrian troops were killed, and around 100,000 civilians were uprooted from their homes in the Golan Heights during and after the hostilities.

The Syrian armed forces' poor showing in 1967 has been attributed to negligence, lack of overall coordination, and poor high-level command. Observers considered the failure the result of Syria's twenty-year military tradition of politicization at the expense of professionalization.

The 1967 defeat also led to increased support for irregular Palestinian guerrilla forces that, in 1964, had been formally united under the banner of the PLO. Syria was the major Arab supporter of the PLO immediately after the June 1967 War, although this relationship was often marked by violent conflict and upheaval. Syria formed As Saiqa (The Thunderbolt), theoretically a guerrilla unit under the aegis of the PLO but aligned politically with the Baath (Arab Socialist Resurrection) Party and manned largely by

Palestinian volunteers from the Syrian Army (see Special and Irregular Armed Forces, this ch.).

Between 1968 and 1970, the PLO operated against Israel from Jordanian territory, on occasion supported by Jordanian units. Israel conducted some major reprisals, notably the Karameh Operation of March 21, 1968. The PLO created a virtual "state within a state" in Jordan, even organizing an assassination attempt against King Hussein, whose regime felt increasingly threatened by the PLO's activity. In response, Hussein launched an all-out attack on PLO forces in August and September 1970. The latter, Black September, was a bloody eleven-day civil war between Jordanian troops and PLO commandos backed by Syrian armored units that invaded Jordan. As the Syrian invasion developed and the Jordanian Army strove to resist it, Syria and the Soviet Union received unequivocal indications that neither the United States nor Israel would view with equanimity a Syrian invasion of Jordan. Israeli mobilization and American troop, fleet, and air activities led the Soviets to advise the Syrians to pull back. The Syrian invasion of Jordan also caused political strife within Syria. Two months later, the minister of defense, General Hafiz al Assad, who had strongly opposed Syrian involvement in Jordan, assumed the presidency of Syria in a bloodless coup d'état.

Clashes between PLO units and the Jordanian Army continued throughout 1971, but most of the surviving PLO fighters left Jordan for Syria. Syria's new leadership supported the goal of "the restoration of the national and legal rights of Palestinian Arabs" but was ambivalent about the presence of the potentially subversive Palestinians and placed severe restrictions on their activities. As a result, the majority moved to Lebanon.

Another major foreign policy goal was the recovery of Syrian territory on the Golan Heights, occupied by Israel in 1967 and annexed in 1981 (see Foreign Policy, ch. 4). The October 1973 War (known in the Arab world as the Ramadan War and in Israel as the Yom Kippur War) was principally a result of Syria's pursuit of this second goal, which coincided with Egypt's desire to recover the Suez Canal, the Sinai Peninsula, and the Gaza Strip, also taken by Israel in 1967. Other intricacies of Arab politics, including President Assad's desire to end Syria's traditional isolation in the Arab world (and ultimately to attain regional hegemony), also played a part. The International Institute for Strategic Studies, noting the wave of riots by workers and students in Egypt in 1972 and 1973 and Sunni Muslim protests in Syria in early 1973, argued that "The very [political] weakness of Sadat and Assad were important factors in the decision to launch war on Israel."

By 1973 Syria's post-1967 effort to increase the professionalism of its armed forces, largely through the aid of the Soviet Union and Czechoslovakia, had borne fruit. Syrian military leaders felt self-confident and believed that their superpower ally would lend considerable weight in the event of renewed war with Israel. From mid-1973 until the beginning of hostilities, Arab leaders met frequently to plan the coordinated offensive, and Syrian and Egyptian army units began massing along their respective borders during the last days of September. However, Israeli intelligence, military, and political officials misinterpreted these deployments. When the Syrian-Egyptian offensive was launched on October 6 at 2:00 P.M. on Yom Kippur, Judaism's holiest day, 5 Syrian divisions, consisting of some 45,000 men, moved against only 2 Israeli armored brigades of about 4,500 men stationed on the Golan Heights.

The timing, no doubt deliberate on Syria's part, in fact had a different effect than intended. Because most Israelis were either at their synagogues or at home, the roads were clear, and troops could be rushed to the border. Nevertheless, for some twenty-three hours, Syrian forces held the offensive, almost reaching the encampment overlooking the Jordan River Valley at the southern edge of the Golan Heights region, but making little headway beyond the 1967 cease-fire line in the north. About 1,800 Moroccan troops held the peak of strategic Mount Hermon near the common Syrian, Israeli, and Lebanese border. In the central region, Syria recaptured Al Qunaytirah. But reinforced Israeli troops launched successful counterattacks on October 8 and 9 and had pushed Syrian troops back behind the 1967 lines by October 10. Two Iraqi mechanized divisions, a Jordanian armored brigade, and a Saudi Arabian detachment had joined the Syrian offensive line east of Saassa, less than forty kilometers from Damascus, by October 14. To its credit, this Arab defense line held for three days of fierce fighting.

During the war, Syria deployed vast numbers of Soviet-made surface-to-surface missiles. Between October 7 and October 9, several of these hit populated areas in northern Israel. As the Israeli ground forces advanced into Syria, the Israeli Air Force destroyed part of the Syrian missile system, vital oil installations, power plants, bridges, and port facilities at Tartus, Baniyas, and Latakia.

Syria finally accepted the UN cease-fire on October 24, but sporadic fighting continued on the Golan Heights until the disengagement agreement of March 31, 1974. In all, the war was extremely costly to Syria. An estimated 7,000 troops were killed and 21,000 wounded; 600 tanks, 165 fighter aircraft, and 7 naval vessels were destroyed or lost. An additional 845 square kilometers of territory was lost, and much vital economic infrastructure was destroyed.

Syria, however, counted several victories. First, Syria's six years of struggle to professionalize the armed forces paid off when Syrian forces revealed great improvement in battle. In addition, Soviet airlifts and sealifts of military equipment during the hostilities demonstrated the importance of Syria's military relationship with the Soviet Union (see Foreign Influences in the Development of the Armed Forces, this ch.). Also, for the first time in the twenty-five-year-old Arab-Israeli conflict, there had been effective coordination of Arab armies. Finally, under the terms of the disengagement agreement, Israel withdrew from all freshly captured territory and also from a narrow strip of territory, held since 1967 and including Al Qunaytirah, which was incorporated into a demilitarized zone policed by the 1,200-member United Nations Disengagement Observer Force (UNDOF).

Syria's next engagement with Israel was an outgrowth of its aspirations toward regional hegemony, especially with regard to Lebanon. On June 6, 1982, Israel launched Operation "Peace for Galilee," a campaign intended to establish a security zone north of the Lebanese border, a distance of some forty kilometers that would be free of hostile Palestinian and Shia elements. However, this official intention was soon transformed into an overarching strategic plan for a three-pronged attack: one along the coastal plain to destroy the PLO military infrastructure; a central advance to reach the Damascus-Beirut road and establish a presence there; and a third to turn eastward along the Damascus-Beirut highway and cause the Syrian forces in the Biqa Valley to withdraw toward the Syrian border, thereby removing the Syrian military presence in Lebanon.

The Israeli invasion of Lebanon was prompted by a number of elements. First, the Lebanese Christian Phalangists had appealed to Israel for help following the escalation in fighting between the Syrian Army and Phalangist units, placing the mostly Greek Orthodox enclave in Zahlah in the Biqa Valley and the Phalangist-controlled port of Juniyah, north of Beirut, in danger of being overrun by the Syrian Army. Then, both Israel and Syria violated tacit agreements concerning Lebanese air space. Syria placed surface-to-air missile (SAM) batteries in the Biqa Valley, thus hampering regular Israeli reconnaissance flights over Lebanese territory, flights to which Syria previously had acquiesced. In addition, Israeli and PLO clashes intensified with PLO long-range shelling of Israeli border towns and heavy Israeli retaliation against PLO concentrations in Lebanon. Finally, on June 3, members of the Abu

Nidal group, a Palestinian terrorist organization, attempted to assassinate Israeli ambassador to Britain Shlomo Argov.

One of the most significant military events of the conflict was the Israeli aerial attack against the Syrian SAMs, resulting in the destruction of nineteen sites and the damaging of four. Israeli aerial mastery was confirmed in the skies over the Biqa Valley. At the conclusion of the first week of the war, after the participation of approximately one hundred combat aircraft on each side, a total of eighty-six Syrian MiG-21, MiG-23, and Sukhoi-22 aircraft had been shot down with no Israeli losses. At the end of the battle, Israel had lost two helicopters and an A-4 Skyhawk, which was shot down by PLO missile fire.

There were also armored battles with the Syrians in the central and eastern sectors, around Jazzin and Ayn Darah, the latter of which commands the Damascus-Beirut highway, and stretching into the Biqa Valley. The Syrian armored divisions, with a strength of about 700 tanks, were equipped with Soviet-made T-72 tanks, the most modern in the Syrian arsenal. Fighting effectively to prevent the Israeli forces from reaching the Damascus-Beirut highway, the Syrians also used heavy concentrations of antitank weapons manned by special commando units. In other battles, Israeli forces advanced into the vicinity of Beirut, moving beyond the original terms of reference laid down by the Israeli cabinet. Under the direction of Ariel Sharon, the controversial minister of defense, Israeli forces moved into West Beirut, attacking from land and sea, and laid siege to the Palestinian fighters.

By mid-July 1982, through the mediation of United States ambassador Philip Habib, negotiations involving Syria, Israel, Lebanon, and the PLO led to the evacuation of some 8,000 PLO fighters and remnants of the Syrian 85th Brigade, under the supervision of the Multinational Force composed of United States Marines and French and Italian troops. PLO personnel were evacuated by sea to eight Arab countries; the Syrian forces were evacuated by land along the Damascus-Beirut highway to the Biqa Valley in eastern Lebanon.

Following the assassination of Lebanese president-elect Bashir Jumayyil (also spelled Gemayel) on September 14, 1982, Israeli forces once again entered West Beirut, with the declared intention of preventing an outbreak of sectarian strife. However, it was under Israeli coordination that on September 15, the Lebanese Phalangist forces entered the two Palestinian refugee camps in Sabra and Shatila in West Beirut and massacred Palestinian civilians. The Israeli forces withdrew from Beirut on September 3, 1983, and redeployed along a new line along the Awali River. This redeployment followed the breakdown of the May 17, 1983, Lebanon-Israel agreement and the handing over of Beirut to the Lebanese forces and troops of the 3,000-member Multinational Force. Lebanon's abrogation of the agreement under Syrian pressure was considered a major victory for Assad in his quest for regional hegemony.

Israel initially refused to withdraw its troops from southern Lebanon unless arrangements were also made for the withdrawal of Syrian and PLO forces. However, the high human and material cost of deployment in Lebanon, as well as adverse international and domestic public opinion, were major factors in Israel's decision to withdraw most of its forces from southern Lebanon in June 1985, although the Christian forces of Antoine Lahad's pro-Israeli South Lebanon Army (SLA) remained.

By May 1983, Syrian matériel losses amounted to 350 to 400 tanks, 86 combat aircraft, 5 helicopters and 19 SAM batteries; human casualties totaled around 370 killed, 1,000 wounded, and 250 prisoners of war. Israeli losses, meanwhile, amounted to about 50 tanks; Israel's casualties in the overall war in Lebanon reached about 480 killed, 2,600 wounded, and 11 prisoners.

The 1982 Lebanon War represented a number of milestones in military warfare. For example, the new Soviet T–72 tank was battle tested against American-equipped advanced Israeli armor. Also, Israel used new forms of battlefield intelligence (including electronic countermeasures), made effective use of reconnaissance drones, and demonstrated air superiority. The air battles over the Biqa Valley—among the major aerial battles in modern history—involved a confrontation between two highly sophisticated electronic command, control, and communications systems, not just between aircraft and missiles. On the ground, the Syrian Army fought well, and there was effective coordination between armor units and antitank commando units. Observers felt that the weakness of the Syrian Army was an inflexibility in maneuver at the major formation level.

The next clash between Syria and Israel, which occurred in November 1985, was caused by Syrian opposition to Israel's air surveillance in Lebanon. When Syrian fighter aircraft scrambled to prevent Israeli aircraft from flying over eastern Lebanon, two Syrian MiG-23s were shot down in Syrian airspace. Syria responded by deploying mobile SA–6 and SA–8 SAMs into eastern Lebanon and by setting up SA–2 sites along its border with Lebanon. Thereafter, the potential for rapid escalation in Syrian-Israeli hostilities became a source of concern on both sides. Following the Israeli withdrawal from Lebanon, Syrian influence and control expanded to eastern Lebanon and the Biqa Valley, where Syria maintained

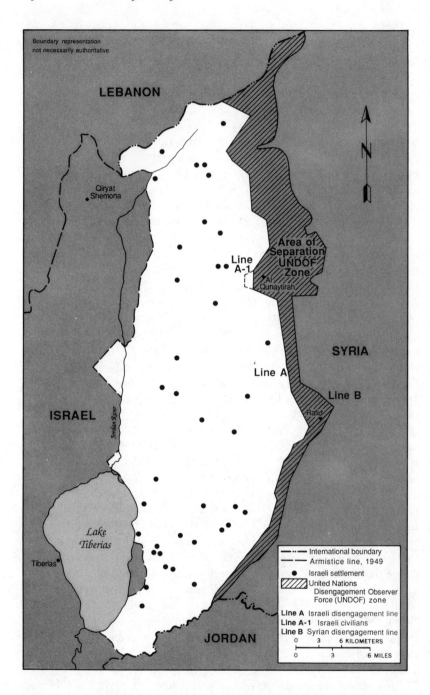

Figure 14. Disengagement Lines and Israeli Settlements on the Golan Heights, 1985

about two divisions; about six divisions were redeployed in the Damascus-Golan Heights region.

In 1987 Israel continued to be Syria's overriding security concern. Syrian leaders reiterated their denunciation of Egyptian president Anwar Sadat's 1977–81 peace initiative as "capitulationist" and continued to demand that all territory occupied by Israel in 1967 be returned. They also considered the fulfillment of the national rights of the Palestinians as a primary objective of any peace talks with Israel. These demands encompassed both military and political considerations. Militarily, Israel's annexation and settlement of the Golan Heights gave it a strategic military position less than 100 kilometers from Damascus (see fig. 14). Politically, Assad and his colleagues wanted the Arab world to support Syria as the leader of the Arab "confrontationist" or "rejectionist" states. They felt their position was justified in light of Egypt's decision to seek a diplomatic solution to the conflict with Israel and Syria's defense of its position in Lebanon against the 1982 Israeli invasion.

Although a major buildup of the Syrian Army following the 1982 Lebanon War resulted in increased confidence in Syria's military capability, outside observers concluded that Syria would lose any future military confrontation with Israel. Israeli armed forces were considered far more skilled and innovative, in terms of manpower and matériel, than those of Syria. Even were there an alliance with other Arab states, such as Jordan, Libya, and Iraq, few analysts doubted in early 1987 that Israel would prove militarily victorious. Nevertheless, Syria's military inferiority has not precluded (as illustrated by its 1973 offensive) intervention in Lebanon, support for terrorist activities, or pursuit of a military option against Israel. Despite its losses on the battlefield, Syria won some political and territorial gains in the October 1973 War, the mid-1970s disengagement agreements, and the 1982 Lebanon War. Syria's continued efforts to massively reinforce its military capabilities with Soviet aid were designed to bolster the military option to retake the Golan Heights without the aid of Egypt, Syria's traditional Arab ally.

Syria and the Lebanese Crisis, 1975–87

Syria's post-1973 confidence in its military capability contributed to its intervention in the civil war that broke out in Lebanon in 1975. Syrian ties to the area comprising modern-day Lebanon had been close for centuries; Lebanon was part of Greater Syria under the Ottoman Empire, and both nations were subject to French Mandate authority between the two world wars (see World War I, Arab

Nationalism, and the French Mandate, ch. 1; Foreign Policy, ch. 4). Thus, Syrian leaders viewed Lebanon's instability as a threat to Syria's internal and external security interests, and Syria considered itself strong enough to impose a military solution on the Lebanese conflict.

In 1975 Syria played a vital diplomatic role throughout the initial stages of the civil war. It acted as mediator for the many cease-fires declared between Lebanon's Christians, who dominated the country politically and economically, and the majority Sunni and Shia (see Glossary) Muslims. The latter sought to transform Lebanon into a Muslim Arab country; their drive for greater power was afforded a military option by the presence of thousands of armed Palestinian guerrillas who had relocated in Lebanon after the PLO's 1970–71 defeat in Jordan. It was not until January 1976, however, when a detachment of fifty Syrian officers was sent to Beirut to help police the twenty-sixth cease-fire, that Syrian military personnel entered Lebanon. On March 16, Syria escalated its involvement by ordering Syrian-backed units of the Palestine Liberation Army (PLA, the standing army of the PLO) and As Saiqa to stop rebel leftist Muslim officers of the Lebanese Army from attacking the palace of the country's Christian president, Sulayman Franjiyah (also spelled Frangie, Franjieh, or Franjiye) (see Special and Irregular Armed Forces, this ch.).

Lebanese Muslims and the PLO opposed the Syrian intervention, which had prevented them from seizing the presidency from the Christians. Much of the Arab world was outraged. The Syrian intervention also gave rise to a crisis of allegiance within PLA and As Saiqa units, which found themselves battling forces closely aligned with the PLO. For their part, Syrian leaders talked of peace and stability in Lebanon, while privately acknowledging that their concept of Syria's own security interests made it necessary to have a moderate Lebanese government compatible with Syrian interests. In their judgment, a radical left-wing Muslim Lebanese government would have been a security risk to the Assad regime, which preferred a Lebanese state subservient to its own regional interests.

Syrian presence in Lebanon grew rapidly. Around 3,000 Syrian regulars crossed Lebanese borders on April 9. In May the Lebanese parliament elected a new, Syrian-backed, Christian president, Elias Sarkis. By October more than 22,000 Syrian troops had entered Lebanon. The Syrian presence was sanctioned by the Arab League as the major component of the Arab Deterrent Force (ADF), to which the league gave a mandate to stop any breach of the peace. The ADF was technically under the command of President Sarkis, but de facto power and control were in the hands of Syrian military commanders.

After the June 1978 slaying by rival Christian militiamen of Christian leader Tony Franjiyah, son of the former president and Syria's firmest supporter in Lebanon, the ADF began a campaign against Lebanese Christians that included massive artillery barrages on Christian-held territories in East Beirut and other areas. With this action, Syria in effect "switched sides" in the ongoing civil war. The reason for this switch was the call by Lebanese Christians, whose confidence had been bolstered by increasingly overt Israeli support, for a partition of Lebanon along religious lines. This call constituted the major challenge to Lebanese stability and the authority of the Lebanese government.

The majority of Syrian troops deployed in Lebanon were formed into at least three divisions. Armored brigades and commando units were also present, and naval and air force units were used for transport purposes. Syria's heavy use of artillery, both against Muslim factions in earlier fighting and against Christian factions later, caused widespread criticism that the bombardments were indiscriminately killing civilians and that Syrian troops were pursuing a policy of genocide toward Lebanese Christians.

In 1987 Syria's military presence in Lebanon remained an urgent security issue. In early 1987, the ADF in Lebanon consisted of 25,000 Syrian troops (the troops from Saudi Arabia, Sudan, and the United Arab Emirates had withdrawn). The ADF units were deployed throughout those areas of central and northern Lebanon not under the control of the Christian militias. They were not deployed south of the so-called "red line" at the Litani River, near the Israeli border, or in the area controlled by the Israeli-dominated SLA.

In February 1987, there was an intensification of clashes between militiamen of the Syrian-backed Shia Amal and a coalition of Palestinians, Druzes, and the Lebanese Communist Party. A renewed deployment of an estimated 7,000 Syrian troops in West Beirut and major highways linking Beirut to the mountains and the northbound coastal road from southern Lebanon followed. Lebanese Muslim leaders requested Syrian deployment, which was condemned by some Maronite officials. Under the agreement for the Syrian entry, the militias were to disband their forces and lay down their weapons. To restore order, the Syrian troops, stationed at most intersections, closed down militia offices, confiscated arms caches, and rounded up militia and neighborhood strongmen. There was concern, however, that the Syrians would have difficulty resolving Lebanon's complex set of rivalries and disarming remaining militia strongholds in and around Beirut. For instance, Beirut's southern suburbs remained a stronghold of Shia militants, particularly the growing pro-Iranian Party of God (Hizballah), whose uncontrolled militancy and hostage-taking also had become increasingly troublesome to Damascus. Meanwhile, Christian militiamen still held ground in East Beirut.

In early 1987, few analysts believed Syrian occupation would end until the Lebanese conflict was resolved. In its own security interests, Syria could not afford for either radical leftist or religiously fundamentalist Muslim groups to gain total control of Lebanon. Also, President Assad had invested his political reputation, both at home and within the Arab world, in Syrian-imposed solutions to the civil war. Nevertheless, the Syrian intervention was becoming increasingly costly to Syria's economy as well as to the morale of the participating armed forces. Above all, it weakened Syria's military threat to Israel by dividing its forces into two fronts and diverting resources from recapturing the Golan Heights; at the same time, the intervention increased the possibility of direct confrontation with Israel. In early 1987, following the Israeli withdrawal to south Lebanon, the Syrian order of battle in Lebanon was reported to consist of about two divisions, with a deployment of some six divisions in the Damascus-Golan Heights region.

Some experts believed Syrian leaders preferred to maintain the chaotic situation in Lebanon to preserve Syria's hegemony there. However, other experts believed that the Syrian leaders strongly desired a resolution to the Lebanese conflict so that Syria would be free to concentrate on the conflict with Israel.

Syrian-Iraqi Hostility

Another important Syrian security consideration in early 1987 was Syria's twenty-four-year-old antagonism toward its eastern neighbor, Iraq. Since 1963, when the Baath Party came to power in Syria and became a rival of the Baath Party in Iraq, relations between these two states have been marked by political intrigue, attempts at subversion, assassinations, and concerted propaganda campaigns by each against the other. Since both Syria and Iraq are ruled by the ostensibly pan-Arab Baath Party, the conflict has been over which "true Baath Party" was to dominate the whole movement (see Political Dynamics, ch. 4). Both states considered themselves vulnerable to attack because the border between them is little more than a line drawn across a vast, open, thinly populated desert.

In 1975 a dispute over rights to the waters of the Euphrates River—a waterway essential to both countries—took Syria and Iraq to the verge of war. Syria limited the water flowing out of its newly completed Euphrates Dam (also known as Tabaqah Dam or Thawra Dam), thereby slowing the flow into Iraq. For two months, both countries hurled invective at each other, and Syrian troops massed along the Iraqi border. Only Saudi Arabian mediation induced Syria to release more water from Lake Assad "as a gesture of goodwill."

Throughout the 1970s and 1980s, both sides committed frequent acts of terrorism and subversion. Syria routinely blamed Iraqi agents for a multitude of internal ills. Disaffected army officers who had left either country served as prized sources of intelligence and propaganda. Tensions between Damascus and Baghdad have been exacerbated by Syria's support, including weapons shipments, to Iran in the Iran-Iraq War. Just as damaging to Iraq was the 1982 cutoff of the pipeline that runs through Syria and through which Iraq pumped oil to Mediterranean ports (see Industry, ch. 3).

Syrian-Palestinian Tensions

PLO military forces constitute another potential threat to the stability of the Syrian regime. Hostilities between Syria and Yasir Arafat and the PLO's Al Fatah faction intensified in May 1983, when armed rebellion against Arafat's leadership broke out. With Syrian approval, Fatah dissidents led by Abu Musa overran Al Fatah supply centers in Damascus in late May 1983. In June, July, and early August 1983, Syrian forces also actively supported the anti-Arafat forces fighting in the Biqa Valley and succeeded in driving the Arafat loyalists north into Tripoli. On June 24, Arafat was expelled from Damascus. In Syrian-dominated areas of Lebanon, Syrian officials also confiscated PLO arms and depots. With Syria's active support, Palestinian factions opposed to Arafat's rule, principally the Abu Nidal organization, assassinated high-ranking PLO officials in the Middle East and Western Europe. Syria also sponsored the Damascus-based Palestine National Salvation Front, an anti-Arafat coalition, consisting of such groups as the Popular Front for the Liberation of Palestine and the Democratic Front for the Liberation of Palestine. Although many PLO forces had been expelled from Syria, a PLA brigade, with a force of some 4,500, was still stationed there; however, it was carefully watched, infiltrated by Syrian security officials, and dependent on Syria for arms and supply routes. During the mid-1980s, these measures were effective in preventing any organized PLO insurgency against the Assad regime, but the potential for such a threat remained in early 1987, when many pro-Arafat PLO fighters had begun moving back to Lebanon.

Syrian-Jordanian Tensions

Syrian-Jordanian relations have fluctuated between normal diplomatic relations and armed confrontation. At times each side has attempted to subvert the other and has supported and provided refuge to the other's internal opposition groups. Jordanian interest in Syria began in 1921, when the founder of Transjordan, King Abdullah, sought to advance into Syria, from which his brother had been expelled by the French, and which he regarded as part of the promised Hashimite kingdom. Even as late as 1946, when both countries gained independence, Abdullah did not abandon his plan to become king of Syria. Syria considered Abdullah's schemes for an expanded Hashimite kingdom as intervention in its domestic affairs and officially complained to the Arab League. During the 1950s, Syria mounted a propaganda campaign against Abdullah and granted political asylum to opposition elements from Jordan, including political asylum in 1957 to Jordanian Army officers and civilian politicians who had conspired to topple King Hussein. Tensions mounted in 1958 when Hussein's private jet en route to Europe was intercepted by Syrian MiGs and forced to return to Amman. Also, Syrian-trained groups infiltrated Jordan to carry out subversive acts, culminating in the August 1960 assassination of Jordanian prime minister Haza al Majali, whose killers escaped to Syria.

Syrian-Jordanian tensions were exacerbated in the late 1960s, following the rift between Jordan and the PLO, with Syria supporting the Palestinians against Jordan. In September 1970, Syria sent an armored division into Jordan to reinforce the Palestinian forces under attack by Hussein's army. By July 1971, Syria had broken off diplomatic relations with Jordan over the issue.

The October 1973 War resulted in a gradual improvement in relations, as Jordan contributed to the Syrian military effort. In 1976 Jordan was the only Arab country to support the Syrian invasion and subsequent role in Lebanon. However, another break between Syria and Jordan occurred in 1977, following Jordan's tacit support for Egyptian president Sadat's peace initiative. During this period, Syria charged Jordan with harboring members of the Muslim Brotherhood, who had escaped from Syria. This charge led to new tension in December 1980, and military forces of both sides were deployed along the border. As a counterweight to Syria, Jordan improved its relations with Iraq and became one of its primary suppliers. In 1981 Jordan accused Syria of being behind the kidnapping of the Jordanian military attaché in Beirut and charged Rifaat al Assad, President Assad's brother, with masterminding a plot to assassinate the Jordanian prime minister. By the mid-1980s, rapprochement efforts were again under way (see Foreign Policy, ch. 4).

Syrian-Turkish Tensions

Relations between Syria and Turkey, which share a long border, have ranged from normal diplomatic ties to political and military tension. Conflicts have arisen over border problems, the apportionment of river water flow, smuggling, and charges of internal subversion. Some of these conflicts have historical roots, particularly in Syrian resentment at the arbitrary transfer in 1939 of the province of Alexandretta (or Hatay, as it was named by the Turks) to Turkey by the French Mandate authorities (see Concepts of Nationalism, Unity, and the Arab Nation, ch. 4).

Turkey has charged Syria with supporting Armenian, Kurdish, and Arab terrorist groups operating against Turkey. Turkey believes Syria offers training facilities and arms to Armenian terrorists belonging to the Armenian Secret Army for the Liberation of Armenia and assists them in infiltrating across their common border and into Western Europe for attacks against Turkey and Turkish targets, particularly diplomats. Turkey has also charged that Syria was behind the activities of anti-Turkish Kurdish separatist groups. Syria, in turn, has asserted that Turkey gave refuge to members of the Syrian Muslim Brotherhood and other opposition elements at the height of agitation in Syria in the early 1980s.

Delineating the 1,347-kilometer-long border between the two countries has been another sensitive issue. Border problems have included smuggling illegal narcotics and arms by individuals and militant groups on both sides and (because of the arbitrary border demarcation) illegal crossings by related peoples, leading to clashes between border guards and, at times, military maneuvers. Border crossing has remained a problem in the absence of a Turkish-Syrian agreement on border security and the "right of hot pursuit," which in Turkey's view would prevent acts against it by separatist groups tied to the Syrian government. In the mid-1980s, Syria was implicated in two terrorist attacks in Turkey. In the July 1985 murder of Jordanian diplomat Ziad Sati in Ankara, an arrest warrant was issued for a Syrian diplomat. However, the Syrian was allowed to leave Turkey shortly before the trial because Turkey did not want the incident to affect its relations with Syria. The chief defendant in the trial, who was employed as a translator in the Jordanian embassy, carried a Syrian passport. During the trial, he confessed to having worked for Syrian intelligence, stating that his control officer was a Syrian diplomat in Turkey who had given the order to assassinate Sati. The same Syrian diplomat was also suspected of complicity in the terrorist attack on the Neve Shalom Synagogue in Istanbul in September 1986, in which twenty-two people were killed.

Antiregime Opposition Movements

Opposition movements to the Syrian government in the 1980s were based on ideological, ethnic, or religious motives. However, because of the interrelationships in Syria between ideology and sectarian questions, distinctions among the reasons for dissent were often blurred.

Ideologically Based Opposition Movements

Although the Syrian government has frequently blamed Iraqi agents for many breaches of internal security, several other groups also were real or potential threats to Syrian political stability. In 1987 Syria's armed forces constituted the greatest potential threat to the regime, if only because they had been the kingmakers in every change of government since 1949. By early 1987, however, Assad had not been seriously challenged by the military in his sixteen years in power. This situation can be attributed to effective intelligence agents within the officer corps and to Assad's genuine popularity with the military. Assad is popular because, like Assad, most of the top army officers have been Alawis. Also, tremendous attention has been devoted to building the armed forces, which are well paid. Nevertheless, amid mounting tensions with Iraq, in 1975 there were reports that 200 military and civilian members of the Syrian Baath Party had been arrested and charged with plotting against the government.

The Syrian Communist Party (SCP), having a membership of about 5,000, was the largest communist organization in Syria. Although banned in 1981 when a campaign of arrests was ordered against supporters of its veteran leader, Khalid Bakdash, it was reported in 1986 that as a concession to the Soviet Union, the SCP was restored to favor and had rejoined the ruling National Progressive Front (see The Syrian Communist Party, ch. 4).

Until its banning in the late 1970s, the Communist Party Political Bureau (CPPB) was one of the main ideological opposition groups in Syria. Created in 1974 as a result of a split within the legal SCP, the CPPB provoked the ire of the Assad regime by protesting against Syria's intervention on behalf of the Christian Phalangists in the Lebanese Civil War. In 1987 the first Secretary of the CPPB, Riad at Turk (imprisoned without trial since

October 1980), and about 150 party members continued to be confined in Al Mezzah military prison in Damascus. Nevertheless, the CPPB remained a threat to the regime, and throughout the late 1970s and early 1980s, Turk's sympathizers staged numerous terrorist attacks against Syrian targets. The CPPB also published several pamphlets condemning the Baath regime and printed its own newspaper, *Ar Rayah al Hamrah* (The Red Banner).

In the 1980s, there were additional communist groups in Syria, although they were officially banned and many of their members held in detention. These groups included the Party for Communist Action (PCA), which had about 100 party members still in detention in 1985. In 1980 the Base Organization was formed by Yusuf Murad, a former member of the SCP Central Committee. The Union for Communist Struggle, formed in May 1980, was another opposition group. Its seven members were arrested, three of whom continued to be detained through 1985. In 1983 a communist organization called the Popular Committees took root among Syria's Palestinian refugees. In July 1986, a third division occurred within the SCP when Central Committee members Ibrahim Bakri and Umar Sibai split off over the Palestinian issue and created a new "Central Committee." In mid-1986, as an unknown terrorist group was detonating bombs in public places, the government cracked down on the proliferating and expanding communist opposition movements in Syria and arrested about 1,000 suspected activists.

Ethnic and Religious Opposition Movements

Rivalry among the country's various religious and ethnic minorities has been a perennial source of instability in Syria. During the 1980s, the primary cause of conflict was domination of top-level political and military posts by the minority Alawi community to which Assad belongs (see The Armed Forces and Society, this ch.; Political Dynamics, ch. 4).

More worrisome perhaps was intra-Alawi friction. For example, some Alawis honored the memory of former political figure Major General Muhammad Umran, assassinated in Lebanon in 1972, reportedly by Syrian agents. Likewise, some Baath Party members remained loyal to the faction Assad overthrew in his 1970 Corrective Movement (see Political Dynamics, Background, ch. 4). This group, named the 23 February Movement, supported former Party Secretary Salah al Jadid, former President Nureddin Atassi, and former Prime Minister Yusuf Zuayyin—all three of whom were incarcerated in Syria. Assad has repeatedly, and unsuccessfully, attempted to negotiate with these figures, offering them freedom in return for their approval of his government. In many respects, the Assad regime was more concerned with the activities of the 23 February Movement than with the open revolt of the Muslim Brotherhood. Whereas the fundamentalists carried out terrorist attacks, the 23 February Movement staged several well-planned but abortive coup attempts in the 1980s and, because Umran and Jadid were Alawis, threatened to split the Alawi community.

Sunni Islamic fundamentalists, however, have posed the most sustained and serious threat to the Baath regime. The government referred to these militants as the Muslim Brotherhood (Ikhwan al Muslimin), although this is a generic term describing a number of separate organizations. The most important groups included the Aleppo-based Islamic Liberation Movement, established in 1963; the Islamic Liberation Party, founded in Jordan in the 1950s; Shabab Muhammad (Muhammad's Youth); Jundallah (Soldiers of God); and At Talia al Muqatila (The Fighting Vanguard), established by the late Marwan Hadid in Hamah in 1965 and led in 1987 by Adnan Uqlah. The At Talia al Muqatila group, which did not recognize the spiritual or political authority of the exiled veteran leader of Syria's Sunni fundamentalists, Issam al Attar, bore the brunt of the actual fighting against the regime. In the early 1980s, the Muslim Brotherhood staged repeated hit-and-run attacks against the Syrian regime and assassinated several hundred middle-level government officials and members of the security forces and about two dozen Soviet advisers. The armed conflict between the Muslim Brotherhood and the regime culminated in full-scale insurrection in Aleppo in 1980 and in Hamah in February 1982. The government responded to the Hamah revolt with brutal force, crushing the rebellion by killing between 10,000 and 25,000 civilians and leveling large parts of the city (see The Assad Era, ch. 1).

On the third anniversary of the Hamah rebellion, in February 1985, the government announced an amnesty for Muslim Brotherhood members. About 500 of the Muslim Brotherhood were released from prison, and those who had fled abroad were encouraged to return to Syria. As a result of the amnesty, many members of At Talia al Muqatila surrendered to government authorities.

Following the Hamah uprising, extremist antiregime Muslim groups in Syria seemed fragmented and presented little threat to the Assad regime. The next series of major antiregime terrorist attacks occurred when a truck exploded in northern Damascus on March 13, 1986, followed on April 16 by explosions on buses carrying military personnel. A Lebanese, claiming he had been sent by the Iraqi government, publicly confessed to the March incident and was hanged. Outside observers, however, were unable to verify his or Iraqi complicity. Other potential instigators included

Lebanese Christian groups (in retaliation for the Syrian role in artillery shelling and car bomb explosions in East Beirut), PLO factions such as Al Fatah, and Israel.

Despite these dangers to Syrian internal security, the overall situation in the mid- and late 1980s was stable compared with the situation between 1946 and 1970. The traditional centers of dissatisfaction—students, labor unions, and dissident communist organizations—were thoroughly infiltrated by Syrian security personnel and in early 1987 posed no significant threat to the government. However, Syrian society is a mosaic of social groups whose interests and loyalties have often conflicted. President Assad, more than any leader in Syria's modern history, has been able to focus these conflicting interests and loyalties on national goals. Nevertheless, centrifugal forces, such as sectarianism, persisted in this volatile Arab nation, and the armed forces will probably long remain the ultimate arbiters of power.

The Regular Armed Forces
Size, Equipment, Command Structure, and Organization

By 1987 the Syrian armed forces were increasingly professional and well equipped. The Syrian armed forces totaled 500,000 regulars and 340,000 reserves in 1985. These figures represented a tremendous expansion in manpower, training, and equipment, which had been achieved with considerable financial and military aid from the Arab states and the Soviet Union and several of its East European allies. By early 1987, the vast majority of Syrian military equipment was Soviet manufactured, and the organization and military doctrine of the armed forces followed the Soviet model.

President Assad was commander in chief of the armed forces, retaining the rank of lieutenant general. Directly responsible to Assad was the flamboyant deputy premier and defense minister, General Mustafa Tlas, who also held the title of deputy commander in chief of the armed forces and army. Although a Sunni Muslim, Tlas has been a close friend of Assad since they were assigned as officers to the Egyptian Army (1959–61). Tlas was jailed for his part in an abortive officers' coup in 1962–63 in cooperation with Assad and later helped bring Assad to power. A tank commander, he was appointed lieutenant general and, in March 1972, minister of defense. He received general staff training in Moscow at the Voroshilov Academy and advocated close ties with the Soviet Union and a hard line on the Arab-Israeli conflict. Vice president for military and national security affairs was the president's brother, the volatile Rifaat al Assad. As a result of political infighting over the issue of succession to Assad, Rifaat was living in temporary exile in France in early 1987. The chief of the general staff and chief of the armed forces, Lieutenant General Hikmat Shihabi, was third in command. General Ali Aslan was deputy chief of the general staff. The commander of the ground forces was Major General Yusuf Bin Raghib Shakur. The air force retained its own commander, Major General Ibrahim Hassan. The navy commander was Rear Admiral Mustafa Tayara.

The chief of staff of the armed forces functioned through the general staff, an administrative body that was divided into the usual branches, such as personnel, intelligence, training, and logistics. The general staff did not possess decision-making powers; these were largely confined to the commanders and chiefs of staff acting on behalf of the president. In 1970 a political department was established "to guide members of the armed forces ideologically and to instill in them loyalty toward the present regime."

Army

In 1987 the army was overwhelmingly the dominant service. In addition to its control of the senior-most posts in the armed forces establishment, the army had the largest manpower, approximately 80 percent of the combined services. In 1985 army regulars were estimated at 396,000, with an additional 300,000 reserves. The army had nine divisions. The major development in force organization was the establishment of the special forces division and the organization of ground formations into two corps. The army's active manpower served in two all-arms army corps, five armored divisions (with one independent armored brigade), three mechanized divisions, one infantry–special forces division, and ten airborne–special forces independent brigades.

In addition to being the largest, the army was the best equipped of the three services, with over 4,100 Soviet-built tanks (including 1,000 of the advanced T–72s) and a formidable air defense system of SAM batteries and myriad antiaircraft guns and artillery. In 1987 Syria was scheduled to receive 500 new Soviet SS–23 ballistic missiles with a range of 500 kilometers. Syria was also reported to have begun producing its own chemical weapons, including nerve gases, with the capability to use the chemical agents in missile warheads. The Air Defense Command, within the Army Command but also composed of air force personnel, numbered approximately 60,000. It served in twenty air defense brigades (with approximately ninety-five SAM batteries) and two air defense regiments. The Air Defense Command had command access to interceptor aircraft and radar facilities. Air defenses included SA–5 long-range SAM batteries around Damascus and Aleppo, with additional SA–6 and SA–8 mobile SAM units deployed along Syria's side of the Lebanese border and in eastern Lebanon, and short-range SS–21 surface-to-surface missiles with conventional warheads. The 1,800-member Border Guard (sometimes designated as the Desert Guard or Frontier Force) was also under the Army Command and responsible for patrolling the nation's vast border areas (see table 13, Appendix).

Navy

In 1985 the navy consisted of approximately 4,000 regular and 2,500 reserve officers and men. The navy, lacking parity with the other services, was under the army's Latakia regional command. The fleet was based in the ports of Latakia, Baniyas, Minat al Bayda, and Tartus. Among the more than 40 vessels in the fleet were 2 or 3 Soviet submarines (including 2 Romeo-type diesel-electric submarines, transferred by the Soviet Navy in 1985), 22 missile attack craft (including 8 advanced Osa II missile boats), 2 submarine chasers, 3 mine warfare vessels, 8 gunboats, 6 patrol craft, 4 missile corvettes (on order), 3 landing craft (on order), and, as part of its coastal defense system, Sepal shore-to-sea missiles with a range of 300 kilometers (see table 14, Appendix).

Air Force

The air force, which was independent of the Army Command, consisted of about 100,000 regular and 37,500 reserve officers and men. In 1985 its 9 fighter-ground attack squadrons and an estimated 15 interceptor squadrons totaled approximately 650 combat aircraft. Almost all combat aircraft were Soviet manufactured and included 50 MiG-25 and MiG-25R (Foxbat) interceptors and nearly 200 MiG-23S/U (Flogger) and Su-20 (Fitter-C) ground-attack and multirole aircraft (see table 15, Appendix). In 1986 there were reports that the Soviet Union had agreed to provide Syria at least two squadrons of the advanced supersonic MiG-29 Fulcrum fighter aircraft equipped with top-of-the-line avionics. The air force was equipped with approximately ninety attack helicopters of the Mi-24/Mi-25 Hind and SA–342 Gazelle types. As part of an effort to upgrade its command-and-control network, the air force was reported to have the Tu-126 (Moss) advanced early warning aircraft. Military airfields were located in Aleppo, Blay, Damascus (International Airport), Damascus (Al Mazzah), Dayr az Zawr, Dumayr, As Suwayda, Hamah, Khalkhalah, Latakia, Nasiriyah, Tadmur, Sayqal, T–4 (located on the oil pipeline), and seven additional sites.

Manpower, Recruitment, and Conscription

The vast majority of manpower for the armed forces came from male conscription, which has been compulsory and universal (only the small Jewish community is exempted) since 1946 and was officially reaffirmed by the Service of the Flag Law in 1953. Females are not required to serve, although some do; however, they play more a public relations than a military role. Males must register for the draft at eighteen; each year around 125,000 reach nineteen, which is when the thirty-month conscription period begins. In 1985 it was estimated that of the country's population of over 10.6 million, 1.3 million were males fit for military service.

Before the rise to power of the Baath Party in 1963, middle and upper class youths, who have rarely been attracted to military service, were often exempted from conscription on payment of a fee. Since then, this practice has been eliminated, although youths living abroad in Arab countries continued to be exempted on payment of a fee set by law. University students were exempted, but many attended military training camps during the summer, and all were obligated to do military service upon completion of their studies. Observers stated that those conscripted in the mid-1980s represented a broad cross section of society.

Conscripts faced a series of options in the Syrian Army. After completion of his period of conscription, a man could enlist for five years in the regular service or, if he chose not to enlist, he would serve as a reservist for eighteen years. If he enlisted and became a noncommissioned officer (NCO) during his five-year service, he could become a professional NCO. A volunteer who did not attain NCO status could reenlist but was automatically discharged after fifteen years of service or upon reaching age forty. A professional NCO was retired at age forty-five or, at his own request, after twenty years of service.

Conscripts and enlisted men generally lacked mechanical and technical skills, although beginning in the 1970s the number of conscripts who had completed the six years of primary school increased dramatically, as did the number of secondary and vocational school graduates. The rugged rural origin of most conscripts has conditioned them to endure hardship and accept strict discipline. Military service has given most recruits the opportunity to improve their health and, because they receive technical training during most of their active duty, to leave the service with a marketable skill.

Officers have tended to be less representative of the general society than conscripts, primarily because of the high degree of politicization of the officer corps. Although officers were not required to join

*Women soldiers
of the Syrian armed forces*

the Baath Party, membership was a crucial factor for advancement to flag rank.

In addition to political loyalty, the officer corps was characterized by the dominance of the Alawi and Druze minorities, a condition dating from the French Mandate policy of recruiting these and other minority groups into the colonial military forces. Although many of the officers were Sunni Muslims, most of the key senior posts were held by Alawis.

Military Training

In 1987 three military schools were training commissioned officers for the services: the Military Academy, the Naval Academy, and the Air Force Academy. Young men from eighteen to twenty-three could apply for admission to the school of their choice. Selections were made from those who passed the required entrance examination, were physically qualified, and were considered politically loyal. All three academies conducted a standard two-year course leading to a commission immediately on completion of the course.

The Military Academy, located at Homs, was founded by the French in 1933 and is the oldest and largest of the service institutions. It was primarily a school for training infantry officers. Graduates selected for the other services went on to additional specialized training at other army-operated specialist schools.

Selected graduates were frequently sent for advanced training to military academies in the Soviet Union.

The Naval Academy, at Latakia, began operations in 1962 after the breakup of the union with Egypt and the recall of Syrian students attending the Egyptian Naval Academy. Its facilities and student body were limited, and it has produced only a handful of graduates each year.

The Air Force Academy was located at Nayrab Air Base, near Aleppo. It was established in 1960 and took over the training of air officers, who were formerly sent abroad for schooling, usually to Britain, France, or Egypt. The curriculum provided instruction in theoretical, technical, and scientific subjects and included basic flight training. The academy has trained technical officers as well as pilots. For training in advanced jet aircraft, however, pilots have been sent to Soviet or East European flight schools. Technical graduates have generally attended Soviet schools for advanced technical training, but since 1964, increased technical training has been conducted at Syrian bases.

Reserve officers were trained at a fourth institution, in Aleppo. Candidates, in many cases college graduates, were selected from among incoming annual classes of conscripts. They attended a concentrated nine-month course and were then assigned to units, usually in the infantry, as officer candidates. Those who met the qualifications continued as candidates until one month before completion of their required tours of duty, at which time they received their commissions as reserve second lieutenants.

In the past, the standards maintained in officer training varied widely because of the country's frequent political changes. In addition, the differences in the experiences of officers trained in France, Britain, Egypt, Iraq, the United States, and the Soviet Union created a divergence of military and political doctrines within the officer corps. Since 1963, however, training has become increasingly systematic and standardized along Soviet lines. By 1987 graduates of Syrian military academies emerged as dedicated and professional soldiers.

Conditions of Service, Morale, and Military Justice

The general atmosphere and the amenities associated with military life have steadily and considerably improved since 1946. With rare exceptions, Syrian government and political leaders have recognized the need for favorable conditions of service so as to maintain the loyalty of their primary source of power. Officers, for example, were reported to be able to buy automobiles without the usual 200 percent duty and to obtain interest-free government loans for down payments on living quarters.

The life of the ordinary soldier, however, was not an easy one. His daily routine was concentrated and arduous, and discipline was strict and often severe. However, a long-range program of construction and rehabilitation, initiated during the early 1960s, improved the living conditions on many bases. In 1987 the quarters, food, and pay compared favorably with what a worker could obtain in the civilian economy. Accrual of leave, retirement, medical care, and other benefits also made military service attractive. There were no reliable figures on military pay available in 1987, but the indications were that rates were relatively high by the standards of many other Arab armies. There were also supplementary allowances for both officers and enlisted men, which in many cases totaled more than the basic rate. For example, various specialists, both officers and enlisted, received substantial amounts of technical pay. Additional compensation for flight personnel, paratroops, and men engaged in other kinds of hazardous duty had been established.

Improved conditions of service have improved morale in the ranks. The relative political stability of the 1970s and 1980s has also raised morale. The previous three decades had witnessed frequent changes of government by military coups d'état, leading to purges, imprisonments, or the execution of officers associated with the deposed regime. Under Assad, the top army ranks have felt more secure. The ambitious rebuilding of the armed forces also increased the prestige and morale of the military. Nevertheless, by early 1987, the eleven-year occupation and frequent fighting in Lebanon were reportedly affecting the army's morale. Frequent rotation of troops limited exposure to an unsatisfactory military situation and the corrupting influences of the war-torn Lebanese environment and reduced periods that soldiers were away from their families.

As in the past, in 1987 the typical enlisted man, whether a conscript or a volunteer, came from a traditional authoritarian Muslim family and accepted discipline as a regular requirement of military life. A system of military courts existed to try cases involving disciplinary and criminal offenses in the armed forces. Although the information available in 1987 was incomplete and somewhat dated, observers noted the existence of two kinds of military courts. In one, a single judge heard cases involving routine disciplinary matters and minor criminal offenses. The other, which was composed of three judges, tried felonies and other major crimes. Judges in both courts were officers who had earned a law degree. Two additional kinds of military courts—state security courts and the Supreme State Security Court—were established in the early 1970s to hear cases involving breaches of security, that is, political crimes (see Crime and Punishment, this ch.). Both civilian and military personnel were subject to trial by these special courts.

Uniforms and Rank Insignia

Service uniforms for Syrian officers generally follow the British style, although army combat clothing follows the Soviet model. Each uniform has two coats: a long one for dress and a short jacket for informal wear. Army officer uniforms are khaki in summer, olive in winter. Air force officers have two uniforms for each season: a khaki and a light gray for summer and a dark blue and a light gray in winter. Naval officers wear white in summer and navy blue in winter. Lower ranks wear the traditional bell bottoms and white blouse. The uniform for naval chief petty officers is a buttoned jacket, similar to that worn by United States chief petty officers. Officers have a variety of headgear, including a service cap, garrison cap, and beret (linen in summer and wool in winter). The color of the beret varies by season and according to the officer's unit.

Commissioned officers' rank insignia are identical for the army and air force. These are gold on a bright green shoulder board for the army and gold on a bright blue board for the air force. Officer ranks are standard, although the highest is the equivalent of general, a rank held in 1986 only by the commander in chief and the minister of defense. Navy officer rank insignia are gold stripes worn on the lower sleeve. The highest ranking officer in the Syrian Navy is the equivalent of captain. Army and air force rank for warrant officers is indicated by gold stars on an olive green shield worn on the upper left arm. Lower NCO ranks are indicated by upright and inverted chevrons worn on the upper left arm (see fig. 15).

Although some twenty-five orders and medals are authorized, generally only senior officers and warrant officers wear medal ribbons. The following are some important Syrian awards: Order of Umayyads, Medal of Military Honor, War Medal, Medal for Courage, Yarmuk Medal, Wounded in Action Medal, and Medal of March 8, 1963.

Foreign Influences in the Development of the Armed Forces

Various foreign countries were essential to the development of the armed forces of the late 1980s. As the former colonial power, France had been the dominant foreign influence during the formative years after Syria's independence. Later, Britain and the United States also aided the military, largely by serving as sources

COMMISSIONED OFFICERS

SYRIAN RANK	MULAZIM	MULAZIM AWWAL	NAQIB	RAID	MUQADDAM	AQID	AMID	LIWA	IMAD	FARIQ AWWAL
ARMY AND AIR FORCE										
U.S. RANK TITLES	2D LIEUTENANT	1ST LIEUTENANT	CAPTAIN	MAJOR	LIEUTENANT COLONEL	COLONEL	BRIGADIER GENERAL	MAJOR GENERAL	LIEUTENANT GENERAL	GENERAL
SYRIAN RANK	MULAZIM	MULAZIM AWWAL	NAQIB	RAID	MUQADDAM	AQID				
NAVY										
U.S. RANK TITLES	ENSIGN	LIEUTENANT JUNIOR GRADE	LIEUTENANT	LIEUTENANT COMMANDER	COMMANDER	CAPTAIN				

WARRANT OFFICERS AND ENLISTED PERSONNEL

SYRIAN RANK	JUNDI	JUNDI AWWAL	ARIF	RAQIB	RAQIB AWWAL	MUSAID	MUSAID THANI	MUSAID AWWAL
ARMY, AIR FORCE AND NAVY	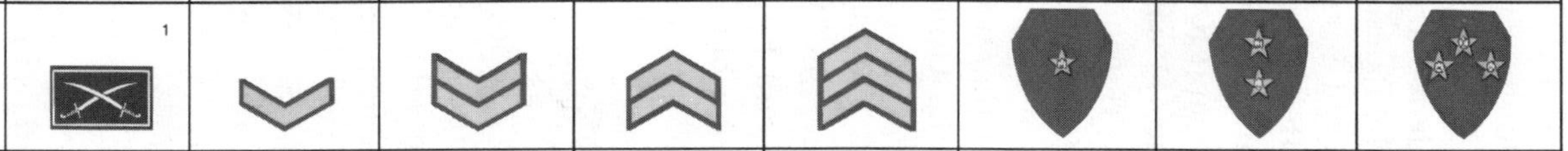 [1]							
U.S. ARMY RANK TITLES	BASIC PRIVATE	PRIVATE	CORPORAL	SERGEANT	SERGEANT 1ST CLASS	WARRANT OFFICER (WO-1)	CHIEF WARRANT OFFICER (CWO-2)	CHIEF WARRANT OFFICER (CWO-3)
U.S. AIR FORCE RANK TITLES	AIRMAN BASIC	AIRMAN 1ST CLASS	SERGEANT	STAFF SERGEANT	MASTER SERGEANT	WARRANT OFFICER (WO-1)	CHIEF WARRANT OFFICER (CWO-2)	CHIEF WARRANT OFFICER (CWO-3)
U.S. NAVY RANK TITLES	SEAMAN RECRUIT	SEAMAN	PETTY OFFICER 3D CLASS	PETTY OFFICER 2D CLASS	PETTY OFFICER 1ST CLASS	WARRANT OFFICER (WO-1)	CHIEF WARRANT OFFICER (CWO-2)	CHIEF WARRANT OFFICER (CWO-3)

NOTE: [1] Air Force and Navy no rank insignia.

Figure 15. Military Ranks and Insignia

of professional officer training. During the 1958–61 union with Egypt, Egyptian doctrine and training were influential. By 1987, however, the Soviet Union was the predominant foreign influence, as it had been for over two decades. At times, Syrian-Soviet relations have been strained, and Syria has guarded its freedom to make policy independent of the Soviets, particularly with regard to Iraq, Lebanon, and the Palestinians. However, Soviet military assistance and the presence of Soviet military advisers continued to be essential to the growth and professionalization of the armed forces. East European countries, notably Czechoslovakia, the German Democratic Republic, and Romania, have also provided some matériel and training (see Foreign Policy, ch. 4).

The Soviet-Syrian military relationship began in March 1955, when the Soviets offered to extend considerable economic and military assistance in support of Syria's refusal to join the Baghdad Pact, an alliance that was being formed under the general auspices of Britain and the United States. Initial arms shipments arrived from Czechoslovakia in 1956, but East European aid was on a small scale until the rise of Baathist president Nureddin Atassi in 1966. During the June 1967 War, the threat of Soviet intervention on behalf of Syria and Egypt was partly responsible for halting the Israeli advance on both fronts. After the June 1967 War, Soviet military aid to Syria grew substantially, and the Soviets established a sizable military presence there.

Assad's rise to power led to a strengthening of political and military ties with the Soviet Union. Contributing to these closer relations was Egypt's sudden ouster of Soviet military advisers in July 1972, which caused an increased Soviet interest in Syria. The months preceding the October 1973 War saw a significant increase in Soviet arms flow to Syria. During the war, Soviet military advisers supervised the operations at SAM sites and were present at Syrian command posts.

The most significant Soviet involvement in October 1973, however, was its airlift of almost 4,000 tons of military equipment and its sealift of considerably more to rearm the Syrian and Egyptian armies. Within a year after the cease-fire, the Soviets had more than replaced Syria's massive equipment loss.

However, Syria's intervention in the Lebanese Civil War against leftist Muslim forces in 1976 led to a strain in Soviet-Syrian relations. For more than a year, the Soviets suspended deliveries of military matériel, while Syria retaliated by reducing its Soviet military presence and halting training for its military in the Soviet Union. To replace Soviet support, Saudi Arabia supplied most of the funds to maintain Syria's troops in Lebanon. By 1987, however, Saudi financial aid was believed to have decreased.

During the Syrian-Soviet rapprochement in 1978, Libya reportedly supplied the equivalent of US$500 million to US$1 billion to pay for Syria's Soviet-supplied weaponry, including 12 MiG-27s.

Syria was also able to pay for Soviet weaponry as a result of the October 1978 Arab summit in Baghdad that pledged payments to Syria (as well as to Jordan and the PLO) if it agreed to reject the Camp David Agreements of September 1978. Under the Baghdad agreement, Syria was allotted US$1.8 billion annually. Only a few countries, however, notably Saudi Arabia and Kuwait, maintained regular payments; consequently, Syria has received only US$700 to US$800 million per year in Baghdad agreement aid (see Balance of Payments, ch. 3).

From 1979 to 1983, the Soviet Union delivered US$9.2 billion in arms transfers (out of a total of US$10.5 billion pledged). Czechoslovakia was the next largest supplier, with US$470 million in military aid. China delivered US$90 million, Poland US$30 million, and Romania US$20 million. In addition, Syria received US$200 million in military aid from France, US$180 million from Britain, and US$40 million from the Federal Republic of Germany.

In addition to arms, Syria received military advisers and technicians from the Soviet Union and Eastern Europe and sent military personnel to those countries for training. The number of such advisers and technicians in Syria was estimated at 3,500 in the aftermath of the October 1973 War; 2,500 in 1976; 2,000 to 3,000 in 1978; 5,300 in 1984; and 2,300 in 1986. With regard to training, the United States Central Intelligence Agency has estimated that 6,600 Syrian military personnel were trained in the Soviet Union between 1955 and 1985, and a further 1,515 were trained in other East European countries.

Some observers saw the 1980 Treaty of Friendship and Cooperation between Syria and the Soviet Union as the culmination of the two countries' relationship. From the Syrian perspective, however, this treaty had a deep-seated flaw; there was no reference in it to Syria's position in Lebanon. Syria wanted and had requested a "strategic agreement" with the Soviet Union to offset any United States-Israeli agreement. Yet no such Soviet-Syrian agreement was signed, and no broader alliance evolved, although the Soviet Union increased its military assistance following Syria's 1982 defeat in Lebanon. While maintaining its sovereignty, Syria expressed appreciation for Soviet assistance by granting the Soviets facilities to base reconnaissance aircraft and expanding the ports of Latakia and Tartus to accommodate large Soviet ships.

Umayyad Square, Damascus, site of the Ministry of Defense
Courtesy Murhaf Jouejati

In 1983 and 1984, the Soviet Union increased involvement by installing SA–5, SA–6, SA–9, and SS–21 missile systems in Syria. The missile systems, which had adequate range to cover a major part of the region, were at first manned and protected by Soviet advisers and troops and have only gradually been turned over to Syrian control. The large Soviet resupply of SAM systems was interpreted by the United States, Israel, and Jordan as a Soviet response to the massive destruction of Soviet-built SAMs in the 1982 Lebanon War, among other reasons. Syria acquired additional T–72 tanks following Assad's October 1984 visit to Moscow.

In 1983 Syria's rejection of the Camp David Agreements, its alleged support of international terrorism, and its close friendship with the Soviet Union led the United States Congress to prohibit any new aid; since 1979 no new American aid has been assigned to Syria. Meanwhile, despite, or perhaps because of, the dominant Soviet influence on the armed forces, Assad has repeatedly sought to diversify Syria's source of armaments, for instance, by negotiations with France. However, Syrian-French arms deals broke down over the issue of Syrian support for anti-French terrorist groups. In general, Syrian efforts to purchase Western defense technology have been unsuccessful.

Special and Irregular Armed Forces

Defense Companies

In 1987 the Assad government controlled or sponsored several important special military units in addition to the regular armed forces. Until they were disbanded and reorganized as a standard division in 1984, the most important special forces were the Defense Companies (Saraya ad Difa), which consisted of about 15,000 to 25,000 specially trained and equipped officers and men. Established in 1971, the Defense Companies were organizationally independent of the regular armed forces and under the command of Rifaat al Assad, the president's brother. In 1984 Rifaat was relieved of his command and replaced by Lieutenant Colonel Muayyin Nassif, his deputy commander and brother-in-law. Nassif, in turn, was replaced by General Hikmat Ibrahim. Foreign observers viewed this elite military unit as the president's private army. The Defense Companies were renamed Unit 569 and reorganized as a standard armored division with four armored brigades and three mechanized brigades.

Until reformation as Unit 569, Defense Companies personnel had been recruited independently of the regular armed forces. Recruitment was believed to be predominantly among Alawis, the ethnic community presumed most loyal to Assad. Observers reported that the Defense Companies had been equipped with some of the most modern weapons available to the Syrian Army, including T-72 tanks, SAMs, and attack helicopters, and could call on regular forces for logistical help and military support.

The Defense Companies had been garrisoned outside Damascus, presumably with the primary mission of countering attempted coups or other challenges to the central government. These special forces, however, also had military missions beyond the role of a praetorian guard. For example, they acquired combat experience during Syria's first armed intervention in Lebanon (June–October 1976). Defense Companies units also had been involved in internal security, such as carrying out house-to-house searches during the nationwide strikes and demonstrations in Aleppo in March 1980 and in June 1980 killing between 600 and 1,000 Tadmur Prison inmates suspected of belonging to the banned Muslim Brotherhood. In 1982 units had been deployed in Hamah during the armed uprising by the Muslim Brotherhood, and they participated in the massacre of 10,000 to 25,000 civilians there.

The Defense Companies had also been deployed against Jordan. In late February 1981, some of their senior commanders, including Colonel Adnan Barakat, were alleged to have been involved in an abortive assassination attempt against Jordanian prime minister Mudir Badran. Members of the Defense Companies also reportedly had been sent abroad to monitor Syrian political exiles and to impede their activities. In Lebanon, Defense Companies units had supported pro-Syrian Lebanese militias, such as the Tripoli-based Arab Knights of the Arab Democratic Party (founded in 1981 by Rifaat al Assad and composed largely of Lebanese Alawis of Syrian origin), and the Lebanese Baath Party and its militia, the Assad Battalion.

Republican Guard

The Republican Guard was responsible for Assad's security and together with the Defense Companies provided bodyguards assigned on the basis of personal loyalties and affiliations to leading members of the regime and top officials. The Republican Guard was commanded by Adnan Makhluf, the president's brother-in-law. Political allies and associates of Rifaat al Assad, on the other hand, were given bodyguards from the Defense Companies.

As Saiqa

A third organization, As Saiqa (The Thunderbolt), was formed in 1966 by the pro-Syria Baath Party National Conference as a military wing of the Palestinian faction of the Syrian Baath Party. Although ostensibly under the umbrella of the PLO (it is represented on the PLO Executive Committee and Military Department), As Saiqa was firmly under Syrian Army control. In 1987 As Saiqa was led by three officials: Isam al Qadi, the secretary general; Muhammad al Khalifa, the representative on the PLO Executive Committee and the Military Department; and Majid Muhsin, the head of operations in Lebanon. Muhsin was the brother of Zuhair Muhsin, who was appointed head of As Saiqa in 1970 by Assad, following the new regime's purge of its Palestinian leadership in an attempt to place As Saiqa firmly under Syrian Army control. Zuhair Muhsin was killed in July 1979 by an unknown assailant in Cannes, France.

As Saiqa's Palestinian credentials have depended on its ability to balance its PLO activities with the state policies of its Baathist Syrian sponsors. As Saiqa's special units participated on Syria's behalf in some of the Syrian-Palestinian clashes during the Lebanese Civil War, in particular in the Syrian siege of Ad Damur, previously a Maronite township but later occupied by the PLO and the Palestinians, who had set up camps and headquarters there. Many of As Saiqa's troops defected to other Palestinian guerrilla groups during these clashes in early June 1976. In July–August 1976, the troops that remained switched sides and assisted in the defense of the Palestinian Tall az Zatar refugee camp against Phalangist attack. Units of As Saiqa participated in the Syrian-backed 1983 armed rebellion against Arafat's leadership by dissident elements within the PLO. By 1983 observers estimated that 70 percent of As Saiqa's members were Syrians.

Sponsorship of Terrorism

In the mid-1980s, much media attention was paid to Syria's alleged use of terrorism to achieve diplomatic, military, and strategic objectives in the Middle East and elsewhere. Although the exact Syrian role was murky, in the mid-1980s Syria's intelligence and security networks were strongly implicated in the support of Middle Eastern and other international terrorist groups in Western Europe. In fact, Syria was one of the countries on the terrorism list issued by the United States government, first compiled in 1979.

Within Syria's intelligence and security services, sponsorship of terrorism reportedly was conducted by air force intelligence, of which Major General Muhammad al Khawli, an air force officer, has served as chief since 1970. Khawli, an Alawi, was considered Assad's most important adviser, and his office was adjacent to Assad's in the presidential palace in Damascus, where he was presidential adviser on national security and head of the National Security Council. Since 1976 Khawli has been the architect of Syria's policy in Lebanon. He also was credited with crushing the uprising by the Muslim Brotherhood in Hamah in 1982, and, according to the *Times* of London, under his command air force intelligence operatives had directed at least twenty-nine terrorist operations as of late 1986. These intelligence operatives reportedly worked in the offices of Syrian Arab Airlines abroad and also as military attachés in Syrian embassies. Thus, Syria had a formidable intelligence network with which to direct and fund terrorist groups and provide them such assistance as explosives and weapons, false passports and official Syrian service passports, diplomatic pouches, safe houses, and logistical support. Lieutenant Colonel Haitham Sayid, deputy chief of air force intelligence and its operations director, was second in command to Khawli. In Lebanon, Khawli's power was exercised by Brigadier General Ghazi Kanaan, head of Syrian intelligence in Lebanon.

Military intelligence services were headed by General Ali Duba, an Alawi, who was, in effect, the country's chief of internal security. Military intelligence was headquartered in the Ministry of Defense complex in the center of Damascus and reputedly exercised immense authority because it operated from within the military establishment. Reportedly, military intelligence services handled radical Palestinian terrorist groups, such as Ahmad Jibril's Popular Front for the Liberation of Palestine—General Command. General Khawli and Lieutenant Colonel Sayid were allegedly also the paymasters of the Abu Nidal terrorist organization, also called the Fatah—Revolutionary Council. According to the United States Department of State, Syria provided the Abu Nidal organization with logistical support and permission to operate facilities in Damascus (the Syrian government asserts the facilities were limited to cultural and political affairs). It is also claimed that the Syrian government helped the Abu Nidal organization maintain training camps in Lebanon's Biqa Valley, an area controlled by Syrian armed forces, and supplied travel documents permitting Abu Nidal operatives to transit freely through Damascus when departing on missions.

Western government and intelligence sources admit that they cannot pinpoint Assad's complicity in planning terrorist operations but consider it unlikely that he was not informed in advance of major terrorist acts. If these reports are true, it was equally unlikely that Major General Khawli would act without clearing a potentially risky operation with Assad.

Various news organizations have claimed that, as part of its overall support network, in the 1980s Syria provided training camps for Middle Eastern and international terrorists. There were reportedly five training bases near Damascus and some twenty other training facilities elsewhere, including the Biqa Valley. In late 1986, *U.S. News and World Report* stated that since October 1983, when Israel withdrew from Beirut, large numbers of international terrorists known to Western intelligence sources have turned up in Damascus. These include members of radical Palestinian and Lebanese terrorist groups, which depended on Syria for refuge and logistical and financial support, as well as other free-lance terrorists. Other sources report that a number of other terrorist groups have received training in Syrian camps or in Syrian-controlled areas in Lebanon including such West European terrorist groups as the Red Army Faction (also known as Baader-Meinhof) and the Action Directe, as well as the Armenian Secret Army for the Liberation of Armenia, the Japanese Red Army, the Kurdish Labor Party, the Pakistani Az Zulfikar, the Tamil United Liberation Front of Sri Lanka, the Moro National Liberation Front for the Philippines, the Popular Front for the Liberation of Oman, the Democratic Front for the Liberation of Somalia, and the Eritrean Liberation Front. Furthermore, the Lebanese Armed Revolutionary Faction (LARF) was based in the Lebanese village of Qubayat, within the area of Syrian control. Syria also permitted Iran to operate training camps in eastern Lebanon for the Shia Party of God (Hizballah) organization.

Syria's goal was to employ as surrogates terrorists whose operations left few traces to Syria. In June 1986, the *Washington Post* reported that Middle East analysts had noted three distinct kinds of relationships between Syria's intelligence and security services and terrorist groups. In the first kind of relationship, there was direct Syrian involvement because Syrian intelligence created new radical Palestinian factions, such as As Saiqa, which were, in effect, integrated components of the Syrian armed forces and hence direct Syrian agents. The radical Palestinian Abu Musa group, which was almost totally dependent on Syria, was another example of such a relationship. In the other two kinds of relationships, Syria used terrorists as surrogates to avoid direct blame. In the second relationship, Syria collaborated with and provided logistical and other support to terrorist groups that maintained independent organizational identities but were directed by Syrian intelligence, which formulated general guidelines as to targets. Reportedly, Abu Nidal's Fatah—Revolutionary Council and the LARF were examples of such collaboration. The third kind of relationship involved selection of free-lance terrorists, mainly Palestinians and Jordanians, to carry out a specific operation. Examples of this kind of relationship included the convicted Lebanese assassin of Bashir Jumayyil, Nizar Hindawi, convicted in 1986 of trying to blow up an Israeli commercial airliner in London, and Hindawi's half-brother, Ahmad Hasi, convicted of bombing the German–Arab Friendship Society office in West Berlin.

The firmest proof of Syrian sponsorship of terrorism occurred at the trials of Hindawi in Britain and Hasi in West Berlin. Evidence introduced in Britain, and other information not made public, linked Hindawi with the Syrian intelligence services. Because of the evidence, the British government severed diplomatic relations with Syria. Hasi's case implicated Haitham Sayid, deputy chief of Syrian Air Force intelligence, for whom an international arrest warrant was issued by West Berlin authorities. After Hasi's conviction, the West German government downgraded its relations with Syria.

A series of terrorist explosions in Paris in September 1986 were linked to a Marxist Maronite terrorist group, the LARF. LARF was implicated in the assassination of a number of American, West European, and Israeli diplomats in Western Europe, and its operations were reputedly known to Syrian intelligence. In a magazine interview in September 1986, Pierre Marion, former director of the French General Directorate of External Security, charged that in the early 1980s, Syrian intelligence agents had helped terrorist groups to operate in France as part of a Syrian effort to punish France for its involvement in Lebanon.

Although Syrian links to terrorists in Western Europe were relatively recent, observers believe that Assad has long used terrorism to further Syrian policy objectives in the Middle East. Over the years, Jordanian officials have accused Syria of assassinating Jordanian diplomats. PLO leaders have accused Syria of the assassination of Arafat's chief of staff and close aide, Saad Sayil (also known as Abu Walid), killed near a Syrian checkpoint in the Biqa Valley in 1982. According to the report by the United States Department of State on "Patterns of Global Terrorism: 1983," several attacks by members of the Abu Nidal organization reflected Syrian opposition toward the pro-Arafat Al Fatah faction of the PLO. In 1983 these attacks included the assassination at the International Conference of Socialists in Portugal of PLO observer Issam Sartawi, who had advocated dialogue with Israel. The same report also charged Syria with encouraging the radical Shia Lebanese group, Islamic Jihad, to carry out the 1983 suicide bombing attacks against the United States embassy in Beirut and the headquarters of the United States and French contingents of the Multinational Force in Beirut, which resulted in 557 casualties.

The Armed Forces and Society

Syria's maintenance of a substantial military establishment has affected the nation's political, social, and economic development, but the military's greatest impact has been on Syrian society's political orientation. Except during the first three years of independence, the head of government has been a military officer. From March 1949 to November 1970, power struggles among the factions of the highly politicized officer corps led to fifteen changes of government by military coups and undermined the organizational structure and military capability of the armed forces (see After Independence, ch. 1). Conversely, the relative political stability since Assad assumed power in early 1971 and the regime's emphasis on building up the military have contributed to increased professionalization of the armed forces. However, the absence of coups d'état between 1971 and 1987 did not indicate the military's decline as a political force. In fact, the armed forces remained the mainstay of Assad's regime. His success in maintaining their loyalty was largely the result of his ability to mobilize popular support for his leadership, the creation of a powerful and pervasive domestic intelligence and security apparatus, and, until its 1984 reconstitution as a division, the formation of the Defense Companies. The other pillar of Assad's power, the Baath Party, has close associations with the armed forces through the party's military branch. Thus the army and the party have direct institutional linkages (see The Baath Party Apparatus, ch. 4).

Despite the effectiveness of the military-political interrelationship, occasional evidence of political dissent within the officer corps existed. These problems stemmed from long-standing tensions between the Sunni Muslim majority and the minority Alawis who held most senior posts. In July 1977, the *Manchester Guardian Weekly* reported that Syrian officials had uncovered within the armed forces clandestine organizations believed to have participated in the assassination of a number of senior Alawi officers. Such activity, if it indeed existed, has important political implications for the future of the Assad regime. For example, a power struggle among factions centering on personalities among Alawi officers is an ever-present danger. Whatever may happen, it seemed clear that the armed forces, because of their capability for violent coercion, would continue to be the ultimate arbiters of political power in Syria.

The most significant sociological impact of the armed forces has been the social mobility that the officer corps has provided the nation's lower classes. Syria's upper classes have consistently disdained the military as a career. Hence, the majority of cadets and officers are of peasant and village origin; a military career has afforded them rapid social mobility to positions of political power and influence. In 1975 one observer stated that in the view of many younger officers, the importance of the military lay as much in its role as an instrument for social change as in its military role against Israel.

In particular, the armed forces have been the best vehicle for social mobility for Syria's Alawi community. Although they constitute about 11 percent of the population and are traditionally the poorest of Syria's ethnic minorities, hundreds of Alawis have risen from an impoverished childhood in the rural areas surrounding Latakia to the pinnacles of power as military officers.

While furthering social mobility, the armed forces have had a largely negative effect on economic development. For instance, the fledgling defense industry has not had much positive impact, either as an economic resource or as a source of armaments. Also, the military's requirement for increasing numbers of skilled technicians and mechanics to maintain and operate a growing inventory of modern weapons constitutes a drain on the already limited pool of skilled workers; the technical training some conscripts receive and use on their return to civilian life has not offset the drain. The rapid growth of the armed forces from about 80,000 in 1967 to 500,000 in 1986 inevitably slowed economic growth because of the loss of manpower in all sectors of the economy (see Labor Force, ch. 3).

By all standard indicators, the economic burden of defense was large. Although government defense expenditures declined during the five years after the June 1967 War, they jumped markedly in 1973, beginning a rapid ascent that continued in 1985 and 1986 (see table 16, Appendix). According to the United States Arms Control and Disarmament Agency, from 1982 to 1985, defense expenditures reportedly grew from US$2.7 billion to US$4.2 billion. According to the Syrian government's 1986 *Statistical Abstract*, however, estimated national security expenditures were only US$3.7 billion. Between 1985 and 1986, defense expenditures were inflated by the high cost of maintaining nearly 25,000 troops in Lebanon. In 1985, for example, defense expenditures consumed about 30 percent of all central government expenditures (see Budget, ch. 3). In 1986 there were reports that defense would account for over 55 percent of total government expenditures in Syria's 1987 budget, and that government spending on defense was driving Syria into heavy debt and an acute economic crisis.

Syria has consistently ranked among the countries with the highest burdens of defense on society. Economic and military analysts contended that the Syrian government's growing defense expenditures have severely limited expenditures in other areas vital to the nation's social and economic progress. According to data compiled by Ruth Leger Sivard in *World Military and Social Expenditures, 1986* for example, in 1983 Syrian military expenditures per capita were the equivalent of US$249 (ranked twenty-seventh in the world), while public expenditures for education were US$102 (ranked fifty-second) and for health were US$7 (ranked ninety-fifth).

In spite of these figures, observers agreed that the government's officially reported defense expenditures markedly understated the actual resources devoted to national defense. The same observers also suspected that the reported expenditures did not include such important items as construction projects for military use.

Civil Police and Internal Security Apparatus

Since independence, Syria's police and internal security apparatus have undergone repeated reorganization and personnel changes, reflecting the security demands of each succeeding regime. During the relative political stability of the 1970s and 1980s, police and security services were credited with having grown and become

Syrian infantrymen practicing antiarmor tactics

professional, but in 1987 only the bare outlines of their institutional makeup were known.

The largest intelligence-gathering and internal security organization was the National Security Directorate, employing about 25,000 personnel. Other security organizations were under the supervision of the Ministry of the Interior. These organizations included a national police force, responsible for routine police duties. It incorporated the 8,000-member Gendarmerie, which had originally been organized by the French Mandate authorities to police rural areas. During the 1960s, the civil police forces were believed to have been used extensively to combat internal security threats to the government, but during the 1970s and 1980s, these forces assumed a more conventional civil police role; this change in role coincided with increased professionalization and the parallel development of an effective and pervasive internal security apparatus. Nevertheless, the police continued to receive training in such functions as crowd and riot control.

In 1987 the internal security apparatus consisted of myriad organizations with overlapping missions to gather intelligence concerning internal security and to engage in activities (largely covert) to apprehend and neutralize opponents of the regime. According to Amnesty International, there were several security force networks in Syria. Each had its own branches, detention cells, and interrogation centers, located throughout the country, and each also had its own intelligence service. Each organization was directly responsible to the president and his closest advisers. The organizations operated independently and had no clear boundaries to their areas of jurisdiction and no coordination among them. For example, although the civilian security police dealt with internal security matters, the responsibilities of military intelligence headed by General Ali Duba were not limited to matters affecting the armed forces but also included internal security. In the mid-1980s, Western sources reported that the power and pervasiveness of Syria's internal security apparatus inspired fear among the Syrian population.

Crime and Punishment

Data published in the government's *Statistical Abstract* do not lend themselves to a realistic analysis of Syria's crime problems. The total number of persons reported to have been convicted in penal cases rose steadily from about 56,000 in 1952 to nearly 275,000 in 1969 and then dropped dramatically to about 165,000 in 1971, at which level it remained through 1975, apparently reflecting Assad's loosening of pre-1970 police controls.

The 1985 statistics, the most recent statistics available in early 1987, cited a total of 187,944 convictions of Syrian nationals in penal cases. Nearly three-fourths of these convictions were for crimes and contraventions neither mentioned in the penal code nor further identified. Of the other convictions, the largest category was for "crimes against religion and family" (not further defined). Other frequent crimes were acts endangering or causing loss of life, robbery, insolence, and crimes against public security.

A rapid increase in crimes against religion and family was the only trend discernible in the data for the 1970–85 period. The figures for the number of convictions in nineteen other classifications of crime remained stable. Accounts of crimes committed in Syria published in Western publications were limited to crimes against state security, such as assassinations and bombings, and to such crimes as bribery and embezzlement as exposed by the Committee for the Investigation of Illegal Profits. The latter committee was set up by the government in September 1977 to investigate a reported growth in corruption by government officials and business leaders.

In 1986 petty offenses were tried in magistrate courts, also called peace courts, found in all population centers. Courts of the first instance, located in twenty-four major urban areas, tried more serious crimes and acted as courts of appeal from the magistrate courts (see The Judiciary, ch. 4). The courts of appeal heard appeals from both lower courts. Juveniles, defined as those between the ages of seven and eighteen, were tried in separate juvenile courts.

The Court of Cassation acted as Syria's supreme court. Located in Damascus, it reviewed appeals to determine if the lower courts had applied the law correctly. If an error were found, the case was sent back for retrial to the court of original jurisdiction.

The judicial system and constitutional rights to some extent were abrogated and superseded by martial law imposed when the National Council of the Revolutionary Command invoked Syria's State of Emergency Law on March 8, 1963. By early 1987, Assad had not repealed this condition. The State of Emergency Law provided for the selection by the president of a martial law governor (the prime minister) and a deputy martial law governor (the minister of the interior). Article 4 of the State of Emergency Law empowered the martial law governor or his deputy to issue written orders to impose restrictions on freedom of individuals with respect to meetings, residence, and travel. It sanctioned preventive arrest, censorship, withdrawal of licenses for firearms, evacuation or isolation of areas, and requisition or sequestration of movable property, real estate, and companies, with compensation to be deferred indefinitely.

Article 6 of the State of Emergency Law defined as violations of martial law "offenses against the security of the state and public order, or public authority, and actions which disturb public confidence, or constitute a general danger." More specifically, Article 6 prohibited "actions considered incompatible with the implementation of the socialist order in the state" and opposition to the unification of the Arab states or any of the aims of the revolution. Furthermore, it enjoined communicating with or benefiting from any organization or foreign state for the purpose of undertaking any action, verbal or physical, that was hostile to the aims of the revolution. Article 6 also proscribed attacks on places of worship, command centers, military establishments, or other government institutions. Finally, currency regulations violations and hoarding of or profiteering in foodstuffs fell under martial law.

Because the 1963 martial law directives gave blanket authority to the martial law governor, in 1979 Assad vowed to "apply firmly the sovereignty of law" and to "strengthen the authority of the judiciary." He issued orders limiting the jurisdiction of the state security courts and annulled martial law in cases not actually affecting state security. Moreover, the written orders implementing extraordinary measures were subject to review by the Administrative Court of Justice (Majlis ad Dawlah), which had ruled in several instances that the martial law governor's powers did not exceed the limits specified in Article 4. In such cases, the administrative court could rule the martial law governor's actions illegal and invalid and award compensation to the injured party.

Martial law offenses were tried at state security courts, whose presiding members were appointed by presidential decree. The verdicts of state security courts were not subject to appeal but were ratified by the president, who could suspend or vacate the verdict, order a retrial, or reduce the penalty. The decision of the president was irreversible.

In 1987 criminal and judicial procedures continued to be modeled after those of France. Following an arrest, the police presented their evidence to a public prosecutor, who conducted his own investigation. If the prosecutor decided to proceed, he referred the case to the appropriate court. Decisions were made by a majority of the three judges of the court, who ruled on questions of law and fact. There was no trial by jury. In the mid-1980s, about 90 percent of all criminal court cases resulted in a conviction. Although the legal code provides for due process, it is not always followed. For example, in its *Country Reports on Human Rights Practices for 1986,* the United States Department of State stated that "under the state of emergency in force since 1963 . . . an individual may be held indefinitely without charge or trial, especially in political and security cases." Penalties were severe. They included loss of civil rights, fines, imprisonment for up to life, forced labor, exile, and death by hanging or firing squad. Public hangings in Damascus Square of convicted thieves, murderers, assassins, and spies continued to be a common occurrence in 1987. Amnesty International reported that fifteen "officially confirmed executions" took place in 1985.

Observers have asserted that the Syrian penal system was geared toward punishment rather than rehabilitation. In *Country Reports on Human Rights Practices for 1986,* the United States Department of State provided little detailed information about prison conditions but reported that those charged with or convicted of criminal offenses have been detained in isolation from those charged with political and security offenses. Health care, food, and access by family to persons held in ordinary prisons were reported to be adequate, whereas conditions at prisons where political and security prisoners were held were reported to be more severe, and family visits were prohibited. In its 1986 human rights report, the Department of State also noted that "there have been numerous credible reports of torture, primarily during arrest and interrogation," and (referring to the 1985 Amnesty International report) it added that "use of torture by the Syrian security forces is routine."

In 1985 the Syrian government declared two general amnesties, but only one benefited political prisoners, covering between 200 and 500 members of a faction of the banned Muslim Brotherhood (see Antiregime Opposition Movements, this ch.). In 1986 Amnesty

International estimated that there were thousands of political prisoners under Syria's state of emergency legislation, including 290 prisoners of conscience.

*　　*　　*

English-language literature on Syrian national security was extensive in 1987. Valuable information regarding the development of the Syrian armed forces, their political role, and the sociology of the military is contained in the works by Gordon H. Torrey, Nikolaos Van Dam, Moshe Ma'oz and Avner Yaniv, John F. Devlin, Eliezer Be'eri, J.C. Hurewitz, Itamar Rabinovitch, Benedict F. FitzGerald, Amos Perlmutter, and George M. Haddad. The most informative and reliable sources on current Syrian national security issues are the annual *Middle East Military Balance*, published by Tel Aviv University's Jaffee Center for Strategic Studies, the annual *Middle East Contemporary Survey*, published by Tel Aviv University's Shiloah Center for Middle Eastern and African Studies, the annual *Strategic Survey* and *The Military Balance*, both published by the International Institute for Strategic Studies, and the annual *World Military Expenditures and Arms Transfers*, published by the United States Arms Control and Disarmament Agency. All these sources have been widely used for a variety of information, particularly on the changing size and equipment inventories of military organizations and national security doctrines and concerns. (For complete citations and further information, see Bibliography.)

Appendix

Table 1. Metric Conversion Coefficients and Factors

When you know	Multiply by	To find
Millimeters	0.04	inches
Centimeters	0.39	inches
Meters	3.3	feet
Kilometers	0.62	miles
Hectares (10,000 m²)	2.47	acres
Square kilometers	0.39	square miles
Cubic meters	35.3	cubic feet
Liters	0.26	gallons
Kilograms	2.2	pounds
Metric tons	0.98	long tons
	1.1	short tons
	2,204.	pounds
Degrees Celsius	9	degrees Fahrenheit
(Centigrade)	divide by 5 and add 32	

Table 2. Schools and Students, 1975, 1980, and 1985

	1975	1980	1985
Schools			
Primary	6,750	7,689	8,747
Secondary	1,050	1,330	1,707
Students			
Primary			
Male	736,478	854,584	1,051,267
Female	475,092	626,912	872,975
Total primary	1,211,570	1,481,496	1,924,242
Secondary*			
Male	85,192	97,623	122,912
Female	34,817	56,241	88,182
Total secondary	120,009	153,864	211,094
University			
Male	48,410	70,036	91,917
Female	12,746	24,731	39,807
Total university	61,156	94,767	131,224

*No statistics given for lower secondary schools.

Source: Based on information from Syria, Office of the Prime Minister, Central Bureau of Statistics, *Syrian Statistical Yearbook, 1986,* Damascus: 1986, pp. 339–445.

Table 3. *Medical Personnel and Hospital Beds, 1975 and 1985*

	1975	1985
Physicians		
Total	2,400	6,163
Persons per	3,065	1,666
Dentists		
Total	765	1,975
Persons per	9,614	5,198
Pharmacists		
Total	1,255	2,621
Persons per	5,861	3,917
Nurses, total	1,267	8,326
Midwives, total	877	2,201
Hospital Beds		
Total	7,479	11,891
Persons per	995	863

Source: Based on information from Syria, Office of the Prime Minister, Central Bureau of Statistics, *Syrian Statistical Yearbook, 1986,* Damascus: 1986, pp. 450, 452.

Table 4. *Gross Domestic Product at Market Prices by Sector, Selected Years, 1963–85*
(in millions of Syrian pounds) [1]

Sector	1963	1970	1980	1984	1985 [2]
Agriculture [3]	4,690	3,842	10,369	9,563	10,097
Industry [4]	2,060	4,537	8,373	7,622	7,997
Construction	752	918	3,574	4,528	4,811
Trade	3,964	4,802	12,693	14,259	13,750
Transportation and					
communications	1,273	1,731	3,555	4,698	4,825
Finance and insurance	1,000	1,420	3,266	3,029	3,035
Government	1,367	2,416	8,480	11,806	11,371
Other services	258	371	960	1,208	1,208
TOTAL	15,364	20,037	51,270	56,713	57,094

[1] For value of the Syrian pound—see Glossary.
[2] Provisional
[3] Includes forestry and fishing.
[4] Includes extractive industries and electric power.

Source: Based on information from Syria, Central Bureau of Statistics, *Statistical Abstract 1986,* Damascus: 1986, pp. 624–625.

Table 5. Estimated Labor Force and Employment by Sector, 1970, 1975, and 1983
(in thousands)

Sector	1970 [1]	1975 [2]	1983
Agriculture, forestry and fishing	748	916	662
Mining and quarrying	9	12	15
Manufacturing	181	211	296
Electricity, gas and water	7	10	22
Construction	107	130	325
Trade (including restaurants and hotels)	139	189	219
Transportation, storage and communications	61	78	134
Financial services	9	10	19
Community and personal services	202	238	494
Not Stated	5	45	83
Total Employed	1,468	1,839	2,172
Unemployed and seeking first job	115	136	46
TOTAL LABOR FORCE	1,583	1,975	2,269

[1] Based on full census.
[2] Estimated from sample survey.

Source: Based on information from Syria, Central Bureau of Statistics, *Statistical Abstract 1977*, Damascus: 1977, pp. 138–139; Central Bank of Syria, *Quarterly Bulletin 1984*, vol. 22, no. 3–4, Damascus: 1984, p. 60; International Labour Organisation, *Yearbook of Labour Statistics*, Geneva: 1985, p. 90.

Table 6. Summary of Proposed Government Budget Receipts, 1983–1985
(in millions of Syrian pounds) [1]

	1983	1984	1985
Tax revenues			
Business taxes	2,800	3,800	4,300
Personal income taxes	400	450	550
Real estate taxes	230	350	400
Other direct taxes	733	915	993
Indirect taxes	5,088	5,377	4,164
Total tax revenue	9,251	10,892	10,407
Nontax revenues			
Surpluses from public sector	12,170	9,118	13,111
Investment revenue	2,533	4,298	4,100
Other nontax revenues and fees	1,436	4,488	5,063
Total nontax revenues	16,139	17,904	22,274
Domestic loans	7,682	7,682	7,682
Loans and grants	1,866	1,710	1,981
TOTAL	37,253	41,289	42,984

[1] For value of the Syrian pound—see Glossary.
[2] Essentially foreign credits and grants to the degree they are included in the budget.

Source: Based on information from Syria, Central Bank of Syria, *Quarterly Bulletin*, vol. 22, no. 3–4, Damascus: 1984, p. 47; Syria, Central Bureau of Statistics, *Statistical Abstract 1985*, Damascus, 1985, p. 477.

Table 7. Summary of Proposed Budget Expenditures, 1983–85
(in millions of Syrian pounds)*

Ministry or Agency	1983	1984	1985
Administrative, legislative and judicial	6,630	7,481	7,030
National security	11,176	13,325	13,778
Education and information	3,236	3,351	3,756
Social welfare	336	419	447
Economy and finance	1,989	2,400	2,217
Agriculture and irrigation	1,936	3,211	3,985
Industry and mining	3,270	3,369	2,730
Transportation and public works	7,382	6,312	7,142
Other	2,311	2,049	1,900
TOTAL	38,363	41,289	42,984
Development	18,581	17,850	19,436
Current	18,672	23,439	23,548

*For value of the Syrian pound—see Glossary.

Source: Based on information from Syria, Central Bureau of Statistics, *Statistical Abstract 1985*, Damascus: 1985, pp. 470–476; and Syria, Central Bank of Syria, *Quarterly Bulletin*, No. 3–4, Damascus: 1984, p. 46.

Table 8. Land Use, Selected Years, 1970–84
(in thousands of hectares)

Kind of Land	1970	1975	1980	1984
Forests	468	445	466	498
Steppe and Pasture [1]	5,450	8,631[1]	8,378	8,317
Uncultivable Land	3,773	3,487	3,520	3,534
Cultivable Land	8,827	5,955[1]	6,154	6,169
Uncultivated	2,918	479	470	514
Cultivated	5,908	5,476[1]	5,684	5,655
Fallow	2,610	1,776[1]	1,791	1,920
Under crops	3,299	3,700	3,893	3,735
Irrigated	451	516	539	618[2]
Nonirrigated	2,848	3,184	3,354	3,117
Specified Crops				
Grains	2,502	2,745	2,701	2,457
Legumes	229	223	172	256
Cotton	249	208	141	179
Vegetables	115	200	284	259
Fruit	259	351	481	546
Other industrial crops	42	86	107	96
TOTAL AREA	18,518	18,518	18,518	18,518

[1] Some land reclassified after 1974.
[2] Data as given although less than shown by kinds of crops.

Source: Based on Syria, Central Bureau of Statistics, *Statistical Abstract 1977*, Damascus: 1977; *Statistical Abstract 1985*, pp. 124, 132, 137, 141.

Table 9. Production of Agricultural Products, 1981–84
(in thousands of tons)

Products	1981	1982	1983	1984
Wheat	1,087	1,556	1,612	1,068
Barley	1,406	661	1,043	303
Lentils	61	53	61	36
Tomatoes	723	790	831	728
Potatoes	311	279	315	322
Sugar Beets	564	860	1,158	1,268
Onion	175	187	159	136
Cotton	356	422	526	451
Tobacco	12	14	14	13
Olives	208	471	152	311
Grapes	404	423	384	400
Washed wool	12	13	14	13
Eggs*	1,546	1,684	1,727	1,804
Milk	1,097	1,132	1,161	1,003

*In millions.

Source: Based on information from Syria, Central Bank of Syria, *Quarterly Bulletin*, no. 3–4,
Damascus: 1984, pp. 47–54

Table 10. Crude Oil Production and Export, 1980–1985

Year	Production (barrels per day)	Value of Crude Exports (in millions of Syrian pounds)*	Crude Oil Exports
1980	166,000	5,235	68.9
1981	158,000	5,044	63.1
1982	166,000	4,082	61.1
1983	168,000	4,131	51.3
1984	161,000	3,608	49.6
1985	n.a.	n.a.	n.a.

n.a.—not available
*For value of Syrian pound—see Glossary.

Source: Based on information from International Monetary Fund, *International Financial
Statistics Yearbook, 1986,* Washington: 1986, p. 645; and Economist Intelligence Unit,
Country Profile: Syria 1986, London: 1986, pp. 26–31.

Table 11. Imports and Exports by Use, Selected Years, 1975–84
(in millions of Syrian pounds) [1]

	1975	1980	1982	1984
Imports [2]				
Final consumption	1,073	3,492	2,586	3,246
For further processing	3,310	10,129	10,752	11,140
Investment goods	1,790	2,544	2,417	1,768
Total imports	6,173	16,165	15,755	16,154
Exports				
Raw materials	3,054	6,323	5,190	5,232
Products for further processing	108	259	328	429
Finished goods	279	1,691	2,436	1,614
Total exports	3,441	8,273	7,954	7,275

[1] For value of the Syrian pound—see Glossary.
[2] Probably excludes items for defense.

Source: Based on information from Syria, Central Bureau of Statistics, *Statistical Abstract 1977*, Damascus: 1977, pp. 338–39; Syria, Central Bureau of Statistics, *Statistical Abstract 1985*, Damascus: 1985, pp. 278–79.

Table 12. Balance of Payments, 1980–1985
(in millions of United States dollars)

	1980	1981	1982	1983	1987
Goods and Services					
Exports of goods (f.o.b.)*	2,112	2,230	2,032	1,928	1,859
Imports of goods (f.o.b.)* ...	−4,010	−4,843	−3,703	−4,152	−3,801
Services (net)	−145	−62	−405	−330	−438
Private Transfers (net)	774	582	446	461	327
Government Grants (net)	1,520	1,819	1,379	1,278	1,201
Total Goods and					
Services	251	−251	−251	−815	−852
Long-term capital	−25	48	−8	309	326
Short-term capital	431	531	148	310	581
Balance of capital account	406	579	140	619	907
Errors and omissions	−915	−285	208	66	−68
Counterpart items	15	−64	−190	−15	–
Changes in resources	243	45	93	146	13

*f.o.b.—free on board

Source: Based on information from International Monetary Fund, *International Financial Statistics Yearbook 1986*, Washington: 1986, p. 645.

Table 13. Major Army Equipment, 1986

Type	Designation	Quantity
	GROUND FORCES	
TANKS		
High quality	T–72/Improved T–72	1,000
	T–62	1,000
Medium quality	T–55	2,100
Armored personnel carriers	BMP–1	1,500
Armored reconnaissance vehicles	BTR–152 BTR–40/–50/–60 OT–64 BRDM–2	2,000
		TOTAL: 7,600
ARTILLERY		
Guns and heavy mortars	180mm S–23 gun 152mm M–1973 howitzer 152mm M–1943 howitzer 130mm M–46 gun 122mm M–1974 howitzer 122mm D–30 howitzer 240mm mortar 160mm mortar	TOTAL: 1,200
Antitank weapons	Sagger Spigot HOT MILAN	TOTAL: 2,000
Surface-to-surface missiles and rockets	FROG–7	23
	SS–1 (Scud B)	18
	SS–21	12
Surface-to-air short-range missiles	SA–14/–13/–9/–7	11
Anti-aircraft short-range guns	ZSU 57–2SP; ZSU 23–4 SP;ZU 23–2	TOTAL: 1,000

Table 13. (Continued)

Type	Designation	Quantity
AIR DEFENSE COMMAND		
Surface-to-air long-range missiles (batteries)	SA-2/-3	63
	SA-5	3
	SA-8	n.a.
	SA-11	n.a.
Interceptor aircraft	MiG-25/-25R	50
	MiG-21MF/S/U	310

n.a.—not available

Source: Based on information from Mark Heller, Aharon Levran, and Ze'ev Eytan, *The Middle East Military Balance, 1985,* Boulder, Colorado: Westview Press, 1986, pp. 239–40, 243; International Institute for Strategic Studies, *The Military Balance, 1986–1987,* London: 1986.

Table 14. Major Navy Equipment

Type	Designation	Quantity
Frigates	Petya-1 class	2
Fast patrols boats with Styx surface-to-surface missiles	Komar class	6
	Osa I class	6
	Osa II class	8
Mine warfare vessels	T-43 class minesweeper	1
	Vanya class minesweeper	2
Submarines	Soviet F class (on order)	2-3
Gunboats	P-4 class MTB	8
Patrol craft	CH class 130.9 ft.	3
	Zhuk	3
	Nanuchka missile corvettes (on order)	4
Advanced armament	SS-N2 Styx SSM	n.a.
Coastal defense	Sepal ground-to-sea missile	n.a.

n.a.—not available

Source: Based on information from Mark Heller, Aharon Levran, and Ze'ev Eytan, *The Middle East Military Balance, 1985,* Boulder, Colorado: Westview Press, 1986, pp. 243–44; International Institute for Strategic Studies, *The Military Balance, 1986–1987,* London: 1986.

Table 15. Major Air Force Equipment, 1986

Type	Designation	Quantity
Fighter/ground attack	MiG-23S/U (Flogger) MiG-27 (Flogger D) Su-20 (Fitter C)	TOTAL: 190
	MiG-17 Su-7B (Fitter A)	TOTAL: 100
Interceptors	MiG-25/-25R (Foxbat) MiG-21MF/S/U (Fishbed)	50 310
Transports	An-24/26 (Coke/Curl) IL-14 (Crate) IL-18 (Coot) IL-76 (Unconfirmed) Mystere Falcon 20 Yak-40 (Codling)	TOTAL 32
Trainers	L-29 Delfin L-39 Albatross Piper Navajo SIAT/CASA/MBB 223 Flamingo Yak-11 (Moose) Yak-18 (Max)	60 40 2 48 n.a. n.a.
Attack helicopters	Mi-24/Mi-25 (Hind) SA-342 Gazelle	45 45
Medium transport helicopters ..	Mi-8 (Hip) Mi-4 (Hound) Mi-2 (Hoplite)	110 10 10
Antisubmarine warfare helicopters	Kamov Ka-25 (Hormone) Mi-14 (Haze)	5 10

n.a.—Not available

Source: Based on information from Mark Heller, Aharon Levran, and Ze'ev Eytan, *The Middle East Military Balance, 1985,* Boulder, Colorado: Westview Press, 1986, p. 242; International Institute for Strategic Studies, *The Military Balance, 1986–1987,* London: 1986.

Table 16. Budgeted Defense Expenditures, 1981–85
(in United States Dollars)

Year	Total Expenditures (in millions)	Expenditures per capita	Percentage of Syrian GNP*	Percentage of Middle East GNP	Percentage of Government Expenditure
1981	2.3	284	13.9	12.8	37.7
1982	2.7	303	15.0	14.1	34.5
1983	4.0	413	21.3	15.6	41.0
1984	4.3	405	22.4	15.6	41.7
1985	4.2	369	21.1	12.3	42.0

*GNP—gross national product.

Source: Based on information from United States, Arms Control and Disarmament Agency, *World Military Expenditures and Arms Transfers, 1986.* Washington, 1987, p. 95.

Bibliography

Chapter 1

Abd-Allah, Umar F. *The Islamic Struggle in Syria.* Berkeley: Mizan Press, 1983.

Abu Jaber, Kamal S. *The Arab Baath Socialist Party.* Syracuse: Syracuse University Press, 1966.

Altounyan, Taqui. "To Aleppo Once Again," *Middle East International* [London], No. 26, August 1973, 20–22.

Amnesty International. *Report from Amnesty International to the Government of the Syrian Arab Republic, 1983.* London: November 1983.

Amos, John W. *Arab-Israeli Military Political Relations: Arab Perceptions and the Politics of Escalation.* New York: Pergamon Press, 1979.

Antonius, George. *The Arab Awakening.* New York: Capricorn, 1963.

Atiya, Aziz. *Crusade, Commerce, and Culture.* Bloomington: Indiana University Press, 1962.

Barker, A. J. *Arab-Israeli Wars.* New York: Hippocrene Books, 1981.

Communique of the Islamic Revolution in Syria and its Success. *Bayan al-Thawrat al-Islamiyah fi Suriya wa Najahuha.* Damascus: Command of the Islamic Revolution in Syria, 9 November 1980.

Bleaney, C. H. (comp.) *Modern Syria: An Introduction.* Durham, United Kingdom: University of Durham, 1979.

Burke, Edmund III. "A Comparative View of French Native Policy in Morocco and Syria, 1912–1925," *Middle Eastern Studies* [London], 9, No. 2, May 1973, 175–86.

Cass, Alain. "Assad's Difficult Choice," *Middle East International* [London], No. 55, January 1976, 9–11.

Dawisha, Adeed I. *Syria and the Lebanese Crisis.* London: Macmillan, 1980.

Dawisha, Karen. "The USSR in the Middle East: Superpower in Eclipse," *Foreign Affairs,* 61, No. 2, Winter 1982–83, 438–51.

Deeb, Marius. *The Lebanese Civil War.* New York: Praeger, 1980.

———. "Lebanon's Continuing Conflict," *Current History,* January 1985, 13–15.

Dekmejian, Richard H. *Fundamentalism in the Arab World.* Syracuse, N.Y.: Syracuse University Press, 1985.

Dessouki, Ali E. (ed.). *Islamic Resurgence in the Arab World.* New York: Praeger, 1982.

Devlin, John F. *The Ba'th Party: A History from Its Origins to 1966.* Stanford, California: Hoover Institution Press, 1976.

———. *Syria: Modern State in an Ancient Land.* Boulder, Colorado: Westview Press, 1983.

295

Drysdale, Alasdair. "Syria's Troubled Baathi Regime," *Current History*, January 1981, 32–35, 37–38.

Eigeland, Tor. "Ebla, City of the White Stones," *Aramco World Magazine*, 29, No. 2, March–April 1978, 10–19.

Farsoun, Samih, and Walter Carroll. "The Civil War in Lebanon," *Monthly Review*, 28, No. 2, June 1976.

Fedden, Robin. *Syria and Lebanon.* (3d ed.) London: John Murray, 1965.

Field, Michael. "Focus on Syria under Assad," *Middle East International* [London], No. 14, July 1972, 26–27, 30.

Freedman, Robert O. *Soviet Policy Toward the Middle East Since 1910.* (3d ed.) New York: Praeger, 1982.

George, A. R. "The Nomads of Syria: End of a Culture?" *Middle East International* [London], No. 22, April 1973, 21.

Glubb, John Bagot. *Syria Lebanon Jordan.* New York: Walker, 1967.

Greenwood, Bart. "The Fickle Stream," *Middle East International* [London], No. 22, April 1973, 23–25.

Grey, Lawrence. "The Destruction of Kuneitra," *Middle East International* [London], No. 41, November 1974, 24–26.

Haley, P. Edward, and Lewis W. Snider (eds.). *Lebanon in Crisis: Participants and Issues.* Syracuse, N.Y.: Syracuse University Press, 1979.

Hayani, Ibrahim. "Syria's Traditional Role," *Middle East International* [London], No. 38, August 1974, 9–11.

Herzog, Chaim. *The Arab-Israeli Wars: War and Peace in the Middle East.* New York: Random House, 1982.

Hinnebusch, Raymond A. "Local Politics in Syria: Organization and Mobilization in Four Village Cases," *Middle East Journal*, 30, No. 1, Winter 1976, 1–24.

Hitti, Philip K. *Makers of Arab History.* New York: Harper and Row, 1971.

_____. *Syria: A Short History.* London: Macmillan, 1959.

Holden, David. "Lebanon's Future in Syria's Hands," *Middle East International* [London], No. 57, March 1976, 6–9.

Holmstrom, David. "Syria—Unity, Liberty, and Socialism," *Middle East International* [London], No. 22, April 1973, 11–13.

Humphreys, R. Stephen. *From Saladin to the Mongols. The Ayyubids of Damascus: 1193–1260.* Albany: State University of New York Press, 1977.

Hureau, Jean. *La Syrie aujourd'hui.* Paris: Editions J. A., 1977.

Joarder, Safiuddin. "The Syrian Nationalist Uprising (1925–1927) and Henri de Jouvenel," *Muslim World*, 67, No. 3, July 1977, 185–204.

Kaylani, Nabil M. "The Rise of the Syrian Ba'th, 1940–1958: Political Success, Party Failure," *International Journal of Middle East Studies*, 3, No. 1, January 1972, 3–23.

Keilany, Ziad. "Socialism and Economic Change in Syria," *Middle Eastern Studies* [London], 9, No. 1, January 1973, 61–72.

Khadduri, Majid. *Political Trends in the Arab World*. Westport, Connecticut: Greenwood Press, 1983.

Khoury, Philip S. *Syria and the French Mandate*. Princeton: Princeton University Press, 1986.

Legum, Colin, and Shaked Haim (eds.). *Middle East Contemporary Survey, 1976–77,* 1. New York: Holmes and Meier, 1978.

Legum, Colin, Shaked Haim, and Daniel Dishon (eds.). *Middle East ·Contemporary Survey, 1979–80,* 4. New York: Holmes and Meier, 1981.

_____. *Middle East Contemporary Survey, 1980–81,* 5. New York: Holmes and Meier, 1982.

Longrigg, S. H. *Syria and Lebanon Under French Mandate*. Oxford: Oxford University Press, 1958.

Ma'oz, Moshe. *Syria under Hafiz al-Asad: New Domestic and Foreign Policies.* Jerusalem: Hebrew University of Jerusalem Press, 1986.

Malone, Joseph J. *The Arab Lands of Western Asia.* Englewood Cliffs, New Jersey: Prentice-Hall, 1973.

Mansfield, Peter. "Resurgent Syria," *Middle East International* [London], 8, No. 4, October 1977, 545–63.

Naomi, Joy. *Syrian Intervention in Lebanon.* New York: Oxford University Press, 1986.

The Middle East, 6th ed., Washington: Congressional Quarterly, 1986.

Middle East and North Africa 1983–1984 (13th ed.) London: Europa, 1983.

Newhall, Richard A. *The Crusades.* New York: Holt, Rinehart and Winston, 1963.

Perera, Judith. "The Shifting Futures of Syria's Muslim Brotherhood," *Middle East,* May 1983, 25–28.

Peters, F. E. "The Nabateans in the Hawran," *American Oriental Society Journal,* No. 97, July 1977, 263–77.

Petran, Tabitha. *Syria.* New York: Praeger, 1972.

_____. "Syria: Anxious but Resolute," *Middle East International* [London], No. 41, November 1974, 26–28.

_____. "Syria: A Skeptical Ally," *Middle East International* [London], No. 49, July 1975, 12–14.

_____. "Syria: Closing the Ranks," *Middle East International* [London], No. 53, November 1975, 7–8.

Rabinovitch, Itamar. *The War for Lebanon, 1970–1983*. Ithaca: Cornell University Press, 1983.

Reid, Donald M. "The Syrian Christians and Early Socialism in the Arab World," *International Journal of Middle East Studies*, 5, No. 2, April 1974, 177–93.

_____. "Syrian Christians, the Rags-to-Riches Story, and Free Enterprise," *International Journal of Middle East Studies*, 1, No. 4, October 1970, 358–67.

Roberts, David. *The Ba'th and the Creation of Modern Syria*. New York: St. Martin's Press, 1987.

Roberts, Gordon. "The Druzes—A Community Apart," *Middle East International* [London], No. 26, August 1973, 23–25.

Runciman, Steven. *A History of the Crusades*. 3 vols. New York: Harper and Row, 1964.

Sachar, Howard M. *The Emergence of the Middle East, 1914–1924*. New York: Knopf, 1969.

Salih, Shakeeb. "The British-Druze Connections and the Druze Rising of 1896 in the Hawran," *Middle Eastern Studies* [London], 13, No. 2, May 1977, 251–57.

Salihi, Kamal Suleiman. *Syria under Islam*. Delmar, New York: Caravan, 1977.

Seale, Patrick. *The Struggle for Syria*. London: Oxford University Press, 1965.

Shorrock, William I. *French Imperialism in the Middle East: The Failure of the French Policy in Syria and Lebanon, 1900–1914*. Madison: University of Wisconsin Press, 1976.

_____. "The Origin of the French Mandate in Syria and Lebanon: The Railroad Question, 1901–1914," *International Journal of Middle East Studies*, 1, No. 3, July 1970, 133–53.

Simon, Reena S. "Hashemite Conspiracy: Hashemite Unity Attempts, 1921-58," *International Journal of Middle East Studies*, 5, No. 3, June 1974, 314–27.

Spagnolo, J. P. "French Influence in Syria Prior to World War I: The Functional Weakness of Imperialism," *Middle East Journal*, 23, No. 1, Winter 1969, 45–62.

Springborg, Robert. "Baathism in Practice: Agriculture, Politics, and Political Culture in Syria and Iraq," *Middle Eastern Studies*, [London], 17, No. 2, April 1981, 191–209.

Strategic Survey 1982–1983. London: International Institute for Strategic Studies, 1983.

Tibawi, A. L. *A Modern History of Syria, Including Lebanon and Palestine*. London: St. Martin's Press, 1969.

Torrey, Gordon H. "The Ba'th—Ideology and Practice," *Middle East Journal*, 23, No. 4, Autumn 1969, 445–70.

Van Dam, Nikolaos. *The Struggle for Power in Syria: Sectarianism, Regionalism, and Tribalism in Politics, 1961-1978.* London: Croom Helm, 1979.

Ziadeh, Nicola A. *Urban Life in Syria under the Early Mamluks.* Westport, Connecticut: Greenwood Press, 1970.

Chapter 2

Addison, Charles Greenstreet. *Damascus and Palmyra.* New York: Arno Press, 1973.

Al-Ahsan, Syed Azim. "Economic Policy and Class Structure in Syria, 1958-1980," *International Journal of Middle East Studies,* 16, August 1984, 301-23.

Akhrass, Safouh. *Revolutionary Change and Modernization in the Arab World.* Damascus: Atlas, 1972.

Anderson, J. N. D. "The Syrian Law of Personal Status," *Bulletin of the School of Oriental and African Studies* [London], 27, No. 1, 1955, 34-49.

Antonius, George. *The Arab Awakening.* New York: Capricorn, 1963.

Arberry, A.J. (ed.). *Religion in the Middle East: Three Religions in Concord and Conflict.* 2 vols. London: Cambridge University Press, 1969.

Baer, Gabriel. *Population and Society in the Arab East.* New York: Praeger, 1964.

Bahnassi, Afif. *Damascus: Ash-Sham.* (Libraire Universelle). Tunis: Smail, 1982.

Batto, Bernard Frank. *Studies on Women at Mari.* Baltimore: Johns Hopkins University Press, 1974.

Bell, Gertrude Lowthian. *Syria.* New York: Arno Press, 1973.

Berger, Morroe. *The Arab World Today.* New York: Doubleday, 1964.

Betts, Robert Brenton. "The Indigenous Arabic-Speaking Christian Communities of Greater Syria and Mesopotamia." (Unpublished Ph.D dissertation). Baltimore: John Hopkins University, 1968.

Bliss, Frederick Jones. *The Religions of Modern Syria and Palestine.* New York: AMS Press, 1977 (reprint).

Brockelmann, Carl. *History of the Islamic Peoples.* New York: Putnam, 1939.

Cleland, W. Wendell. "Social Conditions and Social Changes," *Journal of International Affairs,* 6, No. 1, Winter 1952, 7-20.

Copeland, W. *The Land and People of Syria.* Philadelphia: Lippincott, 1972.

Costello, V. F. *Urbanization in the Middle East.* New York: Cambridge University Press, 1977.

Crary, Douglas D. "The Villager." Pages 43–59 in Sydney N. Fisher (ed.), *Social Forces in the Middle East,* III. Ithaca: Cornell University Press, 1955.

Daher, Adel. *Current Trends in Arab Intellectual Thought.* (Research Program on Economic and Political Problems and Prospects of the Middle East, RM–5979–FF, December 1969.) Santa Monica: Rand, 1969.

Devlin, John. F. *Syria: Modern State in an Ancient Land.* Boulder, Colorado: Westview Press, 1983.

Dewdney, J. C. "Syria: Patterns of Population Distribution." Pages 130–42 in J. I. Clarke and W. B. Fisher (eds.), *Populations of the Middle East and North Africa.* New York: Africana, 1972.

Dodd, Peter C. "Family Honor and the Forces of Change in Arab Society," *International Journal of Middle East Studies,* 4, January 1973, 40–54.

Dodge, Bayard. "The Settlement of the Assyrians on the Khabbur," *Journal of the Royal Asian Society* [London], 27, 1940, 301–20.

Economist Intelligence Unit. *Quarterly Economic Review of Syria* [London], 1–4; 1985–86.

Fisher, W. B. *The Middle East: A Physical, Social, and Regional Geography.* New York: Dutton, 1956.

"From Tel-Aviv Yedi'ot Aharanot in Hebrew," Foreign Broadcast Information Service, *Daily Report: Middle East and Africa,* 5, No. 161 (FBIS–MEA–86–161), August 20, 1986, I4.

George, A. R. "The Nomads of Syria: End of a Culture?" *Middle East International* [London], No. 22, April 1973, 21.

Gibb, Hamilton A. R. "The Heritage of Islam in the Modern World," Pt. 1, *International Journal of Middle East Studies,* 1, No. 1, January 1970, 1–14.

_____. "The Heritage of Islam in the Modern World," Pt. 2, *International Journal of Middle East Studies,* 1, No. 3, July 1970, 221–37.

Gibb, H. A. R., and J. H. Kramers (eds.). *Shorter Encyclopedia of Islam.* Ithaca: Cornell University Press, 1953.

Haddad, George. *Fifty Years of Modern Syria and Lebanon.* Beirut: Dar al Hayat, 1950.

Haddad, Robert M. *Syrian Christians in Muslim Society: An Interpretation.* Princeton: Princeton University Press, 1970.

Halpern, Manfred. *The Politics of Social Change in the Middle East and North Africa.* Princeton: Princeton University Press, 1963.

Hansen, Henny. *An Ethnographical Collection from the Region of the Alawites.* Copenhagen: Munksgard, 1976.

Hitti, Phillip K. *History of Syria.* New York: Macmillan, 1951.
_____. *History of the Arabs.* New York: Macmillan, 1956.
_____. *Islam: A Way of Life.* Minneapolis: University of Minnesota Press, 1970.
Hodgson, Marshall G. S. *The Venture of Islam.* 3 vols. Chicago: University of Chicago Press, 1974.
Holt, P. M., Ann K. S. Lambton, and Bernard Lewis (eds.). *The Cambridge History of Islam.* 2 vols. London: Cambridge University Press, 1970.
Horton, Alan Williams. "A Syrian Village in Its Changing Environment." (Ph.D. dissertation.) Cambridge: Harvard University, 1961.
Hottinger, Arnold. "How the Arab Bourgeoisie Lost Power," *Journal of Contemporary History,* 3, No. 3, 1968, 111–28.
Hourani, A. H. "Race, Religion and Nation-State in the Near East." Pages 1–19 in A. M. Lutfiyya and C. W. Churchill (eds.), *Readings in Arab Middle Eastern Societies and Cultures.* Paris: Mouton, 1970.
Hudson, J. "Syria," *Focus,* 18, No. 8, April 1968, 1–12.
Human Relations Area Files. *Area Handbook on Syria.* 2 vols. (HRAF Subcontractors Monograph, Dropsie College.) New Haven: HRAF Press, 1956.
Hurewitz, J. C. *Middle East Dilemmas.* New York: Harper, 1953.
Issawi, Charles. "The Arab World's Heavy Legacy." Pages 13–25 in Jack H. Thompson and Robert D. Reischauer (eds.), *Modernization of the Arab World.* New York: D. Van Nostrand, 1966.
_____. "Social Structure and Ideology in Iraq, Lebanon, Syria, and the UAR," *Journal of International Affairs,* 19, No. 1, 1965, 39–46.
Joseph, John. *The Nestorians and Their Muslim Neighbors.* Princeton: Princeton University Press, 1961.
Joint Publications Research Service—JPRS (Washington). The following items are from the JPRS series:
Translations on the Near East.
"Emigration of Arab Technicians: Why and How?" *al-Thawrah,* Damascus, December 8, 1970. (JPRS 52617, No. 578, March 15, 1971.) "Premier Salam Returning from Damascus Satisfied with Results of Talks, Al Asad Says No Kidnapping and No interference in Lebanese Affairs," *Al Nahar,* Beirut, December 5, 1970 (JPRS 52247, 1971).
Kramer, Martin. *Syria's Alawis and Shi'ism.* Tel Aviv: Tel Aviv University, December 1984.
LaFay, Howard. "Syria," *National Geographic,* 154, 3, September 1978, 326–61.

Lapidus, Ira. *Middle Eastern Cities: A Symposium on Ancient, Islamic, and Contemporary Middle Eastern Urbanism.* Berkeley: University of California Press, 1969.

Lerner, Daniel. *The Passing of Traditional Society.* Glencoe, Illinois: Free Press, 1958.

_____. *Race and Color in Islam.* New York: Harper and Row, 1971.

Lewis, Bernard (ed.). *Islam and the Arab World.* New York: Knopf, 1976.

Lewis, Norman. "The Isma'ilis of Syria Today," *Journal of the Royal Central Asian Society* [London], 39, January 1952, 69–77.

Longuenesse, Elizabeth. "The Syrian Working Class Today." Pages 17–24 in *MERIP Reports,* No. 134, Washington: Middle East Research and Information Project, No. 15. July–August 1985.

Ma'oz, Moshe, and Avner Yaniv (eds.). *Syria under Assad.* New York: St. Martin's Press. 1986.

Massignon, L. "Nusairi." Pages 453–56 in H. A. R. Gibb and J. H. Kramers (eds.), *Shorter Encyclopedia of Islam.* Leiden: E. J. Brill, 1974.

Munayyir, Muhammad Arif ibn Ahmad. *The Hejaz Railway and the Muslim Pilgrimage.* Detroit: Wayne State University Press, 1971.

Musil, Alois. *The Manners and Customs of the Rwala Bedouin.* New York: American Geographical Society, 1928.

Nahas, M.K. "The Family in the Arab World," Pages 232–46 in Ailon Shiloh (ed.), *Peoples and Cultures of the Middle East.* New York: Random House, 1969.

"Nomadic Populations in Selected Countries in the Middle East and Related Issues of Sedentarization and Settlement." Pages 105–17 in *Studies on Selected Development Problems in Various Countries in the Middle East.* New York: United Nations, 1970.

Patai, Raphael. *Golden River to Golden Road: Society, Culture, and Change in the Middle East.* Philadelphia: University of Pennsylvania Press, 1969.

Petran, Tabitha. *Syria.* New York: Praeger, 1972.

Prins, A. H. D. "The Syrian Schooner: Problem Formulation in Maritime Culture Change." Pages 404–23 in Ailon Shiloh (ed.), *Peoples and Cultures of the Middle East.* New York: Random House, 1969.

Prothro, Edwin Terry, and Lutfy Najib Diab. *Changing Family Patterns in the Arab East.* Beirut: American University of Beirut, 1974.

Reid, Donald M. "The Syrian Christians and Early Socialism in the Arab World," *International Journal of Middle East Studies,* 5, No. 2, April 1974, 177–93.

————. "Syrian Christians, the Rags-to-Riches Story, and Free Enterprise," *International Journal of Middle East Studies,* 1, No. 4, October 1970, 358–67.

Roberts, Gordon. "The Druzes—A Community Apart," *Middle East International* [London], No. 26, August 1973, 23–25.

Salih, Shakeeb. "The British-Druze Connection and the Druze Rising of 1896 in the Hawran," *Middle Eastern Studies* [London], 13, No. 2, May 1977, 251–57.

Savory, Roger. "Land of the Lion and the Sun." Pages 245–72 in Bernard Lewis (ed.), *Islam and the Arab World.* New York: Knopf, 1976.

Sayigh, Yusif A. *The Determinants of Arab Economic Development.* London: Croom Helm, 1978.

Schultz, T. P. *Fertility Patterns and Their Determinants in the Arab Middle East.* (Rand Abstract, RM-5978-FF.) Santa Monica: Rand, 1970.

Shahgaldian, Nikola B. "Sectarian Politics and the Islamic Challenge in Syria," *Middle East Insight,* 4, No. 2, 1984, 20–29.

Sharabi, Hisham. "Islam and Modernization in the Arab World." Pages 26–36 in Jack H. Thompson and Robert D. Reischauer (eds.), *Modernization of the Arab World.* New York: D. Van Nostrand, 1966.

Smith, Wilfred Cantwell. *Islam in Modern History.* Princeton: Princeton University Press, 1957.

Spears, Edward Louis. *Fulfillment of a Mission.* Hamden, Connecticut: Archon, 1977.

Sweet, Louise. (ed.). *The Central Middle East: A Handbook of Anthropology.* 2 vols. New Haven: Human Relations Area Files, 1968.

————. "A Day in a Syrian Peasant Household." Pages 99–104 in Ailon Shiloh (ed.), *Peoples and Cultures of the Middle East.* New York: Random House, 1969.

————. *Tell Toqaan: A Syrian Village.* (Anthropological Paper No. 14.) Ann Arbor: Museum of Anthropology, University of Michigan, 1960.

"Syria." Pages 179–85 in David Tarr (ed.), *The Middle East.* Washington: Congressional Quarterly, 1986.

Syria. Ministry of Social Affairs and Labor Statistical Division. *The Annual Statistical Bulletin of the Ministry of Social Affairs and Labor,* 22. Damascus: 1984.

Syria. Office of the Prime Minister. Central Bureau of Statistics. *Statistical Abstract,* 38, Damascus: 1985.

Tibawi, A. L. *A Modern History of Syria, Including Lebanon and Palestine.* New York: St. Martin's Press, 1969.

United Kingdom. Admiralty. Naval Intelligence Division. *Syria.* (Geographical Handbook Series.) London: 1943.

Van Nieuwenhuijze, C. A. O. *Social Stratification and the Middle East.* Leiden: E. J. Brill, 1965.

Zeine, Zeine N. *The Struggle for Arab Independence.* Delmar, New York: Caravan, 1977.

Zeltzer, Moshe. "Minorities in Iraq and Syria." Pages 10–50 in Ailon Shiloh (ed.), *Peoples and Cultures of the Middle East.* New York: Random House, 1969.

Zenner, Walter P. "Syrian Jews in Three Social Settings," *Jewish Journal of Sociology* [London], 10, No. 1, 1968, 101–20.

Chapter 3

Al-Ahsan, Syed Aziz. "Economic Policy and Class Structure in Syria, 1958–1980," *International Journal of Middle East Studies,* 16, August 1984, 301–23.

Amin, Samir. *Irak et Syrie, 1960–1980.* Paris: Editions de minuit, 1982.

Askari, Hossein, and John T. Cummings. *Middle East Economics in the 1970s: A Comparative Approach.* (Praeger Special Studies in International Economics and Development.) New York: Praeger, 1976.

Beaumont, Peter. "The Euphrates River—An International Problem of Water Resources Development," *Environmental Conservation,* 5, Spring 1978, 35–44.

Carr, David W. "Capital Flows and Development in Syria," *Middle East Journal,* 34, No. 4, 1980, 455–64.

Central Bank of Syria. *Quarterly Bulletin.* 23. Nos. 1–4, Damascus: 1985.

El-Akhrass, Hisham. *Syria and the CGIAR Centers.* Washington: World Bank, 1986.

Evans, Robert B. *Cotton in Syria.* Washington: Washington Foreign Agricultural Service, 1978.

Firro, Kais. "The Syrian Economy under the Assad Regime," Pages 36–68 in Moshe Ma'oz and Avner Yaniv (eds.), *Syria under Assad,* New York: St. Martin's Press, 1986.

Gottheil, Fred. "Iraqi and Syrian Socialism: An Economic Appraisal," *World Development,* 9, September–October 1981, 825–37.

Hannoyer, Jean. *Etat et secteur publique industriel en Syrie.* (Beirut: Centre d'études et de recherches sur le Moyen-Orient Contemporain). Lyon: Presses universitaires de Lyon, 1979.

_____. "Grands projets hydrauliques en Syrie," *Maghreb-Machrek,* [Paris], No. 109, July–September 1985, 24–42.

Hansen, Brent. "Economic Development of Syria." Pages 330–67 in Charles A. Cooper and Sidney S. Alexander (eds.), *Economic Development and Population Growth in the Middle East.* New York: American Elsevier, 1972.

Himadeh, Said B. *Economic Organization of Syria.* New York: AMS Press, 1973.

Hinnebusch, Raymond A. "Rural Politics in Ba'thist Syria: A Case Study in the Role of the Countryside in the Political Development of Arab Societies," *Review of Politics,* 44, 1982, 110–30.

International Labour Organisation. *The Syrian Arab Republic: Project Findings and Recommendations.* Geneva: United Nations Development Programme, International Labour Organisation, 1982.

_____. *Economic Development of Syria.* Tel Aviv: David Horowitz Institute for the Research of Developing Countries, 1975.

International Monetary Fund. *International Financial Statistics Yearbook.* Washington: 1986.

_____. *Balance of Payment Statistics Yearbook, Parts 1 and 2.* Washington: 1985.

Kanovsky, Eliyahu. *The Economic Development of Syria.* Tel Aviv: University Publishing Projects, 1977.

_____. *Economic Development of Syria.* Tel Aviv: David Horowitz Institute for the Research of Developing Countries, 1975.

_____. "What's Behind Syria's Current Economic Problems?" Pages 280–347 in Haim Shaked and Daniel Dishon (eds.), *Middle East Contemporary Survey, 1983–84,* 7. Tel Aviv: Tel Aviv University, 1986.

Keilany, Ziad. "Land Reform in Syria," *Middle Eastern Studies,* [London], 16, October 1980, 209–24.

_____. "Socialism and Economic Change in Syria," *Middle Eastern Studies* [London], 9, No. 1, January 1973, 61–72.

Khader, Bichara. *La question agraire dans les pays Arabes.* Louvain-la-Neuve, Belgium: Université Catholique de Louvain, 1984.

Longuenesse, Elizabeth. "The Syrian Working Class Today." Pages 17–24 in *MERIP Reports,* No. 134. Washington: Middle East Research and Information Project, July–August 1985.

_____. "Syrie: secteur public industriel, les enjeux d'une crise," *Maghreb-Machrek,* [Paris], No. 109, July–September 1985, 5–23.

Manners, Ian R., and Tagi Sagafi-Nejad. "Agricultural Development in Syria." Pages 255–78 in P. Beaumont and K. McLachlan (eds.), *Agricultural Development in the Middle East.* New York: John Wiley and Sons, 1985.

"Manpower and Employment Planning in Iraq and the Syrian Arab Republic." Pages 22–44 in *Studies on Development Problems in Countries of Western Asia, 1975.* New York: United Nations, 1977.

Métral, Françoise. "Etat et paysans dans le Ghab en Syrie: approche locale d'un projet d'état," *Maghreb-Machrek* [Paris], No. 109, July–September, 43–63.

Sayigh, Yusif A. *The Economics of the Arab World: Developments since 1945.* London: Croom Helm, 1978.

Syria. Arab Office for Press Documentation. *Fifth Five Year Economic and Social Development Plan of the Syrian Arab Republic, 1981–1985.* Damascus: 1981.

Syria. Ministry of Agriculture and Agrarian Reform. *The Annual Agricultural Statistical Abstract, 1981.* Damascus: 1982.

_____. *The Annual Agricultural Statistical Abstract 1982.* Damascus: 1983.

Syria. Office of the Prime Minister. Central Bureau of Statistics. Statistical Abstract, 1968, 21, Damascus: 1969.

_____. *Statistical Abstract, 1976,* 29, Damascus: 1977.

_____. *Statistical Abstract, 1979,* 32, Damascus: 1980.

_____. *Statistical Abstract, 1985,* 38, Damascus: 1985.

_____. *Statistical Abstract, 1986,* 39, Damascus: 1986.

United States. Agency for International Development. *Syria: Agricultural Sector Assessment.* 5 vols. Washington: 1980.

United States. *Syria Agricultural Sector Assessment, Vol. 1.* Washington: 1980.

Wilson, Rodney. *Development Planning in the Middle East: The Impact of Foreign Influences.* London: Institute for the Study of Conflict, 1983.

World Bank. *The Economic Development of Syria.* Baltimore: Johns Hopkins Press, 1955.

(Various issues of the following publications were also used in the preparation of this chapter: *An Nahar Arab Report and Memo* [Beirut]; *Arabia: The Islamic World Review* [London]; *Country Profile: Syria* [London]; *Country Report: Syria* [London]; *Financial Times* [London]; *Foreign Agriculture*; *Foreign Economic Trends*; *International Financial Statistics*; Joint Publications Research Service, *Near East/South Asia Reports*; *Middle East Economic Digest* [London]; *Middle East Economic Outlook*; *Middle East Economic Survey* [Cyprus]; *MidEast Markets*; *Mineral Trade Notes*; *New York Times*; *Outlook and Situation Report: Middle East and North Africa*; *Quarterly Economic Country Report: Syria* [London]; *Syrie et Monde Arabe* [Damascus]; United Nations *Handbook of International Trade and Development Statistics;* United Nations

Yearbook of International Energy Statistics; *Washington Post.*; World Bank, *World Development Report.*

Chapter 4

Abd-Allah, Umar F. *The Islamic Struggle in Syria.* Berkeley: Mizan Press, 1983.

Adams, Michael. "The Arab-Israeli Confrontation, 1967–77." Pages 35–49 in *The Middle East and North Africa, 1977–78.* London: Europa, 1977.

Amnesty International. *Report from Amnesty International to the Government of the Syrian Arab Republic.* London: November 1983.

Babikian, N. Salem. "A Partial Reconstruction of Michel Aflaq's Thought: The Role of Islam in the Formation of Arab Nationalism," *Muslim World,* 67, No. 4, October 1977, 280–94.

Bar-Simon-Tov, Yaacov. *Linkage Politics in the Middle East: Syria Between Domestic and External Conflict, 1961–1970.* Boulder, Colorado: Westview Press, 1983.

Batatu, Hanna. "Some Observations on the Social Roots of Syria's Ruling Military Group and the Causes for Its Dominance," *Middle East Journal,* 35, No. 3, Summer 1981, 331–44.

Ben-Dor, Gabriel. *Political Participation under Military Regimes.* Beverly Hills: Sage, 1976.

Burrowes, Robert, and Gerald DeMaio. "Domestic/External Linkages: Syria, 1961–1967," *Comparative Political Studies,* 7, No. 4, January 1975, 478–507.

Cass, Alain. "Syria." Pages 332–42 in *Middle East Annual Review, 1976.* Saffron Walden, United Kingdom: 1976.

Cooley, John K. "Shifting Sands of Arab Communism," *Problems of Communism,* 24, March–April 1975, 22–42.

Dawisha, Adeed I. "The Motives of Syria's Involvement in Lebanon," *Middle East Journal,* 38, No. 2, Spring 1984, 228–36.

———. *Syria and the Lebanese Crisis.* London: Macmillan, 1980.

———. "Syria under Assad, 1970–78: The Centers of Power," *Government and Opposition* [London], 13, No. 3, Summer 1978, 341–54.

Devlin, John F. *The Ba'th Party: A History from Its Origins to 1966.* Stanford, California: Hoover Institution Press, 1976.

———. "The Political Structure in Syria," *Middle East Review,* 17, No. 1, Fall 1984, 15–21.

———. "Syria: Consistency at Home and Abroad," *Current History,* 85, No. 508, February 1986, 67–70, 84–85.

_____. *Syria: Modern State in an Ancient Land.* Boulder, Colorado: Westview Press, 1983.

Drysdale, Alasdair. "The Succession Question in Syria," *Middle East Journal,* 39, No. 2, Spring 1985, 246-57.

_____. "The Asad Regime and Its Troubles." Pages 3-11 in *MERIP Reports,* No. 110. Washington: Middle East Research and Information Project, November-December 1982.

Ehrnman, Bruce. "Syria and the United States: The Awkward Relationship," *Middle East Insight,* 4, No. 5, 1986, 14-20.

Faksh, Mahmud A. "The Alawi Community of Syria: A New Dominant Political Force," *Middle Eastern Studies* [London], 20, No. 2, April 1984, 133-53.

_____. "The Military and Politics in Syria: The Search for Stability," *Journal of South Asian and Middle Eastern Studies,* 8, Spring 1985, 3-21.

Freedman, Robert O. "Moscow, Damascus, and the Lebanese Crisis of 1982-1984," *Middle East Review,* 17, No. 1, Fall 1984, 22-39.

Galvani, John. "Syria and the Baath Party." Pages 3-16 in *MERIP Reports,* No. 25. Washington: Middle East Research and Information Project, February 1974.

Garfinkle, Adam. "The Forces Behind Syrian Politics," *Middle East Review,* 17, No. 1, Fall 1984, 5-13.

Golan, Gatalia. "Syria and the Soviet Union since the Yom Kippur War," *Orbis,* 21, No. 4, Winter 1978, 777-802.

Gubser, Peter. "Minorities in Power: The Alawites of Syria." Pages 17-48 in R. D. McLaurin (ed.), *The Political Role of Minority Groups in the Middle East.* New York: Praeger, 1979.

Haddad, George. *Revolutions and Military Rule in the Middle East: The Arab States, II, Part I. Iraq, Syria, Lebanon, and Jordan.* New York: Robert Speller and Sons, 1971.

Heller, Peter B. "The Permanent Syrian Constitution of March 13, 1973," *Middle East Journal,* 28, No. 1, Winter 1974, 53-66.

Hinnebusch, Raymond A. "Local Politics in Syria: Organization and Mobilization in Four Village Cases," *Middle East Journal,* 30, No. 1, Winter 1976, 1-24.

_____. *Political Organization in Syria: A Case of Mobilization Politics.* Pittsburgh: University of Pittsburgh Press, 1975.

_____. "Political Recruitment and Socialization in Syria: The Case of the Revolutionary Youth Federation," *International Journal of Middle East Studies,* 11, No. 2, April 1980, 143-74.

_____. "Syria under the Ba'th: State Formation in a Fragmented Society," *Arab Studies Quarterly,* 4, No. 3, Summer 1982, 177-97.

Hottinger, Arnold. "Syria: On the Verge of a Civil War?" *Swiss Review of World Affairs*, 32, No. 4, July 1982, 12–13.

Hudson, Michael C. *Arab Politics: The Search for Legitimacy.* New Haven: Yale University Press, 1977.

Ismael, Tareq Y. *The Arab Left.* Syracuse: Syracuse University Press, 1976.

Kaylani, Nabil M. "The Rise of the Syrian Ba'th, 1940–1958: Political Success, Party Failure," *International Journal of Middle East Studies*, 3, No. 1, January 1972, 3–23.

Korn, David. "Syria and Lebanon: A Fateful Entanglement," *World Today* [London], 42, Nos. 8–9, August–September 1986, 137–42.

Kramer, Martin. "Syria's Alawis and Shi'ism." Pages 237–54 in Martin Kramer (ed.), *Shi'ism, Resistance, and Revolution.* Boulder, Colorado: Westview Press, 1987.

Landau, Jacob. "Syria in Some Soviet Publications," *Middle Eastern Studies* [London], 13, No. 2, May 1977, 258–60.

Lawson, Fred H. "Social Bases for the Hamah Revolt." Pages 24–28 in *MERIP Reports*, No. 110. Washington: Middle East Research and Information Project, November–December 1982.

_____. "Syria's Intervention in the Lebanese Civil War, 1976: A Domestic Conflict Interpretation," *International Organization*, 38, No. 3, Summer 1984, 451–80.

Longuenesse, Elizabeth. "The Class Nature of the State in Syria." Pages 3–11 in *MERIP Reports*, No. 77. Washington: Middle East Research and Information Project, May 1979.

Macintyre, Ronald R. "Syrian Political Age Differentials, 1958–1966," *Middle East Journal*, 29, No. 2, Spring 1975, 207–14.

Ma'oz, Moshe. "Society and State in Modern Syria." Pages 29–91 in Menachem Wilson (ed.), *Society and Political Structure in the Arab World.* New York: Humanities Press, 1973.

Ma'oz, Moshe, and Avner Yaniv (eds.). *Syria under Assad.* New York: St. Martin's Press, 1986.

Michaud, Gerard. "The Importance of Bodyguards." Pages 29–33 in *MERIP Reports*, No. 110. Washington: Middle East Research and Information Project, November–December 1982.

Neumann, Robert G. "Assad and the Future of the Middle East." *Foreign Affairs*, No. 62, Winter 1983–84, 237–54.

Nir, Amiran. *The Soviet-Syrian Friendship and Cooperation Treaty: Unfulfilled Expectations.* Tel Aviv: Jaffee Center for Strategic Studies, Tel Aviv University, May 1983.

Olmert, Yosef. "Syria." Pages 671–709 in Haim Shaked and Daniel Dishon (eds.), *Middle East Contemporary Survey, 1983–84.*

No. 8, (Dayan Center for Middle Eastern and African Studies, The Shiloah Institute.) Tel Aviv: Tel Aviv University, 1986.

Olson, Robert W. *The Ba'ath and Syria, 1947-1982: The Evolution of Ideology, Party, and State.* Princeton: Kingston Press, 1982.

Perry, Glen E. "Syria." Pages 434-36 in Richard F. Staar (ed.), *Yearbook on International Communist Affairs, 1985.* Stanford: Hoover Institution Press, 1986.

Petran, Tabitha. *Syria.* New York: Praeger, 1972.

Rabinovitch, Itamar. "The Foreign Policy of Syria: Goals, Capabilities, Constraints, and Options." Pages 38-46 in Charles Tripp (ed.), *Regional Security in the Middle East.* New York: International Institute for Strategic Studies, St. Martin's Press, 1984.

_____. "The Limitations of Power: Syria under al-Asad," *New Middle East* [London], 54, March 1973, 36-37.

_____. "Syria." Pages 265-82 in Edward A. Kolodzies and Robert E. Harkavy (eds.), *Security Policies of Developing Countries.* Lexington, Massachusetts: Lexington Books, 1982.

_____. *Syria under the Baath, 1963-66: The Army-Party Symbiosis.* Jerusalem: Israel Universities Press, 1972.

Ramet, Pedro. "The Soviet-Syrian Relationship," *Problems of Communism,* 35, No. 5, September-October 1986, 35-46.

Reed, Stanley. "Dateline Syria: Fin de Regime?" *Foreign Policy,* No. 39, Summer 1980, 176-90.

Rothenberg, Mavis. "Recent Soviet Relations with Syria, "*Middle East Review,* 10, No. 4, Summer 1978, 5-9.

Sadowski, Yahya M. "Cadres, Guns and Money: The Eighth Regional Congress of the Syrian Ba'th." Pages 3-8 in *MERIP Reports,* No. 134. Washington: Middle East Research and Information Project, July-August 1985.

"Salah ad Din Bitar's Last Interview." Pages 21-23 in *MERIP Reports,* No. 110. Washington: Middle East Research and Information Project, November-December 1982.

Seelye, Talcott W. "The Syrian Perspective on the Peace Process," *American-Arab Affairs,* No. 17, Summer 1986, 55-61.

_____. "U.S.-Syrian Relations: The Thread of Mu'awiyyah," *American-Arab Affairs,* No. 4, Spring 1983, 40-45.

Shahgaldian, Nikola B. "Sectarian Politics and the Islamic Challenge in Syria," *Middle East Insight,* 4, No. 2, 1985, 20-29.

Shiff, Ze'ev. "Dealing With Syria," *Foreign Policy,* No. 55, Summer 1984, 92-113.

Sinai, Anne, and Allen Pollack (eds.). *The Syrian Arab Republic: A Handbook.* New York: American Academic Association for Peace in the Middle East, 1976.

Stiefbold, Annette. "Lebanon, Syria, and the Crisis of Soviet Policy in the Middle East," *Air University Review,* No. 28, September–October 1977, 62–70.

Stoakes, Frank. "The Civil War in Lebanon," *World Today* [London], 32, No. 1, January 1976, 8–17.

Torrey, Gordon H. "Aspects of the Political Elite in Syria." Pages 151–61 in George Lenczowski (ed.), *Political Elites in the Middle East.* Washington: American Enterprise Institute for Public Policy Research, 1975.

_____. "The Ba'th—Ideology and Practice," *Middle East Journal,* 23, No. 4, Autumn 1969, 445–70.

United States. Congress. 94th, 1st Session. Senate. Committee on Foreign Relations. *A Select Chronology and Background Documents Relating to the Middle East.* (2d rev. ed.) Washington: GPO, 1975.

United States. Congress. 95th, 1st Session. House of Representatives. Committee on International Relations. *Report of a Study Mission to Israel, Egypt, Syria, and Jordan.* Washington: GPO, 1977.

Van Dam, Nikolaos. *The Struggle for Power in Syria: Sectarianism, Regionalism, and Tribalism in Politics, 1961–1978.* London. Croom Helm, 1979.

Vatikiotis, P.J. "The Politics of the Fertile Crescent." Pages 225–63 in Paul Y. Hammond and Sidney S. Alexander (eds.), *Political Dynamics in the Middle East.* New York: American Elsevier, 1972.

Yamak, Labib Zuwiyya. *The Syrian Social Nationalist Party: An Ideological Analysis.* (Harvard Middle Eastern Monograph series, No. 16.) Cambridge: Harvard University Press, 1966.

Yodfat, Aryeh. *Arab Politics in the Soviet Mirror.* Jerusalem: Israel Universities Press, 1973.

Younger, Sam. "The Syrian Stake in Lebanon," *World Today* [London], 32, No. 11, November 1976, 399–406.

(Various issues of the following publications were also used in the preparation of this chapter: *An Nahar Arab Report and Memo* [Beirut]; *Christian Science Monitor; Daily Summary of World Broadcasts, Part 4: The Middle East and Africa* [London]; *Defense and Foreign Affairs Daily; Defense and Foreign Affairs Weekly;* Foreign Broadcast Information Service, *Daily Report: Near East and South Asia;* Joint Publications Research Service, *Near East/South Asia Report; Keesing's Contemporary Archives; Middle East Contemporary Survey; Middle East Economic Digest* [London]; *Middle East International* [London]; *Middle East Reporter* [Beirut]; *Quarterly Economic Country Report: Syria* [London]; *New York Times;* and *Washington Post.*)

Chapter 5

Abd-Allah, Umar F. *The Islamic Struggle in Syria.* Berkeley: Mizan Press, 1983.

Adams, James, et al. "Assad's Assassins," *Sunday Times* [London], October 26, 1986, 27.

Amin, Eqbal. "Iraq and Syria: The Long Estrangement," *Africa Asia,* No. 31, July 1986, 63.

Amnesty International. *Amnesty International Report, 1985.* London: 1985.

_____. *Amnesty International Report, 1986.* London: 1986.

_____. *Syria: An Amnesty International Briefing.* London: November 1983.

Banks, Tony. "Syria Upgrades Forces Facing Golan Heights," *Jane's Defence Weekly* [London], December 28, 1985, 1386–87.

Be'eri, Eliezer. *Army Officers in Arab Politics and Society.* New York: Praeger, 1970.

Ben-Dor, Gabriel. "Civilianization of Military Regimes in the Arab World," *Armed Forces and Society,* 1, No. 3, Spring 1975, 317–27.

Bernstein, Richard. "The Terror: Why France? Why Now." *New York Times Magazine,* October 19, 1986, 31.

Bruce, James. "Huge Weapons Race with Israel Is Driving Syria Deeper into Debt," *Jane's Defence Weekly* [London], December 6, 1986, 1,336.

Cobban, Helena. *The Palestine Liberation Organization: People, Power, and Politics.* New York: Cambridge University Press, 1984.

Devlin, John F. *The Ba'th Party: A History from Its Origins to 1966.* Stanford, California: Hoover Institution Press, 1976.

Dyer, Gwynne. "Syria." Pages 682–95 in John Kegan (ed.), *World Armies.* New York: Facts on File, 1979.

Economist Intelligence Unit, *Country Report: Syria* [London], No. 2, 1986.

Fisk, Robert. "Air Slaughter Plot Points to Syria's Iron Man," *Times* [London], October 25, 1986, 5.

FitzGerald, Benedict F. "Syria." Pages 41–61 in Richard A. Gabriel (ed.), *Fighting Armies: Antagonists in the Middle East; A Combat Assessment.* Westport, Connecticut: Greenwood Press, 1983.

Glassman, Jon D. *Arms for the Arabs: The Soviet Union and War in the Middle East.* Baltimore: Johns Hopkins University Press, 1975.

Haddad, George M. *Revolutions and Military Rule in the Middle East: The Arab States, II, Part I. Iraq, Syria, Lebanon, and Jordan.* New York: Robert Speller and Sons, 1971.

Haseklorn, Avigdor. "Syrian Missiles: Shifting Balance in the Middle East," *World & I,* January 1987, 148–53.

Heller, Mark, Aharon Levran, and Ze'ev Eytan. *The Middle East Military Balance, 1985.* Boulder, Colorado: Westview Press, 1986.

Herzog, Chaim. *The Arab-Israeli Wars.* New York: Vintage Books, 1984.

Hurewitz, J. C. "Military Roulette: Syria and Iraq." Pages 145–62 in J. C. Hurewitz (ed.), *Middle East Politics: The Military Dimension.* New York: Octagon Books, 1974.

International Institute for Strategic Studies. *The Military Balance, 1986–1987,* London: 1986.

_____. *Strategic Survey 1986–87.* London: 1987.

Jenkins, Loren. "Arafat Links Syria, Libya to Attacks," *Washington Post,* January 5, 1986, A1, A21.

Kent, Jay. "The Assad Factor," *Middle East,* No. 135, January 1986, 47–49.

Kifner, John. "Can Syria Untie the Lebanese Knot?" *New York Times,* February 23, 1987, A10.

Lambeth, Benjamin S. *Moscow's Lessons from the 1982 Lebanon Air War.* Santa Monica: Rand, 1984.

Ma'oz, Moshe, and Avner Yaniv (eds.). *Syria under Assad.* New York: St. Martin's Press, 1986.

Merari, Ariel, et al. *Inter 85: A Review of International Terrorism in 1985.* Boulder, Colorado: Westview Press, 1986.

Moreaux, J. M. "The Syrian Army," *Defence Update International* [Cologne], No. 69, 1985, 26–31, 42–43.

Miller, Judith. "The Istanbul Synagogue Massacre: An Investigation," *New York Times Magazine,* January 4, 1986, 14.

Nir, Amiran. *The Soviet-Syrian Friendship and Cooperation Treaty: Unfulfilled Expectations.* Tel Aviv: Jaffee Center for Strategic Studies, Tel Aviv University, May 1983.

O'Dwyer-Russell, Simon. "Fears Grow over Golan War," *Jane's Defence Weekly* [London], June 28, 1986, 1,240.

Ottaway, David B. "Syrian Connection to Terrorism Probed," *Washington Post,* June 1, 1986, A1, A24–A25.

Pajak, Roger F. "Soviet Military Aid to Iraq and Syria," *Strategic Review,* 4, No. 1, Winter 1976, 51–59.

Perlmutter, Amos. *Political Roles and Military Rulers.* Totowa, New Jersey: Frank Cass, 1981.

Perry, Glen E. "Syria." Pages 434–36 in Richard F. Staar (ed.), *Yearbook on International Communist Affairs, 1985.* Stanford: Hoover Institution Press, 1986.

_____. "Syria and Lebanon," *Current History,* 86, No. 517, February 1987.

Rabinovitch, Itamar. "Syria and Lebanon," *Current History,* 86, No. 517, February 1987.

_____. "Syria's Quest for a Regional Role." Paper presented at Woodrow Wilson Center for International Scholars, December 11, 1986.

Ramet, Pedro. "The Soviet-Syrian Relationship," *Problems of Communism,* 35, No. 5, September–October 1986, 35–46.

Raviv, Chaim. "The Arab Soldier: The Race to Reach Quality," *Bamachane,* No. 23, February 5, 1986, 10 (in Hebrew).

Rosen, Steven J. "What the Next Arab-Israeli War Might Look Like," *International Security,* 2, No. 4, Spring 1978, 149–74.

Schiff, Ze'ev, and Ehud Ya'ari. *Israel's Lebanon War.* New York: Simon and Schuster, 1984.

Sinai, Anne, and Allen Pollack (eds.). *The Syrian Arab Republic: A Handbook.* New York: American Academic Association for Peace in the Middle East, 1976.

Sivard, Ruth Leger. *World Military and Social Expenditures, 1986.* Washington: World Priorities, 1986.

Syria. Office of the Prime Minister. Central Bureau of Statistics. *Statistical Abstract,* 1986, 39, Damascus: June 1986.

Torrey, Gordon H. *Syrian Politics and the Military, 1945–1958.* Columbus: Ohio State University Press, 1964.

United States. Arms Control and Disarmament Agency. *World Military Expenditures and Arms Transfers, 1986.* Washington: GPO, April 1987.

United States. Central Intelligence Agency. *Handbook of Economic Statistics, 1986.* Washington: GPO, September 1986.

United States. Department of State. *Country Reports on Human Rights Practices for 1986.* (Report submitted to United States Congress, 100th, 1st Session, Senate, Committee on Foreign Relations, and House of Representatives, Committee on Foreign Affairs.) Washington: GPO, February 1987.

_____. *Warsaw Pact Aid to Non-Communist LDCs, 1984.* Washington: GPO, May 1986.

_____. *Syrian Support for International Terrorism, 1983–1986.* (Special Report, No. 157.) Washington: GPO, December 1986.

United States. Department of State. Bureau of Public Affairs. Office of Public Communication. *Background Notes: Syria.* (Department of State Publication, No. 7761.) Washington: GPO, June 1986.

"The Unmasking of Assad," *U.S. News and World Report,* November 10, 1986.

Van Dam, Nikolaos. *The Struggle for Power in Syria: Sectarianism, Regionalism and Tribalism in Politics, 1961–1978.* London: Croom Helm, 1979.

Weinberger, Naomi Joy. *Syrian Intervention in Lebanon: The 1975–76 Civil War.* Oxford University Press, 1986.

Who's Who in the Arab World, 1986–1987. Beirut: Publitec Publications, 1987.

(Various issues of the following publications were also used in the preparation of this chapter: *Armed Forces; Defense and Foreign Affairs; Journal of Defense and Diplomacy;* Foreign Broadcast Information Service, Joint Publications Research Service, *Near East/South Asia Report; Daily Report: Middle East and Africa; Times* [London]; *Manchester Guardian, Middle East Contemporary Survey; Middle East Journal; Middle Eastern Studies* [London]; *New York Times*; and *Washington Post.*)

Glossary

Alawi(s)—Member of a Shia (*q.v.*) sect that is the largest religious
minority in Syria. President Hafiz al Assad and many other
leaders of the ruling political party are adherents. Alawis believe
in divine incarnation and the divinity of Ali, and hence they
are viewed as heretical by most other Muslims.

Alawite—See Alawi.

amir—Literally, commander. Frequently used as title by tribal
chief. Also used by rulers of principalities or small states and
governors of provinces. In Saudi Arabia and elsewhere used
by princes of the royal family.

barrels—See barrels per day.

barrels per day—Production of crude oil and petroleum products
is frequently measured in barrels per day. A barrel is a volume
measure of forty-two United States gallons. Conversion of barrels to metric tons depends on the density of the special product.
About 7.3 barrels of average crude oil weigh one metric ton.
Heavy products would be about seven barrels per metric ton.
Light products, such as gasoline and kerosene, would average
close to eight barrels per metric ton.

currency—See Syrian pound.

Druze(s)—Member of a religious community located in the southern part of Syria that is the third largest religious group of the
country. Druze beliefs contain elements of Shia (*q.v.*) Islam,
Christianity, and paganism.

fiscal year (FY)—Same as calendar year since 1963.

GDP (gross domestic product)—A value measure of the flow of
domestic goods and services produced by an economy over a
period of time, such as a year. Only output values of goods
for final consumption and intermediate production are assumed
to be included in final prices. GDP is sometimes aggregated
and shown at market prices, meaning that indirect taxes and
subsidies are included; when these have been eliminated, the
result is GDP at factor cost. The word gross indicates that
deductions for depreciation of physical assets have not been
made. *See also GNP.*

GNP (gross national product)—GDP (*q.v.*) plus the net income
or loss stemming from transactions with foreign countries. GNP
is the broadest measurement of the output of goods and services by an economy. It can be calculated at market prices,
which include indirect taxes and subsidies. Because indirect

317

taxes and subsidies are only transfer payments, GNP is often calculated at factor cost, removing indirect taxes and subsidies.

Greater Syria—Term used by historians and others to designate the region that includes approximately the present-day states of Jordan, Israel, Lebanon, and Syria before those states were formed.

hadith—Tradition based on the precedent of the Prophet Muhammad's nondivinely revealed deeds and words that serves as one of the sources of Islamic law (sharia).

hijra—Literally, to migrate, to sever relations, to leave one's tribe. Throughout the Muslim world, hijra refers to the migration of Muhammad and his followers to Medina. In this sense the word has come into European languages as hegira and is usually and somewhat misleadingly translated as flight.

Imam—A word used in several senses. In general use and lower-cased, it means the leader of congregational prayers; as such, it implies no ordination or special spiritual powers beyond sufficient education to carry out this function. It is also used figuratively by many Sunni (q.v.) Muslims to mean the leader of the Islamic community. Among Shias (q.v.) the word takes on many complex and controversial meanings; in general, however, when capitalized, it indicates the particular descendant of the House of Ali who is believed to have been God's designated repository of the spiritual authority inherent in that line. The identity of this individual and the means of ascertaining his identity have been the major issues causing divisions among Shias.

International Monetary Fund (IMF)—Established along with the World Bank (q.v.) in 1945, the IMF is a specialized agency affiliated with the United Nations and is responsible for stabilizing international exchange rates and payments. The main business of the IMF is the provision of loans to its members (including industrialized and developing countries) when they experience balance of payments difficulties. These loans frequently carry conditions that require substantial internal economic adjustments by the recipients, most of which are developing countries.

Ismaili(s)—Member(s) of a branch of Shia (q.v.) Islam. Ismailis recognize seven Imams (q.v.) and venerate Ismail as the Seventh; other Shias recognize Musa al Kazim as the Seventh Imam. Ismailis are often called Seveners, and other Shias are known as Twelvers.

jihad—The struggle to establish the law of God on earth, often interpreted to mean holy war.

shaykh—Leader or chief. Word of Arabic origin used to mean a tribal, political, or learned religious leader. Also used as an honorific.

Shia (or Shiites, from Shiat Ali, the Party of Ali)—A member of the smaller of the two great divisions of Islam. The Shias supported the claims of Ali and his line to presumptive right to the caliphate and leadership of the Muslim community, and on this issue they divided from the Sunnis (*q.v.*). Shias revere Twelve Imams, the last of whom is believed to be hidden from view.

Shiite—See Shia.

Sunni (from sunna, orthodox)—A member of the larger of the two great divisions of Islam. The Sunnis supported the traditional method of election to the caliphate and accepted the Umayyad line. On this issue they divided from the Shias (*q.v.*) in the first great schism within Islam.

Syrian pound (LS)—Has consisted of 100 piasters since first issued by the French in 1920. Par value of LS2.19 to US$1 was established with the IMF in 1947. Par value was the official exchange rate until 1954 when it became LS3.58 to US$1. In the 1960s and 1970s the official exchange rate ranged between LS3.82 to US$1 in 1962 to LS3.95 to US$1 in 1978. In 1981 Syria returned to a multitier exchange rate, establishing a parallel rate for the pound to float freely against major world currencies. In 1987 there were four government-established exchange rates for the Syrian pound: the official rate (used for imports) was LS3.92 to US$1; the parallel rate (used for commercial ventures) was LS5.40 to US$1; the tourist rate (used by tourists but also diplomats and for commercial transactions) was LS9.75 to US$1; and the "neighboring country" rate (private sector imports and the trading rate of the pound in other countries and illegally inside Syria) was LS21.50 to US$1.

World Bank—Informal name used to designate a group of three affiliated international institutions: the International Bank for Reconstruction and Development (IBRD), the International Development Association (IDA), and the International Finance Corporation (IFC). The IBRD, established in 1945, has the primary purpose of providing loans to developing countries for productive projects. The IDA, a legally separate loan fund but administered by the staff of the IBRD, was set up in 1960 to furnish credits to the poorest developing countries on much easier terms than those of conventional IBRD loans. The IFC, founded in 1956, supplements the activities of the IBRD through loans and assistance specifically designed to encourage the growth of productive private enterprises in the less developed countries. The president and certain senior officers of the IBRD hold the same positions in the IFC. The three institutions are owned by the governments of the countries that subscribe their capital. To participate in the World Bank group, member states must first belong to the International Monetary Fund (IMF—*q.v.*).

Yazidi(s)—Member(s) of a small religious group. The religion is little known to outsiders but contains elements of Islam, Judaism, and Christianity and also includes the veneration of the Peacock Angel.

Abadah, 78
Abbasids, 4, 11-12, 95
Abdul Hamid II, 18, 95
Abdullah, 20
Abu Ali Hasan, 12
Abu Bakr, 10, 90
Abu Musa, 251
Abu Nidal, 223, 243-44, 251, 272, 274; training camps, 272
Administrative Court of Justice (Majlis ad Dawlah), 279
Aflaq, Michel, 32, 34, 35, 195, 196-97, 199
Aga Khan, 95
Agricultural Cooperative Bank, 137-38, 169
agriculture (see also cotton; irrigation; land reform), xiv, xxi, 56, 77, 109, 125, 127-28; barley, xiv; budget, 119, 124, 127, 128, 129-30, 145; cereals, 56; cooperatives, 136, 139-40; cultivation, 135; drainage, 111, 127, 135; expansion, 110; financing, 137-38, 141; government role, 137-40, 145-46; gross domestic product (GDP), xiv, 112, 129-30; labor force, 112, 127; land reclamation, 111, 130; marketing organizations, 138; mechanization of, 110; outlook, 145-46; price controls, 128, 138-39, 141; rainfall, 140; research projects, 141; sugar beets, 143, 157; wheat, xiv, 139, 141
Al Ahd (The Covenant), 18
Ahmad, Ahmad Iskander, 210
Ahmar, Abdallah al, 206, 212, 222
air force, xvi; air bases, 259; combat aircraft, xvii, 259; manpower, 259; origins, 237; pilot shortages, 38; training, 262; uniforms and rank insignia, 264
Air Force Academy, 262
airports and aviation, 173, 177-78
Akkad, 6
Alawis, xvi, 17, 26, 62, 86, 96-97; attacks from Muslim Brotherhood, 45; and the Baath Party, 36, 37; Christian elements, 96; kin-groups, 97; and the military, xxii, 275; political domination, xx, 255-56; religious beliefs, 97

Aleppo, xxii, xx, 6, 12, 16, 44, 68, 69, 86, 100, 129, 133; 1945 demonstrations in, 26; population, 58; religious settlements, 86
Alexander the Great, xix, 7, 96
Alexandretta (see also Iskenderun), 24, 27, 253; self-government, 24
Algeria, 143, 163
Ali, 10, 90, 91, 94, 97
Ali, Ali ibn Abid al, 44
Ali, Shaykh Salih ibn, 21
alphabet, 7; Armenian, 68
Amal, 249
American Petroleum Institute (API), 147
Amir, Abdul Hakim, 30
Amu Darya, 4
Amuda, 66, 86
Ancient Syria. See Greater Syria
Anti-Lebanon Mountains, 55
Antioch, 8
Arab Academy, 19
Arab countries (see also names of individual countries), xv; imports, 162, 163; relationship, 29, 39, 41
Arab Cultural Unity Agreement, 101
Arab Democratic Party, 270
Arab Deterrent Force (ADF), 42, 164, 248-49
Arab Fund for Economic and Social Development, 160, 167
Arab-Israeli conflict (see also June 1967 War, October 1973 War, and names of individual countries;), xvi, xxiii, 186, 220-22; 1948 War, 197; economic effects, 110; foreign policy, 220
Arab League (League of Arab States), 26, 237, 248, 252
Arab Legion, 238
Arab Liberation Army, 238
Arab Liberation Movement (ALM), 28
Arab National Movement, 20
Arab Satellite Organization (ARAB-SAT), 178
Arab Socialist Party (ASP), 41, 197-98
Arab Summits: Baghdad, 1978, 165-66, 267; Fez, Morocco, 1982, 221
Arabian Peninsula, 18
Arabs, 62, 64-65; attitude to non-Arabs, 64-65; and language, 65

Published Country Studies

(Area Handbook Series)

550-65	Afghanistan	550-174	Guinea
550-98	Albania	550-82	Guyana
550-44	Algeria	550-151	Honduras
550-59	Angola	550-165	Hungary
550-73	Argentina	550-21	India
550-169	Australia	550-154	Indian Ocean
550-176	Austria	550-39	Indonesia
550-175	Bangladesh	550-68	Iran
550-170	Belgium	550-31	Iraq
550-66	Bolivia	550-25	Israel
550-20	Brazil	550-182	Italy
550-168	Bulgaria	550-69	Ivory Coast
550-61	Burma	550-30	Japan
550-50	Cambodia	550-34	Jordan
550-166	Cameroon	550-56	Kenya
550-159	Chad	550-81	Korea, North
550-77	Chile	550-41	Korea, South
550-60	China	550-58	Laos
550-26	Colombia	550-24	Lebanon
550-33	Commonwealth Caribbean, Islands of the	550-38	Liberia
550-91	Congo	550-85	Libya
550-90	Costa Rica	550-172	Malawi
550-152	Cuba	550-45	Malaysia
550-22	Cyprus	550-161	Mauritania
550-158	Czechoslovakia	550-79	Mexico
550-52	Ecuador	550-49	Morocco
550-43	Egypt	550-64	Mozambique
550-150	El Salvador	550-88	Nicaragua
550-28	Ethiopia	550-157	Nigeria
550-167	Finland	550-94	Oceania
550-155	Germany, East	550-48	Pakistan
550-173	Germany, Fed. Rep. of	550-46	Panama
550-153	Ghana	550-156	Paraguay
550-87	Greece	550-185	Persian Gulf States
550-78	Guatemala	550-42	Peru

550-72	Philippines	550-62	Tanzania
550-162	Poland	550-53	Thailand
550-181	Portugal	550-89	Tunisia
550-160	Romania	550-80	Turkey
550-51	Saudi Arabia	550-74	Uganda
550-70	Senegal	550-97	Uruguay
550-180	Sierra Leone	550-71	Venezuela
550-184	Singapore	550-32	Vietnam
550-86	Somalia	550-183	Yemens, The
550-93	South Africa	550-99	Yugoslavia
550-95	Soviet Union	550-67	Zaire
550-179	Spain	550-75	Zambia
550-96	Sri Lanka	550-171	Zimbabwe
550-27	Sudan		
550-47	Syria		

☆U.S. GOVERNMENT PRINTING OFFICE: 1988 - 0 - 201-418